Controversies and Decisions

Controversies and Decisions

The Social Sciences and Public Policy

CHARLES FRANKEL, *Editor*

A Study Prepared under the Auspices of the
American Academy of Arts and Sciences

Russell Sage Foundation   New York

Russell Sage Foundation
230 Park Avenue, New York, N.Y. 10017

The Contributors

Kenneth E. Boulding is Professor of Economics, and with the Institute of Behavioral Sciences, University of Colorado.

Harvey Brooks is Benjamin Peirce Professor of Technology and Public Policy, Harvard University.

Jonathan Cole is Associate Professor of Sociology, Barnard College and Columbia University.

Stephen Cole is Professor of Sociology, State University of New York at Stony Brook.

Lee J. Cronbach is Vida Jacks Professor of Education, Stanford University.

Paul Doty is Mallinckrodt Professor of Biochemistry and Director of the Program for Science & International Affairs, Harvard University.

Yaron Ezrahi is Professor of Political Science, Hebrew University of Jerusalem.

Charles Frankel is Old Dominion Professor of Philosophy and Public Affairs, Columbia University.

H. Field Haviland is Professor of International Politics, Fletcher School of Law and Diplomacy, Tufts University.

Hugh Hawkins is Professor of History and American Studies, Amherst College.

Harry G. Johnson is Charles F. Grey Distinguished Service Professor of Economics, University of Chicago, and Professor, University of Geneva.

Robert Nisbet is the Albert Schweitzer Professor in the Humanities, Columbia University.

Nicholas Rescher is University Professor of Philosophy, University of Pittsburgh.

Edward Shils is Distinguished Service Professor in the Committee on Social Thought and in the Department of Sociology, University of Chicago.

Adam Yarmolinsky is Ralph Waldo Emerson University Professor, University of Massachusetts.

Contents

Acknowledgments   ix

Introduction, *Charles Frankel*   3

The Autonomy of the Social Sciences, *Charles Frankel*   9

The Role of Values in Social Science Research, *Nicholas Rescher*   31

The Reward System of the Social Sciences,
 Jonathan R. Cole and Stephen Cole   55

The Ideal of Objectivity among American Social Scientists
 in the Era of Professionalization, 1876–1916, *Hugh Hawkins*   89

Max Weber and the Roots of Academic Freedom, *Robert Nisbet*   103

Five Decades of Public Controversy Over Mental Testing,
 Lee J. Cronbach   123

The Jensen Controversy: A Study in the Ethics and Politics
 of Knowledge in Democracy, *Yaron Ezrahi*   149

Scholars as Public Adversaries: The Case of Economics,
 Harry G. Johnson   171

Science Advising and the ABM Debate, *Paul Doty*   185

Scholarly Rights and Political Morality, *Kenneth E. Boulding*   205

Federal-Academic Relations in Social Science Research,
 H. Field Haviland   219

The Federal Government and the Autonomy of Scholarship,
 Harvey Brooks   235

How Good Was the Answer? How Good Was the Question?,
 Adam Yarmolinsky   259

Legitimating the Social Sciences: Meeting the Challenges
 to Objectivity and Integrity, *Edward Shils*   273

Index   291

Acknowledgments

In the preparation of this volume the editor has acquired a number of obligations. From the start I have received the advice and encouragement of the steering committee established by the American Academy of Arts and Sciences, composed of Guido Calabresi, Daniel Bell, Talcott Parsons, Corinne Schelling, and John Voss. The president of the Academy, Harvey Brooks, in addition to contributing a paper and taking part in the round tables that have marked the progress of this project, has been a constant ally and source of ideas. I owe an extra debt to John Voss, whose care and nurture of American Academy projects represent a triumph of statesmanlike perspective as well as scholarly judgment, and to Corinne Schelling, whose interest, humor, and energy never seem to flag and whose imagination and good sense have been indispensable. Cyrille White also gave me excellent editorial assistance when it was much needed.

The individual papers in this volume are the responsibility of their respective authors. In no sense can the positions taken in the pages that follow be said to represent official views of the Academy. Nevertheless, if the Academy cannot be burdened with the liabilities of authorship, it does deserve the credit that goes to authors' guardian angels. Its prestige and resources, its staff and its experience in conducting joint intellectual ventures, have all been available in the editing and writing of this book, and the gift has been of exceptional value.

Particularly worthwhile have been the three round table meetings at which the general plans for the project, its problems, and, ultimately, most of the essays in this book were discussed. Attending one or more of these meetings, in addition to the members of the steering committee and the contributors to this volume, were Graham Allison, Stephen Baratz, Alexander Bickel, Hendrik Bode, Clark Byse, William Capron, Ian Clark, Karl Deutsch, Sigmond Diamond, Robert

Dorfman, Joseph Goldstein, Stephen Graubard, Virginia Held, Fred Ikle, Milton Katz, Seymour Martin Lipset, Leon Lipson, Michael McElroy, Robert Morison, Charles Frederick Mosteller, Richard Neustadt, Ithiel de Sola Pool, Don Price, Maurice Rosenberg, Jack Ruina, Eleanor Bernert Sheldon, Eugene Skolnikoff, Laurence Tribe, James Q. Wilson, Albert Wohlstetter, and Roberta Wohlstetter. The editor is grateful to these colleagues for their advice and wisdom.

Finally, grateful acknowledgment is due from the Academy and the editor to Russell Sage Foundation, which provided the funds that made the project possible.

Charles Frankel

New York City
April, 1976

Controversies and Decisions

Introduction

Charles Frankel

For most of its history American social science has been comparatively free of the kind of concern that is conspicuous in the social inquiries conducted in countries where there is the memory of a single established religion that has dominated education and politics. In such countries people tend to see, in the background of all social issues, fundamental choices between godliness and god-lessness, order and progress, idealism and materialism, the classes and the masses. Every problem, no matter how narrow, tends to become vested with transcend-ent meaning; every disagreement, no matter how compromisable it may be in its own terms, is seen as linked to numberless other issues about which there can be no compromise but only struggle and either victory or defeat. This kind of intel-lectualized ferocity has not been the mark of American social science. Nor has it been characteristic for our homegrown sociologists or political scientists to raise the ultimate question about the authority and moral propriety of the scientific study of man that has been raised by such scholars as Weber, Durkheim, or Franz Neumann, who come from traditions in which social investigators tend to be conscripted, whether they wish it or not, into separate camps opposed on all basic issues.

Since the Russian Revolution, however, and especially since the 1930s, which saw the Great Depression, the advent of Nazism, and the coming of ideo-logical Marxism to these shores, American social science has been acquiring some of the traits of European social science. During the last decade this tendency has greatly accelerated. The Vietnam war, urban decay, racial confrontations, and the economic slowdown have created an atmosphere in which the idea that social in-

3

telligence can be used to the advantage of all groups and the disadvantage of none has lost its immediate plausibility. Yet it was that idea which to a great extent underlay the faith in social science and the belief in its inherent impartiality and beneficence.

There have also been more specific reasons for the changed climate in the social sciences. There have been significant and disorienting changes in the relation of social science to the polity and economy since World War II. Governmental agencies and commissions, the courts, nonprofit organizations and business enterprises, all have come to lean heavily on the results of scholarly research and the assistance of individual scholars. The impact of scholarly work on the mass media and general public attitudes has also grown markedly. Witness phenomena such as the widespread acceptance of no-fault insurance, the expectation that Keynesian techniques will be employed to doctor the economy, and popular concerns about environmental degradation and the depletion of resources. Scholarship and the scholar have thus been projected to the center of the public policy arena. The social scientist, above all, has become conspicuous.

Obviously, this is a salutary situation in many respects. Philosophers and social thinkers since the time of Plato have dreamt of a day when disciplined inquiry would become an influential element in public affairs. Nevertheless, the consequences of this marked shift in the public position of social science are ambiguous. On one side, social science's prestige and influence are greater; on the other side, in proportion as it has moved closer to the practical decision-making processes of society, its claim to "neutrality" has been questioned and its cognitive authority attacked. Indeed, the doubts about the independence of the social sciences have probably grown even more rapidly within the social science community than outside it.

An incomplete list of the controversies that have exposed the divisions within the social science community would include the Moynihan Report on black families; the study by James Coleman of the problems surrounding the achievement of equality of educational opportunity; the angry quarrel among distinguished scholars, conducted under the lights of congressional committee rooms, over the desirability of the ABM; the report of the Kerner Commission, prepared by a staff composed largely of social scientists, indicating that the United States is a "white racist" nation; the wounding charges and counter-charges that marked the argument over the role of scholars in the United States' adventure in Vietnam; and the accusations and counter-accusations surrounding the discussion of the bearing of genetic factors on intelligence. It is doubtful that there is any professional association of social scientists or any major department of social science in the country that has not been touched by one or another of these controversies. Perhaps only in economics has a certain decorousness and sense of common professional purpose survived in good shape, and reports on the quiet in the territory of economics vary with the reporter.

As the bitter controversies among social scientists during the last decade attest, the inherited rules of the road within the social science community have become unclear. There is dispute about standards of fair debate; about the individual scholar's right to choose his own subjects of inquiry; about the obligation to take sides or refrain from taking sides in political controversies; about the distinction between analysis and advocacy; and about whether some questions are too indecent to be asked and some hypotheses too ugly to be examined. It is against this background that the present volume has emerged. The fundamental reason for undertaking the studies that comprise this volume is the recognition that the supporting consensus for the social sciences has cracked open.

To be sure, the bitterness that marked controversies a few years ago has somewhat abated, so that the atmosphere in which this volume has been completed is not that in which it was first conceived. Nevertheless, the fundamental issues remain unresolved, as is evidenced by the continuance of serious and persistent debate among social scientists about the cognitive reliability of their disciplines, about their utility in relation to contested issues of policy, and about the proper norms by which they should be guided in commenting on public affairs or engaging in active political advocacy. The persistence and significance of these unresolved issues is attested equally by the inconsistency and indecisiveness of university faculties and learned societies in dealing with such questions as who should have access to their forums and whether they should take corporate positions on social issues. The reasons for these continuing problems are deeply rooted in the history, methodology, and environmental circumstances of the social sciences.

The effort in this book, accordingly, has been to explore a group of related questions bearing on social science controversies and their relation to public policy. Among these questions are the relation of "values" to "facts" in social science inquiry; the historical background of received ideals of neutrality and *Wertfreiheit;* the governing norms and actual procedures by which the collective worth of different social science disciplines is in fact carried forward; the interplay of theoretical and practical considerations in the application of social science methods and findings to specific issues in the political arena; modes of self-government and self-education within the social sciences; the moral obligations of social investigators in political contexts; and the ways and means of protecting and advancing the autonomy of the social sciences.

It will be plain that nothing like a "party line" is present in the answers given to these questions in the essays that follow. One or two, indeed, diverge fairly strongly from the main trend of opinion. That main trend, however, is that, despite the severe practical challenges presented by new conditions, the ideals of autonomy and objectivity are still valid for the social sciences and represent the only rationale for social scientists' claims either to academic freedom or to special attention for their views. Moreover, these ideas are best served by using the internal machinery of disciplined observation and debate available to the social sciences rather than by creating forms of external supervision and restraint. This opinion applies not only to the conduct of research and the critique of its results, but to the statements and behavior of social scientists when they openly enter the theater of political controversy. Obviously they there become subject to the forms of criticism and attack normal in the political arena. But if they use the authority of their disciplines where that writ does not go they are also properly subject to the professional criticism of their peers. What is needed to make such normal professional inhibitions and controls effective is not the promulgation of new regulations committing learned bodies to high-sounding political principles. What is needed is greater attention and sensitivity to the line between professional competence and political credo. Social scientists have a duty to the first and a right to the second, but they ought to know which is which.

In sum, the consensus among the contributors to this volume is that the heart of the issue lies in the self-critical disciplines of the social science community itself and in its capacity to distinguish between what may reasonably be asserted on the basis of one's discipline and what should be put into the domain of opinion or political preference. In practice, of course, the drawing of such a line is usually a matter of considerable subtlety. No sharp and precise agreement can be expected even within fields with a highly developed theoretical structure, such as economics, and drawing the line grows in difficulty as fields, such as history, are approached, to say nothing of directly practical fields, such as urban planning. Moreover, these difficulties, not inconsiderable even in periods of social tranquillity, become immeasurably greater when disagreements are ventilated in the press or before congressional committees, or when they have to do with matters on which the scholar's own fellow-citizens are risking prison or resorting to civil disobedience or violence.

Nevertheless, the difficulty of a task, though it may mean that a goal can only be approximated, does not prove that the goal as such is invalid. Social science loses its *raison d'être* if no valid distinction in principle can be made between knowledge and prejudice or disinterested counsel and biased advocacy. In actual practice the sophisticated methodologies of social sciences, though they sometimes disguise biases, also regularly expose, criticize, and dissipate them. The distinctive role of social science is maintained in essence by the procedures of mutual criticism characteristic of the communal scientific endeavor.

A similar set of considerations, in the eyes of most of those who have contributed to this volume, applies to the question, much debated in recent years, concerning the choice of subjects for research. Should scholars look into topics—for example, the genetic determinants of IQ—if the results of their research are susceptible to plainly immoral uses, and if, indeed, the mere fact that they are treating certain hypotheses as open questions may lead to the further victimization of people who have already suffered too much? The predominant opinion expressed or implied in this volume is that no subject can be ruled out a priori simply on the grounds of its feared social consequences. Research subjects are parts of chains of research; they have by-products that cannot be foreseen; their social consequences often turn out to be different from those expected. External political or moral taboos not only limit potentially significant intellectual inquiries but beg precisely the distinctive political question that advancing knowledge raises: What policies should be adopted if we wish to be guided not by our illusions but by the facts?

If, for example, it were to turn out that intelligence is mainly inherited, but that slowness of mind was curable by genetic therapy, would it not be an inexcusably cruel—and anti-egalitarian—social policy to ignore the hereditarian thesis on the ground that it supports the belief in human inequality? To be sure, we do not now know to what extent the hereditarian thesis is true, much less whether it is applicable to the complex, elusive, and usually ill-defined issues of racial and ethnic differences. The example suggests, however, what has again and again turned out to be true. The progress of knowledge changes the very terms of debate, including the standards that are pertinent to an evaluation of the moral significance of such progress.

Even more important, perhaps, than the convergence of opinion that marks this volume, however, is the collective act of self-confrontation that it represents. The academic problem—the intellectual problem—of our time is not defined by the hostility to the received scholarly consensus exhibited by small and diminishing numbers of students. It is defined by the much larger, and much more astonishing, lack of confidence that has been exhibited by the press, the educated public, the leaders of moderate political parties, and, not least, by academics themselves in the claims that academia has traditionally made for itself. And in the vanguard are large segments of the social science professoriate. They are not sure they are right to be doing what they are doing; they are no longer persuaded that the professional norms governing them make sense logically or morally; they have come to doubt the possibility of studying human society from a position independent of political commitment. The earth shocks recently felt by universities and learned societies in every liberal democratic country attest to the depth of this crisis of conscience and confidence. The shocks would not have been so shattering and would not have moved from Berkeley to Paris and Berlin to Tokyo with such irresistible force if the permanent citizens of academia, the scholars, were not already feeling unsure of the ground beneath them.

The social function of the social sciences, it was once widely supposed, is to contribute to the larger society an ingredient of impartial inquiry and judgment that, it was hoped, might help mediate otherwise intractable quarrels. How well, in theory and in practical fact, can the social sciences reasonably be expected to perform this role? That is the question addressed by this book. It is an academic issue that can hardly be described as academic.

The Autonomy of the Social Sciences

Charles Frankel

Most social scientists understandably welcome the public attention, which, for the last two decades or so, has been paid to them and their works. The world has changed: Gone are the days when corporation executives showed how smart they were by expressing their scorn for long-haired "experts" who had never met a payroll. Today civic bodies call on social scientists to recite on the cause and cure of ailments ranging from the insecurity of nations to the reading problems of children, and the standard operating procedure for people who make important decisions, whether in banks or labor unions, is to have a social scientist on tap to ask for advice. To be sure, the deference paid to the social sciences is in part ritualistic. As often as not people turn to them not to receive guidance in determining policy but to sanctify a policy they have already decided to follow. Nevertheless, the present situation is bound to be gratifying to the social science ego. No less than doctors, lawyers, or garbage-collectors, social scientists like to know that they are appreciated.

However, there is a flavor of irony in the present situation. The evidence grows—some of it is contained in this book—that social scientists are beginning to feel that they are appreciated perhaps beyond their due. Economics is probably the best established of the social sciences, yet at the American Economic Association's convention in 1973, its new president, Walter Heller, once chairman of the Council of Economic Advisers under President Kennedy, said,

> Economists are distinctly in a period of re-examination. The energy crisis caught us with our parameters down. The food crisis caught us too. This was a year of infamy in inflation forecasting. There are many things we really don't know.[1]

---

[1] *New York Times*, December 29, 1973, p. 31.

The self-doubts that have emerged go beyond such doubts as to the practical capacity of the social sciences to deliver useful knowledge. They go to the question of whether "science" is the right word to describe the social studies. An observation by the political philosopher Charles Taylor in a widely quoted article is typical.

> A given framework of explanation in political science tends to support an associated value position, secretes its own norms for the assessment of politics and policies.[2]

Nor is the attack directed simply at the possibility of attaining unbiased results; it is also aimed at the assumption that objectivity is a morally desirable ideal. Alvin Gouldner has said that the *Wertfreiheit* sought by the positivistic sociologists who have dominated sociology in the past can be traced to their "anomic adaptation" to political failure and powerlessness. Society would not accept the sociologists' values. Accordingly, they accepted society's. That is what their *Wertfreiheit* has meant pragmatically. Every social theory, in Professor Gouldner's view, is controlled by "domain assumptions" representing not the results of controlled professional inquiry but the influence of the prevailing ideology and the inquirer's social position. The cure, he avers, is not to get rid of such assumptions, which is impossible. It is to accept their inescapable presence and to choose assumptions proper to a world seeking to be born rather than to one that is collapsing.[3]

Invective and incivility have marked controversies in the social sciences in the last decade. The phenomenon is significant, in the final analysis, because it reflects a deep suspicion that social science is a pretense. In the days when the social science community was poor and an object of public scorn, it was held together by common beliefs and ideals, which, now that it is prosperous, appear to have come apart. The first generation of gods in the American social science pantheon—e.g., Burgess, Ely, James Harvey Robinson, Wesley Mitchell, Boas, Thorndike, John Dewey—taught that social scientists possessed a common logic of inquiry and that this logic should allow them, despite their individual prejudices, to arrive at mutually acceptable conclusions. They thought, too, that the country would be better off if social scientists, emancipated by their scientific methods and objectives from sectarianism, were listened to more and the politicians and interest groups were listened to less. As Professor Shils indicates in his essay, even apparent critics of this "objectivism," such as Veblen and Beard, emphasized the biases in social inquiry mainly because they were concerned with purging it of such biases and regarded objectivity as an intelligible goal. In

---

[2] Charles Taylor, "Neutrality in Political Science," in *Philosophy, Politics, and Society,* eds. P. Laslett and W. G. Runciman (New York, 1967), p. 48.

[3] Alvin Gouldner, *The Coming Crisis of Western Sociology* (New York, 1970), pp. 34–46, 102, and *passim.*

Europe as well, although there was nothing similar to the American consensus on these propositions, the major figures, e.g., Weber, Durkheim, Keynes, essentially supported them.

But when these old propositions are restated in contemporary terms they strike an odd note. In 1966, in an article in *The American Sociological Review* entitled "The Decline of Politics and Ideology in a Knowledgeable Society," Robert Lane wrote:

> . . . the dominant scholarly interpretation of policy-making processes has changed in the direction of emphasizing the greater autonomy of political leaders and legislators; with respect to the role of pressure groups, the power elite, and the electorate . . . if leaders and other legislators are less bound by the domain of pure politics . . . they are freer to be guided by the promptings of scientists and findings from the domain of knowledge.[4]

Read today, such words sound like the expression of a small and dying sect's despairing hopes. The elements of an indurated ideology are discernible: the prophecy about the coming to power of one's own emancipated group; the definition of the eternal enemy—politics, interest groups, the competition for advantage; the reading of the omens to show that the enemy is finally in retreat; the assurance that the victory of one's own side is a victory for everybody.

Which view is correct? Were two generations of social scientists who believed in the possibility and desirability of objectivity the victims of a comforting professional illusion? Or were they right to think that social science, for all the blindnesses of social scientists, had something distinctive to contribute to political controversy, something that was more than a brief for a partisan cause or a reflection of reigning fashions in ideas and social faiths? On the answer to this question depends the possibility of defining and establishing the autonomy of the social sciences.

To gain perspective on it a number of issues must be canvassed:

the nature and sources of the older consensus supporting the objectivity of the social sciences;
the historical reasons for the decline of this consensus;
the logic of the argument against *Wertfreiheit;*
the character of the idea of "ideology";
the sources of self-discipline within the social sciences;
the significance of recent controversies as seen in the long view.

2.

The old consensus within the house of social science was not mainly epistemological in its origins. It was moral and political, and the professional

---

[4] Vol. 31, p. 658 (October 1966).

social scientist shared it with a large audience of laymen. The general neutrality and beneficence of social science, its utility as a means for the accomplishment of defensible ends, was presupposed. It was presupposed because the ends of American society were thought essentially legitimate and because the American constitutional system was believed to be adequate to the needs of justice and peaceful reform.

Viewed in the perspective of its history, a special characteristic of American social science strikes the eye when European social science is put alongside it. As Professor Johnson observes in his chapter, British economists to this day tend to insist on dividing themselves along political lines. In contrast, American social scientists, whatever their political leanings at election time, have historically tended to think of their adversaries not as a definite political group but as generic enemies, such as superstition, ignorance, and the inertia of the past. It was at the height of the Progressive movement, to be sure, that social science emerged in America as a fully self-conscious and institutionalized activity. In that period, it was often explicitly allied with the cause of reform. Nevertheless, Veblen, Charles Beard, or Arthur Bentley, although they knew that they were rubbing powerful people's sensibilities the wrong way, did not think of themselves, as most of their counterparts in France or Germany were wont to do, as representatives of a particular political group, social class, or intellectual cadre. They saw themselves as workers within the American civic process, which belonged to nobody and to everybody, and while they recognized the conflicts of interest within American society, they did not view the basic social system as closed to the victory of new groups by peaceful and politically conventional means. In consequence, they rarely raised the kind of classic question raised by their "outsider" European contemporaries, such as Max Weber, about the grounds of social authority or the rationale for democracy and equality.

The image of a nonpartisan yet reform-oriented social science took shape in the United States within such a perspective. It was a science not concerned with rejecting the basic assumptions of the political system. Its purpose was only to eliminate cultural lag and to remove the disagreements about facts that kept reasonable men apart. There is a sense, indeed, in which the idea of a nonpolitical social science may be said to have constitutional status in the United States. As Don K. Price has noted, a place for impartial empirical research is written into the American Constitution, which provides for a population census every ten years for the purpose of apportioning representatives among the several states. In the American republic, as Dean Price suggests, statistics might be said to be "the ultimate basis for sovereign power."[5]

The point is more than a legalistic one. Deprived of an established church and functioning in a rapidly changing society in which hereditary lines are looked upon with suspicion, social authority in the United States requires new forms of

---

[5] Don K. Price, *Government and Science* (New York, 1954), p. 5.

support. American social science, in thinking of itself as providing a common set of tested procedures and conclusions by which a convergence of views could be promoted, has attempted to answer a special need of American society. And that conception of the task of social scientists was inherently persuasive to them because they shared with a much larger audience certain unspoken presuppositions: that American society, for all its violence, materialism, and freebooting, was an open society in which outsiders could, sooner or later, make their way in and up; that it was essentially a society of abundance in which one group's advance was not necessarily another group's loss; and that it was a democratic one where members could expect, in time, to be able to communicate with their fellows, and to understand and be understood, about the basic values of life. People solved problems in America; they learned to talk to one another across the barriers created by different backgrounds. The idea of a social science at once activist and objective, reformist and politically neutral, flourished in the atmosphere in which such convictions were held.

3.

There is no need to review at length the experiences of the last decade, which have shaken these convictions. The diminished sense of American possibility is a product of Vietnam and Watergate, assassinations and riots, extravagant promises and limping performance by one administration, and Tartuffian homilies on the virtues by its corrupt successor. And beneath these events there have been deeper trends: the apparent intractability of the problem of chronic poverty; the rapid decline in the amenities and spaciousness of life felt by large sections of the middle class; the growth of physical insecurity; the hardening of social divisions; inflation; stagflation. The idea of an objective, independent social science is easier to absorb in a society in which people do not believe that they are arrayed against adversaries with whom they can never, under any circumstances, see eye to eye. But in a society grown accustomed to massive forms of distrust and confrontation and to apparently radical differences in personal and public conceptions of right and wrong, the question has inevitably arisen: Social science for whom, and social progress in whose version?

There must also be mentioned the trauma suffered or self-inflicted by academia. In 1956 the late Jacob Bronowski wrote:

> By worldly standards of public life, all scholars in their work are oddly virtuous. They do not make wild claims, they do not cheat, they do not try to persuade at any cost, they appeal neither to prejudice nor to authority, they are often frank about their ignorance, their disputes are fairly decorous, they do not confuse what is being argued with race, politics, sex or age, they listen patiently to the young and to the old who both know everything.[6]

---

[6] *Science and Human Values,* rev. ed. (New York, 1965), p. 59.

It would take a Rip Van Winkle who had slept through the 1960s to write such a passage today. *"They do not confuse what is being argued with race, politics, sex or age. . . ."* On balance, the scholarly community made the public discourse not less but more venomous. To the general foreboding that the society is breaking apart we must now add the fear that the social science world does not have even its own unifying professional standards.

Other factors further help to explain the erosion of the inherited consensus. The simple phenomenon of social scientists' success itself is one. The rationale that grows up around an emerging science is not usually the same as that which surrounds one that has arrived. Descartes announcing the promise of the new physics is not like Leibniz celebrating its triumphs; still less is he like Kant reflecting on its limits. The ideal of a "value-free" social science, whether or not we think it intellectually defensible, functioned for most of its history as a "utopia" in Karl Mannheim's technical sense of the term. It was a system of belief and aspiration expressing the outlook of people struggling for acceptance, not the least in the academic community itself. Unlike the physicists, social scientists did not possess a commanding scientific theory allowing them to speak the truth as they saw it without regard to politics, religion, or conventional belief. Unlike philosophers or students of the literary classics, neither could social scientists call upon a putatively transcendent moral and literary tradition. In this setting, a conception of a social science progressively more independent in its methods, and progressively more influential in the evolution of public policy, had a special function in unifying and justifying the scattered efforts of the social science tribe.

Such a philosophy, like other "utopias," inevitably has trouble weathering success. Once social scientists became confident that they had something of unique value to offer and once the public began to listen to them, the disparity between the actual performance of social scientists and their professed ideal was bound to become more obtrusive. Indeed, once established, the social sciences, for their own health, need something different from the old rationale. They are parts of a going social system. If their integrity is to be protected, they need a professional doctrine stressing less the possibility of objectivity than the dangers to that objectivity. In terms of their social function, current doubts about the received consensus can be understood in part as the social sciences' self-therapy. They are efforts to guard the honesty of the social sciences in a period when they are living in close alliance with the powers that be and are therefore living dangerously.

The conditions in which social scientists have competed for the benefits of success have also contributed to the erosion of the old consensus. The nation, after World War II, became officially committed to full employment at home and the pursuit of the cold war abroad. Sums of money beyond most social scientists' dreams were made available for research that might conceivably contribute to these purposes. Even more important, the new relationships between social scientists and their patrons were developed precipitately. The wealth available to the social sciences brought the styles of business competition to the campus and mortgaged the universities' economic and educational futures to the activities of academic entrepreneurs. Over the course of two decades, in consequence, the sense of academic community has been undergoing dissolution. It was this as much as anything that weakened the academic organism's resistance to the violent disruptions of the late 1960s. In the best of times a university is like an opera company. It is composed of people with large egos who have the habit of dominating the stage in front of respectful audiences, and also have a talent for taking umbrage easily. The grants economy of the post-World War II era made matters worse. The structure of mutual forebearance within the social science community was therefore already considerably weakened when the political tornadoes turned loose by Watts and Vietnam arrived.

And to these stresses must be added, finally, those that emerge when people think themselves close to where the action is. A note comes into a man's voice when he hopes that the Secretary of Defense is listening. In proportion as social scientists have come to involve themselves in extramural activities, extramural considerations have intruded more obviously into professional disagreements. In consequence, social scientists have it more on their minds these days that when they are reading a paper at a scholarly meeting they are also committing a political act. In the eyes of an increasing number, indeed, the political act is the most important aspect of their professional lives. The emergence of the social scientist as unembarrassed public advocate even while he wraps the authority of his discipline around himself is a conspicuous mark of the present era in social inquiry.

Inside and outside the house of social science, therefore, there is unease as to just where social science ends and the political thoroughfare begins. The idea that at some point we can draw a line—the idea that one *should* draw a line—has come unstrung. The boundaries of social science, the relation of its research findings to policy decisions, and the responsibilities of social scientists as political beings have become subjects for reassessment.

[margin, handwritten:] This is the change: the positive assertion that there is no line — and shouldn't be!

4.

But the historical explanation of why a set of beliefs once prevailed and why it has lost its currency does not settle a separate question—the inherent validity of the beliefs in question. The problems that have recently erupted reflect two hundred years of intellectual history. What has broken loose in the social science community is not, in essence, a new quarrel. It has been going on since the time of the Encyclopedists; it can be traced, indeed, farther back, to the debate between Hobbes and his contemporaries over whether there existed a higher moral law antecedent to human desire and convention. The issues have to do with two connected themes—the relation of "facts" to "values" and the distinction, if any, between a social science and a social ideology. Are doubts warranted about the validity of the social science ideal of independence and political detachment?

The ideal rests on a distinction between description and prescription, "is" and "ought." The most trenchant statement of the rationale for this distinction is probably still that of David Hume.

> In every system of morality which I have hitherto met with I have always re-mark'd that the author proceeds for some time in the ordinary way of reasoning, and establishes the being of a God, or makes observations concerning human affairs; when of a sudden I am surpriz'd to find that instead of the usual copula-tions of propositions, *is,* and *is not,* I meet with no proposition that is not con-nected with an *ought* or an *ought not.* This change is imperceptible; but is, how-ever, of the last consequence. For as this *ought* or *ought not* expresses some new relation or affirmation, 'tis necessary that it should be observ'd and explain'd; and at the same time that a reason should be given for what seems altogether incon-ceivable, how this new relation can be a deduction from others which are entirely different from it. But as authors do not commonly use this precaution, I shall presume to recommend it to the readers; and am persuaded that this small atten-tion wou'd subvert all the vulgar systems of morality and let us see that the dis-tinction of vice and virtue is not founded merely on the relations of objects, nor is perceiv'd by reason.[7]

The doctrine enunciated in this passage, which has united thinkers from Hume to Max Weber, has been called, pejoratively, "Hume's guillotine." Those who condemn it assert that it declares all moral beliefs to be arbitrary and that it implies that the study of human behavior should be cut off from concern with normative issues. Although those who have put forward this indictment are numerous and have belonged to all political categories, they have shared a com-mon inattentiveness to the actual arguments on which Hume's thesis turns.

One common mode of attack on Hume's doctrine, for example, is to say that it presupposes a psychological theory, now wholly outmoded, that the human mind functions as a mere passive container into which experience is poured. Hume, it is alleged, misunderstood the role that human interests and a selective point of view play in inquiry, and mistakenly supposed, therefore, that it was possible neatly to separate "fact" from "value." This description of Hume's psychological presuppositions is, however, inaccurate. Hume spoke of reason as "the slave of the passions," and often detailed at length the part human desires play in the formation of human beliefs. He explicitly assigned active functions to the mind. Perhaps the most important thesis in his philosophy, that having to do with the logic of induction, turns on what Hume called "the tendency to feign"— the mind's disposition, for the sake of its own vital needs, to leap ahead of the evidence and presume, without deductive warrant, the uniformity of nature.

In any case, whatever Hume's psychological theories were, they have no

---

[7] David Hume, *A Treatise of Human Nature* (London, 1739); reprinted Oxford 1896, ed. Selby-Bigge, Bk. 3, pt. 1, section 1, p. 469.

logical bearing on his argument that "ought" does not follow from "is." As the passage quoted suggests—it is the key passage in Hume's statement of his thesis —the argument is entirely self-sufficient and says nothing about psychological theory. It merely applies to the specific question of "ought" and "is" the broader logical principle that no deduction can be valid which contains terms in its conclusion not contained in its premises. Accordingly, if Hume is right, the support that factual statements give to moral conclusions cannot be demonstrative. Hume's doctrine rests exclusively on such considerations of logic, and its point, if valid, is therefore invulnerable to attack on psychological or sociological grounds. Appeals to the subsequent discoveries of Darwin, Marx, or Freud are irrelevant in appraising a position that is wholly concerned with the relation of premise to conclusion and not with the content of the premises.

But the question intrudes: Do we not, as a matter of daily fact, move from factual assertions to value judgments? And do we not think that this is a reasonable thing to do, and that, indeed, it is the very definition of rationality in the conduct of life? If the social sciences are to serve a function in this regard, must we not reject Hume's doctrine? It is the sense that "Hume's guillotine" clashes with such commonplaces of thought and behavior, and that it erases the distinction between reasonable and unreasonable people, that explains much of the dissatisfaction with it. Similarly, the now widely expressed criticisms of *Wertfreiheit* appear to be based on the belief that the separation of "facts" and "values" demeans social science, reducing it to the wholly servile role of finding the efficient means for reaching given ends, but denying it the right to take a position about the merits of these ends themselves.

Once again, however, we confront objections addressed to a point not at issue. Hume himself, certainly, did not draw such consequences from his argument. He wrote repeatedly on moral and social issues, appealing to facts, expressing moral judgments or making recommendations for policy, and plainly believing that, in advising people about the ends they ought to pursue, he was engaging in a rational enterprise. And, quite independently of Hume's own practice, the distinction between "is-statements" and "ought-statements" carries no logical consequence either prohibiting a scientific interest in values or restricting the concept of reasoned argument to nonevaluative discourse. These consequences follow only if one fails to distinguish between *hypothetical* and *categorical* value judgments. Hume's principle rules out only the latter.

Scientific objectivity with regard to value judgments does not mean, therefore, the refusal to make them. It means the much subtler business of seeking to make explicit, as far as possible, the value presumptions on which policy recommendations depend. The distinction made by Hume, in sum, is parallel to the distinction made by Max Weber between the ethics of "absolute ends" and the ethics of "responsibility." Factual information is relevant to policy because it permits the informed appraisal of alternatives in terms of consequences without which choice is blind or capricious. Of course, the use of scientifically winnowed information in the evaluation of comparative costs and benefits requires that some presupposed set of standards, in a particular context of choice, be accepted as controlling; and since these standards, from the logical point of view, are merely assumed, the conclusions drawn with their help have only a hypothetical status.

Without misleading ellipsis, therefore, we cannot speak, in the abstract, of "the findings of science" and apply them as authoritative revelations to particular problems. But the standards we presuppose can themselves be examined in relation to their factual conditions and consequences, so that they, too, are not immune to scientific scrutiny. Nor does this involve infinite regress. In the contexts of practical choice, the situations are rare where no values can be taken as desirable. Choices are made by people in definite historical settings and with restricted options. And, as with our inductive beliefs about the sun or the characteristics of fire, we have good reason to base our actions on certain values so long as we lack specific reasons to doubt them. If the fundamental postulate on which the ideal of social science objectivity rests is indeed Hume's "guillotine," it would seem to be a sound one.

But this discussion cannot be regarded as complete until we see that it turns on a question much larger than the distinction between "facts" and "values." It touches on the distinction between disciplined and undisciplined discourse. Hume's point is the general one that, in any inquiry, if one uses a term in a given way, one must stay with that use all the way through. In the case of words like "good" and "ought," if one begins by using them descriptively—as in "This ointment is good for a rash," or "You ought to get up earlier if you want to get to work on time"—one cannot, *in medias res*, turn around and use them to stand not for the relation of means to ends but for the obligatoriness of the ends. To be sure, in any imaginative inquiry, viewed as a psychological process, there are qualities of uncertainty, confusion, search, trial, and retrial. In such a process, terms change their meanings, and the definitions with which one ends are not those with which one begins. But an inquiry viewed as an unfolding process in time is not the same as an inquiry viewed as an object of critical appraisal. In the latter perspective, the concern is to determine whether the evidence warrants the conclusion. The logical principle that terms should retain constancy of meaning applies to inquiry so perceived. It is a principle for the regulating of inquiry, for subjecting it to rules designed to move it to determinate conclusions. It is in this setting that the distinction between "facts" and "values" emerges.

These considerations are immediately pertinent to recent highly sophisticated efforts to blunt the thrust of Hume's principle. Not only in social science, but in philosophy, arguments have been presented that appear to give sustenance to the increasingly popular opinion in intellectual circles that the line between "is" and "ought" is thin and elusive. As Antony Flew remarks,

The word seems to have gone round that the idea that there is a radical difference between *ought* and *is* is old hat, something which though still perhaps cherished by out-group backwoodsmen has long since been seen through and discarded by all with-it mainstream philosophers.[8]

At bottom, the "word" in question seems to derive from two kinds of consideration. The first is that the categories of discourse discerned by Hume are too few. Language falls into more than the logical-analytic, the factual-descriptive, and the normative-prescriptive forms of discourse. The second is that examples of ordinary discourse are not neatly categorizable. Language is too "open-textured." These insights are valid and have contributed greatly to the more precise understanding of the powers and richness of human language and thought. For the most part people communicate in mixed modes, never have any trouble understanding one another when they do so, and would be unable to think or act effectively if this liberty were denied to them. A carpenter, seeking to saw through a hard board, finds the saw that will do it and says "descriptively," "*That's* a saw." An appraiser says evaluatively, "The price of this house is too high," but when asked why, he gives as his reason the factual statement, "Its roof leaks." If the distinction between "descriptive" and "prescriptive" is taken to describe features of discourse that can be detected, as it were, by immediate inspection, it is radically misleading.

However, if it is not intended in this way, but as a tool for the regulation of inquiry so that it yields determinable conclusions whose reliability can be assessed, its rationale remains. This is what is ignored, it seems to me, even in such accomplished arguments as those of Professor John Searle in opposition to Hume's distinction between "is" and "ought." To prove that Hume is wrong, Professor Searle offers as an example a series of statements which, he says, proceed without logical fallacy from the descriptive statement, (1) "Jones uttered the words 'I hereby promise to pay you, Smith, five dollars'" to what would be generally accepted as the "evaluative" conclusion, (5) "Jones ought to pay Smith five dollars." The intervening steps would be filled in by (2) "Jones promised to pay Smith five dollars," a statement that follows from (1); by (3) "Jones placed himself under (undertook) an obligation to . . . etc."; and (4) "Jones is under an obligation to . . . etc."[9] At no point, Professor Searle asserts, is an additional normative premise smuggled into the argument.

Professor Searle puts the question raised by his argument as follows:

One feels there must be some trick involved somewhere. We might state our uneasiness thus: How can my granting a mere fact about a man, such as the fact

---

[8] *The Is-Ought Question,* ed. W. O. Hudson (New York, 1969), p. 135.

[9] John B. Searle, "How to Derive 'Ought' from 'Is,'" in Hudson, *The Is-Ought Question,* p. 121 and *passim.*

that he uttered certain words or that he made a promise, commit *me* to the view that *he* ought to do something?[10]

The answer, he argues, is that there are certain sorts of facts that are, in his language, "institutional facts." When people act in relation to these facts, their activities are rule-defined and rule-bound. Accordingly, to state the fact that they have so acted is also to state that they have incurred duties, rights, commitments, and responsibilities. By way of contrast, eating, in most societies, is governed by standards of proper manners, but the activity of eating can be defined, performed, and observed apart from these standards. It is not an "institutional fact." On the other hand, chess, baseball, marriage, promising, acquiring a debt, entering into a partnership, forming a corporation,[11] are activities that cannot be defined, performed, or observed apart from understanding the existence and character of the rules that govern them. Rules of this sort are constitutive of the activities they regulate. Consequently, if it is true of a man that he said, in the appropriate circumstances, "I promise to pay . . . etc.," then it follows that he ought to pay. In Professor Searle's words,

> I started with a brute fact, that a man uttered certain words, and then invoked the institution in such a way as to generate institutional facts by which we arrived at the institutional fact that the man ought to pay another man five dollars. The whole proof rests on an appeal to the constitutive rule that to make a promise is to undertake an obligation.[12]

But the problem is in the meaning to be attached to the slippery phrases "I . . . invoked the institution" and "an appeal to the constitutive rule." Is Professor Searle observing the behavior in question as one who belongs to the relevant institution and has internalized its norms? As a bystander indifferent to the institution? As an enemy of it? As the representative of another institution whose norms collide in the instant case with the norm of keeping a promise? "Invoking the institution" and "an appeal to the constitutive rule" may mean making them explicit in order to explain (perhaps to a visitor from Mars) the behavior in question, including the obligations that the participants accept. Here to invoke a constitutive rule is to invoke a premise in a prediction. Or it may mean employing the rule, as it were, from inside the institution and joining the participants in pressing for conformity to it. Here the rule serves as a norm. And we might "invoke the rule" in other ways too—for example, to show the wickedness of the institution in question as seen from the perspective of other rules or institutions.

Constitutive rules, says Professor Searle, "are such that to commit myself

---

[10] Ibid., p. 128.

[11] Only some of these examples are Professor Searle's. I extend the list to show the full thrust of his point.

[12] Searle, p. 131.

...ay in which admission to the circle of "competent judges" is determined
...he degree to which the group's tests are insulated from external challenge.
...litical right-mindedness is an indispensable prerequisite for recognition as
...mber of the guild, or if political tests are employed for the supposed pur-
...of insuring a "fair" representation of different points of view, ideological
...ies are built into the appraisal system of the discipline. Again, if the
...rds by which ideas are accepted or rejected in the disciplines are unaffected
...velopments in other disciplines, these standards have privileged status and
...e qualified as "ideological." (Thus carbon tests are products of chemical
...ch, but are relevant to the appraisal of anthropological hypotheses about
... of fossil remains.) "Ideology" is a term to be applied to ideas that move
...sed circles—that have their own preselected critics and tests so that it is
...teed in advance that they will survive. Scientific ideas, in contrast, live
...t these protections.

...Without discounting the amount of tribal prejudice that exists in the social
...es, the evidence is that, overall, their institutions of self-governance and
...ctual criticism are in the scientific pattern. If they are regarded as sta-
... and examined at a given moment, the ideological accretions in them
... considerable. If they are seen as changing systems of ideas driven by the
...c of challenge and criticism, they emerge as bodies of knowledge that,
... as they retain their autonomy, are insured against permanent capture by
...ology.[17]

...gainst this background, we may turn to the question of the forms of self-
...e available in the social sciences with regard to the discussion of con-

---

...ciences. At the conclusion of his much-discussed *The Structure of Scientific Revo-*
...Thomas S. Kuhn asks, "Does it really help to imagine that there is some one full,
...true account of nature and that the proper measure of scientific achievement is
...: to which it brings us closer to that ultimate goal? . . . the entire process [of the
...ent of science] may have occurred, as we now suppose biological evolution did,
...enefit of a set goal, a permanent fixed scientific truth, of which each stage in the
...ent of scientific knowledge is a better exemplar." (Chicago, 1962), pp. 170–171.
...ct of Professor Kuhn's position on current debate within the social sciences is
...deserves a separate examination on its own.
...would note in passing—unhappily, space does not allow a discussion of the
...e length it deserves—that Professor Kuhn's theory of "paradigms" does not,
...ndermine this point. Even if these "paradigms" are sustained by force of essen-
...ical processes within the relevant scientific community, they do collapse under
...the strain is produced not simply by competition with other groups with dif-
...rests and perspectives but by the difficulties experienced in fitting new observa
...nvestigations into the received models.

---

to the view that Jones made a promise involves committing myself to what he
ought to do (other things being equal)." But why? Surely a man might agree
that Jones made a promise as defined within the American socio-legal system and
yet say that Jones ought not to keep it because that socio-legal system is iniquitous and its obligations should be ignored whenever possible. To this objection,
Professor Searle's response is that there is a distinction between an "external"
and "internal" point of view towards "institutional facts." To ask "Ought one to
accept the institution of promising?" is to ask an "external" question, in which
the constitutive rule is not accepted as a binding norm, but is instead made a
subject of examination and appraisal. It is to be sharply contrasted, Professor
Searle indicates, with "internal questions asked within the framework of the institution"—for example, "Ought one to keep one's promises?"[13] But if this is
the case, we have merely substituted the language of "internal-external" for the
language of "is-ought" or "fact-value," while retaining the essential distinction
at issue.

That distinction is between, on one hand, expressing, internalizing, or participating in a system of obligations and, on the other, regarding that system as
itself subject to question and possessing moral legitimacy only so far as it meets
the test of some external set of norms. However we describe this distinction, it
reemerges the moment one refuses to say, as Professor Searle refuses, that any
specific moral system carries with it its own internal guarantee of validity. The
difference between his view and Hume's, then, is hard to see.

Indeed, the distinction between "is" and "ought" can itself be seen as derivative from the more basic rule of inquiry that terms must retain a fixed meaning
within any particular course of argument. This is, if one wishes to put it in
Professor Searle's language, a "constitutive rule" of inquiry. Just as people within
the institution of "promising" are not engaging in promising when they use
expressions with the word "promise" but see no connected obligation, so people
are not engaging in the institutional practice known as inquiry when they disregard shifts in the meanings of terms as they go along. For the function of this
institutional practice is to arrive at conclusions testable by a community of observers employing the same rules, and the test cannot be made if the community
cannot pin down what is being asserted. The *Wertfreiheit* of the social sciences
insists on little more than the application of this rule of inquiry to the subjects
that social scientists investigate, including the desirability of specific social institutions and values.

---

[13] "Taken literally, as an internal question, as a question about promises and not
about the institution of promising, the question, 'Ought one to keep one's promises?' is as
empty as the question, 'Are triangles three-sided?' To recognize something as a promise is to
grant that, other things being equal, it ought to be kept" (Ibid., p. 127).

5.

But logic, it may be replied, is one thing and the actual and inescapable condition of social scientists as human beings caught in a world of partisan claims is another—and much more to the practical point. Behind many of the recent controversies between social scientists there lies the belief that since all social ideas are socially conditioned, all social ideas, inevitably, are interest-loaded —partisan, inherently one-sided, in short "ideological." Often as the concept of ideology is analyzed and presumably refuted, it comes back with the hardiness of a perennial flower. And it is, in fact, one of the permanent ideas in the Western tradition of thought.

The notion of tragic blindness, on which Greek tragedy rests, indicates how old the recognition is that people can, though thoroughly conscious and under no one else's control, act as though hypnotized. They perform actions whose causes, meaning, and consequences they misunderstand, and are unable to do anything else, because they hold a picture of reality in which the actions they are pursuing appear to be the only proper or possible course. These blindnesses may be self-defeating, preventing people from satisfying their important needs; they may be self-protective, permitting the individual to seek purposes that, if undisguised, he would not seek or would not seek without embarrassment. In either case, they are self-deceptions.

Obviously, this idea of psychological blindness reflects an important truth of human experience. It is fundamental to both comedy and tragedy. In their classic forms these have presupposed an audience sitting on the outside of the action and able to tell the difference between appearance and reality although the personages in the play cannot. Bottom is Bottom although the Fairy Queen, under a spell, does not know this. Oedipus has killed his father and taken his mother as wife, and all the world watching the play knows this, although he does not. Similarly, a fundamental idea in the religions of conversion and revelation is that people can live in darkness without knowing it and that the darkness is of their own willful yet helpless making so that they can be saved only by those who bring light from the outside. As in comedy or tragedy, an external spectator is presupposed.

It is helpful to see the concept of "ideology" against this background. It is the descendant of the dramatic and religious ideas of the disabling blindness, self-imposed yet unwilled. "Ideology" asserts the existence of this phenomenon as a collective matter. Conceptions of social reality reflect not that reality but the needs and perspectives of the groups, classes, or nations that construct them. And social science, according to this view, is in a way more ideological than other modes of interpreting reality because it parades under the banner of universal truth, and thus better serves the ideological function of masking the interests and intentions behind it. But the problem in such a generalized imputation of

"false consciousness" to social science is that, as in th spectator must be presupposed who is able accurately from the illusory. Without this assumption no content cept of "false consciousness." The fundamental issue, th of this external knowledge as reliable and as superio beliefs composing the alleged ideology.

Broadly speaking, there are two ways to support may point to a putatively superior science, e.g., a gen and criticize the findings of particular social sciences allegedly superior science, however, is itself maintaine a theater, it is the actors who are at fault if they do never the audience that is obtuse, insensitive, or un "ideology" that is offered from such a base is, howe the method of authority.

The second way is by a process of internal crit This may go on within an individual science, as wher that the overwhelming proportion of American soci politics concentrate on reform movements or on neglect "integrative institutions," such as religion a mist notes that his compeers give central importanc a conception of "consumer sovereignty" apparently phenomena as advertising or the setting of prices by cal forces like management, labor, and governme tween disciplines, as when a historian points to sociologist's generalizations or a sociologist indicat ent explanation of events would be given if mo impact of bureaucracy on the events under study. kind of critique is that it is always partial and pi technique for the reduction of the ideological eler not a special technique apart from the norma criticism.

However, authoritative judgments of truth rest with a community of competent judges. The agreement among a self-defining and self-selecti itself simply a way of enshrining an ideology? I the guild's collective imprimatur of approval—i madness"?[16] The key elements in determining

[handwritten margin note: Kuhns:
1) Belief in "natural" laws
2) Reality of scientific process (development)]

---

[14] S. M. Lipset, "Political Sociology," in *Socio* eds. R. K. Merton, Leonard Brown, and Leonard S. 81–114.

[15] The works of J. K. Galbraith are, of course,

[16] The question has been given new strength b

to the view that Jones made a promise involves committing myself to what he ought to do (other things being equal)." But why? Surely a man might agree that Jones made a promise as defined within the American socio-legal system and yet say that Jones ought not to keep it because that socio-legal system is iniquitous and its obligations should be ignored whenever possible. To this objection, Professor Searle's response is that there is a distinction between an "external" and "internal" point of view towards "institutional facts." To ask "Ought one to accept the institution of promising?" is to ask an "external" question, in which the constitutive rule is not accepted as a binding norm, but is instead made a subject of examination and appraisal. It is to be sharply contrasted, Professor Searle indicates, with "internal questions asked within the framework of the institution"—for example, "Ought one to keep one's promises?"[13] But if this is the case, we have merely substituted the language of "internal-external" for the language of "is-ought" or "fact-value," while retaining the essential distinction at issue.

That distinction is between, on one hand, expressing, internalizing, or participating in a system of obligations and, on the other, regarding that system as itself subject to question and possessing moral legitimacy only so far as it meets the test of some external set of norms. However we describe this distinction, it reemerges the moment one refuses to say, as Professor Searle refuses, that any specific moral system carries with it its own internal guarantee of validity. The difference between his view and Hume's, then, is hard to see.

Indeed, the distinction between "is" and "ought" can itself be seen as derivative from the more basic rule of inquiry that terms must retain a fixed meaning within any particular course of argument. This is, if one wishes to put it in Professor Searle's language, a "constitutive rule" of inquiry. Just as people within the institution of "promising" are not engaging in promising when they use expressions with the word "promise" but see no connected obligation, so people are not engaging in the institutional practice known as inquiry when they disregard shifts in the meanings of terms as they go along. For the function of this institutional practice is to arrive at conclusions testable by a community of observers employing the same rules, and the test cannot be made if the community cannot pin down what is being asserted. The *Wertfreiheit* of the social sciences insists on little more than the application of this rule of inquiry to the subjects that social scientists investigate, including the desirability of specific social institutions and values.

---

[13] "Taken literally, as an internal question, as a question about promises and not about the institution of promising, the question, 'Ought one to keep one's promises?' is as empty as the question, 'Are triangles three-sided?' To recognize something as a promise is to grant that, other things being equal, it ought to be kept" (Ibid., p. 127).

5.

But logic, it may be replied, is one thing and the actual and inescapable condition of social scientists as human beings caught in a world of partisan claims is another—and much more to the practical point. Behind many of the recent controversies between social scientists there lies the belief that since all social ideas are socially conditioned, all social ideas, inevitably, are interest-loaded —partisan, inherently one-sided, in short "ideological." Often as the concept of ideology is analyzed and presumably refuted, it comes back with the hardiness of a perennial flower. And it is, in fact, one of the permanent ideas in the Western tradition of thought.

The notion of tragic blindness, on which Greek tragedy rests, indicates how old the recognition is that people can, though thoroughly conscious and under no one else's control, act as though hypnotized. They perform actions whose causes, meaning, and consequences they misunderstand, and are unable to do anything else, because they hold a picture of reality in which the actions they are pursuing appear to be the only proper or possible course. These blindnesses may be self-defeating, preventing people from satisfying their important needs; they may be self-protective, permitting the individual to seek purposes that, if undisguised, he would not seek or would not seek without embarrassment. In either case, they are self-deceptions.

Obviously, this idea of psychological blindness reflects an important truth of human experience. It is fundamental to both comedy and tragedy. In their classic forms these have presupposed an audience sitting on the outside of the action and able to tell the difference between appearance and reality although the personages in the play cannot. Bottom is Bottom although the Fairy Queen, under a spell, does not know this. Oedipus has killed his father and taken his mother as wife, and all the world watching the play knows this, although he does not. Similarly, a fundamental idea in the religions of conversion and revelation is that people can live in darkness without knowing it and that the darkness is of their own willful yet helpless making so that they can be saved only by those who bring light from the outside. As in comedy or tragedy, an external spectator is presupposed.

It is helpful to see the concept of "ideology" against this background. It is the descendant of the dramatic and religious ideas of the disabling blindness, self-imposed yet unwilled. "Ideology" asserts the existence of this phenomenon as a collective matter. Conceptions of social reality reflect not that reality but the needs and perspectives of the groups, classes, or nations that construct them. And social science, according to this view, is in a way more ideological than other modes of interpreting reality because it parades under the banner of universal truth, and thus better serves the ideological function of masking the interests and intentions behind it. But the problem in such a generalized imputation of "false consciousness" to social science is that, as in the theater or religion, a spectator must be presupposed who is able accurately to distinguish the real from the illusory. Without this assumption no content can be given to the concept of "false consciousness." The fundamental issue, therefore, is the validation of this external knowledge as reliable and as superior in its authority to the beliefs composing the alleged ideology.

Broadly speaking, there are two ways to support such an assumption. One may point to a putatively superior science, e.g., a general philosophy of history, and criticize the findings of particular social sciences from this standpoint. The allegedly superior science, however, is itself maintained free from scrutiny. As in a theater, it is the actors who are at fault if they do not give satisfaction; it is never the audience that is obtuse, insensitive, or unreasonable. The critique of "ideology" that is offered from such a base is, however disguised, a critique by the method of authority.

The second way is by a process of internal criticism within social science. This may go on within an individual science, as when a political sociologist notes that the overwhelming proportion of American sociologists who are students of politics concentrate on reform movements or on right-wing extremism and neglect "integrative institutions," such as religion and law,[14] or when an economist notes that his compeers give central importance in their analytic models to a conception of "consumer sovereignty" apparently unaffected by such empirical phenomena as advertising or the setting of prices by the clash of organized political forces like management, labor, and government.[15] It may also go on between disciplines, as when a historian points to the temporal limitations of a sociologist's generalizations or a sociologist indicates to a historian that a different explanation of events would be given if more attention were paid to the impact of bureaucracy on the events under study. What is significant about this kind of critique is that it is always partial and piecemeal. It is a social scientific technique for the reduction of the ideological elements in social science, but it is not a special technique apart from the normal apparatus of scientific self-criticism.

However, authoritative judgments of truth and falsity in the social sciences rest with a community of competent judges. The question therefore remains: Is agreement among a self-defining and self-selecting group of "competent judges" itself simply a way of enshrining an ideology? Is "truth" in a social science only the guild's collective imprimatur of approval—in Santayana's phrase, its "normal madness"?[16] The key elements in determining the answers to this question are

---

14 S. M. Lipset, "Political Sociology," in *Sociology Today: Problems and Prospects,* eds. R. K. Merton, Leonard Brown, and Leonard S. Cottrell, Jr. (New York, 1959), pp. 81–114.

15 The works of J. K. Galbraith are, of course, prominent examples.

16 The question has been given new strength by having been raised recently about the

the way in which admission to the circle of "competent judges" is determined and the degree to which the group's tests are insulated from external challenge. If political right-mindedness is an indispensable prerequisite for recognition as a member of the guild, or if political tests are employed for the supposed purpose of insuring a "fair" representation of different points of view, ideological affinities are built into the appraisal system of the discipline. Again, if the standards by which ideas are accepted or rejected in the disciplines are unaffected by developments in other disciplines, these standards have privileged status and can be qualified as "ideological." (Thus carbon tests are products of chemical research, but are relevant to the appraisal of anthropological hypotheses about the age of fossil remains.) "Ideology" is a term to be applied to ideas that move in closed circles—that have their own preselected critics and tests so that it is guaranteed in advance that they will survive. Scientific ideas, in contrast, live without these protections.

Without discounting the amount of tribal prejudice that exists in the social sciences, the evidence is that, overall, their institutions of self-governance and intellectual criticism are in the scientific pattern. If they are regarded as stationary and examined at a given moment, the ideological accretions in them will be considerable. If they are seen as changing systems of ideas driven by the dynamic of challenge and criticism, they emerge as bodies of knowledge that, so long as they retain their autonomy, are insured against permanent capture by any ideology.[17]

6.

Against this background, we may turn to the question of the forms of self-discipline available in the social sciences with regard to the discussion of con-

Kuhn:
1) *Belief in "natural" laws*
2) *Reality of scientific process (development)*

natural sciences. At the conclusion of his much-discussed *The Structure of Scientific Revolutions*, Thomas S. Kuhn asks, "Does it really help to imagine that there is some one full, objective, true account of nature and that the proper measure of scientific achievement is the extent to which it brings us closer to that ultimate goal? . . . the entire process [of the development of science] may have occurred, as we now suppose biological evolution did, without benefit of a set goal, a permanent fixed scientific truth, of which each stage in the development of scientific knowledge is a better exemplar." (Chicago, 1962), pp. 170–171. The impact of Professor Kuhn's position on current debate within the social sciences is great and deserves a separate examination on its own.

[17] I would note in passing—unhappily, space does not allow a discussion of the issue at the length it deserves—that Professor Kuhn's theory of "paradigms" does not, I believe, undermine this point. Even if these "paradigms" are sustained by force of essentially political processes within the relevant scientific community, they do collapse under strain, and the strain is produced not simply by competition with other groups with different interests and perspectives but by the difficulties experienced in fitting new observations and investigations into the received models.

troverted social issues or the advocacy of particular policies and causes. It is useful in approaching this question to draw a distinction between two ways in which social scientists, in relation to public policy decisions, may unwarrantedly lend the authority of their discipline to what are essentially extra-scientific political biases. The first is in their formulation of research agenda and definition of theoretical issues. The second is in the explicit judgments they make with regard to questions of practical policy.

Examples of the first are the following.

—Sociologists during the past two decades have devoted much effort and ink to exploring the causes for the growth of "conformity" on the American scene. However, there is no strong weight of evidence that conformity *has* grown. The belief that it has is part of a general moral-political outlook shared by most sociologists, but it is not a finding of empirical sociology.[18]

—Fundamental questions are sometimes systematically ignored, both for ideological and practical reasons. For example, "schools do a great deal of testing and use the results, for better or worse, in the diagnosis and counseling of individual students, but rarely for analytical purposes—to compare the effectiveness of different programs or different schools, or to identify progress or retrogression of the system over time."[19] Seeking an objective answer to the question, "Is the nation better educated than it used to be?," the authors of *Toward a Social Report* scoured the literature and found almost nothing worth reporting. The reason is that national assessments of education by means of tests administered periodically to a national sample of children and adults have regularly been fought by the teaching profession. "School officials, fearful that, for them, 'assessment' meant 'report cards,' rejected all designs that have permitted comparisons among schools or systems."[20]

—The distinctive intellectual tools available to a discipline often prefigure the explanation of a phenomenon that it will give. Economists, in studying whether punishment deters crime, tend to begin with the assumption that it will do so; it is their habit to explain behavior in terms of the comparative costs of alternatives, and they treat punishment as part of a pricing system. In contrast, sociologists have characteristically begun with the assumption that punishment does not deter, because they tend to explain behavior in terms of attitudes socially transmitted and supported by relevant reference groups. For them, therefore, the pronouncement is almost automatic that punishment does not work, because it does not get at "the causes" of crime, which lie in social dislocation, anomie,

---

[18] S. M. Lipset, "Political Sociology," pp. 81–114.

[19] Alice M. Rivlin, *Systematic Thinking for Social Action* (Washington, 1971), p. 49.

[20] See Martin T. Katzman and Ronald S. Rosen, "The Science and Politics of National Educational Assessment," *The Record* 71 (May 1970) : 571–86.

family conditions, etc.[21] Another example of the way in which established interests in existing methods may preclude systematic inquiry is offered by the phenomenon of advertising. What is its impact on the market? On the concept of "consumer sovereignty"? On the national distribution of resources? Advertising is a giant presence on the contemporary economic scene, and billions are spent on the assumption that it creates demand. Nevertheless, there has not been much empirical examination of the effects of advertising by economists.

—Techniques, e.g., Paretian optimality, that are used to provide putatively neutral content to concepts such as "social welfare," in fact may incorporate fundamental moral judgments, such as that it is right for men to hold their values subject to trade-offs. Similarly, the concept of the GNP, as a number of economists have pointed out, shows a bias in favor of tangible goods as against more intangible goods, such as environmental beauty and serenity.

In these ways the social sciences function, like poetry in Shelley's description, as unacknowledged legislators of the race. They exercise, all unconsciously, an influence on one or the other side of contested issues. The protections against this, however, cannot be found in terms of a model of social science in which it presents immaculate conceptions of social reality free from provincialism and special pleading. The protections reside in the patterns of mutual criticism normally employed within these sciences. Their "objectivity" is a function of the communal forum provided by a discipline for the vetting of ideas. Broadly speaking, the operative questions are three.

1. Are there well-established facts and theories in the science capable of serving as independent generators of inquiries and as effective frameworks for the conduct of mutual criticism? In practice social sciences differ widely in the degree to which they have succeeded in building such analytical structures. Economics, for example, is relatively well advanced in comparison with anthropology. The possession of a powerful analytical structure means that the science has within it a factor making for its development along lines independent of existing practical demands or moral beliefs. It does not mean, of course, that practitioners of the science will agree on practical matters. Physicians, presumably, accept the same principles of anatomy, but do not invariably agree on the cure for a specific case of curvature of the spine. Similarly, economists may disagree on measures to be taken about a specific recession.

2. Even if the discipline is divided into sects and schools, are the procedures governing recruitment into the discipline and debate and criticism within it reasonably adapted to the pursuit of consensus on facts and theories? Thus, the

---

21 See Gordon Tullock, "Does Punishment Deter Crime," *The Public Interest* 36 (Summer 1974): 103–11; also, James Q. Wilson, "Crime and the Criminologists," *Commentary* 58 (July 1974): 47–53.

chapter in this volume submitted by Jonathan and Stephen Cole gives strong, though admittedly partial, evidence that the sociological profession, in its procedures for recruitment and the recognition of achievement, has arrived at a relative consensus on basic criteria and has squared its practice fairly well with its announced principles. Nor is there evidence that other principles could be substituted that would be better designed to attain progressive convergence of instructed opinion. Empirical inquiries of the kind conducted by the Coles show that the question whether a given discipline is an ideology in disguise is capable of at least partial resolution by empirical methods.

3. Is the wider cultural and social context such that the members of a given intellectual discipline, while enjoying autonomy in the determination of acceptable doctrine within their fields, are nevertheless exposed to a variety of perspectives and to constraints requiring them with some regularity to review the definitions, presumptions, and purposes of the discipline? The means for controlling unconscious partisanship in a social science consist fundamentally in the normal procedures of publication and criticism within the field. However, this principle needs to be supplemented by another. The "normal" procedures of publication and criticism can degenerate into routine forms of inspection to insure conformity to inherited conventions unless there is pressure from the outside. It was ideas in physics that helped generate, through Hobbes and the Physiocrats, the methods of modern economics. It was ideas in economics—specifically Malthus'—that prepared the way for Darwin's theory of biological evolution. The degree to which practitioners of a social science are insulated from people in other disciplines is therefore a possible sign of encrusted bias. Similarly, a highly controlled or undiversified culture is another condition for the scientific disease known as hardening of the categories. In this sense, liberty and social democracy are conditions for a social science capable of policing itself.

The importance of bringing to bear on a social science a variety of perspectives gives weight to the claim that the social sciences, if only for their own health, are mistaken to eschew direct involvement in questions of practical moment in the political arena. Scholars as a group live in a special sub-culture, and their general view of social problems can be self-perpetuating unless some among them bring back into the culture perspectives drawn from a different kind of experience. This therapeutic exercise is vitiated, however, when social scientists unwarily mix ideological and scientific motifs in the judgments they offer. Examples in recent controversies are numerous.

—Social scientists working on questions related to the control of pornographic books and films usually emphasize the insufficiency of evidence that such materials do determinate harm. In dealing with the effects of television violence, however, they tend, although the evidence is also equivocal, to lean in the other direction. The well-known fact that academic people generally take a more respectful attitude towards books and films than toward television would appear to have something to do with this difference.

—Social scientists, for example, those attached to the Kerner Commission, have lent the authority of their disciplines to pronouncements such as that America is a "white racist" nation. This is to deal in epithet, not precise and carefully qualified scientific description, and it implies comparative judgments that are not stated and for which no evidence is produced. It deals with complex and subtle issues of practical policy by substituting a general moral judgment, reached by a priori methods, for detailed analysis and evaluation of the concrete social claims and interests actually in competition.

—Policy analysis, sometimes in deference to existing institutional practices and government policies, sometimes in deference to what are taken to be the technical limits of a discipline beyond which analysis should not go, may offer recommendations based on a systematically foreshortened view of alternatives. This lies at the heart of the controversy over the ABM between the ORSA group and Professors Wiesner and Rathjens, aspects of which have been discussed by Professor Doty in this volume. The question of the capacities and intentions of the Soviet Union with regard to the construction of a missile system good enough to destroy the United States' retaliatory capability is not resolvable by appeal to purely technical questions of weaponry. The sociological and political prerequisites and consequences of such a Soviet effort are at least as pertinent. Moreover, the diplomatic implications of mounting an ABM system with regard, for example, to the SALT talks, are also relevant. Unless what is left out of consideration is carefully specified, an insistence on scientific "purity"—the avoidance of any judgments that are not one's technical business—can be a disguised way of sanctifying unspoken political presuppositions and preferences.

Again, however, there is no general panacea for dealing with these problems. A greater self-awareness as to their prepossessions and a greater willingness to avow them is desirable in individual social scientists working in the public arena. It would be desirable if it were taken to be a norm of professional ethics that individuals should indicate as clearly as they can when it is that they speak as members of a discipline and when it is that they are addressing issues with regard to which they can offer, at best, only an enlightened citizen's opinion. But this is often a difficult and delicate judgment to make, especially when the individual is judging himself. Ultimate reliance must be placed on the discipline's collective procedures for mutual criticism. That they often work slowly it would be hard to deny. Nothing is more evident day to day than the influence of the *Zeitgeist,* particularly that prevailing in academia, on the public pronouncements of social scientists. Happily, however, the *Zeitgeist* as it affects American social scientists appears to change fairly rapidly, and the methods internal to the disciplines for separating bias from scientific findings can reasonably be expected to be effective over the long term.

7.

If the foregoing analysis is in general correct, the questions that have been raised in recent years about the posture of social scientists in relation to value-loaded questions in the arena of public controversy do not put in jeopardy the basic concept of an autonomous social science enterprise. They point to the need for greater self-discipline, but they do not show that the social sciences have been or should be converted into forms of propaganda and preaching. The attack on *Wertfreiheit* has been motivated, at least some of the time, by the laudable purpose of encouraging social scientists to examine vital moral and political issues, and to do so from a point of view in which the premises and values on which existing institutions are based are themselves thrown into question. But this purpose is grossly distorted when an alternative to *Wertfreiheit* is offered which, in effect, demands that social scientists bind themselves to some set of antecedent values that they accept as unquestioned absolutes. On the whole, this has been the alternative that has been offered, and it means not the cure of social science but its dissolution.

When it is said that the social scientist should lend himself professionally only to "moral" or "socially desirable" purposes, the critic assumes precisely what is subject to inquiry—namely, the content to be given, in a particular context of choice, to the terms "moral" and "socially desirable." The difficult problems in professional life do not present choices between the indisputably moral and the indisputably immoral. Rather, they present conflicts between norms each of which has some prima facie claim to be taken seriously and weighed in the balance. The social sciences' relations to controversial issues are best seen, I believe, in this perspective. The danger is not that something of finer stuff known as "values" will be extruded from the work of social scientists. It is that the commonplace human attitudes that social scientists share with everyone else—hopes, hunches, allegiances, prejudices, principles, active faiths—will either be concealed below the surface or treated as though their validity were assured. Indeed, from a logical point of view, the attack on *Wertfreiheit* is but the other side of the doctrine that the social sciences, in their policy-making role, can be totally dissevered from all but purely technical and factual considerations. Both views hold that values are not themselves subject to disciplined study and criticism.

Indeed, although the controversies between social scientists about matters of public policy have lately become a bit more muted, the long-term stakes over which the battles have been fought remain of the greatest importance. There is a sense in which the severest, even the vulgarest, critics of the social sciences may be said to be right. The social sciences, however autonomous they may succeed in being, are inextricably involved in politics. Politics—the deliberate, conscious process of competition to influence the ordering of values—supervenes when customary rule breaks down and a consensus on things small or large disappears. In coming to decisions, in Aristotle's phrase, "as to what it is to do and what it is to abstain from," society turns to a variety of sources of instruction, secular and sacred. The essential condition for the emergence of social science exists when the authority of the principles, ideas, and information received from conventional sources has eroded.

But this is only the essential condition for its emergence. It must still compete for the society's attention and respect. Social scientists, although they may seek nothing more than a fair hearing for what they have to say, are thus in the political business whether they realize it or not. They are upsetting apple carts, undermining positions of power, and moving money, opinion, and prestige in this direction or that. In this sense Dr. Ezrahi is right: There is a "culture" of social scientists, and this "culture" may run athwart tendencies deeply implanted in the "political" culture. But to remind social scientists that politics is not science, and not, therefore, their proper game, is an ill-conceived counsel. Social scientists, representing as they do a source of social description, explanation, and diagnosis different from other sources to which societies also appeal, are in politics. They can escape this destiny only by taking vows of silence. They compete in the political arena because, like priests, journalists, or professional politicians, they cannot help but make the claim that they know something valuable that should be used to govern the polity.

To forsake this claim would be more than to deny the reality or value of social science. It would be to turn away from an abiding enterprise of liberal civilization. Particularly over the last one hundred years, liberal civilization has been engaged in a complex and dangerous venture—on the one side, to incorporate the many into society, to serve their interests and, as far as possible, to speak their will; on the other side, to cut into the sway of magic, mystery, and authority and to rely on them less in the governance of men. Along with the notions of professionalism, civility, and rule by law, the idea of an independent and objective quest for the social truth is part of the family of principles on which liberal society has relied to hold it together as it engages in this effort.

Indeed, the idea of an independent social science is part of the central faith on which liberal civilization, since its origins in Greece, has rested. This is faith in the possibility of a society's standing, as it were, apart from itself, of its attaining a perspective on its doings not wholly reducible to rationalization, self-congratulation, or self-promotion. Something like this—the chance to live twice, the chance to escape the obsessions of place and time and to see things in the aspect of eternity—is what has drawn enlightened men in all cultures to the hope for immortality. The notion of an autonomous science of man is a liberal, secular civilization's effort to achieve something like this perspective of immortality on itself.

The Role of Values
in Social Science Research
Nicholas Rescher

INTRODUCTION

The ramifications of the fact-value distinction within the social sciences move in two major directions. On the one hand lies the issue of the status of values as targets of social science research and in particular the question of whether the social scientist is in a position not simply to study the values held by others but also to invoke values himself, to do some actual evaluating of his own with respect to his objects of investigation. On the other hand lies the issue of the status of values not as targets of research but as operative factors in the shaping of the research effort itself. Both of these issues form part of the overall theme of this essay.

PART I: VALUES AS AN OBJECT OF EVALUATION

The Problem

Everyone agrees that the social sciences can investigate the values held by a social group, just as they can study its eating mores or rites of passage, in a "purely descriptive" and nonevaluative manner, as a sort of reportage on the evaluative discourse and value-related behavior in actual currency within the group. But the crucial question remains whether the "scientist-outsider" can legitimately go beyond such description to *evaluate* the values of the group and criticize them in ways other than with regard to their internal coherence. In short, as an outsider can he pass some sort of valid reasoned judgment upon them? Can he legitimately say such things as "Yes, they do indeed value X, but it's quite wrong of them to do so (and not just because X is inconsistent with Y which they value even more highly)" or "They prefer X to Y but in doing so are ill-advised (misguided, mistaken)"? In short, can the social scientist himself legitimately and warrantedly give us not merely a descriptive *report* on the values of a social group, but an actual evaluation or criticism of them? I want to argue here that he not only can but to some extent must do so.

The Contingent Foundation of Human Purpose

The question of the range of human purposes cannot be settled on theoretical, a priori grounds. To specify normatively the objectives that people are well advised to pursue in life demands in the first instance a purely empirical inquiry into what they say and do and requires us to examine the facts of the matter regarding the nature of man and the character of the human condition. Any serviceable clarification of the scope of people's aims and goals must root in these facts of the matter: Wherever we end, we must begin with man as we find him and with the structure of human life as we find it.

Empirical inquiry about human values and purposes is more than a mere listing of discrete items. Above all, it requires information regarding the relative role played by these values and purposes in situations of mutual conflict. Internal relations of weight and precedence ("higher and lower") must be taken into due account. Our purposes are not created equal: Some are in a dominant or controlling position vis-à-vis others. What is thus at issue is not just a schedule (or list) of purposes and values but a *structure*. Within such a structure, an internal comparison or relative evaluation is possible. And the realization of this possibility leads to the rational systematization of purposes and desires in the framework of an empirically based understanding of man's nature and of the human condition. (To give but one crude example, we prize *survival* over mere *enjoyment* and so would value, in terms of internal consistency, what is survival-conducive over what is (merely) enjoyment-conducive.)

But a crucial issue remains open. Given the (empirical) fact that a society does have a certain value, what can one say about the *genuineness* of this value? Can the "mere fact" of its being valued show that it is deserving of recognition as normatively authentic, appropriate, and legitimate?

Mill's "Fallacy" and Its Lessons

Few texts in modern social theory have received more discussion than the following passage of J. S. Mill's classic essay on *Utilitarianism*.

The only proof capable of being given that an object is visible, is that people actually see it. The only proof that a sound is audible, is that people hear it: and so of the other sources of our experience. In like manner, I apprehend, the sole evidence it is possible to produce that anything is desirable, is that people do actually desire it. If the end which the utilitarian doctrine proposes to itself were not, in theory and in practice, acknowledged to be an end, nothing could ever convince any person that it was so. No reason can be given why the general happiness is desirable, except that each person, so far as he believes it to be attainable, desires his own happiness.[1]

A whole pack of philosophical critics have descended upon this passage of Mill's, reproving him for committing a crude fallacy in reasoning by making the move from being *desired* to being *desirable,* a step, it is said, that blatantly ignores the Humean divide between fact and value, between *truth* and *norm,* between what *is* the case and what *ought* to be the case.

This matter is centrally important for our present purposes. We have granted that the issue of what human purposes are is a matter of contingent empirical fact. But suppose we are not content to let the matter rest here, at this factual level; suppose that, like Mill, we seek to obtain conclusions of normative weight.

The first thing is to recognize that the step

$$\text{desired} \rightarrow \text{desirable}$$

is not a matter of an automatic inference (as, for example, in talking about whole numbers the step "prime $\rightarrow$ indivisible by 4" would be). The link is not *deductive* but *evidential:* The factual status of being desired carries evidential weight towards the normative status of being desirable. For example, there is obviously a relation of a prima facie sort that would prevail in the absence of suitably powerful countervailing considerations. (If something is desired, then in the absence of any and all indications to the contrary it should be recognized as desirable. In the face of the fact of desire the burden of proof regarding desirability shifts to the other foot.) The fact of being desired is certainly not a determinant or guarantee of what is desirable (*worthy* of being desired, *properly* and *warrantedly* desired). But actual desire at least constitutes *presumptive evidence* of desirability, evidence which (1) must be allowed to prevail in the absence of any counter-indications, and (2) must otherwise be weighted against them in the balance scale, so as to constitute a consideration to which *some* weight must be accorded in any case. In short, though not a *guarantee* of the normative status of desirability, the empirical fact of being desired must at least be viewed as an *evidential factor* that has *some* tendency to move toward this conclusion.

---

[1] J. S. Mill, *Utilitarianism* (London, 1863), ch. IV. For references to the extensive literature on the ideas of this passage, see the bibliography in *Mill's Ethical Writings,* ed. J. B. Schneewind (New York, 1965).

The Fundamentality of Respect of Persons

But the matter does not rest there—at this simply evidential level. Considerations of respect for the worth of man and the dignity of his condition impel us towards acceptance of a practical principle along something like the following lines.

> Those purposes that people widely share in their thinking and take seriously in their actions are to be respected as at least presumptively legitimate.

This principle is not a factual (empirically constitutive) *thesis* about how things work in the world, but represents a procedural (normatively regulative) *postulate* as to the course of our actions: It does not say what *is the case* but stipulates *what ought to be done* (viz., that these purposes *are to be treated as* legitimate). Accordingly it might be designated as a regulative "Postulate of Respect," that is, respect for the intrinsic dignity of the human person. Its legitimation roots in a mixture of utilitarian considerations for smoothing the channels in which human affairs run their course and idealistic considerations as to the inherent worth and dignity of man (which function quite apart from any utilitarian implications).[2]

The purport of this postulate is not to have us take the stance that whatever is is automatically right in the domain of human goal and purposes. The applicability of the precept is nothing automatic but is restricted by considerations of the *appropriateness of circumstances,* with a view to such conditions as the following.

1. the *mode* in which the purposes are held—the way in which they are subscribed to—is such as to indicate their fundamentality (e.g., through their stability).
2. the pursuit of these purposes, while it need not advance the welfare interests of people, should not, in general, do them harm.
3. the purposes at issue must have some deep foothold in the structure of the human condition: They should not be altogether parochial and idiosyncratic to the group in question; a wide variety of other ethical codes, even those which do not accord a comparably prominent place to the objectives at issue, must provide a background against which the according of some positive value to them can be rationalized.

We are carried back to the preceding thesis that the Postulate of Respect establishes a relationship of a prima facie sort that prevails only in the absence of suitably powerful countervailing considerations, considerations which such conditions of applicability serve to illustrate in somewhat more specific detail.[3]

---

[2] The idea of respect for persons is a fundamental and pervasive theme in the philosophy of Kant. For approaches to this Kantian theme in contemporary social theory, see John Rawls, *A Theory of Justice* (Cambridge, Mass., 1971), esp. ch. V, pp. 395–452. See also R. S. Downie and E. Telfer, *Respect for Persons* (London, 1969).

[3] It must be stressed that we are only saying that being desired is one route to desirability, not that it is the *only* route. Something could redound to the welfare (or other

It is crucial that the warranting principle at issue is *practical* and relates to the inherently telic and norm-oriented area of human purposes. We would, of course, take a rather different view of the seemingly analogous principle.

> Those propositions that people widely accept in their thinking and implement in their actions are to be accepted as correct.

The critical difference between these principles resides in the classical distinction between man's will and his intellect. The point is that the very concept of a "legitimate human purpose" turns on what is *authentic for people* in terms of their actual desires and actions. On the other hand, the concept of a "correct human belief" does not pertain in any straightforward way to posture vis-à-vis the world, but on "the actual facts of the matter," precisely because factual beliefs (unlike purposes, goals, aims, ideals, etc.) make an other-directed claim about how things go in the world rather than an inner-directed claim about the condition of man as such. Accordingly there is a radical disanalogy between the transition

thought to be true → actually true

and the transition

thought to be desirable → actually desirable

Though an inferential gap certainly exists in both cases, it is far wider in the case of truth than in the case of desirability—wider not in the statistical sense that fewer people are perverse than misinformed, but in the sense of the scope and scale of the added conditions to be satisfied for the transition to be properly warranted. The difference in the validation conditions between actual truth and actual desirability are such as to make for a clear difference between the two cases. The realm of norms and values is autonomous of "the actual facts of the matter" in a way that the realm of beliefs and truth claims cannot be. (Though to say this is, as we have seen, not to say that factual considerations do not serve as data for normative ones. They do serve as data, but their ability to do so rests on the espousal of a postulate of practical and regulative import that has no counterpart on the strictly factual side.)

In the framework of present concerns the Postulate of Respect provides the social theorist at the regulative or methodological level with a bridging principle across the fact-value divide. It furnishes a vehicle for moving from the *actuality* of a certain evaluative stance within a social group to constitute, at least in the first instance, a case for the *legitimation* of the values at issue with relation to the social group at issue.

---

proper interests) of people—and so be eminently desirable—without its ever having entered into their consciousness, let alone their actually desiring it (e.g., public sanitation in fifteenth-century Europe). Indeed, it is crucially important to our overall argument that desire-satisfaction—which, after all, is usually of hedonic orientation—is not the only factor in establishment of desirability.

The Social Sciences as Policy Oriented

Insofar as the social sciences are not "merely descriptive," proceeding in purely behavioristic manner, to limit themselves to the descriptive depiction of human action (overt and verbal), they must also consider the rationale of human purposes that underlie the actions of men. And this "insofar" is substantial. For the very taxonomy of social description is theory-laden with respect to the purposive aspects of human action. The categories used in the description of social phenomena are fundamentally teleological. To account in a satisfactory way for what people do, the social scientist cannot avoid casting his descriptive account of actual behavior in terms that reflect the purposive springs of human action.

Moreover, the social sciences are inherently policy-significant. Insofar as successful social research reveals "the way in which things work in the world," its findings bear upon what will happen "in certain circumstances" and thus provide a basis for taking practical steps in the arrangement of human affairs. But the rationalization of policy always requires some degree of commitment at the purposive level: One cannot proceed to guide policy in altogether purpose-hypothetical terms ("If X is your operative purpose, do X") but must be in a position to determine the legitimacy of espousing certain purposes under certain circumstances. Comprehensively effective policy guidance cannot confine itself to considerations of the rationality (effectiveness) of means; it must also face the issue of the rationality (validity) of ends.

The rational guidance of policy cannot rest with a strictly descriptive accord of the value and purposes that people actually have without any normative screening between the valid and the invalid. There can be no analysis of the cost-benefit implications of policy alternatives without reference to the relevantly operative modes of utility. This policy-oriented aspect of the social sciences means that the appropriate techniques for the rational appraisal of human purposes must be at hand within the overall resources of the methodological instrumentalities of social research.

Now it is a consequence of the Postulate of Respect that the discovered actualities of a society's strivings, admirings, and purposes (i.e., its values) deserve weight, that they be regarded as, prima facie, candidates to be legitimated as proper values. But this must not be misconstrued to maintain that actual evaluations are final, that in the normative sphere whatever is is right. The crucial difference remains between considerations that are relevant in determining validity and those that are conclusive or final.

Human Purpose: Preferences Are Not Enough

Although preferences are important for the understanding of welfare, their proper place in the scheme of things must not be exaggerated, as a not inconsiderable sector of modern economics has been inclined to do. For example, when mooting the problem of his book on *Social Choice and Individual Values,* it soon becomes apparent that by "individual values" Kenneth Arrow simply means *preferences* of the tea-over-coffee variety. This will not do if our aim is to establish the conception of group *welfare* in anything like its normal sense: The road from preference to welfare is too long and winding. A man's welfare may, indeed standardly does, bear *some* relationship to his preferences, but that does not result in their mutual assimilation. Preference is too gross an instrument to capture the subtle nuances of welfare. If Jones prefers apples to oranges—be it in general or in point of, say, appearance or flavor—this does not go far to indicate what his welfare consists in. Welfare is a thing of stability and solidity; preferences can be things of the fleeting moment, and indeed things that fly in the face of consciously reckoned benefits. (Attempts such as that of deriving welfare from "retrospective preferences in the long run" are, rather transparently, little more than mythology.)

This is why the talk of some economists about preference-combining schemes in terms of "social *welfare* functions" rings a hollow note. There is nothing sacred about preferences. Parents, physicians, and schoolmasters (among others) have long known that welfare is not to be extracted from preferences, not even necessarily from preferences in the long run. Welfare has to do with our real interests. What relates to welfare is objective and interpersonally debatable. But preferences frequently operate in the area of tastes, and fall within the purview of the classic maxim that *de gustibus non est disputandum.* Thus to assign central importance to the project of distilling a conception of social welfare out of individual *preferences* is to espouse a highly questionable ideology in the economic-political sphere.

Democratic societies do not in fact, and surely need not in theory, settle public issues in terms of such preference-pooling procedures. These will, of course, have *some* role in the democratic process, but this need not be an all-pervasive one making individual preference a supremely predominant factor that sweeps all else before it. Precisely because preferences need not reflect interests and welfare, there is nothing intrinsically objectionable about this.

For reasons such as these I regard the preoccupation of welfare economists with the problems of preference determination and aggregation as a red herring that has drawn them off the track of their proper concerns. In taking *preference* too seriously they have not taken welfare seriously enough.

The natural extension of welfare economics seems clearly to lie in the area of social applications of cost-benefit analysis, with social costs and social benefits both reckoned on a society-wide scale that does not insist upon deriving each detail by aggregation from individual considerations. The forging of the necessary tools, such as adequate procedures of social accounting, is obviously a task for the inheritors of "political economy." It would seem both plausible and eminently desirable that a revitalized welfare economics should orient itself in this direction and should address itself directly to the multifaceted elements of public welfare, instead of contending with the unrewarding complexities of preference pooling.[4]

The Scope of Human Purpose: Welfare is Not Enough

At this stage, the question of the comprehensiveness of the concept of welfare itself still remains. When concerned about the legitimation of our purposes, is a consideration of their welfare-related implications enough, or are there further substantial factors that must be taken into account? We must face the critical question of whether human *welfare,* comprehensive though it is, affords a wholly sufficient criterion of evaluation for social policy guidance.

Human purposes fall into two groups, somewhat along the lines of classical distinction between necessities and luxuries. The one category of purpose relates to the essentials of human welfare: to the strictly *practical goals* that have to do with the material interests of man, with what is needed to make life not only minimally possible but even satisfactory. With this first category we have to do with the hedonic dimension as it relates to the material interests of man not just in regard to the biomedical aspect of what makes life possible but also the economic aspect of what makes life pleasant in terms of the availability of goods and services. The governing concept in this area of basic needs comprises those factors that relate to man's welfare.

The second category of purpose relates to the transcendent concerns of man in matters that lie outside the range of his material requirements for food, shelter, clothing, goods, services, etc., and so go beyond the area of welfare and the whole sphere of "enjoyment." Here we have to do not with man's needs for the basic requisites of a satisfactory life but with his enhanced desires for a life that is rewarding and meaningful. Not only happy but good people and not only enjoyable or *satisfactory* but *satisfying* lives are important in the ethical scheme of things. Correspondingly, in assessing the quality of life one operates with an essentially two-factor criterion in which both welfare and human excellence play a significant part.

No matter how we shape in its details our overarching vision of the good life for man, welfare will play only a partial and subsidiary role because a satisfactory condition of affairs as to welfare is compatible with a substantial impoverishment outside the region of welfare minima. Indeed, a person, or a society, can be healthy, prosperous, and literate, but yet lack all those resources of personality, intellect, and character that, like cultivation of mind and fostering of human congeniality, make life rewarding as well as pleasant. Toward people or nations who have—even to abundance—the constituents of welfare, we may well feel envy, but our *admiration* and *respect* could never be won on this ground

---

[4] See Chap. XVIII, "A Philosopher Looks at Welfare Economics," in N. Rescher, *Essays in Philosophical Analysis* (Pittsburgh, 1969), for a further discussion of issues related to this section, which in fact draws upon the dicussion given there.

alone. Neither for individuals nor for societies is "the pursuit of happiness" the sole and legitimate guide to action; its dictates must be counterbalanced by recognizing the importance of doing those things upon which in after years we can look back with justifiable pride.

This points to an enlarged view of "the social good" that goes every bit as far outside the area of social welfare as any traditional view of "the good life" for man goes beyond the basics of individual welfare. On this view, a civilized society comes to qualify as such only when it devotes some reasonable proportion of its human and material resources to the cultivation of the fields of human excellence.

Accordingly, the legitimation of these nonutilitarian values does not rest on any appeal to utilitarian, welfare-related considerations. It rests ultimately upon the pattern of values to which people actually subscribe and find their rationale in an appeal to purposes and interests whose standing derives from the Postulate of Respect, through invocation of the de facto reality of human purposes of this "loftier" sort.

These considerations indicate that there is no valid theoretical reason for construing the practical area of welfare-related goals as exhausting the domain of legitimate human purposes. The values that a policy-oriented social science must be prepared to recognize as appropriate within the normative sector of the inquiry cannot validly be restricted to the welfare area alone.[5]

Instrumental vs. Pragmatic Justification: The Question of Reductionism

The tendency of the line of thought developed in the preceding section is that the domain of our strictly practical welfare-oriented purposes cannot validly be regarded as exhausting the entire range of human purposes: An extra-pragmatic dimension of legitimate human purpose must be admitted. The range of purposive justification is broader than its specifically pragmatic subdomain precisely because the range of legitimate human purpose as a whole is broader than the range of the specifically practical purposes that relate to human welfare. The reason is that, of course, the latter encompasses the ideal sector as well. Accordingly, instrumental (or *purposive*) justification, in the general terms of conducing to the realization of human purposes at large, is of broader scope than pragmatic justification in terms of specifically practical purposes.[6]

What justifies this insistence that society recognize the claims of excellence?

---

[5] The issues mooted in the present section are developed in a wider context in Chap. 9 of the author's book, *Welfare: The Social Issues in Philosophical Perspective* (Pittsburgh, 1972).

[6] Kant certainly stressed, as sharply as one could ask for, the Humean divide between the empirical domain and theoretical reason. But that the latter domain must itself be divided into a practical and a transpractical area, the former of which is in some sense controlling for theoretical reason (and the latter of which is determinative with respect to ethics proper) represents a perspective that goes beyond Kantian positions.

Certainly not an appeal to social welfare: It smacks of brazen hypocrisy to argue that art galleries, botanical gardens, theoretical physics, or the classical stage inevitably somehow advance the *welfare* of people. If the allocation of substantial social resources to museums, symphony orchestras, or institutes of advanced studies is justified—as I am convinced it is—the justification cannot proceed on the basis of welfare advancement; it should not be given with reference to *welfare* at all (no matter how indirect), but given, rather, in terms of something else that is just as important: *an investment in social ideals.* A nation in which certain of the arts, or historical studies, or pure mathematics go uncultivated could conceivably contrive matters so that the welfare of no specific individual is diminished thereby, but would nevertheless be a society whose *standing as a society* is impoverished by this lack. This is something in which every member of the society has a stake—albeit a *nonwelfare* stake. For the individual this is a matter not of comfort or well-being but of self-image, self-realization, self-identity, and just plain pride. What is at issue here is not a practical, utilitarian defense in terms of welfare benefits to people, but an "idealistic" defense in terms of the general principle of human ideals. No impoverishment of purse is as harmful as an impoverishment of spirit, and no route more surely leads to this tragic destination than the despising and neglect of the sectors of human achievement that compel admiration even in those of us who only look on disinterestedly from the sidelines.

The question remains: How is an appeal to welfare-transcending considerations of "quality" and "excellence" to be validated in the setting of a democratic society? Ideally, of course, through the existence of a general consensus in their favor. But on the basis of what sorts of rational considerations can this be motivated? Various possibilities exist. For one thing an appeal to the cumulative aspects of a generally beneficial cultural evolution might be of service. And there are also more purely pragmatic (and hence ultimately "welfare"-oriented) arguments for an appeal to excellence, having to do with the morale and esprit of a society, which may be ultimately necessary for its material prosperity and political coherence. Indeed, recent sociological studies suggest that work that generates a good self-image may be much more important to welfare than income and that plans for guaranteed income may be totally ineffective or even counterproductive without a guaranteed opportunity to become a contributing member of society. They also indicate that *relative* income is a far more important index of material satisfaction than *absolute* income—indeed that what is considered a "barely sufficient" income to get along (for a family of four) has remained at exactly 55 percent of median family income for the last thirty-five years, since data have been collected (Lee Rainwater).[7]

---

[7] Several parts of the paper, specifically including the present paragraph, are indebted to helpful comments by Harvey Brooks on a draft version of this essay.

To be sure, in the *logical* order the "higher" welfare-transcending values do not require the sort of benefit-conduciveness support indicated for them in the preceding paragraphs. Their value status as such is autonomous and would be secure even if no utilitarian defense could be given for them. But this, though true enough in the abstract, would provide but cold comfort in the context of political motivation. From this angle it is fortunate that things valuable "in themselves" can and frequently do turn out to be able to yield pragmatically beneficial side effects as well.

The basis of our position is a pluralistic conception of human values that is not prepared to accept welfare and its congeners (happiness, satisfaction, "utility") as the sole pivot about which all other legitimate goals must be made to revolve as instrumental means to this monolithic end. Instead, we see a value pluralism that envisages a diversity and variety of intrinsic (noninstrumental) goods, insisting that one must recognize as authentic human desiderata in their own (noninstrumental) right goods that (like knowledge,[8] artistic creativity, and excellence in various lines of human endeavor) may well fail in the final analysis to prove themselves as welfare-promoting or happiness-conducive. Though welfare is by no means *omni-determinative,* it does remain *central.* But our position espouses a fundamentally pluralistic conception of human purposes and values that regards the purely practical sector (of welfare, happiness, satisfaction, "utility," etc.) as only one incomplete part of a larger picture, and accordingly envisages the process of means-constituting justification with reference to *these* ends (viz., *pragmatic* justification proper) as only one particular version of goal-oriented justification in general (viz., *instrumental* justification). From this standpoint, the identification of pragmatic with instrumental justification commits a serious error of omission in failing to recognize the welfare-transcending status of certain values. This failure marks a regrettable narrowing of sympathy in appreciating the creative potentialities of the human spirit. It manifests an incapacity to achieve a vision of human nature that sees the task of man on this planet in larger terms than those of feathering his own nest in the pursuit of happiness.

The Upshot

The conclusion toward which these considerations point can now be summarized. The key point is that normative analysis is not only a possible but an appropriate part of social inquiry viewed in its global totality. As a practitioner of an inherently policy-oriented discipline, the social scientist cannot appropri-

---

[8] It deserves noting that there is no contradiction in holding with respect to factual knowledge that its methodological canons are validated in practical terms, but that a mastery of the substantial cognitive disciplines that result has a value that transcends the practical.

ately shut his eyes to the evaluative aspects of his discipline. The assessment of the rationality of de facto ends and the legitimation of de facto purposes poses issues that might in practice be ignored but not in theory justified. The conceptual tools for describing the life style of a social group and those needed for a rational assessment of the quality of its life are ultimately inseparable. Evaluative analysis is not something occult, which the social scientist would do well to shun. The evaluative framework of reference is ultimately inseparable from the scrutiny of the realities of the social situation as we encounter it in social inquiry. That, for example, the (descriptive) conditions making for illness or impoverishment are also (normatively) bad is so striking and obvious that any attempt to keep these aspects antiseptically separated is an exercise in futility.[9] The rational analysis of evaluation need not be value free as the price of remaining scientific: The critical scrutiny of values can maintain its normative as well as its descriptive dimension without transgressing the proper boundaries of scientific inquiry.[10]

PART II: THE ROLE OF VALUES IN THE CONDUCT OF RESEARCH

The Evaluative Dimension of Scientific Research[11]

This part of the discussion will survey the terrain constituting the evaluative dimension of scientific research. In particular, we will see that questions of a strictly evaluative nature arise in connection with scientific research at the following crucial junctures:

1. the choice of research goals;
2. the selection of research methods;
3. the specification of standards of proof;
4. the dissemination of research findings;
5. the control of scientific misinformation;
6. the allocation of credit for research accomplishments.

In short, it seems warranted to assert that, at virtually every stage in the conduct of scientific research, from initial inception of the work to the ultimate reporting of its completed findings, issues of a distinctively evaluative nature may present themselves for resolution.

---

[9] It is no accident that the normatively pejorative weight cannot be factored out from the descriptive residue of such terms as "filthy," "unsanitary," "putrid."

[10] For a further working-out of this theme see the methodological chapters in *Values and the Future: The Impact of Technological Change on American Values,* eds. K. Baier and N. Rescher (New York, 1969).

[11] The discussion of this second part of this essay draws upon my paper on "The Ethical Dimension of Scientific Research" in *Beyond the Edge of Certainty,* ed. R. Colodny (Englewood Cliffs, 1965).

It is frequently asserted that science is distinguished by its objectivity. The professional scientist—so it is said—must go about his work in a rigidly impersonal and unfeeling way, moved only by his love of knowledge and the delights of discovering the secrets of nature. This widely accepted image of scientific inquiry as a cold, detached, and inhumane affair is by no means confined to the scientifically uninformed outsiders, but finds many of its most eloquent spokesmen within the scientific community itself. Social scientists in particular tend to be outspoken supporters of the view that the scientist does not engage in making value judgments, and that science, real science, deals only with what is and has no concern with what ought to be. Any recitation of concrete instances in which the attitudes, values, and temperaments of scientists have influenced their work or affected their findings is dismissed via the scornful dichotomy that such matters may bear upon the psychology or sociology of scientific inquiry, but have no relevance whatever to the substance of science. This conviction that scientific inquiry is "value free" has such wide acceptance as to have gained for itself the title of *the thesis of the value neutrality of science.*

The main point that I propose to argue here is simply that this supposed division between the evaluative humanistic disciplines on the one hand and the nonevaluative sciences on the other is based upon mistaken views regarding the nature of scientific research. In placing too great an emphasis upon the abstract logic of scientific inquiry, many students of scientific method have lost sight of the fact that science is a human enterprise, carried out by flesh and blood men, and that the products of scientific research must therefore inevitably exhibit some unquestionably normative complexion. It will be shown that evaluative problems crop up at numerous points within the framework of scientific research and that the scientist does not and cannot put aside his common humanity and his evaluative capabilities when he sets to work in his "official" capacity.

Preliminary Clarifications

Before embarking on a consideration of the evaluative dimension of scientific research, a number of preliminary points are in order.

To begin with, it deserves note that many of the evaluative issues regarding scientific research are specifically ethical in nature. Now in considering ethical issues within the sciences, I do not in general propose to take any notice at all of the various moral problems that arise in relation to what is *done with* scientific discoveries once they have been achieved. Questions of what is done in the way of *application* with the products of scientific research are frequently not problems that arise *within* science and are then not evaluative choices confronting the scientist himself. This fact puts them outside of my limited area of our immediate concern.

However, it is worth noting that this line between the theoretical and the applied is particularly tenuous or even nonexistent in many areas of social science research. If we are considering, for example, the sociopolitical stability of a certain nation, then it is clear that our findings, insofar as valid, are of direct and immediate applicability, be it by those who seek to maintain the social order as established or by those who seek to overthrow it. And insofar as the research is inherently application oriented, the question of the moral coloration of its probable applications is a not irrelevant aspect of the evaluative side of the subject.

Evaluative Problems Regarding Research Goals

Perhaps the most basic and pervasive way in which evaluative problems arise in connection with the prosecution of scientific research is in regard to the choice of research problems, the setting of research goals, and the allocation of resources (both human and material) to the prosecution of research efforts. This evaluative problem of choices relating to research goals arises at all levels of aggregation—the national, the institutional, and the individual.

As regards the national level, it is a commonplace that in most advanced countries the state is heavily involved in the sponsorship of research. In the United States, for example, the level of federal expenditure on research and development has in recent years stood at around 10 percent of the federal budget and some 3 percent of the gross national product. If this seems like a modest figure, one must consider the historical perspective. The rate of increase of this budget item in the recent past has been around 10 percent per annum, which represents a doubling time of seven years. Since the doubling time of our GNP is around twenty years, *at these present rates* our government would be spending all of our money on science and technology a few decades hence. And since the man who pays the piper inevitably gets to call at least some of the tune, public decision makers are confronted with difficult choices of an evaluative (and frequently *ethical*) nature regarding the direction of these research efforts. Let me indicate some obvious issues.

In the Soviet Union, 35 percent of all research and academic trained personnel is engaged in the engineering disciplines, compared with 10 percent in medicine and pharmaceutical science. Does this 3.5 to 1 ratio of technology to medicine set a pattern to be adopted by the United States? Just how are we to "divide the pie" in allocating federal support funds among the various areas of scientific work?

In our country, the responsibility for such choices is, of course, localized and rests mainly not in the scientific community itself but in the political process. Scientific opinion enters only marginally. The President's Science Advisory Committee (PSAC) and the Federal Council for Science and Technology among others help to establish a frame of reference for an overall science budget and thereby for making the difficult decisions regarding resource allocation. These decisions, which require weighing space probes against biological experimentation and atomic energy against oceanography, are among the most difficult choices that have to be made by, or on behalf of, the scientific community. The entrance of power-political considerations may complicate, but cannot remove, the evaluative issues that are involved in such choices, though it is only fair to say that scientists are involved in the choice process to a far lesser degree than is generally believed. Representatives of the scientific community were never consulted regarding the allocation of funds to the 90 percent of the R & D budget represented by large-scale development programs of recent American experience. It is an open secret that PSAC did everything it could to oppose the manned space program, and it was opposed to many of the large military programs, such as the ABM, the aircraft nuclear propulsion program, the nuclear rocket program, the supersonic bomber programs, the SST, the Skybolt missile program, the Civil Defense program, and numerous other large-scale programs, such as the C-5 aircraft, the TFX, and others, that have since become national scandals. It did advocate unmanned space science programs with a set of published priorities that were directly reversed by political decision makers. In fact the scientific community has had little or no influence over the gross allocation of resources for technology. It has had some influence on the distribution of the less than 0.3 percent of the GNP that has gone into internally motivated science. The rest have been political decisions regarding major national goals, and the allocation of R & D resources has merely followed these goals, not the other way around.

The problems of fixing upon research goals and designing appropriate routes of inquiry by way of resource allocation arise not only at the national level, but recur in the institutional and individual spheres as well. Many forces are operative here: market forces (e.g., in terms of the availability of funding), peer-group pressures, intellectual styles and fashions within disciplines, "political" considerations of various kinds, and even to some extent public opinion. The weighing of these factors is a process that underlies—however tacitly, covertly, and obliquely—the design of research programs and is a process that is inherently evaluative in its nature.

Evaluative Problems Regarding Research Methods

Let me now indicate a second sort of evaluative and in large measure *ethical* problems arising in scientific research—those having to do with the *methods* of the research itself. Problems of this kind arise perhaps most acutely in biological or medical or psychological experiments involving the use of experimental animals. They have to do with the measures of omission and commission for keeping experimental animals from needless pain and discomfort. In this connection, let me quote Margaret Mead.

> The growth of importance of the study of human behavior raises a host of new ethical problems, at the head of which I would place the need for consent to the research by both observer and subject. Studies of the behavior of animals other than man introduced a double set of problems: how to control the tendency of the human observer to anthropomorphize, and so distort his observations, and how to protect both the animal and the experimenter from the effects of cruelty. In debates on the issue of cruelty it is usually recognized that callousness towards a living thing may produce suffering in the experimental subject, but it is less often recognized that it may produce moral deterioration in the experimenter.[12]

It goes without saying that problems of this sort arise in their most acute form in experiments that risk human life, limb, well-being, or comfort. But problems of a significantly analogous character come up in psychological and social science experiments in which the possibility of a compromise of human dignity or integrity is present.

Evaluative Problems Regarding Standards of Proof

I turn now to a further set of ethical problems relating to scientific research—those that are bound up with what we may call the standards of proof. These have to do with the amount of evidence that a scientist accumulates before he deems it appropriate to announce his findings and put forward the claim that such-and-so may be regarded as an established fact. At what juncture should scientific evidence be reasonably regarded by investigators—and by the editors, referees, etc., who sit astride the channels of publication—as strong enough to give warrant for a conclusion, and how should the uncertainties of this conclusion be presented?

This problem of standards of proof is evaluative, and not merely theoretical or methodological in nature, because it bridges the gap between scientific understanding and action, between thinking and doing. The scientist cannot conveniently sidestep the whole of the ethical impact of such questions by saying to the layman, "I'll tell you the scientific facts and then *you* decide on the proper mode of action." As medical examples perhaps most clearly show (e.g., the choice between the surgical and the radiological route to treating a certain cancer patient), these issues are usually so closely interconnected that it is the scientific expert alone who can properly adjudge the bearing of the general scientific considerations upon the particular case in hand.

Every trained scientist knows, of course, that "scientific knowledge" is a body of statements of varying degrees of certainty—including a great deal that is quite unsure as well as much that is reasonably certain. But in presenting par-

---

[12] *Science* 134 (1961) : 164.

ticular scientific results, and especially in presenting his own results, a researcher may be under a strong temptation to fail to do justice to the precise degree of certainty and uncertainty involved.

On the one hand, there may be some indulgence of the natural human tendency to exaggerate the assurance of one's own findings. Moreover, when much money and effort have been expended, it can be embarrassing—especially when talking with the nonscientific sponsors who have footed the bill—to detract from the significance or suggestiveness of one's results by dwelling on the insecurities in their basis. The multiple studies and restudies made in recent years in order to assess the pathological and genetic effects of radioactive fallout afford an illustration of a struggle to pinpoint the extent of our knowledge and our ignorance in this area. And the excessively optimistic predictions that have been used to justify large-scale public measures of social experimentation afford another example.

On the other hand, it may in some instances be tempting for a researcher to underplay the certainty of his findings by adopting an unreasonably high standard of proof. This is especially possible in medical research, where life-risking actions may be based upon a research result. In this domain, a researcher may be tempted to "cover" himself by hedging his findings more elaborately than the realities of the situation may warrant.

Evaluative Problems Regarding the Dissemination of Research Findings

A surprising variety of evaluative—and in large measure ethical—problems revolve around the general topic of the dissemination of research findings. It is so basic a truth as to be almost axiomatic that, with the possible exception of a handful of unusual cases in the area of national security classification, a scientist has not only the right, but even the duty, to communicate his findings to the community of fellow scientists, so that his results may stand or fall in the play of the open marketplace of ideas. Modern science differs sharply in this respect from science in Renaissance times, when a scientist shared his discoveries only with trusted disciples and announced his findings to the general public only in cryptic form, if at all.

This ethical problem of favoritism in the sharing of scientific information has come to prominence again in our day. Although scientists do generally publish their findings, the processes of publication consume time, so that anything between six months and three years may elapse between a scientific discovery and its publication in the professional literature. It has become a widespread practice to make prepublication announcements of findings or even pre-prepublication announcements. The ethical problem is posed by the extent and direction of such exchanges, for there is no doubt that in many cases favoritism comes into the picture and that some workers and laboratories exchange findings in a preferential way that amounts to a conspiracy to maintain themselves ahead of the state of the art in the world at large. There is, of course, nothing reprehensible in the natural wish to overcome publication lags or in the normal desire for exchanges of ideas with fellow workers. But when such practices tend to become systematized in a prejudicial way, a plainly ethical problem comes into being.

Let us consider yet another ethical problem regarding the dissemination of research findings. Questions regarding scientific or technical merits thus tend to get treated not just in the proper forum of the science journals, but also in the public press and in congressional or foundation committee rooms. Not only does this create the danger of scientific pressure groups devoted to preconceived ideas and endowed with the power of retarding other lines of thought, but it also makes for an unhealthy emphasis on the spectacular and the novel—unhealthy, that is, from the standpoint of the development of science itself. For such factors create a type of control over the direction of scientific research that is disastrously unrelated to the proper issue of strictly scientific merits.

The fact is that science has itself become vulnerable in this regard through its increasing sensitivity to public relations matters. Let me cite just one illustration—that of the issue of the fluoridation of municipal water supplies. Some scientists appear to have chosen this issue as a barricade at which to fight—when the prestige of science is engaged.

Some years ago, local referenda in the state of Massachusetts gave serious defeats to the proponents of fluoridation. Not only were proposals to introduce this practice defeated in Wellesley and Brookline, but Andover, where fluoridation had been in effect for five years, voted discontinuance of the program. These defeats in towns of the highest educational and socioeconomic levels caused considerable malaise in the scientific community, and wails of anguish found their way even into *Science,* the official journal of the American Association for the Advancement of Science. This annoyance over what is clearly not a *scientific* setback, but merely a failure in public relations or political effectiveness, sharply illustrates the sensitivity that scientists have developed in this area.

Evaluative Problems Regarding the Control of Scientific "Misinformation"

Closely bound up with the evaluative problems regarding the dissemination of scientific information are what might be thought of as the other side of the coin—the control, censorship, and suppression of scientific misinformation.

The vast scale of scientific work in relation to the great but still limited potential for its public dissemination means that a substantial degree of quality control is necessary. Vast though the professional literature has become, the journals of top quality are still relatively few and can publish only a small fraction of submitted material. All manner of controls have sprung into prominence, reflected in the organizational procedures of the journals themselves, the mechanisms of refereeing and reviewing, the conduct of scholarly meetings that control debate within disciplines and shape the process of reputation formation, etc.

To give just one historic illustration of the importance of such considerations, I will cite the example of the nineteenth-century English chemist J. J. Waterson. His groundbreaking papers on physical chemistry, anticipating the development of thermodynamics by more than a generation, were rejected by the referees of the Royal Society for publication in its Proceedings, with the comment (among others) that "the paper is nothing but of nonsense." As a result, Waterson's work lay forgotten in the archives of the Royal Society until rescued from oblivion by Rayleigh some forty-five years later. J. B. S. Haldane, whose edition of Waterson's works in 1928 decisively rehabilitated this important researcher, wrote as follows.

> It is probable that, in the long and honorable history of the Royal Society, no mistake more disastrous in its actual consequences for the progress of science and the reputation of British science than the rejection of Waterson's papers was ever made. The papers were foundation stones of a new branch of scientific knowledge, molecular physics, as Waterson called it, or physical chemistry and thermodynamics as it is now called. There is every reason for believing that, had the papers been published, physical chemistry and thermodynamics would have developed mainly in this country (i.e., England), and along much simpler, more correct, and more intelligible lines than those of their actual development.[13]

Many other examples could be cited to show that it is vitally important that the gatekeepers of our scientific publications be keenly alive to the possible but unobvious value of unfamiliar and strange seeming conceptions.

It is worth emphasizing that this matter of "controlling" the dissemination of scientific ideas poses special difficulties due to an important, but much underrated, phenomenon: *the resistance to novelty and innovation by the scientific community itself*. No feature of the historical course of development of the sciences is more damaging to the theoreticians' idealized conception of science as perfectly objective—the work of almost disembodied intellects governed by purely rational considerations and actuated solely by an abstract love of truth. The mere assertion that scientists can resist, and indeed frequently have resisted, acceptance of scientific discoveries clashes sharply with the stereotyped concept of the scientist as the purely objective, wholly rational, and entirely open-minded man. Although opposition to scientific findings by social groups other than scientists has been examined by various investigators, the resistance to scientific discoveries by scientists themselves is just beginning to attract the attention of sociologists.[14]

---

[13] Quoted by Stephen G. Brush in *American Scientist* 49 (1961): 211–212.

[14] To anyone interested in this curious topic, I refer the eye-opening article by Bernard Barber, "Resistance by Scientists to Scientific Discovery," *Science* 134 (1961).

The history of science is, in fact, littered with examples of this phenomenon. Lister, in a graduation address to medical students, bluntly warned against blindness to new ideas such as he had himself encountered in advancing his theory of antisepsis. Pasteur's discovery of the biological character of fermentation was long opposed by chemists, including the eminent Liebig, and his germ theory met with sharp resistance from the medical fraternity of his day. No doubt due in part to the very peculiar character of Mesmer himself, the phenomenon of hypnosis, or mesmerism, was rejected by the scientifically orthodox of his time as so much charlatanism. At the summit of the Age of Reason, the French Academy dismissed the numerous and well-attested reports of stones falling from the sky (meteorites, that is to say) as mere folk stories. And this list could be prolonged ad nauseam.

Scientists clearly have a duty to protect both their own colleagues in other specialties and the lay public against the dangers of supposed research findings that are strictly erroneous, particularly in regard to areas, such as medicine and nutrition, where the public health and welfare are concerned. And quite generally, of course, a scientist has an obligation to maintain the professional literature of his field at a high level of content and quality. The editors and editorial reviewers in whose hands rest the access to the media of scientific publication clearly have a duty to preserve their readership from errors of fact and trivia of thought. But these protective functions should ideally be balanced by respect for the free play of ideas and by a real sensitivity to the possible merit of ideas that do not fall into the common groove.

Here as elsewhere one encounters the phenomenon that one man's truth is another's folly. Science as actually practiced does not answer to the naive picture of a disinterested collaboration of abstract intelligence but comes close to being an adversary procedure between highly interested parties with substantial rewards at stake (prestige, fat consulting fees, ample research awards, etc.). The social sciences in particular are no stranger to the clash between "schools of thought" engaged in heated advocacy and refutation. The evaluative issue of the impartial implementation of communally agreed standards of proof remains an ideal standard honored in the breach no less frequently than in the observance.

At no point does the ethical problem of information control in science grow more difficult and vexatious than in respect to the boundary line between proper science on the one hand and pseudo-science on the other. The plain fact is that truth is to be found in odd places and that scientifically valuable materials turn up in unexpected spots.

No one, of course, would for a moment deny the abstract thesis that there is such a thing as pseudo-science and that it must be contested and controlled. The headache begins with the question of just what is pseudo-science and what is not. We can all readily agree on some of the absurd cases so interestingly described in Martin Gardner's wonderful book *Fads and Fallacies in the Name of*

Science (New York, 1957). But the question of exactly where science ends and where pseudo-science begins is at once important and far from simple. There is little difficulty indeed with Wilbur Glenn Voliva, Gardner's Exhibit No. 1, who during the first third of this century thundered out of Zion (Illinois) that "the earth is flat as a pancake." But parapsychology, for example, is another study and a much more complicated one. And the handful of United States geneticists who, working primarily with yeasts, feel that they have experimental warrant for Lamarckian conclusions, much to the discomfort of the great majority of their professional colleagues, exemplify the difficulties of a hard and fast compartmentalization of pseudo-science in a much more drastic way.

One cannot avoid the equally disconcerting fact that reputable scientists have advanced, and their fellow scientists accepted, findings that were strictly fraudulent. One instructive case is that of the French physicist Rene Blondlot, which is interestingly described in Derek Price's book *Science Since Babylon* (New Haven, 1961). Blondlot allegedly discovered "N rays," which were supposed to be something like X rays. His curious findings attracted a great deal of attention and earned for Blondlot himself a prize from the French government. But the American physicist Robert W. Wood was able to show by careful experimental work that Blondlot and all who concurred in his findings were deluded. It is thus to be recognized not only that pseudo-science exists, but that it sometimes even makes its way into the sacred precincts of highly orthodox science. This, of course, does not help to simplify the task of discriminating between *real* and *pseudo*-science.

But let us return to the inherent evaluative and ethical issues. These have to do not with the uncontroversial thesis that pseudo-science must be controlled, but with the procedural question of the *means* to be used for the achievement of this worthy purpose. It is with this problem of the means for its control that pseudo-science poses real ethical difficulties for the scientific community.

The handiest instrumentalities to this end and the most temptingly simple to use are the old standbys of thought control: censorship and suppression. But these are surely dire and desperate remedies. It is no doubt highly unpleasant for a scientist to see views that he regards as "preposterous" and "crackpot" disseminated and even gaining a considerable public following. But surely we should never lose sensitivity to the moral worth of the methods for achieving our ends. It is undeniably true that scientists have the duty to prevent the propagation of error and misinformation. But this duty has to be acted on with thoughtful caution. It cannot be construed to fit the conveniences of the moment. And it surely cannot be stretched to give warrant to the suppression of views that might prove damaging to the public "image" of science or to justify the protection of one school of thought against its critics. Those scientists, who pressured the publisher of Immanuel Velikovsky's fanciful *Worlds in Collision* by threatening to boycott the firm's textbooks unless this work was dropped from its list, resorted to measures that I should not care to be called on to defend. But the case is perhaps an extreme one. However, the control exercised by editors and guardians of foundation pursestrings is more subtle, but no less effective and no less problematic.

The main point in this regard is one that needs little defense or argument in its support. Surely scientists, of all people, should have sufficient confidence in the ability of truth to win out over error in the marketplace of freely interchanged ideas as to be unwilling to forego the techniques of rational persuasion in favor of the unsavory instrumentalities of pressure, censorship, and suppression. Simply to be intelligently sensitive to the ethical requirements is already to go a good way toward meeting them.

Evaluative Problems Regarding the Allocation of Credit for Scientific Research Achievements

The final set of evaluative problems arising in relation to scientific research that I propose to mention here relates to the recognition of scientific work by allocation of credit for the achievement of research findings.

For one thing, moral philosophers as well as students of jurisprudence have long been aware of the difficulties in assigning to individuals the responsibility for corporate acts, and thus to allocate to individual wrongdoers the blame for group misdeeds. This problem now faces the scientific community in its inverse form—the allocation to individuals of credit for the research accomplishments resulting from conjoint, corporate, or combined effort. Particularly in this day of collectivized research, this problem is apt to arise often and in serious forms.

And there is also the second, even more legalistic aspect of the problem: that of the codes of scholarly controversy and competition that canalize the stance of the scientific community toward the rivalry of individuals and "schools." We have to do here with the inherently evaluative issue of the distribution of recognition and credit among competing theories and approaches.

Let no one be put off by stories about scientific detachment and disinterestedness. For example, the issue of credit for their findings has for many centuries been of the greatest importance to scientists. Doubts on this score are readily dispelled by the prominence of priority disputes in the history of science, illustrated by such notorious episodes as the bitter and long-continuing dispute between Newton and Leibniz and their followers regarding priority in the invention of the calculus. To return to the present, the problem of credit allocation can come up nowadays in forms so complex and intricate as to be almost inconceivable to any mind not trained in the law. For instance, following out the implications of an idea put forward as an idle guess by X, Y, working under W's direction in Z's laboratory, comes up with an important result. How is the total credit to be divided? It requires no great imagination to think up some of the kinds of problems and difficulties that can come about in saying who is to be credited with what in this day of corporate and collective research. This venture lends itself to clever literary exploitation in the hands of a master, such as C. P. Snow.

It deserves stress that this issue of credit allocation does not derive its importance solely from considerations of abstract justice, but is of great practical importance for the conduct of scientific work in its present-day institutionalized setting. For credit is crucial to considerations of status and prestige that govern the distribution of rewards, not only the personal, but those that serve to shape the ongoing process of scientific work itself: research opportunities, claims upon scarce resources, and influence within the profession.

Retrospect on the Evaluative Dimension of Scientific Research

It is, of course, quite correct to observe that the preceding discussion of the evaluative aspects of science deals not with the *substantive* side of scientific propositions but with its organizational and procedural side. It is concerned with how the work is done in the kitchen, so to speak, and not with what is dished out "up front" on the platters of the professional literature. It deals with the *sociology* of science, not with its content. All this must be granted. But the basic fact of the role of evaluation in the conduct of scientific work cannot be gotten rid of by drawing neat distinctions. The regrettable circumstance remains that too many persons, working scientists and theorists of scientific method alike, have focused their attention so sharply upon the abstracted "logic" of an idealized "scientific method" that the evaluative dimension of science as a human enterprise has been underemphasized.

Of course, someone might object as follows: You are quite right that science is a social system made up of individuals, and in its internal operations it is no different from other social systems. The "objectivity" of science is something that pertains to the overall process of science, not to individual scientists. Your discussion makes the mistake of confusing the institution with the individuals making it up. This objection takes far too optimistic a view of the matter. What *deus ex machina* can guarantee that collective objectivity will mysteriously emerge from the admittedly imperfect dealings of fallible individuals? One cannot, of course, *disprove* that systemic objectivity might somehow emerge at the institutional level through the mysterious workings of a benign hidden hand, creating at the global level a value-free upshot in which all the imperfect valuations of individual workers are cancelled out. But this surely remains, in the final analysis, rather a trusting hope than a well-founded expectation.

Science is invariably *our* science, the enterprise of flesh and blood creatures, and not of disembodied intelligences. So long as this remains so, scientific inquiry will have an inextricably evaluative aspect. The rational course is not to gainsay this, but to learn to reckon with it.

The Reward System of the Social Sciences

Jonathan R. Cole and Stephen Cole

For the past eight years, we have been conducting a series of studies of the social organization of contemporary American science.[1] These studies have concentrated on the problem of social stratification in science, and particularly on the processes by which scientists achieve high status and on the consequences for scientists of occupying varying levels in the stratification system. We have been concerned primarily with the degree to which the reward system of science is universalistic. In such a reward system, scientists will be evaluated solely on the basis of their scientific role performance. Since the primary goal of science is the production of new knowledge, those who contribute most to this goal should be the most heavily rewarded. In a universalistic reward system, functionally irrelevant criteria (those which have no bearing on the ability of the scientist to perform scientific roles), such as race, sex, and religion, should play no part in the allocation of rewards.

A first series of studies indicated that physics closely matched the ideal of universalism. The quality of published research explained considerably more of the variations in success within the scientific pecking order than did any other variable. We have recently extended the scope of our investigation and have completed an analysis of the reward systems of five scientific fields: physics, chemistry, biochemistry, psychology, and sociology. In the first section of this

---

[1] Jonathan R. Cole and Stephen Cole, *Social Stratification in Science* (Chicago, 1973).

paper we summarize the results of this investigation; in the second section we report results of a study of how nonscientific statuses, such as sex, race, and religion, influence allocation of rewards in the social and natural sciences; and finally, in concluding, we speculate on the significance of this research for some of the larger issues that form the focus of this volume.[2]

I. REWARD SYSTEM OF FIVE DISCIPLINES

A scientific reward system is universalistic to the extent that quality of performance is the sole determinant of rank in the scientific community. Since contributing to the advance of knowledge is the primary function of the scientist, if science does indeed have a universalistic reward system, the quality of published work should be the most important criterion used in evaluation. There has been a long-standing belief that scientific reward systems are dominated by the "publish or perish" principle. If you want to get ahead, you must churn out an endless stream of articles and books. It is sometimes said that the emphasis is on quantity of publication rather than quality.

The extent to which quantity or quality of a scientist's research determines the course of his career may have a crucial influence on the rate of advance in a scientific discipline. The most important scientific problems are usually those that are difficult to solve. If success in science depends as much on the quantity of publications as on their quality, then young scientists may not be motivated to work on the important but difficult problems. Why should one spend several years working on a problem that is difficult and the outcome of which is in doubt when one can tackle a series of simple problems that have a higher probability of leading to quick publication? To what extent then does the quantity and the quality of scientific research influence success in the various scientific fields?

We thought that intellectual differences among fields might have a significant influence on the structure of their reward systems. In such highly developed fields as physics and chemistry, there would be a substantial consensus on who is doing important work, and sheer quantity of publications would therefore have an insignificant effect on the distribution of rewards. In less developed fields, such as psychology and sociology, there might be less agreement on who is doing important work. In the absence of such agreement, sheer quantity of publications would have a greater influence on distribution of rewards.

---

[2] In this paper we have space only to summarize the results of these investigations. We do not fully report on sampling, methods, and data. A complete report of these investigations is currently being prepared for publication. Further information on any of the studies discussed may be obtained from the authors.

We studied samples of scientists who have been promoted from associate to full professor at Ph.D. granting institutions between 1965 and 1969.[3] We studied recent full professors, because we wanted to analyze the currently existing reward systems in each field—not the reward systems that may have existed at the time when older scientists became full professors. We did not study ranks below full professor, because we wanted to study professionally mature scientists. We studied scientists at Ph.D. granting institutions because the overwhelming majority of scientific research is produced at these universities. After listing all scientists that met the sampling criteria, we stratified the list by the prestige rating of the academic department, using the 1968 American Council of Education survey.[4] We then randomly selected twenty scientists from each of the high, medium, and low ranked groups of departments. The results in each field are based upon this sample of sixty scientists.

Information on career history, age, and rewards received for each scientist was collected from *American Men and Women of Science.* The quality of published work was measured by the number of citations listed for each scientist in the *Science Citation Index* (SCI). Extensive research has been done in the past indicating that citations are a valid rough indicator of the quality of work.[5] The number of citations is highly correlated with all other measures of quality that sociologists of science have employed. As long as we keep in mind that high quality research is being defined as research that other scientists find useful in their current work, citations are a satisfactory indicator. Citations do not measure the "absolute" or "objective" quality of research, but they do measure the currently assessed value of work of one's colleagues.

Quantity of research output was easily obtained for physics, chemistry, biochemistry, and psychology as these fields have very well organized and complete abstracting journals. All that was necessary was to count the number of papers listed for each scientist in each volume of the abstracting journal from the year that the scientist received his Ph.D. through 1969. For sociology, the abstracting journal is not as adequate. We therefore requested that each scientist send us a copy of his vita.

A third independent variable in the study was the scientific origin of the scientist or the rank of the department from which he received his Ph.D. To the extent that mobility in science is of the "contest" rather than the "sponsored" variety, where a scientist earned the Ph.D. should have no *independent* effect on

---

[3] Because of the ease of obtaining data, there were slight differences in the years for each field. Biochemistry included scientists promoted between 1964 and 1968; the chemists were promoted between 1963 and 1967.

[4] Kenneth D. Roose and Charles J. Andersen, *A Rating of Graduate Programs* (Washington, 1970).

[5] Cole and Cole, *Social Stratification,* ch. 2.

where he ends up in the stratification system.[6] Although it is possible, indeed likely, that the more highly rated departments get better students, this should only play a role in the acquisition of a first, not a final, position. In a universalistic reward system, students from top ranked departments who do not produce should be downwardly mobile and those from lower prestige departments who do produce should be upwardly mobile.

We consider three dependent variables. The first is "perceived quality." This is a subjective assessment of the quality of a scientist's work, made by a sample of his colleagues. To measure this variable, we sent a questionnaire to random samples of approximately 300 faculty members listed in the directories of their professional associations. The raters were asked to answer the following question for each of the sixty scientists: "By circling the appropriate number, please indicate the relative importance of the work of the following scientists: Has made very important contributions; Has made average contributions; Work has been relatively unimportant; Unfamiliar with work but have heard of this scientist; Have never heard of this scientist." Perceived quality was defined as the mean rating received by a scientist.

We thought that perceived quality would be primarily dependent upon the actual impact of a scientist's published work: the number of citations the work has received. But other variables, such as the sheer quantity of work or the scientist's academic origin, might also play a role. The more universalistic a reward system is, the less effect these other variables will have on the perceived quality of a scientist's work.

The other two dependent variables are different aspects of scientific success. One is reputational and consists of having your work widely known. The other component is the more tangible one of position: To be successful is to occupy a prestigious position in the scientific community. To measure reputational recognition or what we term "visibility," we used responses to the same question that yielded the indicator of perceived quality. Visibility was merely the percentage of all scientists returning the questionnaire who either rated the scientist or had heard of the scientist. Positional success was measured by the rank of the scientist's academic department in the 1969 ACE survey. By some criteria, all of the scientists we have studied have achieved positional success; all of them are full professors at Ph.D. granting institutions. Yet there are important differences among them. Some of them are full professors at highly prestigious schools, such as Berkeley and Chicago, and others are full professors at much less prestigious institutions.

---

[6] L. Hargens and W. O. Hagstrom, "Sponsored and Contest Mobility of American Academic Scientists," *Sociology of Education* 40 (1967) : 24–38.

Quality and Quantity of Published Research

In all five fields, there is a relatively high correlation between the quantity and the quality of published work. The correlation coefficients vary between .53 and .72. Although we find the lowest correlations in the two social sciences—psychology (.53) and sociology (.54)—they are not significantly different from that observed for physics (.59). Although quality and quantity of published research are correlated in all fields, the correlation is not perfect, which indicates that in each field there are some scientists who produce many relatively insignificant papers and some scientists who produce only a few highly significant papers. We now want to see how quantity and quality of published research influence the distribution of rewards in each field.

The zero-order correlations between quantity and quality of work and the three forms of recognition are presented in Table 1. In every case the correlation between quality of output and recognition is at least slightly higher than that between quantity and recognition. What is more important is that there are no systematic differences between the social and the natural sciences. Quantity cannot be said to be a more important determinant of success in the social sciences than it is in the natural sciences.

Table 1: Correlations Between Quantity and Quality
and Three Measures of Recognition

| | Perceived Quality | | Visibility | | Rank of Department | |
	Quantity	Quality	Quantity	Quality	Quantity	Quality
Biochemistry	.51	.70	.44	.61	.38	.39
Chemistry	.47	.55	.55	.62	.21	.31
Physics	.41	.53	.53	.63	.20	.34
Psychology	.37	.55	.44	.52	−.16	.21
Sociology	.51	.59	.48	.55	.42	.51

To illustrate the way in which the reward systems of the five disciplines operate, we performed a multiple regression analysis of the determinants of visibility. The four independent variables used were quality, quantity, perceived quality, and rank of the scientists' academic departments. It turned out that not only are there no differences between the social and natural sciences, but there are virtually no differences at all among the five fields. The multiple r achieved for the five fields varies from a low of .74 for biochemistry to a high of .78 for chemistry. Apparently, the determinants of visibility are the same in these five fields.

As the final step in our analysis, we present in Figure 1 a causal model depicting the operation of the scientific reward system in each discipline. Let us begin our discussion of the model with an analysis of the determinants of perceived quality. What variables influence the perception that we have of the quality of our colleagues' work? In a rational system the "actual" quality or the utility that the work has for other scientists will be the prime determinant of perceived quality. A path analysis that we performed indicated that in all five fields quality of work, as measured by citations received, is the strongest determinant of perceived quality. It is true, however, that the path coefficient (a measure of the independent effect of an independent variable on a dependent variable) found for sociology was the lowest. However, the path coefficient found for psychology was higher than those found for chemistry and physics. Likewise, we found that although quantity of output had the largest independent effect on perceived quality among sociologists, it had the lowest independent effect on psychology. The variations among the five fields formed no pattern.

What does the model tell us about the extent to which mobility in the various sciences is of the contest or sponsored variety? In general, the rank of the department where the scientist earned the Ph.D. has a negligible effect on the perceived quality of work. It is highest in sociology and lowest in psychology. This indicates that people who publish useful work will be perceived as making high quality contributions regardless of where they received their training.

As the absence of a path from rank of doctoral department to visibility indicates, the social origin of a physicist has no independent effect on reputational recognition. There are several possible explanations of the independent effect of social origin on positional recognition. It could be a result of the informal sponsor system that exists in academe. The sponsor system works most strongly in the attainment of a first academic position. A graduate student's sponsor will make contacts leading to the student's employment. Since sponsors at top ranked departments are more likely to have contacts at other top ranked departments, their students have an easier time getting jobs at prestigious institutions. Analysis of other data we have collected indicates that the effect of rank of doctoral department on prestige of current department is almost entirely mediated by the influence of rank of doctoral department on a scientist's first job.[7] Of course, the prestige of a scientist's first job has a strong independent effect on the prestige of his current job. Thus, we may conclude that sponsorship is primarily important in getting a first job and has little effect on later job acquisition. Also, once a scientist attains a specific rank in the stratification system, structural processes operate to keep him there. These processes are exemplified by the different criteria usually employed in considering the promotion of insiders and when hiring outsiders. Since insiders are more likely than outsiders to be considered in terms of their teaching and service to the department and university as

---

[7] Cole and Cole, *Social Stratification,* pp. 117–118.

Figure 1: The Scientific Reward System

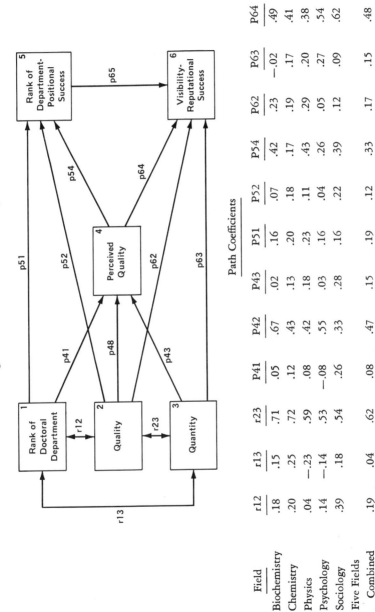

Path Coefficients

Field	r12	r13	r23	P41	P42	P43	P51	P52	P54	P62	P63	P64	P65
Biochemistry	.18	.15	.71	.05	.67	.02	.16	.07	.42	.23	−.02	.49	.15
Chemistry	.20	.25	.72	.12	.43	.13	.20	.18	.17	.19	.17	.41	.26
Physics	.04	−.23	.59	.08	.42	.18	.23	.11	.43	.29	.20	.38	.07
Psychology	.14	−.14	.53	−.08	.55	.03	.16	.04	.26	.05	.27	.54	.15
Sociology	.39	.18	.54	.26	.33	.28	.16	.22	.39	.12	.09	.62	.03
Five Fields Combined	.19	.04	.62	.08	.47	.15	.19	.12	.33	.17	.15	.48	.12

well as their publication records, the former can be promoted on the basis of a considerably weaker publication record than that expected of outsiders. Likewise, is is difficult for good scientists below the top level to make the necessary contacts to be upwardly mobile from low ranked to high ranked departments.

There is a slight inaccuracy in this model which results from insufficient data. The three dependent variables: perceived quality, reputational success, and positional success, located at the right in the model, actually interact. Thus, a scientist who obtains a position at a high ranked department may experience a rise in the perceived quality of his work. Likewise, a scientist who becomes more visible may subsequently be offered a position in a high ranked department. To adequately study the interaction of these variables, we would have to follow the careers of samples of scientists over an extended period of time, measuring the variables at frequent intervals. Not having such data, we must assume a set of unidirectional causal relationships. Taking this shortcoming into consideration, we may still, however, learn something of how the reward systems work in the various disciplines.

In general, we find it most difficult to explain variance on positional recognition. While we can usually explain more than 50 percent of the variance on reputational recognition, we rarely can explain more than 25 percent of the variance on positional success. There is certainly far from a one-to-one relationship between the quality of a scientist's work and the prestige of the place where he holds a job. As we have pointed out elsewhere, this is partly a result of self-selection. Some scientists who could get a job at a top ranked department choose for one reason or another to work at a lower ranked one. Also, studies currently underway indicate that there are higher levels of particularism at this point in the social system than some of our previous work indicated. These preliminary investigations indicate that there clearly are some superior scientists who are tenurable at many major departments, a large body who are clearly unproductive and nontenurable at major departments, and a group of scientists who are on the border. Since there are not enough clearly superior scientists available to fill all the positions at major departments, some borderline people get jobs there and others do not. It is in differentiating between the borderline people that particularism enters the scene. However, thus far, there is no evidence that there is any more particularism operating in the social sciences than operates in the natural sciences. Quality of work explains no more variance on rank of department in physics than it does in sociology.

Sheer quantity of research turns out to have no independent effect on positional recognition in any of the five fields. The direct effect of quality of work as measured by citations on both positional and reputational recognition is slight in all the fields. The effect of quality on rewards is mediated by the perceived quality of work. This allows us to make a subtle but important modification in analyzing the way in which universalism works in science. There can be little doubt that the quality of work *as it is perceived by other scientists* is the most important variable in determining the allocation of rewards. There is also little doubt that to have one's work highly evaluated, one must actually produce work that other scientists find useful, i.e., work that is highly cited. The production of work deemed useful is a necessary condition for earning a reputation as a good scientist. It is also true, however, that variables other than the actual substantive content of the work produced, influence the subjective evaluation of one's work. Two of these variables are the rank of doctoral department and intelligence as it becomes evident in interaction. (For example, data from our other studies demonstrate the independent effect of intelligence.)[8] Other variables influencing the subjective perception of quality are rewards the scientist has received. This brings us to a consideration of the process of accumulative advantage.

In almost every case in which the scientific reward system seems to depart from universalism, we can find the operation of accumulative advantage. In science as in other areas of life, those who are initially successful have greater opportunities for future success. Thus, students who get into good graduate departments have better chances of getting good jobs. Scientists who are perceived as having done high quality work achieve both positional and reputational recognition. But scientists who are successful are more likely to have their work perceived favorably, independently of the content of the work. There is also feedback between the two forms of recognition. Thus, scientists who are at top ranked departments will be more visible, independently of other variables, and scientists who are visible are more likely to get jobs at top departments, independently of other variables. We may conclude that doing good science brings rewards and once those rewards are received, they have an independent effect on the acquisition of further rewards. It makes little difference whether positional or reputational recognition comes first; the attainment of one aids in the attainment of the other. We may also conclude that the process of accumulative advantage seems to work the same way in the social sciences as it does in the natural sciences.

Looking at the causal model as a whole, to what extent can we conclude that the five fields we have studied have similar reward systems? Are they samples drawn from the same population? There are no standard procedures for comparing path models. What we have done is to create a correlation matrix for all variables in the path model. Then treating each correlation coefficient as an observation, we computed a correlation between the matrix obtained in one field with that obtained in another. For example, we found that the correlation between the fifteen correlation coefficients for physics and the fifteen for biochemistry was $r = .93$. All correlations obtained were high with the lowest being that between psychology and sociology. This is exactly the opposite of what we should find if the social sciences have reward systems that differ from those in the natural

---

[8] Jonathan R. Cole, *Woman's Place in the Scientific Community* (New York, 1976).

sciences. The results of this analysis lead us to conclude that at least as far as the variables included in our path model go, there are no systematic or significant differences in the way the reward systems of the five disciplines we have studied operate.

Before concluding this section, we must consider one additional question. Why is it that we did not find the hypothesized field differences? Preliminary investigations suggest three answers. (1) There do not appear to be significant differences in levels of consensus in the natural and social sciences. Although there is probably more consensus within narrow specialties in the natural sciences than within specialties in the social sciences, the natural sciences have become so highly specialized that the level of consensus in the field as a whole is reduced. The social sciences, on the other hand, are still in a state of development where workers in one specialty are capable of understanding the work of their colleagues in other specialties. Because there are similar levels of consensus in the various fields, perceived quality of work has a similar effect on the distribution of rewards. (2) All academic fields we have studied operate primarily in universities and colleges. Sociologists up for promotion and physicists up for promotion usually go through similar decision-making processes. Since the different scientific fields are located in the same organization, their reward systems tend to take on a similar character. (3) Scientists working in various fields have similar values. Scientists in all fields place value on originality and contributing to scientific progress. Thus, it is not surprising that in all fields quality of work is the primary criterion on which rewards are distributed.

The studies that we have briefly summarized here lead to the conclusion that in all five of the scientific disciplines we have studied, quality of published work is the most important determinant of scientific recognition. We have found no evidence that the two social sciences, psychology and sociology, have any less universalistic reward systems than the three natural sciences, physics, chemistry, and biochemistry. Thus far, however, we have only considered the operation of variables that are internal to the institution of science. In the next section of this essay we report the results of studies aimed at discovering the influence of non-scientific statuses on scientific success.

II. DISCRIMINATION AGAINST WOMEN AND MINORITIES IN AMERICAN SCIENCE[9]

We have analyzed how a scientist's rank in the stratification system is influenced by a set of variables characterizing his position within the institution

---

[9] Some of the data presented in this section were previously discussed in Cole and Cole, *Social Stratification,* ch. 5. Parts of this section are taken verbatim from that source. A far more detailed discussion of the position of women in science may be found in Cole, *Woman's Place.*

of science. It is, of course, possible that scientists could be discriminated against on the basis of their nonscientific statuses. In a truly universalistic system, statuses, such as race, sex, and religion, which are by assumption functionally irrelevant for the performance of scientific roles, would have no independent influence on the distribution of rewards. To what extent are women and minority group members discriminated against in science? Critics of the treatment of women and minorities jump from the known fact that the proportion of women and black scientists is much lower than the proportion these groups represent in the population at large to the assumption that discrimination is occurring.

Although there is unquestionably widespread discrimination against women and racial minorities in the United States, this does not mean that such discrimination occurs in every institution or is evenly distributed within an institution.[10] One task of the sociologist is to locate the points where discrimination does or does not occur. In this section, we try to estimate the extent to which women doctorates, blacks, and Jews are discriminated against in academic science departments.[11] Even if no evidence of discrimination turns up, it would, of course, be possible that discrimination was occurring in science prior to the receipt of the Ph.D. The results reported in this paper are preliminary: They emerge from an ongoing research project on stratification processes in American science.

Determining discrimination turns out to be a complicated problem. Obviously, not every person in the population is qualified to be a scientist. Therefore, comparing the proportion of a particular group in the population and in science tells us little about the extent of discrimination. We must define carefully the particularity of the group: For example, if we assume that possession of a Ph.D. is a prerequisite for a university science job, then we must examine the distribution of rewards only among those with Ph.D.'s. In other words, a social fact that a particular group is underrepresented in science could be the result of social processes at work outside of science. Two types of processes must be considered: social selection and self-selection. Graduate school admissions procedures provide an example of how these two processes might influence the proportion of any group entering science. If graduate schools systematically reject qualified women and blacks, this would certainly constitute discrimination, the social selection of these groups out of science. However, small proportions of women and blacks in graduate school may also be a result of self-selection. If women and blacks choose not to apply for admission to graduate school, we cannot jump from the fact of

---

[10] Gunnar Myrdal, *An American Dilemma* (New York, 1944) and H. M. Blalock, Jr., *Toward a Theory of Minority Group Relations* (New York, 1967).

[11] Functionally irrelevant statuses have been discussed at length in the lectures of Robert K. Merton at Columbia University. They refer to those status characteristics of individuals that are unrelated to the ability to perform adequately specific roles. For one study of women that has used this concept, see Cynthia F. Epstein, *Woman's Place: Options and Limits in Professional Careers* (Berkeley, 1970).

their underrepresentation to the conclusion of discrimination. The failure of women and blacks to apply to graduate school may be explained by discrimination occurring earlier in life or by a value system influencing the career choices made by members of these groups.

Sex Status and Scientific Recognition

There is a striking paucity of women in contemporary American science, and even fewer women among the scientific elite. Currently, in the United States, for example, only about 12 percent of science Ph.D.'s are women. Women comprise only 3 percent of 1970 Ph.D.'s in physics and astronomy; 8 percent in chemistry; about 15 percent in the biological sciences; 18 percent in sociology; and 24 percent in psychology.[12] This pattern has been remarkably consistent over the past fifty years.

The rolls of the National Academy of Sciences and the list of Nobel laureates register very few women. As of 1971, only 8 of the 866 members of the National Academy were women. And as of 1971, only 5 of the 281 scientists who received the Nobel Prize had been women, and of these five, Marie Curie, Irene Joliot Curie, and Gerty Cori shared their prize with their husbands.[13] How can we account for these facts? Does the social system of science discriminate against women?

To determine whether apparent sex discrimination is actual, we collected data from several sources on a sample of 565 men and women scientists in the fields of chemistry, biology, psychology, and sociology. Helen Astin provided us with a sample of women: 83 percent of all 1957 and 1958 women doctorates.[14] We selected male matches for the women who received doctorates in the physical, biological, and social sciences. These male matches were drawn from the doctorate record file of the Office of Scientific Personnel (OSP), which includes data on 99 percent of annual doctorate recipients (about 17,000).[15] Four matching criteria were used: year of doctorate, university where the Ph.D. was earned, field,

---

[12] *Summary Report 1967 Doctorate Recipients from United States Universities,* National Research Council/National Academy of Sciences, prepared in the Research Division of the Office of Scientific Personnel, OSP-RD-1, May 1968; *Summary Report 1968 Doctorate Recipients from United States Universities,* prepared in the Education and Employment Section, Manpower Studies Branch, Office of Scientific Personnel, National Research Council, Washington, D.C., OSP-MS-2, April 1969.

[13] Harriet A. Zuckerman and Jonathan Cole, "Women in American Science," *Minerva* 13 (1975): 82–102.

[14] We thank Dr. Helen Astin for the help that she has given us in this study. She has provided us with the basic data set and codebook for the women scientists. Her own results for women scientists are reported fully in *The Woman Doctorate in America* (New York, 1969).

[15] Astin's study also made extensive use of the doctoral record file of the Office of Scientific Personnel. We thank Dr. William Kelley and Clarebeth Maguire Cunningham of the OSP for their help in obtaining the basic matches used in this study.

and specialty.[16] Because academic reward systems can be more easily handled than those in government and industry, we report only on the men and women scientists who were academically employed in chemistry, biology, psychology, or sociology departments. Data on selected social characteristics and on social mobility were collected for the entire sample from *American Men of Science* and directories published by professional associations.[17] Publication counts for the years 1957 through 1970 were gathered from the appropriate abstracting journal.[18] Citation data were collected from the *Science Citation Index* (SCI).[19]

To ascertain the extent of recognition received by men and women scientists, consider two forms of recognition: positional and reputational. As an indicator of positional recognition, we use the prestige rank of the scientist's academic department as measured by Cartter's American Council of Education study.[20] An additional indicator is academic rank, although rank must obviously be coupled with prestige of the academic department before it is a meaningful indicator of success. For this sample of scientists, we have only limited data on reputational recognition. We use the number of honorific awards that these scientists have received as an estimate of reputation. This measure is highly correlated with the prestige of a scientist's awards ($r = .70$) and his visibility to peers ($r = .63$).[21]

Sex Status and Prestige of Academic Affiliation

There have been few inquiries into the comparative positions held by men and women scientists, and these report that women tend to occupy lower prestige positions than male peers.[22] However, these studies did not match men and

---

16 The procedure for drawing the sample is described in full in Cole, *Woman's Place.*

17 We used the 11th and 12th editions of the *American Men of Science,* now *American Men and Women of Science.*

18 We used the following sets of abstracts for the publication counts: *Science Abstracts; Chemical Abstracts; Biological Abstracts;* and *Psychology Abstracts.* Publication counts for sociology were obtained by examining the volumes of twenty-seven leading sociological journals over a twelve-year period. Both single-authored and multi-authored papers were counted.

19 Citation data were collected for six years: 1961, 1964, 1965, 1967, 1969, 1970.

20 Universities not included in Cartter's study were rated lower in prestige than those that were ranked, and all colleges were scored lower than universities. While this may involve occasional inaccuracies, in general, universities are the locus of research activities, and a substantial proportion of the eminent scientists in any era can be found at the better large universities.

21 Cole and Cole, *Social Stratification.*

22 Stanley Budner and John Meyer, "Women Professors," as reported in Jessie Bernard, *Academic Women* (University Park, Pa., 1964); Alice S. Rossi, "Status of Women in Graduate Departments of Sociology," *The American Sociologist* 5 (February 1970): 1–12; Alice S. Rossi, "Equality Between the Sexes: An Immodest Proposal," *Daedalus* (1964): 98–143; Alice S. Rossi, "Women in Science: Why So Few?" *Science* 148, no. 3674 (May 28, 1965): 1196–1202.

women scientists for professional age or where they received their training and rarely tried to control for the role performance of the scientists. Our data, which do control for these variables, allow us to determine more adequately the relationship between positional recognition and sex status. We begin with an apparently striking datum: The zero-order correlation between sex status and prestige of academic department in 1965 is virtually zero ($r = -.02$), which suggests that men and women scientists with similar training wind up in academic departments of equal prestige. (Sex status was coded: $1 =$ men; $2 =$ women.) This zero-order correlation coefficient, however, conceals some variation between the four academic fields making up the sample. In chemistry and psychology, women are somewhat less likely than men to be found in top departments. The zero-order correlations for the two fields are $r = -.23$ and $r = -.17$, respectively. In biology, where there is a greater number of women in academic positions than in the other two fields, women do slightly better than men ($r = .06$), and the differential in favor of women is even greater in sociology ($r = .30$).

In 1970, some thirteen years after the doctorate, there still was no relationship between sex status and prestige of academic department ($r = .01$). The pattern of findings within the several fields is similar to those in 1965.

Academic Rank

Intense competition exists for promotion to the higher ranks of associate and full professor among American academicians, especially at prestigious departments. Scientists are not only concerned with achieving high rank, but in doing so as quickly as possible. It is a measure of distinction to be a "young" associate or a "young" full professor.[23]

Since all the scientists in our sample received their Ph.D.'s at the same time (1957–1958) and therefore have about the same professional age, the correlation between sex status and academic rank may be used as a rough indicator of the extent of recognition of the men and women scientists. The zero-order correlation between sex status and academic rank for the entire sample in 1965 is $-.34$: women hold lower academic ranks than men. There are field differences, ranging from an insignificant difference in the ranks of men and women chem-

---

[23] For research that reports data on the relationship between sex status and academic rank, see Carolyn Cummings Perrucci, "Minority Status and the Pursuit of Professional Careers: Women in Science and Engineering," *Social Forces* 49 (December 1970): 245–259; Rita James Simon, Shirley Merritt Clark, and Kathleen Galway, "The Woman Ph.D.: A Recent Profile," *Social Problems* 15 (Fall 1967): 221–236, esp. pp. 228–229; Alan E. Bayer and Helen A. Astin, "Sex Differences in Academic Rank and Salary Among Science Doctorates in Teaching," *Journal of Human Resources* 3 (1968): 191–200. Each of these studies presents problems in interpretation since age, educational background, types of institutional affiliation, and academic role performance are not always adequately controlled, and the number of women sampled is often extraordinarily small.

ists ($r = -.08$) to substantial differences among biologists ($r = -.38$), psychologists ($r = -.36$), and sociologists ($r = -.44$). The zero-order correlation between sex status and academic rank in 1970 declines somewhat from the 1965 level, but remains significant ($r = -.28$), suggesting the possibility that discriminatory practices persist in the promotion of men and women scientists.

Reputational Recognition: Honorific Awards

There are only limited data available on the honorific recognition granted to women scientists. We have already noted their slight representation in the most elite academies of science and in the ranks of Nobelists. Simon reports that women are more likely than men to receive post-doctoral fellowships and memberships in honorary societies.[24] For our sample of scientists, we counted the total number of honorific awards and post-doctoral fellowships listed after their names in *American Men of Science*. For the entire sample, the correlation between sex status and number of honorific awards was $-.05$, men being slightly more likely to have received awards. Once again, field differences exist: The zero-order correlation for chemistry was $-.19$; for biology, $r = -.09$; for psychology, $r = -.07$; for sociology, $r = .28$. In summary, there are only small differences in the level of reputational recognition of men and women scientists in our matched sample. Sociology represents the most consistent divergence from the general pattern of results. While the number of cases on which these sociology correlations are based is very small, the result for sociology may reflect either a heightened sense of social injustice among sociologists or a relatively more able set of women sociologists. This, of course, remains speculation.

The zero-order correlations are summarized in Table 2. The overall pattern indicates that men do only slightly better than women in terms of the prestige rank of their academic departments, the receipt of honorific awards, and significantly better in terms of academic rank. Observed zero-order correlations, such as these, are often the basis for the statement that sex discrimination is operating in the scientific community. Among Astin's sample of women scientists, 25 percent cited experiences of discrimination in hiring practices, 40 percent had experienced differentials in salaries, and 33 percent cited differentials in policies regarding tenure and promotion.[25] Evidence for political scientists, gathered by Mitchell and Starr, indicate that men are as likely as women to believe that women are discriminated against.[26] But the data we have presented thus far, involving only zero-order correlations, are not enough to answer the

---

[24] Simon, et al., "The Woman Ph.D.," pp. 232–233.

[25] Astin, *The Woman Doctorate,* p. 106.

[26] Joyce M. Mitchell and Rachel Starr, "Aspirations, Achievement and Professional Advancement in Political Science: The Prospect for Women in the West," in *Women in Political Science: Studies and Reports of APSA Committee on the Status of Women in the Profession, 1969–71* (Washington, D.C.: American Political Science Association, 1971).

Table 2: Zero-Order Correlations[a] Between Sex Status[b] and Three Forms of
Scientific Recognition[c] for Four Scientific Disciplines

	All Fields	N	Chemistry	N	Biology	N	Psychology	N	Sociology	N
Rank of Department										
1965	−.02	423	−.23	42	.06	215	−.17	131	.30	35
1970	.01	262								
Academic Rank										
1965	−.34	469	−.08	54	−.38	244	−.36	130	−.44	41
1970	−.28	255								
Number of										
Honorific Awards	−.05	438	−.19	41	−.09	239	−.07	122	.28	36

[a] There were missing data for this sample. The correlations are based upon pair-wise computations. The "N" in the right-hand column gives the number of cases on which the Pearson correlation is based.

[b] Sex status was coded: 1–male; 2–female.

[c] Difference in N's between rank of department and academic rank is due to the fact that some scientists were located at medical schools that were not ranked by the ACE.

question of whether women scientists are being discriminated against. Unless it can be shown that the differences in recognition received by men and women scientists are not a result of differential role performance, there is no evidence of discrimination and the social system would be operating in accordance with its universalistic norms. While it is tempting to draw inferences about the presence or absence of discrimination on the basis of simple bivariate relationships, they tell us little about equality or inequality of opportunity.

Since rank in the scientific stratification system depends heavily on the quality of published research—and indeed on its production at a reasonable rate —we must examine the scholarly productivity patterns of men and women scientists. How, if at all, do the publication patterns of men and women scientists differ?

Productivity of Men and Women Scientists

As a cohort, these men and women scientists were neither extraordinarily prolific nor were they below average, in terms of research output. The mean productivity for the 565 academic scientists was nine papers over a span of twelve years. Productivity is very unevenly distributed among the scientists: Few published many scientific papers; a small number published a high proportion of the group's total. For example, in 1959, one or two years after receipt of the doctorate—prolific years for young scientists—53 percent of the sample failed to publish a single paper, and 34 percent published just one. In most years, between 70 and 80 percent of the scientists published nothing. This skewed productivity pattern is exactly the same for both men and women scientists. Roughly, 15 percent of scientists, male and female alike, account for about 50 percent of the total papers produced by scientists of their own sex.

But is there a relationship between sex status and productivity?[27] As a step to the analysis of more complex relationships, we note that male scientists in the matched sample are, on average, more productive than women. For the fourteen-year span, 1957–1970, the median publication rate was eight papers for academic men and three for academic women. Examination of the mean number of scientific publications during these years shows that men scientists consistently published far more than women scientists in all fields, except sociology. (See Table 3.) These differences are summarized for the entire sample of 565 by the Pearson correlation coefficient of —.30.[28]

---

[27] The total number of published papers, both single authored and collaborative, was used as the measure of productivity.

[28] This correlation is based on standardized productivity scores, which had to be computed because of field differences in productivity. The correlation between the standardized and unstandardized scores was .90. The zero-order correlation between scientific productivity from 1958–1970 and scientific productivity from 1958 to 1965 is extremely high ($r =$ .95).

Table 3: Scientific Productivity (1957–1970) of Men and Women
Scientists in Four Fields

	Mean Number of Published Scientific Papers (1957–1970)	
Field	*Men*	*Women*
Total Sample	11.6	5.3
Chemistry	13.6	3.9
Biological Sciences	14.6	6.8
Psychology	9.1	4.2
Sociology[a]	1.5	1.8

[a] The data for sociology were not collected from the sociology abstracts. A list of twenty-seven journals was reviewed during the time span for publications by sampled sociologists. The search for publications, therefore, is not as extensive as in the other fields. The abstracting journals in the other fields contain information for many more journals. The sociology publication rates may be less reliable than those for the other disciplines.

NOTE: The Pearson correlation coefficient between sex status and scientific productivity for the entire sample was $r = -.30$.

There are, of course, several explanations for the lower productivity of women scientists. Consider two that are frequently offered. First, lower publication rates of women result from their family obligations, which prevent them from spending as much time working as men. This hypothesis can be tested by comparing the publication patterns of men and women scientists who have similar family statuses. The men and women scientists were divided into those who were unmarried; married without children; those with one or two children; and those with three or more children. The mean number of publications for the twelve post-doctoral years was computed for each of the eight subgroups. The data in Table 4 testify that sex differences have a much greater influence on publication patterns than do family statuses. Consider the following striking fact: Unmarried women scientists publish far less than men scientists in all family categories. Thus we may tentatively conclude that family status cannot account for the differential rates of productivity of men and women scientists. In fact, family obligations only influence the productivity rates of women having three or more children. Women with smaller families are no less likely to publish than unmarried women. This pattern is found in chemistry, biology, and psychology—fields for which we had enough data to test the hypothesis.

Occupational location is offered as an explanation by Jessie Bernard and others for the lower productivity of women. Women are more frequently found at college settings, where research is not the norm or a prerequisite for promo-

Table 4: Mean Number of Scientific Publications[a] (1957–1970) for Men and Women Scientists, Controlling Marital Status and Family Size

Sex	Total	Un-married	Married with No Children	One or Two Children	Three or More Children
			Marital and Family Status		
Men	$12_{(298)}$	$9_{(32)}$	$15_{(33)}$	$12_{(124)}$	$11_{(109)}$
Women	$5_{(263)}$	$5_{(67)}$	$8_{(38)}$	$6_{(91)}$	$4_{(67)}$

Total	Usable Cases:	561
	Missing Cases:	4
Total Sample		565

[a] These means have been rounded to the nearest integer.

tion.[29] To test this hypothesis, we regressed scientific productivity on institutional affiliation and sex status. Although scientists at universities are in general more prolific ($r = .30$) and produce work that is more frequently cited ($r = .20$) than those located at colleges, the data suggest that institutional affiliation fails to even slightly modify the relationship between sex status and scientific output. The partial regression coefficient between sex status and productivity ($b^*_{p\,s\,cu} = -.28$) is virtually equal to the zero-order correlation between the two variables ($r = -.30$).[30] In short, academic male scientists are more productive than their female colleagues at universities just as they are at colleges.

Other variables, such as differentials in teaching responsibilities, access to research funds, and access to collaboration with other outstanding scientists, might account for the differences in published productivity of men and women, but this must remain untested here for lack of data. It is possible that in order to account fully for the correlation between sex status and the rate of scientific output, it may be necessary to look outside the institutional structure of science and examine carefully the prior experiences and socialization of women in the larger society, which may dampen motivation to succeed and influence their publication performance after they enter science.

Although we cannot explain differences in productivity of men and women scientists, substantial variability exists, of course, in the scientific productivity of

---

[29] Reference in Astin, *The Woman Doctorate*, p. 85.

[30] In presenting the partial regression coefficients we use the following subscripts: s = sex status; p = productivity; q = quality of research; m = marital status; f = family size; r = rank of current department (1965); a = number of honorific awards and post-doctoral fellowships; b = academic rank; c = college affiliation; u = university affiliation.

women scientists. The central issue is whether differential rewards can be explained by differential role performance. When we control for quality and quantity of research output, do men still receive greater recognition than women?

Sex Status and Recognition Controlling For Scientific Role Performance

For the entire sample of academic men and women in four fields, recall that sex status was virtually uncorrelated with rank of department in 1965 ($r = -.02$) or in 1970 ($r = .01$). When productivity of the scientists is controlled, there is, if anything, a slight tendency for women to be overrepresented in higher quality departments ($b^*_{ds.pg} = .06$). This was true for all four fields. The different zero-order correlations in the four fields (see Table 2) do not imply that there is more or less "discrimination" in one field or another. For example, although women biologists in the matched sample are more likely to be found at high prestige departments than their male peers, they could still be the objects of discrimination. For if women biologists are on average more productive and produce higher quality work than their male peers, then it is possible that they are still not being rewarded in direct relation to their performance.

When we regress department prestige on sex status, productivity, and quality of research, the association between sex status and rank of department is reduced significantly in chemistry ($r = -.23$; $b^* = -.06$), psychology ($r = -.17$; $b^* = -.10$), and sociology ($r = .30$; $b^* = .17$). The standardized partial regression coefficients in these fields suggest that sex status is of minimal significance in determining a scientist's rank of department. As we would expect, quantity and quality of research has a far greater independent influence on rank of department than does sex status. In the biological sciences, the pattern is different. Controlling for the amount and quality of work, women are still slightly more likely to be found at higher ranked departments ($r = .06$; $b^* = .15$). The association between sex status and prestige of department in 1970 does not yield evidence of sex-related bias. The partial regression coefficient for sex status, controlling for research performance was insignificant ($b^*_{rs.qp} = .08$). The belief that women are slowly weeded out of the top departments as their careers progress is not supported by these data.

The story becomes more complex when we turn to the issue of advancement to higher academic ranks. The relationship between sex status and academic rank ($r = -.34$) is not reduced by controls on scientific productivity ($b^*_{as.pq} = -.32$). At each level of productivity, women scientists are less likely to receive promotions than men scientists.[31] This pattern holds for each of the four fields: chemistry ($r = -.08$; $b^* = -.13$); biology ($r = -.38$; $b^* = -.39$); psy-

---

[31] This result indicates, of course, that productivity ($r = .10$) and quality of output ($r = .12$) are not strongly correlated with academic rank.

chology ($r = -.36$; $b* = -.31$); and sociology ($r = -.44$; $b* = -.50$). Similar results obtain regardless of how we divide the sample. Thus, sex status definitely influences promotion within the scientific community.

But before we can estimate the extent to which women are discriminated against in promotion to tenured positions, it is necessary to examine influences other than discrimination that could possibly influence these results. One such factor is professional seniority. Most scientists, male and female, with notable exceptions, of course, must put in their years at a given rank before they are put up for promotion. If seniority is an important ingredient in promotion decisions, it probably has more negative consequences for female scientists than for males, since women are more likely to interrupt their professional careers for some period of time closely following receipt of the Ph.D.

Data were available for women on career interruptions; they were not available for men. We made the assumption that all male scientists in the sample had been continuously in the labor force: a reasonable assumption for the period between 1958 and 1965, one of expanding opportunities for new Ph.D.'s. In order to estimate the effects of female career interruptions, we excluded from this analysis all women who had interrupted their professional careers for any time from the receipt of their doctorates to 1965.[32] If seniority affects promotion, we would expect a reduction in the correlation between sex status and academic rank when women with career interruptions are excluded. The data confirm this expectation. When employment history is taken into account, the zero-order correlation between sex status and rank is reduced from $r = -.34$ to $r = -.24$. The influence of sex status on academic rank is further reduced if we examine the relationship at later points in the careers of men and women scientists. The zero-order correlation between sex status and rank in 1970 was $-.24$; when we eliminated those women who had career interruptions prior to 1965, the association was reduced to $-.18$. Finally, when we controlled for the influence of scientific productivity on academic rank in 1970, the effect of sex status is reduced to less than one-half of the original zero-order correlation, $b*_{bs.q} = -.10$. While sex status continues to play some role in determining academic rank in 1970, its independent effect is sharply reduced. In short, these data suggest that seniority weighs heavily in the process of academic promotion and that women scientists more than men are adversely affected by the application of this principle.

Let us turn now to the one indicator of honorific recognition for which we have some empirical data: the receipt of honorific awards and post-doctoral fellowships. For the sample of 565 men and women scientists in four fields, we found a small correlation between sex status and number of honorific awards

---

[32] There is no evidence of any correlation between career interruptions and discrimination that could otherwise account for the drop in the zero-order correlation.

($r = -.05$). When we control for the quality and quantity of published research, the influence of sex status on this form of recognition is completely eliminated ($b^*_{as.qp} = .00$). Sex status has no influence on honorific recognition in any of the four fields. Again, high productivity and quality of research are the primary determinants of honorific recognition. In terms of honorific recognition, there is no evidence that women scientists are discriminated against in the scientific community.

To fully understand the way that sex status could influence scientific recognition, we must consider another social process that operates in the scientific community. In a series of papers and monographs, it has been suggested that scientists who are placed in structurally advantageous positions as a result of outstanding role performance benefit from the process of accumulative advantage. There is, however, a second analytic and darker side of the process of accumulation of rewards in science. It is the accumulation of failures—the process of "accumulative disadvantage."[33]

A social system can operate universalistically at one point in time and still be discriminating. If the conditions for a self-fulfilling prophecy exist at an early point in time, then, of course, a universalistic judgment later on will ultimately produce inferior status for the judged group. For example, suppose women receive less support than men, in terms of access to all kinds of facilities and resources at early points in their training and professional careers. It should not surprise anyone that they would then be less productive than men. Their futures now become predictable.[34]

Several investigators who have spoken to the issue of sex discrimination in science hypothesize that women scientists suffer from compounding career disadvantages. Once denied access to resources and facilities, women must struggle simply to reach parity with their male colleagues. This process has been referred to as the "principle of the double penalty."[35] The principle states that groups, such as blacks and women, not only suffer from direct discrimination but also from the second penalty of being placed initially into second rate structural positions that make it difficult or impossible for them to produce the outstanding work that is necessary for moving out of such positions.

This position is predicated on the assumption that women scientists are not treated in the same way as men in the initial phases of their careers. We must ask whether this is empirically correct. Are women less likely to be admitted to

---

[33] For another discussion of how these processes affect the careers of scientific elites, see Harriet A. Zuckerman, *Scientific Elite: Studies of Nobel Laureates in the United States* (Chicago, forthcoming).

[34] For a full discussion of the structural conditions making for self-fulfilling prophecies, see Robert K. Merton, "The Self-Fulfilling Prophecy," *Social Theory and Social Structure* (Glencoe, 1949), pp. 475–490.

[35] Zuckerman and Cole, "Women in American Science."

top graduate departments of science, independently of their ability? Do women receive less financial support when in graduate school than men? Are women's efforts at research given less support during their training period than men? Are women working on research projects given the less intellectually demanding jobs to perform? Must women more than men choose dissertation topics that are less compatible with their interests? There are no definitive answers to these questions. More research is needed on such matters involving the initial definition of talent and potential of men and women scientists.

Some scanty evidence is available, however, on the extent to which women and men are admitted to and given financial support for their graduate training. Women appear to receive their doctorates from top ranked departments in the same proportion as men. Folger, Astin, and Bayer examined the proportion of men and women Ph.D.'s from departments rated as distinguished or strong in Cartter's ACE study of the quality of graduate education.[36] They found that about 50 percent of each sex were being trained at these top departments. Berelson, in an earlier study of graduate education, also found that women were just as likely as men to receive degrees from one of his "top twelve" schools.[37] Data reported by Astin on admission to medical schools show similar results: In 1964–1965, "47.6 percent of the women applicants were accepted, as compared with 47.1 percent of the male applicants."[38]

The distribution of fellowship support for men and women graduate students offers no prima facie evidence of discriminatory practices. Women are just as likely as men to receive financial support. Astin, comparing the proportion of women and men doctorates receiving either fellowships or graduate assistantships, found that 57 percent of the female doctorates had received aid compared with 58 percent of the men.[39] Jessie Bernard also reported: "The National Science Foundation awards in 1959 were given to women in about the same ratio as to men; 12 percent of the applicants were women, and 12 percent of the awards went to women."[40] Bernard further notes that women receive fellowships to the Center for Advanced Study in the Behavioral Sciences at Stanford in proportion to the numbers of females recommended for fellowships. To add a few more pieces of evidence to that already presented, consider the conclusion reached by James A. Davis in his study of some 34,000 college graduates in 1961. He concluded that "women . . . have no disadvantage or advantage in offerings" of fellowships for graduate education.[41] Simon, as noted earlier, reports that women

---

[36] John K. Folger, Helen S. Astin, Alan E. Bayer, *Human Resources and Higher Education* (New York, 1970).

[37] Cited in Bernard, *Academic Women*, p. 89.

[38] Astin, *The Woman Doctorate*, p. 103.

[39] *Ibid.*

[40] Bernard, *Academic Women*, p. 50.

[41] Davis, James A., quoted in *ibid.*, p. 51.

are slightly more likely than men to receive some form of fellowship support.

Recently, Cynthia Atwood found that during the years 1968–1973 among those admitted to graduate school women were more likely than men to receive financial aid.[42] A report on the status of women in sociology indicated that in 1971–1972 women were admitted to graduate schools in direct proportion in which they applied: 34 percent of the new applicants were women; 37 percent were accepted.[43] And finally, our own data showed no significant differences between the number of post-doctoral honorific awards received by men and women in the matched sample. These data suggest that women are not discriminated against in terms of support necessary to do full-time graduate work.

Thus far we have only considered the influence of one functionally irrelevant status on scientific recognition. There are, of course, other social characteristics of individual scientists that could influence their level of recognition, regardless of the quality of their role performance. We shall briefly discuss two of these: racial and religious status.

Racial Status and Scientific Recognition

Of the various bases of discrimination in American society, none is more salient than racial status. But are racial minorities, and in particular black Americans, treated fairly in the American scientific community? The answer to this question is difficult to determine, because there are almost no detailed, reliable data on the position of blacks in American science. The scattered empirical evidence that does exist all converges upon a single fact: There are few blacks who have Ph.D.'s. Since receipt of the doctorate is a prerequisite for entry into the upper levels of academic science, we first consider the proportions and absolute numbers of doctorates received by blacks.

Crossland surveyed sixty-three Ph.D. granting institutions to compile data on the distribution of blacks in graduate departments. The picture painted is bleak: "1.72 percent . . . of the total enrollment in America's graduate schools of arts and sciences" are black Americans, and "0.78 percent . . . of all Ph.D.'s awarded between 1964 and 1968 went to black Americans."[44] While the absolute number of blacks seeking and obtaining higher degrees has sharply increased

---

[42] Cynthia Atwood, "Women in Fellowship and Training Programs," Association of American Colleges, November 1972, as cited in Lewis C. Solomon, "Women in Graduate Education: Clues and Puzzles Regarding Institutional Discrimination." Unpublished mimeo.

[43] "The Status of Women in Sociology 1968–1972: Report to the American Sociological Association of the Ad Hoc Committee on the Status of Women in the Profession" (Washington, D.C.: The American Sociological Association, 1973).

[44] Fred E. Crossland, "Graduate Education and Black Americans" (New York: Ford Foundation, 1968), p. 2 (mimeo).

since World War II, the percentage of the total number of new doctorates that blacks represent has remained fundamentally unchanged.[45]

There are various estimates of the actual number of blacks within the scientific community; all agree that blacks receive less than 1 percent of science Ph.D.'s conferred in any given year. A recent survey indicates that black Ph.D.'s are not evenly distributed among the various fields of higher education. Twenty-nine percent of black Ph.D.'s have received their doctorates in education; 26 percent, in the social sciences. Approximately 25 percent of black doctorates receive their degrees in one of the physical or biological sciences.[46] Jay estimates that a total of "650 American Negroes obtained doctorate degrees in the natural sciences between 1876 [when the first doctorate to be granted to a black American was conferred at Yale] and 1969. . . ."[47]

Crossland could locate only one black doctorate in physics, eight in chemistry, eleven in biology, six in psychology, and five in sociology, among all recipients of the Ph.D. at sixty-three universities during the two-year period of 1967 and 1968. Consider what a minute fraction this represents when in the same years there were 3,546 doctorates awarded in chemistry, 2,712 in physics and astronomy, 6,797 in biological sciences, 2,745 in psychology and 694 in sociology.[48] Jay's research could identify only 94 black Ph.D.'s in the physical sciences and 252 doctorates in the biological sciences between 1876 and 1969.[49] Clearly, if there is a paucity of women doctorates in American science, there is an even greater scarcity of black Americans in science, even if these estimates are off by a fairly wide margin.

Estimating the treatment of blacks in science is, therefore, virtually impossible. Even if we deal with an entire population rather than samples of scientists, we quickly begin to consider individual cases. Furthermore, there have been no studies on the role performance and productivity of black scientists. What we know is limited indeed: Black doctorates tend to receive their degrees from less distinguished universities; they take longer, on average, to earn their degrees; once they have the doctorate, they are most likely to be located at black colleges far removed from the frontiers of scientific advance.[50]

Black Americans face multiple hurdles along the road to science. If women

---

[45] James M. Jay, *Negroes in Science: Natural Science Doctorates, 1876–1969* (Detroit, 1971), p. 2; Crossland, "Graduate Education," p. 3.

[46] Ford Foundation, *A Survey of Black American Doctorates* (New York, 1970).

[47] Jay, *Negroes in Science,* p. viii.

[48] National Academy of Sciences, National Research Council, Office of Scientific Personnel, *Summary of Doctorates in the United States, 1967, 1968.*

[49] Jay, *Negroes in Science,* pp. 40, 50.

[50] Crossland, "Graduate Education"; Ford Foundation, *Survey;* Jay, *Negroes in Science.*

do not, on average, suffer from a "double penalty," black Americans seem to: Not only must they overcome the disadvantages of their poorer socioeconomic backgrounds, but they must surmount the generally poorer training that they received at less distinguished undergraduate and graduate schools.[51] Although we cannot at this time assess whether there is any actual discrimination against black Americans *within* the scientific community in terms of their just access to scientific resources and facilities and in terms of recognition accorded for outstanding role performance, it is clear that prior to entrance into the scientific community, even the most talented blacks face a set of social and psychological barriers that are difficult to overcome. In short, since there are no data on the ability or the scientific output of black scientists, it is currently impossible to say with any certainty whether or not the positions that blacks occupy in science are the result of a self-fulfilling prophecy.

Religious Status and Scientific Recognition

Although other functionally irrelevant statuses, such as age, may prove to have an independent effect on the evaluation of scientists, we have collected data on only one other nonprofessional status that is sometimes said to influence the status attainment of men and women in academic life: Many scholars have expressed the view that anti-Semitism has been the major form of religious discrimination operating in academic social systems over the past century.[52] In this paper we limit the analysis to a dichotomy on religious status: Jews and Christians. We estimate the effect of being Jewish on location in the scientific stratification system.

The sample of 300 full professors in five disciplines at Ph.D. granting institutions was used to determine the influence of religious status on recognition (see section I). We did not have data on self-reported religious preference. In order to determine the religion of the scientists, we had one Jewish faculty member and two Jewish graduate students independently guess the religion of the scientists from their names. Where two of the three judges agreed that a

---

[51] Harriet A. Zuckerman, "Women and Blacks in American Science: The Principle of the Double Penalty." Paper presented at Symposium on Women and Minority Groups in American Science and Engineering, California Institute of Technology, December 8, 1971, p. 36.

[52] For discussions of anti-Semitism in universities and colleges, see among others, Heywood Brown and George Britt, *Christians Only* (New York, 1931); Carey McWilliams, *A Mask for Privilege: Anti-Semitism in the United States* (Boston, 1948), pp. 38–39; Don W. Dodson, "College Quotas and American Democracy," *The American Scholar* (Summer 1945); Lawrence Bloomingarden, "Our Changing Elite Colleges," *Commentary* (February 1960); Seymour Martin Lipset and Everett Carll Ladd, Jr., "Jewish Academics in the United States: Their Achievements, Culture and Politics," *American Jewish Yearbook* (New York, 1971), pp. 89–128.

name was Jewish, the scientist was so classified.[53] Of course, using this procedure, we are bound to misclassify some of the scientists. But since the three guessers knew nothing about the scientists, there is no reason to believe that the errors would not be randomly distributed. Using this rough procedure, we classified 68 out of the 300, or 23 percent, of the scientists as Jewish. This figure is fairly consistent with independent estimates of the proportion of Jews in academic science. Lipset and Ladd, in their study of some 60,000 academics at colleges and universities throughout the United States, found that approximately 14 percent of the physicists, 8 percent of the chemists, 21 percent of sociologists, and 17 percent of psychologists had Jewish social origins.[54] They also pointed out, however, that Jews are more likely than non-Jews to be located at universities. Since all our scientists are at Ph.D. granting institutions, the figure of 23 percent is at least roughly consistent with the data reported by Lipset and Ladd.

In the analysis, we use three dependent variables: one form of positional recognition, indicated by the prestige rank of a scientist's academic affiliation; one form of reputational recognition, measured by a scientist's visibility to the community; and finally, the perceived quality of his work. The zero-order correlations between religion and the three dependent variables are significantly greater than zero, with Jews receiving more recognition than non-Jews. Jews are also more likely to have their work perceived as being of high quality. The correlation between religion and rank of department is $r = .16$; between religion and visibility, $r = .27$; religion and perceived quality, $r = .19$. These coefficients suggest that Jewish scientists are slightly more likely than non-Jews to be recognized in contemporary science. However, once again these zero-order correlations cannot tell us about equality or inequality of opportunity. It is possible that even though Jews are more likely to be recognized they still may be discriminated against. If twice as many Jews as non-Jews have produced high quality scientific work, then twice as many Jews as non-Jews should be eminent. If Jews are only slightly more likely to be eminent, then discrimination could be operating. We must therefore look at the quality of role performance of Jewish and non-Jewish scientists.

Since, in our data, there is no relationship between religion and the quality of scientific output ($r = .00$) and religion and the quantity of scientific output ($r = .07$), and since Jews are slightly more likely to be recognized than non-

---

[53] For discussion of a similar procedure in identifying Jewish professionals, see Stephen Cole, *The Unionization of Teachers* (New York, 1969), pp. 94–95. The procedure was first introduced by Paul Lazarsfeld. He had people guess the religion of academics from their names. Since he also had data on the actual religious preference of the academics, he was able to estimate the accuracy of this guessing procedure. He found this guessing procedure to yield roughly accurate estimates of the proportion of Jewish and non-Jewish academics.

[54] Seymour Martin Lipset and Everett Carll Ladd, "Jewish Academics."

Jews, we may conclude that there is no evidence that Jewish scientists are discriminated against. As the data of Table 5 indicate, religious status does have a slight independent effect on recognition, but an effect that in no way compares to that of quality of research. While it is, of course, possible that we might find individual cases of anti-Semitism, we may tentatively conclude that currently there is no behavioral discrimination against Jewish scientists as a group in the American academic science community.

Table 5:   Religious Status and Two Forms of Scientific Recognition and
Perceived Quality of Work Controlling for Scientific Output

| Independent Variable | Zero-Order Correlations and Regression Coefficients in Standard Form Dependent Variables | | | | | |
| | *Rank of Department* | | *Visibility* | | *Perceived Quality* | |
	r	*b**	*r*	*b**	*r*	*b**
Quantity[a]	.21	.00	.49	.23	.44	.14
Quality of Work[b]	.35	.34	.59	.43	.58	.48
Religion[c]	.16	.14	.27	.24	.19	.15

[a] Productivity was measured by counting the total number of published papers listed in the journal abstracts of the five scientific fields used for this study.

[b] Quality was measured by counting the total number of citations to the scientists' life's work in the 1965 and 1969 *SCI*.

[c] Religion was coded: 2 = Jews, 1 = all others.

III.   CONCLUSIONS AND POLICY ISSUES

What do the data presented in this paper suggest about the reward systems of the physical, biological, and social sciences? Remember we are dealing only with scientists who have earned their doctorates and have become scientists. We are not considering predoctoral influences on careers. Within this framework the evidence is clear. First, the data are striking in their uniformity. Quality of research performance is the single most significant determinant of recognition in each of the disciplines, considerably more important, for example, than the quantity of a scientist's output. Contrary to initial expectations, there are no significant differences between "hard" and "soft" sciences in the importance of quality as a predictor of various forms of success. The data suggest the existence of a uniform structure of rewards in all fields that is independent of the cognitive content of the field or its degree of intellectual maturation. Second, the functionally irrelevant statuses of sex and religion are not influential in determining several forms of recognition in the stratification system of American science. In the physical, biological, and social sciences, sex differences simply do not influence structural location or honorific recognition, when we control for the intellectual origins and research performance of male and female scientists. However, in all fields studied, sex status does help to predict academic rank, independently of quality and quantity of output. Within the limits of our data, religious status does not seem to impede the careers of men and women in contemporary science. Finally, there are too few black American scientists, and insufficient data on the quality of their work, to test adequately for patterned discrimination based on race.

These findings have a number of policy implications, and it is to these that we now turn.

Affirmative Action Plans

Universities that receive government contracts are now required to file acceptable affirmative action plans with the Department of Health, Education, and Welfare. They must demonstrate that their hiring and promotion procedures are unbiased and, if "deficiencies" are discovered, must develop a plan to eliminate them. On many campuses there is a growing sense that the government, through its control of the purse, is taking action that interferes with the autonomy of universities to determine criteria on which to hire and promote faculty and supporting staff. A feeling that a quota system is being imposed on the universities is widespread. The principle of equality of opportunity is being replaced by a new and different principle of affirmative action.

There is a conceptual difference between equality of opportunity and affirmative action. The multiple historical changes in the concepts of equality of opportunity need not concern us here, except to note that for some time it has implied open competition for positions based solely upon task-related talents.[55] Of course, the breach between creed and practice often has been wide. But up until the 1960s the social composition of an occupation was not an issue as long as the procedures that were followed in recruitment were deemed "fair." In fact, just a few years ago in many states it was illegal to request characteristics, such as race, on application forms for jobs. Things have changed. Affirmative action implies, not simply that every individual has an "equal" try at rewards, but that the social composition of an occupation match the social characteristics of the population. It assumes, for instance, that if 20 percent of sociology doctorates happen to be women, that 20 percent of the members of every department of sociology should turn out to be women. If this is not the case, then sex discrimination is probably being practiced. It assumes that motivation, native ability, and role performance are equally distributed in all social groups and categories

---

[55] For an extended discussion of the concept of equality of opportunity, see Charles Frankel, "Equality of Opportunity," *Ethics* 81 (April 1971): 191–211.

throughout society. From this assumption, it directly follows that all groups should be represented in all job categories roughly in proportion to their relative numbers in the eligible labor pool.

The need to file affirmative action plans requires universities to investigate an area for which they have little hard data. Universities have established over the years a wide variety of "gate-keeping" devices to review the qualifications of their personnel, but the results of these procedures have rarely been systematically analyzed. For the most part, hiring and promotion criteria have been local department matters, with little interference coming from central administrators. Affirmative action policy, however, requires universities to address several old questions in an entirely new way. For instance, how do universities determine who is eligible for jobs on their campus, that is, what is the "labor pool" of potential faculty and supporting staff? Even more difficult is, how does a university go about demonstrating that it does not discriminate against women and minority group members?

Our data, which include measures of quality of research performance but not other significant areas of performance, suggest that universities are actually doing quite well in rewarding excellence. To be sure, there must be many cases of individuals who are discriminated against at specific locations within the academic community. Yet the overall pattern suggests a highly universalistic system. Given the actual state of affairs and the new ideology that holds that proportional representation is evidence of nondiscriminatory practice, we must ask what are some consequences of adopting a policy that implicitly assumes that higher levels of particularism exist than is in fact the case?

Let us examine two sets of consequences for individuals and for the social system of science. First, there are clearly positive consequences for some individuals or sets of individuals. Women and black scholars, especially those with adequate academic credentials, are suddenly rare commodities in the academic marketplace. There is a great deal of demand for their services. Many of these individuals now find themselves in superior departments that were far beyond their earlier expectations. As in other similar supply and demand situations, the salaries and ranks of members of these groups are likely to show relative increases. The relatively minor differences between the academic salaries of men and women, which has been noted in a number of recent studies, may soon totally disappear. In addition, there is now a substantial demand on many campuses for specialists in currently "fashionable" areas within the social sciences. And since many departments tacitly accede to the "insider" doctrine, which holds that only women can fully understand problems of women in society or blacks the problems of blacks, there are increasing opportunities for women, for example, who are specialists on women in society, women in history, women in literature, or women in the labor market. These recent policy changes also affect the black scholar who previously was located at lower prestige black colleges. Opportunities for rapid advance within the academic community, previously beyond the horizon, suddenly appear in full view. But attending this important advance in opportunity for women and minority group members are some negative consequences for the same individuals who benefit most from the new shift in policy.

The use of functionally irrelevant social characteristics as necessary conditions for hiring or promotion can produce for individuals a sense of ambiguity about the basis on which they are being evaluated.[56] It becomes increasingly difficult for women or black scientists, for example, to determine whether they are "hired" for their ability as scholars and teachers or because they are female or of the "right" color. Indeed, there undoubtedly is a growing sense among many female scientists that their sex status has more to do with their success or failure than the quality of their role performance. There is some evidence that such role ambiguity can adversely affect job satisfaction and role performance.[57] Of course, such treatment of women and minorities as special categories produces in those not possessing the "right" characteristic a sense of ambiguity as to how they are being evaluated. Thus, on the aggregate level there can emerge a general sense that universalistic and rational criteria of rewards no longer operate in the social system. Such sentiments, if widespread, can lead to a general decline in the social cohesion within the scientific community and a breakdown of communal norms.

Let us note possible negative consequences of responses to affirmative action policy. If it turns out that there are, in fact, patterned differences in role performance of different social groups—and our data have shown that there are differences at least in scientific productivity between men and women scientists—then the insistence that every university hire and promote individuals in proportion to their numbers in the labor pool could lead to reverse discrimination. Rewards will no longer be based upon performance, but on functionally irrelevant characteristics. Of course, there remains the question of whether these performance differences are a result of discrimination. Our data suggest, however, that differences in productivity of men and women scientists are not the result of unequal treatment within the institution of science. The implication of pursuing a policy such as is implied by affirmative action would be the movement of strong scientific performers to weaker departments—that is, a sharp diffusion of talent, a weakening of the average quality of scientists located at the best departments—in

---

[56] The method by which the government defines the social characteristics that must be examined remains somewhat unclear. There obviously are many religious and ethnic groups with claims to "minority" status. The government has asked universities submitting affirmative action plans to consider in particular the state of women, blacks, and individuals with Spanish surnames.

[57] See, for one example, Daniel Katz and Robert L. Kahn, *The Social Psychology of Organizations* (New York, 1966).

short, a disjunction between the location of talent and the facilities for doing outstanding research. In sum, moving talent to weak research environments, because
they do not possess a requisite social characteristic, may improve the quality of
these lesser institutions at the expense of maintaining a high rate of advance in
science.

Finally, affirmative action policy may produce some unanticipated negative
consequences. Since all universities must set affirmative action goals in situations
that show statistical deficiencies, most universities are seeking qualified scientists
with minority group backgrounds. But at present there simply are not enough
such individuals to fill the needs of universities trying to reach their affirmative
action goals. Until recently, a high proportion of black scholars have been located
at predominantly black colleges and universities. After being offered jobs at
universities that bring increases in prestige and income, many of the holders of
doctorates at black colleges, which still educate a substantial portion of black
college students, are leaving their current positions for these "better" offers. This
represents a major advance for the black professor. Yet, without a significant
increase in the current production of black doctorates, one result of this pattern
of mobility is depletion within black colleges of its most highly trained personnel.

Other Policy Issues

In this essay we have considered the extent to which scientists may be discriminated against on the basis of their social statuses, both those within the institution of science and those external to it. We have ignored the perhaps equally
significant question of whether scientists are discriminated against on the basis
of their ideas. In the social sciences there are two ways in which ideas could
potentially lead to discrimination. Scientists who hold unpopular political ideologies might be discriminated against. Also scientists who adhere to currently unpopular theories and/or methodologies may have their work ignored. Although
we have no data on these types of potential discrimination, we would like to
raise some questions that should be considered in any empirical investigation.
Undoubtedly, there are cases of social scientists who have been dismissed from
their jobs or denied tenure because of "leftist" political views. However, were
these dismissals the result of their unpopular views expressed in their published
work or a result of actions they have taken which violated university regulations?
We would hypothesize that there have been very few cases in recent years where
a social scientist has been dismissed for publishing a politically unpopular piece.

It might be argued that political "purges" cannot be based upon published
work, because scholars with radical views cannot get their papers accepted for
publication by journals controlled by a conservative establishment. If journals
were to reject papers expressing views that are politically unpopular they would

make it impossible for the authors to attain tenure positions in major departments. Such a hypothesis calls for inquiry. To test it we would need independent judgments of both the quality and political implications of papers prior to submission for publication. We do not know what such a study would show. We do know that roughly 85 percent of all papers submitted to major sociology journals, for example, are rejected, which means, of course, that it is hard for radicals, conservatives, and sociologists of all other political persuasions to get their papers published in major journals.

Let us now consider the possibility that social scientists will be discriminated against not because of their ideological beliefs but because of the cognitive content of their work. Take as an example the heavy emphasis in sociology today on quantitative work. Approximately 70 percent of papers published in major journals use quantitative methods.[58] Is it possible that sociologists who do not have quantitative skills or who temperamentally prefer nonquantitative work may be "discriminated" against? Even if it is harder for nonquantitative sociologists to get their papers published, is "discrimination" the right word here? If it is, then we must also conclude that classical biologists are being discriminated against in the age of molecular biology, that physicists sticking with the classical Newtonian mechanics were being discriminated against in the age of quantum mechanics; and that Ptolemaic astronomers were discriminated against in the age of Copernicus. We would not argue that all these statements are untrue but just that they are no more true of the social sciences than they are of the natural sciences. In all sciences, decisions are made that are not based solely upon "rational" criteria, decisions that then affect the life chances of scientists of varying intellectual persuasions.[59] To call such outcomes "discrimination" may be based upon an overly rational and outdated theory of the way science develops.

Thus, although it may not be fruitful to call such decisions and their outcomes "discrimination," it would be highly fruitful to investigate the social process through which intellectual decisions are made by a scientific community. This is particularly important for social science research, which does have important political consequences. Thus we would be interested in studying the ways in which research on the genetic determinants of intelligence or the consequences of marijuana use are evaluated. How do individual scientists formulate their opinions on the validity of such research? Is it true, as Mannheim and others suggest, that our evaluations will be strongly influenced by nonscientific criteria? Before we can better understand the process through which the social science community evaluates politically relevant research we must study the extent

---

[58] Narsi Patel, "Quantitative and Collaborative Trends in American Sociological Research," *The American Sociologist* 7 (November 1972) : 5–6.

[59] Imre Lakatos and Alan Musgrave, *Criticism and the Growth of Knowledge* (Cambridge, Eng., 1970).

to which judgments are made on the bases of scientific or nonscientific criteria, recognizing that there are some points at which these two types of criteria conjoin. In practice it should not be difficult to take at least first steps in such an inquiry. For example, we might ask the extent to which social scientists' evaluations of the work of Jensen are influenced by general political attitudes when we control for a wide range of variables measuring each scientist's professional status and scientific orientation.[60] If it turns out that some lines of research are rejected out of hand on the basis of political criteria, we would argue that such decisions are a barrier to the utility of social science research in solving social problems.

---

[60] A preliminary study of this type has already been conducted by Robert W. Friedricks, "The Impact of Social Factors Upon Scientific Judgment: The 'Jensen Thesis' as Appraised by Members of the American Psychological Association," preprint.

The Ideal of Objectivity among American Social Scientists in the Era of Professionalization, 1876–1916

Hugh Hawkins

The last quarter of the nineteenth century in the United States saw the rise of modern universities, the creation of specialized professional organizations for scholars, and the emergence as separate disciplines of fields once largely united under the rubric "moral philosophy."* The universities responded to demands of a newly industrialized nation, fulfilled long-cherished ideas of the importance of learning, and were part of a nationalistic drive to establish institutions as advanced as any in Europe. The mood of the new universities was one of uncertainty overlaid by brashness, of eagerness to imitate European scholars, especially Germans, and of isolated specialists seeking reassurance through organization and publication—all this, coexisting with assertions that America was already in many ways better than Europe.

The time was ripe for certain questions, and most serious American scholars found themselves struggling with these. Is knowledge to be pursued for its own sake or for its potential usefulness? Should a scholar assert his values or try to suppress them? But to the social scientists these perplexities had particular immediacy. Was society simply to be studied, or should it be rescued from its troubles? These specialists suffered many uncertainties in their newly separate chairs and departments.

---

* Although I have written without an opportunity to read Mary O. Furner's *Advocacy and Objectivity* (Lexington, 1975), Professor Furner generously made suggestions on a late draft of this essay. I thank her for this aid, without involving her in responsibility for this work's shortcomings.

This essay suggests two principal avenues along which American social scientists found reassurance. One was an increasing emphasis on their status as members of a profession. A professional ethic could minimize the need to embrace specific social values; in fact, in the interests of professional solidarity one might well limit his involvement in controversial social causes. A second route by which the dilemmas of fact-versus-value and thought-versus-action were eased for social scientists was their reliance on an unquestioning faith in the reality of progress; such a conviction could easily include automatic transformation of the true into the good, making the pursuit of pure truth conducive to human advancement. Accordingly, most social scientists of the period persisted in the claim both to be coolly objective and to be serving the highest social values.

The social scientists looked somewhat enviously at the natural scientists, who seemed to have acquired the prestige once reserved for professors of ancient languages or theology. Natural scientists were honored for their preciseness, their ability to seek knowledge impersonally, their discoveries of "laws," and the imagined utility of their researches. One method of drawing closer to the natural sciences was through the adoption of the label "science." Even in the traditionally named fields of history and political economy, practitioners often referred to "historical science" or "economic science." The name "social science" was gradually liberated from the "benevolent amateurishness" of the American Social Science Association, a broad gathering of liberal reformers, sound money men, and generalists, which had been founded in 1865. At Columbia, the new school established in 1880 was named the "Faculty of Political Science," in spite of scoffing from Columbia's School of Mines that nothing was science but natural science. In fact, Lester Ward, a practicing paleobotanist and a founder of American sociology, followed Auguste Comte in asserting that sociology was not merely a science, but "the last and highest of the sciences."[1]

Social scientists sometimes sought to improve their credentials by studying the natural sciences. At Johns Hopkins University, which opened in 1876 with a faculty weighted toward physics, chemistry, and biology, some experience in a natural science was originally a requirement for the Ph.D. in every field. Albion Small, a Hopkins Ph.D. of 1889 and founder of the department of sociology at the University of Chicago, declared that the study of natural science was "ideal preparation for sociological research."[2]

Indeed, nomenclature and to a lesser extent specific techniques of the natural

---

[1] Albion W. Small, "Fifty Years of Sociology in the United States (1865–1915)," *American Journal of Sociology* 21 (1916) : 726, 795; John W. Burgess, *Reminiscences of an American Scholar: The Beginnings of Columbia University* (New York, 1934), p. 210.

[2] Hugh Hawkins, *Pioneer: A History of the Johns Hopkins University, 1874–1889* (Ithaca, 1960), pp. 122–23; Jurgen Herbst, "From Moral Philosophy to Sociology: Albion Woodbury Small," *Harvard Educational Review* 29 (1959) : 232.

sciences were adopted by the new-fledged social scientists. Some—especially economists—hoped to make their work as quantitative as that of the natural scientists.
More vaguely, Richard T. Ely, who taught economics at Hopkins, suggested
biology as a model for economists, who should study the earliest development
of "life-forms." Harvard's Charles F. Dunbar, whose appointment in 1871
probably made him the first professor in the United States to deal exclusively with
economics, maintained that the relation of an economic fact to its causes and
consequences was "as certainly a question to be settled by appropriate scientific
methods, as the perturbation of a satellite or a reaction observed by a chemist."[3]

For John W. Burgess, founder of Columbia's new school, the library was
the "laboratory of research." Herbert B. Adams, the Hopkins historian, was far
from alone in calling his seminar a laboratory, but he probably used the term more
persistently than anyone else. "The seminary," he claimed, recalling its theologi-
cal beginnings in Germany, "has evolved from a nursery of dogma into a laboratory of scientific truth." In the early Hopkins seminars, Adams did indeed
have students pass documents from hand to hand and study them minutely, and
he had expeditions bring back artifacts from the early settlements in Maryland
for the scientific enlightenment of seminar members. The new allegiance to
citing sources among historians revealed a willingness to submit their findings
to further testing by others. The scientific spirit with which social scientists hoped
they were imbued has been well summarized by John Higham: "That spirit was
impersonal, collaborative, secular, impatient of mystery, and relentlessly concerned with the relation of things to one another instead of their relation to a
realm of ultimate meaning."[4]

Not all social scientists expressed the need for objectivity with the same
emphasis, but the standard of neutrality appeared in all the new disciplines dealing with man and society. Scholars in these fields, following the example of biologists who had fought religious objections to the theory of evolution, struck out
against the judging of the truth of an idea either by the character of its author or
by its envisioned moral consequences, standards which Walter P. Metzger has
analyzed under the useful label "doctrinal moralism." To let moral presuppositions shape their researches, social scientists believed, would lead to inanities
comparable to those of the devout opponents of Darwinism.[5]

---

[3] Franklin H. Giddings, quoted in R. Gordon Hoxie et al., *A History of the Faculty
of Political Science, Columbia University* (New York, 1955), pp. 286–87; Hawkins,
Pioneer, p. 301; Robert L. Church, "The Economists Study Society: Sociology at Harvard,
1891–1902," in *Social Sciences at Harvard, 1860–1920: From Inculcation to the Open
Mind,* ed. Paul Buck (Cambridge, Mass., 1965), p. 31.

[4] Burgess, *Reminiscences,* p. 212; Herbert B. Adams, "Special Methods of Historical
Study," in *Methods of Teaching History,* ed. G. Stanley Hall (Boston, 1885), p. 143;
John Higham, *History* (Englewood Cliffs, 1965), p. 94.

[5] Richard Hofstadter and Walter P. Metzger, *The Development of Academic Freedom
in the United States* (New York, 1955), p. 353.

A call for an impartial scientific attitude that would lead to investigations made without prepossessions came from E. R. A. Seligman of Columbia during the organizational debate of the American Economic Association in 1885. Small, in recollections of early American sociology, declared that the discipline had become significant only when it entered into the "expansion of DEMAND FOR OBJECTIVITY." He believed that the success of psychology and sociology in lodging the idea of objectivity in reluctant minds was comparable to the gradual decline of horses' shying at automobiles. The Yale historian Charles M. Andrews, looking back over his long career, believed that historians had, at least since the 1890s, gained objectivity, that they had overcome the lack of impartiality among their American predecessors. William A. Dunning, political scientist as well as historian, was startled when one of his students at Columbia suggested that he could discover Dunning's political philosophy in his writings; Dunning considered his methods "a departure from personal opinion and an approach to objectivity." Even the economist and sociologist Edward A. Ross, whose ouster from his professorship at Stanford in 1900 resulted in part from his willingness to become involved in such controversial public issues as free silver and immigration restriction, declared that he unceasingly carried on the spirit of his German mentors, whose keynote had been "that majestic phrase, *wissenschaftliche Objectivität* (scientific objectivity)."[6]

Objectivity did not, of course, rule out general principles or generalizing interpretations, but often the newly professionalized social scientists behaved as if even such an effort to go beyond the reporting and describing of individual facts would make for a distorting bias. In seeking to avoid relating things to a realm of ultimate meaning, they sometimes refrained from indicating their relations to one another. Historians felt that they must escape from the philosophy of history. They often called the name of Leopold von Ranke to their support, overlooking his philosophical idealism and his effort to show the universal in the particular. Americans interpreted him as a dedicated factualist and often became such themselves. Perhaps no label captures the approach of these historians more aptly than "positivistic." However, it must be understood that they usually included Comte's Positivism among the oversystematized theories of history which, they thought, tended to divert scholars from rigorous efforts to discover past reality.[7]

---

6 Seligman, remarks in "Report of the Organization of the American Economic Association," *Publications of the American Economic Association* 1 (1886) : 27; Small, "Fifty Years of Sociology," pp. 748, 789–90, 808–9; Charles M. Andrews, "These Forty Years," *American Historical Review* 30 (1925) : 244, 229; Charles Edward Merriam, "William Archibald Dunning," in *American Masters of Social Science,* ed. Howard W. Odum (New York, 1927), p. 137; Edward Alsworth Ross, *Seventy Years of It: An Autobiography* (New York, 1936), p. 38.
7 Higham, *History,* pp. 98–99.

Richmond Mayo-Smith, an economist who introduced work in statistics at Columbia, made this tendency to stress facts and avoid principles the point of departure for his study of 1888, *Statistics and Economics.*

> It is everywhere recognized that induction is playing an important part in the study of the social sciences. Theoretical treatment is out of favor and we hear on every side of inductive social science, of historical political economy, of comparative jurisprudence. Many authors devote their attention exclusively to the study of mere historical facts, with no attempt to formulate principles from them. Some even deny that the time has as yet arrived for the formulation of principles, and look forward to years of laborious investigation on the part of students before we shall have enough material and in such shape that it will be safe or profitable to draw conclusions. Almost every professed student of political economy or political science feels it necessary, in order to vindicate his scholarship, to devote a portion of his time to such investigations even if they cover only a small field. So we have specialists in each department of historical and economic knowledge. Even where one ventures on a systematic treatise he feels obliged to load his pages with illustrations from historical and contemporary sources.[8]

Characteristic of the new professional consciousness of these social scientists was their insistence that facts were not easily determined and that elaborate training and discipline were necessary in order to establish them. One could not simply rely on common sense; one must have a "scientific method." Truth was indeed "out there," but it was not plain to see. It could only be revealed bit by bit, not by any sudden leap into comprehension.[9]

Few social scientists of the period would have explicitly argued, of course, that discrete facts were the only object of their inquiries. The introductory article to Columbia's new *Political Science Quarterly* in 1886 maintained that in politics and economics, scholars were "able to some extent to trace phenomena to their causes, to group facts under rules, and rules under principles." Most social scientists went beyond mere data, offering inferences of cause and effect, comparisons, and generalizations—with some at times even venturing a "law." But the prevailing temper was one of great caution about making general assertions.[10]

The institutional setting in which American social scientists found themselves in the years after the Civil War helps explain their cautious emphasis on objectivity and empiricism. Their scientific claims helped liberate their scholarship from the control of moral philosophy. That broad field, they declared, was too general to allow precise methods; besides, it was under debilitating religious control and its practitioners tended toward groundless speculation.

---

[8] Richmond Mayo-Smith, "Statistics and Economics," *Publications of the American Economic Association* 3 (1888) : 7.

[9] Jurgen Herbst, *The German Historical School in American Scholarship: A Study in the Transfer of Culture* (Ithaca, 1965), pp. 124–25; Laurence R. Veysey, *The Emergence of the American University* (Chicago, 1965), pp. 145–49.

[10] Munroe Smith, "Introduction: The Domain of Political Science," *Political Science Quarterly* 1 (1886) : 1–2.

Moral philosophy was the opposite of a specialty. The culmination of the college student's educational experience, it attempted to link his earlier training to both religious values and social problems. The course, required of seniors, was generally taught by the college president, who was often not the most scholarly member of the faculty, though presumably the wisest. Some presidents used the course for instilling in students the "respectable" religious and social values (sometimes using textbooks they had written themselves), and they thought of it as the final character-shaping experience of the college years. The resulting course was an amalgam which included bits of history, economics, political theory, ethics, psychology, and theology. There was a generous sprinkling of anecdote, prejudice, and fatherly advice. A student's notes reveal that President Eliphalet Nott of Union College, besides explaining that the larger the group the less likely men were to act rationally, described "the best way to handle mobs in town and gown riots, the evidence for the existence of ghosts, the relation between singing societies and early marriages, and the reason why Methodist ministers die young (they don't laugh enough)." A later generation would see merit in the integrative role of moral philosophy, but most new-style specialists scorned the course with its implication that commonsensical application of values to personal and social problems was the ultimate achievement of an educated man.[11]

The moral philosophy course had begun to lose importance by the middle of the nineteenth century. Economics, for instance, was increasingly offered as a separate subject. After the Civil War new ideals of professionalism, specialization, and careful empirical tests for truth and a view of the student that assumed he was already mature succeeded in breaking the hold of moral philosophy on the teaching of social sciences. (The somewhat later "liberations" of sociology from economics and political science from law and history saw similar ideals used, with historians sometimes finding themselves declared beyond the pale of social science.)[12]

The stress on factuality was also encouraged by the strength of religious faith in the United States. Although in the long run, the anti-Darwinian preachers came generally to be considered as having disgraced themselves, their power to damage institutions of learning remained strong throughout the nineteenth century. To say, in response to suspicions of the godly, that one claimed to make no moral judgments or sweeping assertions about universal law, was to offer a conciliatory defense. To claim both neutrality and expertise raised a double barrier around the new fields. For their part, the university presidents proclaimed that the churches and the scientists were alike seeking God's truth, that most of the

---

[11] George P. Schmidt, *The Liberal Arts College: A Chapter in American Cultural History* (New Brunswick, N.J., 1957), p. 51 (quotation); Schmidt, *The Old Time College President* (New York, 1930), ch. 4; Frederick Rudolph, *The American College and University: A History* (New York, 1962), pp. 140–41.

[12] Higham, *History*, pp. 95–100.

scientists were faithful churchgoers and many of them sons of ministers. Of course, the relationship between scholars and defenders of religion nevertheless remained a tense one. President Daniel C. Gilman of Johns Hopkins required explanations from Herbert B. Adams after one of his students published an article in a Baltimore newspaper about Adams's history classes. In these classes, the student proudly informed the public, the Bible was treated "in no other way than as historic material from which to amass historic knowledge."[13]

There was another reason for social scientists to feel strengthened by claims of objectivity. They were seeking to establish themselves in an era typified by the emergence of civil service reform with its promise of impersonal recognition of merit and disciplined stability. American intellectuals welcomed the idea of carefully ascertained truth, leading to objective laws, with practical application to be left to the discretion of educated men. That this attitude went beyond intellectuals was indicated when in 1889 an attempt was made to found a department of "politics" at the University of Kansas. The public opposed the plan, seeing it as an intrusion of partisanship into the institution. When the department title was changed to "sociology" (it was probably the first in the country to bear that name), there was general satisfaction that the new field would be pursued objectively. Similarly, postwar tensions in Baltimore had evoked from President Gilman a promise that Johns Hopkins University would avoid "sectional, partizan, and provincial animosities."[14]

Also attractive to the public was the vision of the hardworking scholar, an image promoted by university presidents in their public addresses. Obscure though their fields might be, at least the university professors were abiding by the nation's work ethic, and gathering data had the advantage of being more convincing as "work" than was reflective thinking.[15]

While it is generally true that this industrious first generation of professionalized American social scientists emphasized the obligation to be objective and to rely on empirical techniques of research, there were occasionally explicit calls among them for the scholar to bring his values to bear on his researches. Andrew D. White, an elder academic statesman with roots in the American Social Science Association, insisted in the 1880s that a historian was a mere annalist unless he had a philosophy and values that shaped the history he wrote.

13 David B. Potts, "Social Ethics at Harvard, 1881–1931: A Study in Academic Activism," in *Social Sciences at Harvard,* ed. Buck, pp. 92–93; Hugh Hawkins, *Between Harvard and America: The Educational Leadership of Charles W. Eliot* (New York, 1972), pp. 120–21; Hawkins, *Pioneer,* p. 313 (quotation).

14 George M. Fredrickson, *The Inner Civil War: Northern Intellectuals and the Crisis of the Union* (New York, 1965), pp. 201–11; Higham, *History,* pp. 95–96; Small, "Fifty Years of Sociology," p. 760; Daniel Coit Gilman, *University Problems in the United States* (New York, 1898), p. 40 (quotation).

15 Hugh Hawkins, "Charles W. Eliot, Daniel C. Gilman and the Nurture of American Scholarship," *New England Quarterly* 39 (1966): 305–7.

Charles Kendall Adams, White's successor both as professor of history at the University of Michigan and as president of Cornell, made use of a side of German scholarship generally overlooked by Americans when he quoted J. G. Droysen's dictum that the historian had the duty to set public opinion right (and not just on matters of fact). Burgess believed that political science should stress ideals, grand ones of Hegelian dimension. Probably no one brought ethics into the pursuit of a social science more explicitly than did Richard T. Ely, especially during the 1880s at Johns Hopkins. As Ely propagandized for inductive and historical methods in economics, he argued that ethics should not only be studied as a factor in economic relationships, but also be used to shape the economist's choice of subject and his manner of treating it. In his *The Past and the Present of Political Economy* (1884), Ely proclaimed that the newer political economy "does not acknowledge *laissez-faire* as an excuse for doing nothing while people starve, nor allow the all-sufficiency of competition as a plea for grinding the poor. It denotes a return to the grand principle of common sense and Christian precept. Love, generosity, nobility of character, self-sacrifice, and all that is best and truest in our nature have their place in economic life."[16]

The tension between the motive of scientific objectivity and the desire to build ethics into scholarship was sharply revealed by the effort to found a national association of economists in the mid-1880s. The idea of organizing was in large part inspired by the Verein für Sozialpolitik, which had been founded by German economists of the historical school in 1872 and had included the urging of social reforms among its aims. Ely and other American students returning from Germany with these ideals argued zealously against the dominance of the laissez-faire doctrine, especially in the absolute form presented by William Graham Sumner at Yale. As Edward A. Ross recalled the self-image of the young rebels, they were "tackling realities instead of handing on a moth-eaten tradition." They hoped for purposeful change as well as understanding.[17]

The movement that led to the American Economic Association was begun by two German-trained economists at the University of Pennsylvania, Edmund J. James and Simon N. Patten. Their proposed platform was so combatively in favor of state interference in the economy that potential members held back. Ely then took up the idea, broadening the approach and softening the language, but his platform still declared, "We regard the state as an educational and ethical

---

[16] Andrew D. White, "Historical Instruction in the Course of History and Political Science at Cornell University," in *Methods of Teaching History*, ed. Hall, p. 75; Herbst, *German Historical School*, pp. 113, 115; Bernard Crick, *The American Science of Politics: Its Origins and Conditions* (Berkeley, 1959), pp. 97–99; Richard T. Ely, *The Past and the Present of Political Economy* (Baltimore, 1884; *Johns Hopkins University Studies in Historical and Political Science*, vol. 2, no. 3), p. 64.

[17] Gladys Bryson, "The Emergence of the Social Sciences from Moral Philosophy," *International Journal of Ethics* 42 (1932): 316; Ross, *Seventy Years of It*, p. 40.

agency whose positive aid is an indispensable condition of human progress." After debate at the organizing meeting at Saratoga in 1885 led to a yet milder Statement of Principles and a declaration that it was not intended to be binding on any member, the American Economic Association was launched with Francis A. Walker, president of M.I.T., as its president and Ely as its secretary.[18]

The position of the new organization resembled that of Ely's own economic thought; it included a central unresolved contradiction on the matter of objectivity. Ely insisted that the new association was not "colorless," that it stood for something, since it proposed the accomplishment of reforms. Developing a system of social ethics was among his professed aims for the group. Yet in the association's first report, Ely maintained: "It was not proposed to form a society of advocates of any political opinion or set of political opinions, as for example, free-trade or protection . . . [since] this sphere lay outside the realm of science." The association would, Ely affirmed, seek, bear, and diffuse light—"ever the aim of all true science." The contradiction between this notion and Ely's reformist hopes was largely resolved by the ascendancy of the ideal of scientific objectivity. In three years the Statement of Principles was abolished by unanimous vote, and economists of conservative stripe joined. In 1892 the association chose as its second president Charles L. Dunbar, who looked on economics as a deductive study of the laws of material wealth and was eager to keep the discipline uncontaminated by specific policy questions.[19]

A retrospective statement by Ely argued that the development of various national reform organizations had reduced the area of responsibility of the AEA, but a more convincing explanation is found in the drive for professional unity. For economists in the United States to end as in Germany, divided into competing organizations, would seriously weaken a specialty with a newfound and somewhat insecure autonomy. The original modifications in the platform had moved toward greater toleration of varieties of economic thought and toward a professionalism blind to any but guild values. This tendency continued. In time it was largely forgotten that the founders of the AEA had come close to embracing a social cause. The association soon had no more "color" of that sort than the American Philological Association.

J. Laurence Laughlin, who had bitterly opposed Ely and his followers, in-

[18] "Report on the Organization of the American Economic Association," esp. p. 6; Richard T. Ely, "The American Economic Association," 1885–1909: With Special Reference to Its Origin and Early Development: An Historical Sketch," *Publications of the American Economic Association*, 3rd ser., vol. 11 (1910), no. 1, pp. 50–56; Joseph Dorfman, *The Economic Mind in American Civilization*, vol. 3 (New York, 1949), pp. 205–12.

[19] "Report on the Organization of the AEA," pp. 16–19, 5–6; Ely, "The AEA, 1885–1909," pp. 76, 90; Herbst, *German Historical School*, p. 148; Church, "The Economists Study Society," pp. 26, 29–31.

cluded a review of these events in the opening article of the University of
Chicago's new *Journal of Political Economy* in 1892. He recalled the influence
of the "German point of view" in setting American economists against each
other, but he saw unity as now attained. The inductive and deductive methods
had turned out to be less distinctive than had been thought, and the AEA had
dropped its doctrinal attitude. Ironically, after this assertion of the demise of the
reformist element in his profession, Laughlin announced that though the new
journal would welcome discussions of theory, it would be largely devoted to practical problems. Professional solidarity had triumphed, but the ambivalence about
science and social purpose still remained.[20]

An emphasis on science and objectivity helped hold scholarly professions
together, but the public was less likely to be impressed by objective truth than
by results in application. One purpose of the professional organizations was of
course to protect scholars from such pressures. But if most social scientists were
unwilling to dwell on the question of utility, it was largely because it seemed to
them so easily answered. It was implicit in much that was said among social scientists, and sometimes explicit, that once the facts of a matter were known, it was
easy to set things right. Mayo-Smith called for amelioration of social evils through
statistical revelations of cause and effect. Albert Shaw, an Ely student who entered
journalism, went a step further when he suggested a topic to the Johns Hopkins
historical seminar shortly after attaining his Ph.D. He recommended that procedure be divided into two stages, "a scientific study of the facts," followed by
"propositions looking towards an intelligent reform." He made the transition
appear automatic and saw no danger to scientific fact-finding in the prior commitment to reform.[21]

In retrospect, it appears that these sanguine scholars of the late nineteenth
century underestimated the difficulty of keeping personal values out of research.
Few specific checks against distortion through bias were designed and rarely
did a scholar preface reports of his findings with a statement of his social values
or a caveat about the limits of his scientific objectivity. On the other hand, the
exaggerated pose of being value free sometimes silenced investigators who could
have contributed something toward alleviating contemporary social burdens.

One can easily sympathize with scholars' fears of being deflected from their
calling by needs of the workaday world, but too often social scientists tried to
have matters both ways. They pursued truth for its own sake; they respected
verifiable facts above all else; they were hesitant about generalizations, let alone
explicit expression of values. Yet most of them maintained that their scholarship
was going to be immensely important in setting society to rights. It was possible

---

[20] J. Laurence Laughlin, "The Study of Political Economy in the United States,"
Journal of Political Economy 1 (1892) : 7, 8–10, 19.

[21] Mayo-Smith, "Statistics and Economics," pp. 124–25; Hawkins, *Pioneer*, p. 306.

to feel confidence in the social bonus to scholarship largely because of an un-questioned faith in progress. Under the seeming skepticism of the scholar, his seeming dedication to factuality, there often lay an unchallenged conviction that the world was inevitably improving; thus, every discrete fact had its place in the general pattern of history and even the barest economic statistics helped reveal or advance some developing good. The conviction of progress, though not a new thing in the world, had been powerfully enhanced by Darwin's developmental hypothesis. Americans in any case felt they were living the experience of prog-ress; it seemed self-evident in a nation expanding geographically and industrially and filled with individual success stories.[22]

This faith did not hold that whatever was was right, but that whatever was was part of a tendency that was pressing toward the better. Often, the certainty of progress was a substitute for self-consciousness about values, or even a substi-tute for generalization. Ely doubtless felt he was demonstrating the sure demise of laissez-faire economics when he called it "foreign to the spirit of true progress," and Herbert B. Adams believed that isolated historical data would gain con-sequence when brought into "vital connection with the progress and science of the world." Even two sociologists as opposite in tendency as William Graham Sumner and Lester Ward were united in belief in inevitable progress. This faith was particularly comforting to one who considered himself a scientist; he was assured that there was continuing progress in the development of science, and he could not doubt that science itself was a factor in general social progress.[23]

After the turn of the century, during the years that saw the establishment of the American Political Science Association (1903) and the American Socio-logical Society (1905), American social scientists retained their confidence in progress. It was characteristic, then, that they imagined their social science supe-rior to that practiced by their predecessors or by themselves in earlier days. They grew increasingly suspicious of anything that smacked of a philosophy of history or conscious use of values to shape research. At the same time that social scientists became more dedicated to empirical techniques, however, they grew enthusiastic about taking a hand in the social problem-solving of the Progressive Era.

Under the slogan "the Wisconsin Idea," social scientists in universities across the country increasingly served as expert consultants in framing legislation and as members of regulatory commissions. Ely, a professor at Wisconsin since 1892, played only a minor role in this wave of government-by-expert, but his earlier ideas inspired younger men. A journalist who visited the University of Wisconsin in 1909 found many of the social science courses designed to prepare students for participation in new branches of governmental administration and

---

22 Higham, *History,* pp. 101–2; Crick, *American Science of Politics,* p. 38; Veysey, *Emergence of the American University,* pp. 76–77.

23 Hawkins, *Pioneer,* p. 178; H. B. Adams, "Special Methods of Historical Study," p. 126; Crick, *American Science of Politics,* p. 50.

in philanthropic foundations. The students were taught "not merely to study history, but to make it." Abandonment of the old neutrality and noninvolvement appeared to have occurred without loss of thoroughness and fairness. Increasingly, social scientists assumed that undue theorizing posed the principal barrier to attaining truth, whereas social utility could be embraced as a goal without distorting effect.[24]

The early years of the twentieth century saw a drop in the use of the methods of history in other social sciences. But these fields, as their following and independence increased, remained methodologically weak, often relying on empirical studies loosely related to some contemporary problem. When the political scientists formed their association, statements of early leaders showed a new concern for the practical workings of government. One reason for creating the new organization was the opinion that there had been too much concern with utopias and static ideals in dealing with political life. Charles A. Beard of Columbia demanded that political science be separated from "theology, ethics, and patriotism." In a characteristic statement of the era, one that appeared to give preeminence to objective science yet allowed a reformist hope to direct scientific pursuits, Harvard's A. Lawrence Lowell, third president of the association, wrote: "To the scientific mind every phenomenon is a fact that has a cause, and it is wise to seek that cause when attempting to change the fact."[25]

Among historians, Beard, who retained a double disciplinary allegiance, and his colleague at Columbia, James Harvey Robinson, declared for a "New History." They kept the ideal of objectivity, but favored treatment of the parts of the past that might be useful to the present. Thus, a study of the personal motives of the founding fathers could aid in the drive for liberalizing the Constitution through amendment. Albion Small could say with satisfaction in 1916 that the most vivid change in social science during the previous two decades was "the extent to which talk about 'science' has given place to work upon problems." Such tendencies toward present-minded empiricism were no longer particularly traceable to a "German point of view." Fewer American students went to the German universities, and those who did felt less need to form their scholarly ideals there.[26]

Long after the event, Small criticized the founders of the American Economic Association for stressing the improvement of economic activities while

---

[24] Benjamin G. Rader, *The Academic Mind and Reform: The Influence of Richard T. Ely in American Life* (Lexington, 1966), p. 175; Edwin E. Slosson, *Great American Universities* (New York, 1910), pp. 222–23.

[25] Higham, *History*, pp. 106–9, 110, 113; Crick, *American Science of Politics*, pp. 100–101, 103; Frank J. Goodnow, "The Work of the American Political Science Association," *Proceedings of the American Political Science Association* 1 (1904) : 42–43.

[26] Higham, *History*, pp. 111–12, 115; Small, "Fifty Years of Sociology," p. 796; Veysey, *Emergence of the American University*, pp. 124–25.

"neglecting the crying fundamental need of probing into the deeper nature of human society, human resources, and human wants." This sounded much like the calls for objectivity among the early social scientists who had aped the natural sciences. But over the years, Small pursued the fact-value problem intensely and reached a resolution superior to the unexamined faith in progress and the cloak of professional standards relied on by most of his contemporaries.[27]

In 1890 Small had believed that sociology should tend toward the ideals of the Gospels. His early attempts to work out the conflict between this desire and scientific objectivity had not satisfied him, but at least he identified the two extremes that he wanted to avoid. He objected equally to superficial reformers who acted without knowledge and to withdrawn professors with a "pathetic solicitude about the sanctity of science."[28]

In his summing up of 1916, Small had sage advice: "We [sociologists] have mistaken our share of that human aspiration which is normal after mental and moral infancy have been outgrown, for [a] call to the distinctive social function of guiding that aspiration. . . . We have set before ourselves such incandescent pictures of the importance of the far-off divine event, which our longings project, that we have been seduced into moralizing when our job demanded analyzing." Yet there was no need to abjure evaluation, he argued, clarifying the distinction he would make between sociology and ethics.

> I should have no use for sociology if I did not believe that it is an essential factor in that veracious social science which must furnish the content of positive ethical theory. It is necessary to understand primary arithmetic in order to be able to understand what it means to be honest with our neighbor. One cannot be reliable in converting honest intentions into honest acts if one has not the necessary arithmetical knowledge for calculations of the quantities concerned in everyday transactions. It does not follow that the best way to learn arithmetic is to listen to sermons on the virtue of honesty. So with sociology and ethics. The one deals with certain objective structural and functional relationships. The other assigns values to the relationships. In the nature of the case it is a mental impossibility to pay very much attention to observation and analysis of these relationships without beginning to evaluate them, and I see no reason why a teacher, whether of physiology, or psychology, or history, or economics, or sociology, or anything else for that matter, should try to arrest this tendency, provided that it is not allowed to interfere with the requirements of valid scientific method.[29]

At this point one member of the generation of social scientists who had yearned to be objective without relinquishing their values appeared to be contented. Small's involvement with the social sciences had bridged the half century that saw their emergence as professions, and during those years he had shared some of his colleagues' characteristic evasions of the fact-value problem. His

---

27 Small, "Fifty Years of Sociology," p. 768.
28 Herbst, "From Moral Philosophy to Sociology," pp. 234–35.
29 Small, "Fifty Years of Sociology," pp. 852, 854.

ultimate declaration of 1916 had been foreshadowed by some of his contemporaries, though perhaps its argument had never been expressed so well. Small especially clarified matters by pointing to ethical evaluation as natural to the human condition and therefore not avoidable by social scientists, yet he recognized too that care was needed if these inevitable expressions of value were not to distort the design or application of method. The new callings in the social sciences required the sophistication to live with complexity and the capacity to take pains.

Max Weber and the Roots of Academic Freedom

Robert Nisbet

It is a truism that we learn from history chiefly to the extent that we take to history questions shaped in substantial degree by the issues of our own day. History is no seamless web, no iron genealogy. It is, properly regarded, a vast, almost infinitely diverse, collection of human experiences of every kind: political, social, moral, economic, and intellectual. Uniqueness and concreteness may at first sight seem to be the overriding characteristics of each of these experiences in the past. Second thought is more likely to tell us that within these diverse experiences are to be found attributes with a sufficient degree of similarity to experiences of our own to make possible a useful reading of the past. I have recently become convinced that there are striking parallels between Max Weber's Germany and our own contemporary academic America.

1.

Had it not been for my personal experience of living through the storms of the 1960s and seeing their icy grip on the American academic mind, I am sure I should have a very different sense of the meaning of Weber's *"Wissenschaft als Beruf"* than I do have. The essay had little meaning for me when first I read it in the 1930s. Today it seems extraordinarily prophetic. It is hard to conquer belief that in fact Weber is speaking, not to the German academic mind of 1918, but to the American academic mind of the past quarter of a century—which, to be sure, is the unfailing test of the classic.

The immediate inspiration of "Science as a Vocation" was, as we know, an invitation by the students of the University of Munich—to which Weber had only shortly before gone from Heidelberg—to speak on the nature of the academic profession: its rewards, obligations, pitfalls, and general responsibility to society. Very probably what the students had in mind, basically, was what we today call a craft talk, one aimed at acquainting apprentices with some foreknowledge of the nature of the occupation or profession they have chosen. Indeed what Weber responded with is, at least in the opening sections, hardly more than a craft talk, albeit a good one, oriented comparatively and steeped in the kinds of observation regarding financial rewards, teaching loads, and potential career benefits that graduate students to this very moment cherish the nearer they come to the end of their study.

Craft talk is, however, hardly the word for the larger part of Weber's address, for, after the beginning I have just described, he turns to issues that go to the heart of not only academic but all thought in its relation to human purposes and moral values. The essay, as one would expect, is a rich one, diverse in theme and referent, but I take its overriding objective to be that of enjoining upon the academic profession a sense of true mission, a sense somewhat less than Faustian or cosmic, but not the less vital and creative in the social order. It would be hard to find in the long history of the Western university any scholar who ever wore the academic mantle more proudly than Weber did. It is indeed precisely from this pride in true vocation that Weber's warning springs: a warning against the kind of hubris that results when academic man becomes deluded into extravagant visions of his omniscience and omnipotence in society. What Weber is telling us in "Science as a Vocation" is that the scholar is, at his best, just that, a scholar, working within finite and specialized areas. He is not a moral prophet, not an arbiter of taste, not humanitarian per se, not priest or clinical psychologist, not economic entrepreneur, not political leader. Least of all is academic man by his nature the creator of unified moral purpose for a civilization, the purveyor of sacred values for a culture.

If anyone should doubt that Weber is, in this essay, speaking across the Atlantic and down the corridor of time to us, he need but reflect a moment on the claims and pretensions that flowed so abundantly from the American university, from faculty and administrators alike, in the period begun essentially by World War II. Weber is not at any point asking for vows of silence and political chastity from the professoriat. He was himself active in politics. No mind at the turn of the century in Europe was more ardent in declaration of the intellectual's responsibility to society or, for that matter, more tortured by realization of his own and other intellectuals' impotence before the moral and political problems of his time. Nor did Weber rule out completely the possibility that there might come once again into history one of those profoundly charismatic figures who, along with their works and impress, bulk so large in his religious sociology and moral philosophy. Granted that the bureaucratization of mind and spirit, itself consequence of the more fundamental rationalization and disenchantment of the Western mind, made such new charismatic manifestation less and less likely, the possibility yet remained. All Weber is declaring is that such revelation is not, cannot be, the work of the university, of the scientist or scholar.

Science, Weber wrote, "is a 'vocation' organized in special disciplines in the service of self-clarification and knowledge of interrelated facts. It is not the gift of grace of seers and prophets dispensing sacred values and revelations, nor does it partake of the contemplation of sages and philosophers about the meaning of the universe."[1] We will come back shortly to Weber's essay and, specifically, to his notable treatment of values, of *Wertfreiheit,* and of the university's relation to politics. What I should like to do now, though very briefly, is say something about the German university at the turn of the century and the powerful currents of thought in which it found itself. Only thus, I believe, are we in a position to understand the distinctive emphases in Weber's essay and, with this, the relevance both of the essay and its age to our own time.

2.

In no European country in the nineteenth century did so close a linkage exist between university and national culture as in Germany. This linkage had existed in Prussia from the time of the founding of the University of Berlin in 1810, when the doors of that university were first opened to students under the rectorship of the great Fichte. Much the same kind of relationship between academic and cultural life became true of all Germany from about midpoint on in the century, very clearly so after the formation of the modern German state. To write a history of nineteenth-century German thought in the areas of philosophy, history, and the sciences is with only occasional exceptions to write a history of ideas, values, and aspirations sprung overwhelmingly from academe. Such a relationship hardly existed in England. For that country in the nineteenth century it would indeed be possible to write a history of thought and culture without more than the most infrequent of references to Oxford, Cambridge, and London. The same, though in somewhat less degree, was true of France. But in Germany, especially Prussia, linkage between university and nation was not only a major circumstance; it was rooted in an ideal, an ideal that took shape during the first couple of decades in the nineteenth century, whatever may have been anticipations of the ideal earlier.

There is not space here to treat even briefly a history of the German univer-

---

[1] All citations from *Wissenschaft als Beruf* are from the translation by H. H. Gerth and C. Wright Mills in their *From Max Weber: Essays in Sociology* (New York, 1946), pp. 129–156.

sity in the century leading up to Weber's notable address, nor would it be particularly useful in any event. What I want to do is select from among the many
strands available to us in the standard histories of the period those that have most
direct culmination in Weber's essay—or, more accurately, culmination in the
conditions to which he directed attention. There is, allowing only for inevitable
differences of time, place, and idiom, striking relevance to strands of American
thought regarding the university during the past quarter of a century.

One of these strands of German ideal for the university, one that Weber
was a part of and gave luminous expression to, began in the ideas of Wilhelm
von Humboldt, brother of the scientist, Alexander von Humboldt, wise and
learned philosopher in his own right and author of the first systematic policy in
Prussia for the university. To get a notion of Wilhelm von Humboldt's profound
liberality of mind one need only read his *The Sphere and Duties of Government,*
published in 1792. It is a book that was to influence John Stuart Mill deeply,
especially Mill's *On Liberty.* Humboldt had nothing but repugnance for the Rous-
seauian and Jacobin conception of the political state, based upon a monolithic
general will, devoid of either individual or associative liberties, and consecrated
to a kind of permanent revolution against the independent society and its traditions. Later, as in his notable memoirs on the German and the Prussian constitu-
tions (1813 and 1819 respectively), Humboldt moderated the uncompromising
hostility to the political arm of society we see in *The Sphere and Duties of
Government* and relieved the stark individualism of that work by greater attention to the positive values of traditional groups and associations in the social
order. He saw a greater value in government, if wisely deployed, than he had in
his first, passionate reaction to French revolutionary authoritarianism: He came
to realize that the individual by himself—separated from locality, region, institution, and tradition—is not enough on which to found the good state. The
values of social and cultural diversity, which he had absorbed from his friends
Schiller and Goethe and from his reading of Burke, went far to erase his earlier
laissez-faire individualism and negative view of authority of any kind. They
established in Humboldt's mind principles of localism, decentralization, and
pluralism that recognized the importance of inherited institutions and traditions.

These principles were not lacking in his conception of the role of the university in Germany. He became the Prussian secretary of education in 1809, having before that served a number of years as minister plenipotentiary from Prussia
to the Vatican, a period in which he was able to continue his notable scholarship
in a diversity of areas, and with this appointment the liberal, finite, humane, and
rationalist conception of the German university was born—the same conception,
at bottom, we will find informing Max Weber's address to the students at Munich
in 1918. Precisely the same spirit that had directed Humboldt's pluralist vision
of the relation of political state to society in general directed his vision of the

relation of state to university. In Humboldt's view the function of a university was that of teaching and scholarship in the learned disciplines. That and nothing else! To this end, Humboldt thought, the university was entitled to, nay, was obliged to, have a maximum of autonomy within the political realm. Unlike a great many enlightened minds of his day, Humboldt had both respect and an attitude of considerable indulgence for the virtual enclave-like status occupied by the older German universities, especially those which could trace their histories to medieval times. Humboldt did not share the hatred of things medieval we so commonly find among German and, stemming from the Enlightenment, French intellectuals. To minds steeped in the modernism of the Enlightenment, the traditional universities of Europe could seem as obsolete in their consecration to scholarship and curriculum as could traditional guild, church, fief, and locality.

Humboldt was no antiquarian, no medievalist in principle. His mind was as oriented to the present and to the needs of the present as that of any man. But in Humboldt's thinking there is little if any trace of that commitment to history as an irreversible, unilinear process and to progress conceived as imminent and inexorable in history that we find in so much of the writing of the post-Enlightenment late eighteenth and early nineteenth centuries in both France and Germany. He does not equate past and evil, present and good, as do so many of his illustrious contemporaries, whether radical, liberal, or conservative in tendency of mind. But by the same token neither does he equate past and good, present and evil. His was a singularly pragmatic mind, worthy companion to the mind of Stein whose extraordinary reforms in the political and economic spheres so closely matched those sought in education by Humboldt. Their common objectives were emancipation of individuals and groups from authorities that had clearly become stagnant and repressive and establishment of a scene in which creative individuals and groups could realize their potentialities in their respective spheres of interest.

The spirit of laissez-faire animated both Humboldt and Stein, but it was a spirit, unlike the nominally related spirit of laissez-faire in English and French reform, that did not seek to dismember social structure for its own sake, that did not direct policy toward gratuitous fragmentation of old unities, such as towns, guilds, churches, universities, and other forms of traditional association. What we find throughout in the attempted reforms of both Stein and Humboldt is a rooted belief in the values of social and cultural autonomy, of diversity, and of decentralization. Humboldt's early views on the necessity of individuality and of a strictly limited role for political government did not appreciably change in their substance; what we find, during his all too brief tenure of office as minister of education, is greater recognition of the vital roles of the kinds of authority and function to be found in intermediate associations, whether local or functional. It is, as I have suggested, this animating vision that puts Humboldt—and Stein—in the company of those, such as Burke, Tocqueville, and Burckhardt, who also realized that the price of the limited role of central government is diversity and security of man's other memberships in the social order.

Three elements of Humboldt's philosophy of higher education and of the specific nature of the university in his thinking are worth emphasis here. The first and most important I have already hinted at: *autonomy.* "The state must not ever demand from the university that which would serve its purposes directly, but should hold to the conviction that when the universities fulfill their true aims, they will also thereby serve the state in its purposes, and from a far higher point of view."[2] That sentence is to be found in one of Humboldt's official papers. It epitomizes admirably his conviction that the university, like every other major institution in society, has its own "sphere and duties"; it must not, therefore, be either asked or allowed to deviate from this sphere in such a way as to distort or degrade its vital function.

This function, for Humboldt, was, basically, *scholarship:* the discovery, advancement, and teaching of the kind of knowledge to be found in all the learned disciplines, whether liberal or professional in character. Much of Humboldt's patience with, affection for, indeed, the older universities in Germany sprang from respect for what they were doing in this respect. No one could have been more aware than Humboldt—or Weber a century later—that the intellectual costs are sometimes curricular rigidity, seeming isolation from exciting, even creative and prophetic, currents of thought in society and from burning issues of social and economic character, and an ostensible preoccupation with the timeless in philosophy or the antiquarian in history and related disciplines. Nor can Humboldt be said to have cherished such academic aloofness from the topical and contemporary—not by any means. But he was wise enough to know that for every individual willing and able to give devoted study to the past and to those areas of culture that do not often make the headlines, there were, and would always be, a hundred or more among the intellectuals who would joyously grasp the topical and contemporary and who would devoutly seek to make national purpose or some similar overriding aim the sine qua non of thought in all its reaches.

The guiding aim of the university, Humboldt thought, must be *rational* and, at the same time, *humanistic.* The university, properly so-called, is the house of the intellect, not of the religious, moral, political, or military ambition. That Prussia, and for that matter other areas of Germany, desperately needed reforms, reconstruction in government, and a political unity to match its language and culture, Humboldt surely did not question. That the university, pursuing its own function, living in its own proper sphere of duties and responsi-

---

[2] *Gesammelte Schriften* (Berlin, 1903–1936), X, 255. I am indebted to Frederick Lilge's superb book, *The Abuse of Learning* (New York, 1948) for direction to this passage.

bilities, should, and undoubtedly would, be a luminous part of the reconstruction and elevation of German culture, Humboldt did not question either. What he did question, and oppose strenuously, was the notion of deliberate and direct use of the university as an instrument of political or social purpose, however exalted such purpose might be.

Humboldt believed fully in the university's contributions to the social order, to morality, and to government. But he saw this contribution as indirect rather than direct. It is profitable, I think, to compare Humboldt and Cardinal Newman in this respect—the latter in his authorship of the *Idea of a University Defined,* published a half-century after Humboldt's ideas had been given currency in Germany. It is impossible to read Newman's classic without the clear feeling that for him the greatest role of the university—and it is, of course, Oxford above all other universities that Newman has in mind as a model—was moral; that is, its principal function lay in its relation to the students and their preparation for life. Hence Newman's insistence upon the necessity of residential colleges. How else, he asked, could there be that rubbing of shoulders in close community that is vital to the union of intellectual and moral training of the mind? But this said, Newman was steadfast on the primary *objective* of the university, which was nothing less than the pursuit of knowledge with philosophy its core and the dissemination of this knowledge to students. In short, there is in Newman and also in the English university tradition he so deeply admired a concern with the moral, social, and psychological contributions of a university education to the student. But these, Newman argued, must be *indirect;* they must arise in pursuit of learning, of study, and scholarship based upon curriculum itself drawn from the learned disciplines.

In retrospect, if there was one thing lacking in Humboldt's conception of the university it was the sense, so strong in Newman, of the university as an academic *community*. Absence of any tradition of residential colleges in Germany—for that matter on the Continent—contributed strongly to the failure of this sense of community in the university even at its best in Germany and must certainly be accounted as one of the chief causes of the much wider gulf between student and professor in Germany than existed in either England or the United States. Without residential community as the very warp of the university, it was only too easy for the professor to become ever more aloof from students and, for that matter, from everything that did not directly pertain to his research and publication. In the English university in the nineteenth century scholarship existed as one among several almost equally venerated ends. In the German university, even under the best of conditions, scholarship was the sole and sufficient end.

Even so we cannot afford to underestimate the dignity and strength of the university ideal that Humboldt generated in early nineteenth-century Germany and that, a century later, was given such eloquent expression by Weber in his address to the students at Munich. To that ideal, more than to any other, is owed not only the unprecedented outburst of German scholarship and science in the nineteenth century but also, in due time, as the result of diffusion of the Humboldtian ideal to America, the efflorescence of higher education in the United States at the turn of the century.

3.

From the beginning there were powerful currents of opposition in Germany to this ideal of the university as the house of intellect. These currents were many and diverse. Politically, they ranged from conservative nationalism to revolutionary socialism. But along with these were found expressions of opposition to the Humboldtian ideal coming from figures as civilized and humane as Nietzsche and Burckhardt. What these various expressions of opposition all had in common was distaste for the strictly research conception of the university and, more positively, a conviction that knowledge must serve moral and cultural ends beyond itself.

It was at the University of Jena (where Marx was to receive his doctorate in 1842) that the "trans-intellectual" conception of the university first flourished, a conception that sought to unite mind and morality. By 1800, Fichte was there, and both Schelling and Hegel commenced their careers there. It was, let us be reminded, the age of the French Revolution, of the lustrous Napoleon, of the birth of nationalism in the full, modern sense, and it was also the age in which the conception of unilinear, inexorable progress—applied during the seventeenth and most of the eighteenth centuries to knowledge alone—was made the effective context of virtually all treatments of society, state, and institutions. It was not enough to have the ideal of, say, a united nation in Germany. What was necessary was to demonstrate that all German history, all development of culture within the German states, was but a fulfillment of this ideal—a fulfillment to be seen over a long period of time in terms of epochs and stages. If it could be shown that history was indeed the working-out of an imminent principle—be it freedom, justice, equality, national unity, or whatever—then did it not follow that the predestined work of philosophers, teachers, and other intellectuals was that of aiding in this realization of principle?

It is tempting here, under the spell of all the familiar treatments of German nationalism of which Fichte, Hegel, and Treitschke among others were the protagonists, to digress and explore this vein of nineteenth-century thought in Germany. Our subject is, however, the university, and while the German university assuredly was the locus of a large amount of nationalism, as evidenced in the utterances of so many of its professors and students, it held a great deal else as well. When Fichte delivered his momentous *Addresses to the German Nation* in 1808, there was far more than simple nationalism in what he had to say: There was the vision of a social reconstruction hardly less than revolutionary in aim; there was the intoxicating image of a Germany culturally, socially, and psychologically transformed as no nation ever had been before; above all else there was the inevitably magnetizing conception of the university (on which he had already spoken and written at length) as the source of moral and spiritual purpose that would be national in inception, yes, but that could be imagined spreading far beyond German boundaries.

Throughout the nineteenth century this ideal of the university as prophet, seer, and spiritual leader in collective crusade was seen in varied dress: sometimes militarist, sometimes nationalist in the strict sense, but also not seldom socialist and revolutionary. It was, in foundation and nature, diametrically opposite to the Humboldtian ideal of the university as concerned solely with teaching and scholarship in the learned disciplines. I do not mean that university professors and students were drawn up in two separate and hostile camps. I am referring only to two very strong ideals, and it is not strange that both of these ideals can be seen touching in varying degrees the same individuals. Some of the greatest of German scholars, Mommsen and von Gierke among them, allowed their scholarship to become charged by values and aspirations arising from the political events of their own age. It was well known that Mommsen's portrait of Julius Caesar in his classic *History of Rome* reflected his own liberal aversion to Caesarism in any form for Germany, and more than a few other figures striding across the Forum in Mommsen's pages bear a suspicious resemblance to German politicians in Mommsen's day. Great scholar as he was, Mommsen did not shrink from the use of history as a political weapon. Otto von Gierke, whose massive researches into the medieval law of associations had so much to do with inspiring in the English Maitland and the French Duguit the ideas of modern legal pluralism, made it plain that in his researches he was seeking a correct political policy for his own Germany.

Politics and nationalism were not, however, the sole purposes to which the university could be put under this larger ideal of the university's relation to national life. Socialism was another purpose, and there were a good many estimable professors in German universities by the end of the century who had no compunctions about using their chairs of learning to advance beliefs in both the ideal and the imminence of socialist society. *Kathedersozialisten,* socialists of the podium, they were often called, usually with denigratory intent. I would not for a moment disparage the scholarship that could come from such minds as those of Gustave Schmoller and Lujo Brentano, the first at Berlin, the second at Munich. There was certainly nothing crude or exhortative in the teaching done by these two, and there were others like them. They, together with some intellectuals outside the university and also some businessmen and journalists, founded in 1872 the notable *Verein für Sozialpolitik* which served not only as a base of research into social and political questions but as the means of disseminating knowledge about these questions. Weber was to do his first major piece of sociological research under the auspices of the union, a study of agricultural conditions in East Prussia. But with all respect to the socialists of the podium, it cannot be denied that they were doing for their own political ends what a Treitschke was doing for his.

It should not be thought that attack upon the Humboldtian ideal of the university was confined to nationalists, militarists, and socialists—activists in the ordinary sense of the word. There were some very humane and enlightened minds not immersed in active political concerns—among them Nietzsche, Burckhardt, and Stefan George—that also regarded the university's commitment to scholarship with hostility and, occasionally, despair for German culture.

Nietzsche, who had been in the beginning a professor, was particularly harsh on the universities. In his *Twilight of the Idols* he referred to the "steady decline of German earnestness, German profundity, and German passion in things intellectual" in the university, the consequence in large part, he wrote, of the "barrenness" and the "self-satisfied and lukewarm intellectuality" there. In *We Scholars* he compares the orthodox man of learning, whether humanistic scholar or scientist, to the old maid, each respectable no doubt but without creative power. What Nietzsche saw in the university in rising degree was "a commonplace type of man," the sad product of "the instinct of mediocrity of his type."

Almost equally hostile to the universities was Burckhardt. Famous from 1860 on for his splendid study of the Italian Renaissance, he refused all offers to join any of the universities of Europe. He preferred life as a citizen of Basle, regarding himself as one of the city's craftsmen, more pleased by honors at home than by those abroad. He can hardly be thought of as an activist, despising as he did the ideologists of his day, of whatever persuasion, and correctly prophesying that from these ideological militants of left and right would in time issue a new and terrible form of despotism, one based on the masses and led by reincarnate Caesars. Burckhardt was concerned first and last with intellectual, moral, and cultural values, with theories and perspectives, and with the lessons that could be learned from the study of, say, Greek history. He could be even more deadly than Nietzsche in some of his publicized criticisms of those in the universities who thought themselves aristocrats merely by virtue of having "scientifically" ascertained "that the Emperor Conrad II went to the privy at Goslar on May 7, 1030."

Then there was the extraordinarily great, if subtle, influence on the German intellectual mind in the late nineteenth and early twentieth century of Tolstoy's social gospel, one compounded of primitive Christianity, Eros, and a folk anarchism. There are several references to Tolstoy in Weber's "Science as a Vocation," and the reason is clear enough: Tolstoyanism had made inroads among German youth, who were estranged by the increasingly bureaucratized character of both the churches and the social action movements of their day, much as the New

Left in our day has been similarly estranged. The Tolstoyan movement could not but have found the ideal of university scholarship a repugnant one, for whether in its ivory tower humanism presided over by the mandarinate or in its laboratory- and field-based positivism, with objectivity its sole aim, there could appear to be nothing pertinent—relevant, as so many in our day would say—to the need for love, authenticity, and simple freedom among Germans, as the Tolstoyans saw this need.

Finally, something should be said about the influence of the *George-Kreise*. This was the group, the "circle" surrounding the gifted Stefan George, poet, critic, and prophet. Some of the most talented minds of the early twentieth century were to be found in George's circle, among them Gundolf, Hoffmansthal, Rickert, Simmel, Ernst Kantorowicz, ranging from distinguished poets and philosophers to notable historians and sociologists. What they had in common, beyond fascination with Stefan George himself, was a belief that modern German and also Western culture were becoming dominated by nationalism for its own sake, bureaucratization of society, and a spreading philistinism. For George the crowning function of intellect lay in finding or fashioning a new, unifying purpose for human society in the West, starting with Germany, one that would be at once moral, esthetic, and metaphysical, one that would lead Europe to recovery of the sense of community on the one hand and of individual greatness on the other. Inevitably, George and most of his circle, though not all, had little but contempt for the orthodox university and its commitment to knowledge for its own sake.

Weber, as we know from his wife's recollections, was more than a little interested in the *George-Kreise* and in Stefan George himself. Although he disliked the cult-like quality of the circle and the near-adoration of George, he yet admired Stefan George in many ways, and there is record of a number of pleasant, stimulating, and mutually respectful meetings between the two men. After all, a good deal in common lay between Weber's own growing despair over what he perceived as the irresistible spread of political and economic rationalization in the West and the *George-Kreise*'s repudiation of so much of the Germany that had been nurtured by the forces of modernity. The curious mixture of traditionalism and esthetic radicalism we find in George along with the desire for restoration of a true cultural community and of individual greatness in national life was not without root in Weber's own complex spirit.

Where Weber and the *George-Kreise* broke, however, was in respect to the role of the university in a national cultural and moral renascence. As I noted, there was little if any admiration for the Humboldtian ideal of the university in Stefan George and in most of his followers. All learning, all thinking, should be dedicated, they thought, to a cultural reformation of the West, not to knowledge for its own sake, least of all the fact-grubbing they so despised and not to the rampant specialization of science and scholarship they could see in the universities of their day. In this respect the *George-Kreise* was, no matter with what degree of sophistication and civility, in the direct line begun early in the nineteenth century by Fichte and others—the line of thinkers that rejected the Humboldtian ideal as being an evasion, even a betrayal of moral and social responsibility and that saw the true function of the university to be that of prophet to a nation. And this, for all his own anguish at the way things were going in the modern West, was completely repugnant to Weber.

4.

There have been many interpretations of the significance of Weber's "Science as a Vocation," most of the friendly ones centering upon what is generally called the spirit of rationalism contained in the address, the hostile ones upon what is called the meretriciousness, even the hypocrisy of his call for a *wertfrei*, objective, and dispassionate goal for the university scholar. I suggest that the overriding power of Weber's address to the students at Munich comes from its Humboldtian cast of thought, its profound insistence that the university is but one of the major institutions in society, that it has its own embedded function, which is the advancement of knowledge for its own sake, and that it is a perversion of the university's function to declare it and its community of scholars the keeper of the nation's conscience, prophetic builder of a national sense of purpose, guardian of a national morality. Such perversion of the university's function could range, and had ranged for a century in German history, between the civilized, elevated standards of the Fichtes, Nietzsches, and Georges on the one hand and, on the other, of the Jahns and Treitschkes and their willingness to consecrate the university's mission to the goals of militarism, power-nationalism, even anti-Semitism. But whether in elevated or debased form, this activist, prophetic role of the university was one Weber found wholly unacceptable.

The function of the university, he wrote, organized as it is in its special disciplines, is that of "self-clarification" and "knowledge of interrelated facts." The university does not have "the gift of grace of seers and prophets dispensing sacred values and revelations." This was Weber's answer to the Treitschkes and Jahns on the one hand and also on the other to the humane and respected Stefan George. To seek to use the university for the purposes of "academic prophecy" will be, Weber declared, "to create only fanatical sects but never a genuine community."

"To the person who cannot bear the fate of the times like a man, one must say: may he rather return silently, without the usual publicity build-up of renegades, but simply and plainly. The arms of the old churches are opened widely and compassionately for him. . . . In my eyes, such religious return stands higher than the academic prophecy, which does not clearly realize that in the lecture-rooms of the university no other virtue holds but plain intellectual integrity."

How profoundly escapist, derelict in political obligation, and morally irresponsible those words must have seemed to many in Weber's audience that day in Munich in 1918. After all, did not a German nation seem to be lying in ruins, the result of the defeat of the kaiser's Germany that year by the Allies? There was much more than the seeming death of a nation in the minds of Weber's audience; there was also the seeming death of so many of the social and economic causes—social democracy among them—that had flourished prior to World War I. No one who has read any of the literature produced in Germany during the years immediately following the war needs to be told of the mood of defeat and depression only occasionally relieved by the words and actions of the more militant members of both the right and the left. For Weber to refer to all prophecy in the university as wrong and to recommend return to the ancient churches for those who needed prophecy must have seemed the very height of irresponsibility if not treason to many. It was a passionate nationalist from the right, Ernst Krieck, who was the first to attack Weber in print for his words. But at the time of the Weber Centennial in West Germany in 1964, it was the voice of the left, above all that of Herbert Marcuse, which declared Weber an enemy of morality and progress.

How does Weber justify his doctrine of *Wertfreiheit* and insistence that the scholar per se stay clear of ideology and prophecy? Clearly, his position has implications reaching scholarship, science, and research in any quarter whatever. The first observation to make here is that Weber's affirmation of objectivity as the scientist's goal is by no means limited in statement to his address to the students in 1918. In 1904, on the occasion of his assumption of the co-editorship, along with Sombart and Jaffe, of the *Archiv für Sozialwissenschaft und Sozialpolitik,* Weber set forth in that distinguished journal, probably the best of its kind anywhere in the world at that time, some reflections under the title " 'Objectivity' in Social Science and Social Policy." Two years later he wrote his "Critical Studies in the Logic of Cultural Sciences" and, just a year or two prior to his address to the Munich students, "The Meaning of 'Ethical Neutrality' in Sociology and Economics."

These essays deal with substantially more, of course, than the subject of objectivity and *Wertfreiheit.* In their contents are to be found some of the subtlest, most sophisticated, and demonstrably fertile propositions yet set forth in sociology on methodology. Very probably their greatest contributions are the perspicuous limits Weber assigns to science in its relation to history and to philosophy, the nature of the quasi-intuitive method he calls *"Verstehen,"* and the nature of law in social science. But it is evident that along with these interests lies another in the possibility of achieving in the study of the political and social world a science comparable to any physical science in its freedom from the special pleading and partisanship of ideological politics. The great merit of methodology, Weber thought, was its capacity to aid the honest scholar in achievement of this end.

Weber, to repeat, was himself active in the politics of his day, and there could not have been many in that age who felt more deeply and sensitively the issues involved in politics. He had nothing but disdain for the individual mind sterilized of political and moral values and makes it plain that for him callous moral indifference has no relation at all to the kind of scientific objectivity he sought. No normal person can be without value preferences or without the desire to find metaphysical or religious meaning in human events. As Durkheim was writing in France at the very same time, one would indeed be a monster to declare all values equal or to seek to insulate one's affective being from values of any kind.

What Weber is telling us is that the scientist's own deeply held values notwithstanding, there is no reason why the human mind, carefully trained, genuinely dedicated to the search for knowledge, cannot reach reasonably objective statements of factual interrelationships and of causality. Such statements will always necessarily be finite in character, always subject to restatement and to verification by others working in terms of the same objectives, and a universe apart from the kind of moral or metaphysical certitude prized by prophets and partisans. Such statements are nevertheless possible and also eminently desirable as foundations for social policy. Never, Weber wrote in both the essay on "ethical neutrality" and the one on "objectivity," will it be either possible or desirable for the scientist to tell another individual or the world what *should* be done when there are choices to be made among alternative modes of behavior. That, Weber emphasizes tirelessly, is not, cannot be, the scientist's responsibility. What the scientist can offer, however, are statements of relationship among the alternative values and their modes of expression and statements, too, of the probable consequences in fact of choice of one or other of the values and their attached courses of action. In sum, the scientist can advise as to means but not ends!

Can the scientist or scholar, then, ever be actually free of values as a simple reading of *Wertfreiheit* might suggest? Indeed not! It is a fiction to suppose as Descartes pretended to suppose that one can in fact purge his mind of all it has learned and start fresh from a *tabula rasa* formed from the acids of skepticism. But what one can do, if he is but willing, is *become aware* of his ideas and values and then work toward answers of scientific problems, toward propositions of relationship and causality in the full light of not only these, his own, values but also of the other values that may be related in any way to the subject of his study. Basically, all Weber is telling us is that values do indeed exist, and matter profoundly to human beings, and are in one degree or other inescapable, but that they need not chain the disciplined scientist to any predetermined conclusion when, with the advantage of methodological sophistication, he seeks understanding of the world around him. When Weber wrote of objectivity he was not naively supposing likelihood of the scholar's achievement of any absolute state of mind, merely of a degree of disciplined, dispassionate understanding of human behavior that would make such understanding greatly and vitally different from the out-and-out ex parte or ideologically tendentious. This was the Humboldtian ideal that had, despite the many crosscurrents of thought in the nineteenth century I have noted, made the German university at its best a uniquely great institution. But there were many in Weber's day to declare such an ideal no more than unwitting camouflage for forces of the political left. And, a generation later, there were as many voices to argue that Weber's plea for a *wertfrei* science in the study of man had helped pave the way for the Nazism that first erupted five years after Weber's address in the very city in which Weber had spoken to the students.

In short, there was nothing of the merely situational or ad hoc in Weber's plea for the exclusion of politics in the activist sense and also for the exclusion of the moralistic and prophetic from the university when he made his remarks to the students at Munich in 1918. A lifetime of scholarship committed to this very ideal, along with some early writing of an explicitly methodological kind lay behind the remarks. As a historical mind closely acquainted with the course of academic affairs in Germany in the nineteenth century and as a mind deeply involved in the political issues of his own day, Weber knew the ease with which the classroom could become the setting of political and ideological partisanship, made all the greater by the professor's pretence of letting the facts speak for themselves. He knew, in other words, that the very ideal of objectivity—which its enemies repudiated—could become the mask for ideological operations of these selfsame enemies of objectivity.

The difference between the profession of politics and the profession of the *study* of politics is, Weber insisted, vast. At the political forum

> the words one uses . . . are not means of scientific analysis but means of canvassing votes and winning over others. They are not plowshares to loosen the soil of contemplative thought; they are swords against the enemies; such words are weapons. It would be an outrage, however, to use words in this fashion in a lecture or in the lecture-room. If, for instance, "democracy" is under discussion, one considers its various forms, analyzes them in the way they function, determines what results for the conditions of life the one form has as compared with the other. Then one confronts the forms of democracy with non-democratic forms of political order and endeavors to come to a position where the student may find the point from which, in terms of his ultimate ideals, he can take a stand. But the true teacher will beware of imposing from the platform any political position upon the student, whether it is expressed or suggested. "To let the facts speak for themselves" is the most unfair way of putting over a political position to the student.

Then comes Weber's declaration of academic principle, one founded in the very goal of *Wertfreiheit* he had many years earlier set up for the social sciences precisely as Durkheim in France had done at about the same time.

> . . . Now one cannot demonstrate scientifically what the duty of an academic teacher is. One can only demand of the teacher that he have the intellectual integrity to see that it is one thing to state facts, to determine mathematical or logical relations or the internal structure of cultural values, while it is another thing to answer questions of the *value* of culture and its individual contents and the question of how one should act in the cultural community and in political associations. These are quite heterogeneous problems. If he asks further why he should not deal with both types of problems in the lecture-room, the answer is: because the prophet and the demagogue do not belong on the academic platform.
>
> To the prophet and the demagogue, it is said: "Go your ways out into the streets and speak openly to the world," that is, speak where criticism is possible. In the lecture-room we stand opposite our audience, and it has to remain silent. I deem it irresponsible to exploit the circumstance that for the sake of their career the students have to attend a teacher's course while there is nobody present to oppose him with criticism. The task of the teacher is to serve the students with his knowledge and scientific experience and not to imprint upon them his personal political views.

What a powerful and, at its very best, brilliant, even profound, tradition, Weber is speaking against in those words. He was, obviously, addressing himself not simply to the Jahns, Treitschkes, and Kriecks, blatant nationalists all, but also to the Stefan Georges, those who had, ever since Fichte, sought with the highest and often noblest of intentions to make the university the capstone of national purpose, the vessel of intellectual and moral rehabilitation of individuals and societies alike. Weber surely sympathized with the Tolstoyan message of love, agreed with much of the kind of criticism of the university that had come from Heine and Nietzsche in the preceding century and from George and his circle in Weber's own time, and would have been among the first to volunteer to help make the German nation a more civilized and moral nation. He is adamant, however, in his position that such missions, however necessary and noble, are alien to the university, which is the house of scholarship and science, its true inhabitants committed to the vow of *Wertfreiheit*.

5.

Weber, we are told by his wife in her recollections, believed that the great majority of German professors abused the privileges of the chairs they held. This did not affect his own conception of what academic duty was, but it undoubtedly made for a certain added melancholy as he surveyed the setting that the cherished doctrine of academic freedom had in large degree made possible. It will be useful at this point, I think, to say something about that doctrine, the fame of which had penetrated America in the late nineteenth century when universities in the true sense were just coming into being here.

German academic freedom becomes intelligible to us only in light of the peculiar relation German universities held to the government. We must bear in mind that the German universities depended on the government not only for financial assistance but for a substantial degree of direction of policy and program, which latter sprang from the governmental ministries of education in the German states. Nothing like the kind of autonomy Oxford and Cambridge had in England, or for that matter the typical private American college had, was known in Germany. Humboldt had proposed a good deal of such autonomy, but his plans were defeated.

After the Napoleonic wars, a few German universities managed to get charters from their respective governments which provided them with at least some of the functional autonomy in the larger society that older ones had known in the medieval era but that had been assailed by the Reformation state with its declaration of sovereignty proceeding directly from God. In Prussia, at the behest of Humboldt, Stein, and a few other influential figures, Frederick William III agreed to grant a constitution to the universities there, but there is little reason to believe in the genuineness of this, for Frederick made plain that he conceived the primary role of the university to be that of aiding in the moral and social rehabilitation of loyalties to the state. Suffice it to say that what we in fact find during the first half of the century in Prussia is a great deal of interference in the workings of the universities, including the formation of curricula and the appointment and separation of faculty members. Given the highly politicized relation of the university to the central government and the government's determination to use the university as an arm of its administration of society, there is perhaps no great mystery in the fact that within the university itself there was, as we have seen, a highly ideological and activist conception of the role of the university.

From about 1850 on, however, the corporate role of the university in both Prussian and German society as a whole became a somewhat freer one. Gradually there came into existence the doctrines of *Lehrfreiheit* and *Lernfreiheit,* the former relating to the professor's freedom to teach and conduct his research with a minimum of interference and the latter pertaining to the student's right to take courses pretty much where, when, and as he chose during his career, with examination in any course under a given professor a privilege his for the demanding whenever the student felt prepared and disposed.

The first, *Lehrfreiheit,* takes on significance only, really, in a setting comparable to Germany's where a great deal of governing of the universities proceeded directly from the ministry of education. It was the ministry, for the most part, that alone could approve new ventures in the universities, new institutes, curricula, and organizational structures within. Appointment of professors—in contrast to lower-ranking, journeymen-like *Privatdozenten* and others of similar status—was done by the ministry of education, though commonly from a list of nominees provided by a given university. In short, even with the most favorable view of *Lehrfreiheit* in the nineteenth-century German university, it existed within a context of political-administrative direction of the university that would have been unimaginable in England or the America of the private colleges and universities. All, basically, that *Lehrfreiheit* granted was the right of a professor, once he had been officially appointed at this rank by the ministry of education, to teach and otherwise conduct his courses within the realm of his own research specialization. That is, he was exempted from the kind of teaching we think of in connection with general or liberal arts curricular objectives where he might find himself teaching widely in areas only tenuously related to his field or specialization.

Lernfreiheit takes its significance from a scene of German student life very different from that of either the United States or England. Residence for a stated period of years at a single college or university was, in a sense, the very heart of both the English and the American systems. The student was in college not only to study a largely prescribed set of courses but to absorb the values of an intellectual-residential community. Quite the reverse was the case in Germany. Not only was residence for any period of time not required by the German university of the student, such residence was not even honored. Mobility, diversity, and close attachment to single course or professor were the honored values. *Lernfreiheit* meant simply that the student was free to study when and where he desired, to accumulate courses at however many different universities he desired, and that he had the right of being examined for his degree whenever he decided he was prepared.

But while the essence of *Lehrfreiheit* and of *Lernfreiheit* was no more than what I have just described, its theory being strictly an academic one, the practical consequences of both had become, by the late nineteenth century, a great deal wider and inclusive of much more than the simple right of a professor to teach in his research specialization and of a student to study and be examined as he himself chose. The virtual unassailability of a German scholar in his chair, once he had been appointed to the rank of professor, from either local or national pressures gave him a degree of personal autonomy sufficient to cover just about whatever he wanted it to cover. Granted the purely academic character of the beginnings of each aspect of the doctrine of academic freedom and its value in light of early nineteenth-century firings of faculty members and dismissals of students for political reasons, the fact is that by Weber's day the double-barreled doctrine of academic freedom in Germany had become the basis of declared right to teach however a professor wished, no matter how ideologically, politically, or prophetically, and, on the student side, of declared right to engage in whatever activities one wished, no matter how militant and potentially destructive of academic rectitudes these might be. Long before Nazi students began to use the idea of *Lernfreiheit* as a means of bullying professors beginning in the 1920s, there were student groups in one or other German university to adopt the same kinds of tactics in behalf of pacifism, socialism, and other political doctrines.

Weber has little if anything explicit to say on the subject of academic freedom as such in his remarks to the students at Munich, but it is inconceivable that he thought either *Lehrfreiheit* or *Lernfreiheit* a doctrine giving full exemption to professor or student for whatever his political or moral disposition dictated. We know in detail how repugnant he found political or moralistic abuse of academic privilege to be; we know also Weber's almost religious intensity of devotion to the calling of scholar. It is hard in this light to believe other than that Weber regarded the professor's assumption of the role of prophet or demagogue and the student's assumption of the role of militant, with the academy his sanctuary, as reprehensible and a violation of the privilege inherent in the doctrine of academic freedom.

So are such assumptions by professor and student reprehensible in our own day in America. The idea of academic freedom was slow in appearing on the American scene, and the German example had a good deal to do with its acceptance and spread across America. The problem was not often political government so much as it was lay boards of trustees, many of them religious in composition, most of them closely wedded to the principles of laissez-faire capitalism, and few of them at first happy about the conception of a professor's full freedom of teaching. It is remarkable, all things considered, that there were not more instances than there were in the nineteenth and the first part of the twentieth century of faculty members being fired outright by administrations and trustees for teaching what, however honest and scholarly, seemed to contravene moral and political values cherished by trustees and legislators.

Suffice it to say that when the distinctive principle of academic freedom did finally take root in the United States, so largely through labors of the philosophers John Dewey and Arthur Lovejoy, it was in strict keeping with the liberal-rationalist German ideal, the ideal to be found from Humboldt to Weber. There was no profligate libertarianism involved in early manifestos on academic freedom in this country, no insistence that anything and everything said by the professor from his podium in the classroom or done by the professor inside or outside the academy was sacrosanct. None of this: only, in the words of Lovejoy,

> the freedom of the teacher or research worker in higher institutions of learning to investigate and discuss the problems of his science and to express his conclusions, whether through publication or in the instruction of students, without interference from political or ecclesiastical authority, or from the administrative officials of the institution in which he is employed, unless his methods are found by

qualified bodies of his own profession to be clearly incompetent or contrary to professional ethics.[3]

That freedom and tenure alike would someday be demanded by those in the universities concerned with flouting the ideals and works of dispassionate scholarship, with desecrating libraries and laboratories, and bent upon destruction of the university as an institution on the grounds of its inherent subversion of mass equalitarianism, this, surely, could not have been in even the darkest imaginings of the Deweys and Lovejoys early in the century who helped to establish a nationally understood policy of academic freedom in the universities. Was it, in one shape or other, in Weber's mind when he delivered in 1918 his two great addresses at the University of Munich, "Politics as a Vocation" and "Science as a Vocation"? I can only quote from the final words of the former address, violating immediate context perhaps but hardly their spirit or chillingly prophetic character when applied to our own age:

> Not summer's bloom lies ahead of us, but rather a polar night of icy darkness and harness, no matter which group may triumph externally now. Where there is nothing, not only the Kaiser but also the proletarian has lost his rights. When this night shall have slowly receded, who of those for whom spring apparently has bloomed so luxuriously will be alive?

---

[3] "Academic Freedom" in *Encyclopedia of the Social Sciences* (New York, 1930).

Five Decades of Public Controversy Over Mental Testing

Lee J. Cronbach

As the United States mobilized for war in the spring of 1917, Professor Lewis M. Terman of Stanford University filled a briefcase with materials on the group intelligence test his student Arthur Otis had just designed and went East to meet with the other leading psychologists of the time. Within weeks they had organized the Army Alpha Examination for use in testing recruits. Their short mental test did indeed locate men who made satisfactory officers and noncoms. Delighted with this achievement, the psychologists then pressed for civilian testing.

"Teachers must learn to use tests," said Terman. Otherwise, "the universal grading of children according to mental ability must remain a Utopian dream."[1] Terman's individual test for children published in 1916 already was widely used and immediately after the war the group tests were snatched up by school systems and colleges as a basis for pupil classification, guidance, and college admissions. Within thirty months of the first publication of a group test, some four million children had been tested. The test technology became an accepted and increasingly influential feature of American life. The momentum of the tests overrode all criticism.

Today, however, the critics of mental tests are in the ascendant. The California legislature, for example, has voted several times to prohibit group mental testing in schools on the grounds that its effect is to limit the education black children receive. A Republican governor vetoed the bill, which Republican

---

[1] Lewis M. Terman, *The Intelligence of School Children* (Boston, 1919), p. 291.

legislators had opposed. (Such a bill was passed in 1975.) On many fronts, a procedure that came in as an impartial application of scientific findings about talent is now under bitter attack. The irony is all the greater in that the attack comes largely from those who speak for the poor. Proponents of testing, from Thomas Jefferson onward, have wanted to open doors for the talented poor in a system where doors often are opened by parental wealth and status rather than by impartial appraisal.

Public controversy deals in stereotypes, never in subtleties. The Luddites can smash up a device but to improve a system requires calm study. So, following the advice of a professional study committee,[2] the same California legislature that voted in 1972 to outlaw group testing by local districts instituted a new, carefully safeguarded, statewide test of mental ability for first-graders, as these data are needed as a base line in evaluations of reading instruction that the legislature desires. On advice of the same committee, they cancelled a statewide mental test in Grades 6 and 10 that had no proper function. Sound policy is not *for* tests or *against* tests; what matters is how tests are used. But what the public hears is endless angry clamor from extremists who see no good in any test, or no evil.

The topic of this paper is not policies about testing or scientific evidence on individual differences. This volume is concerned with the public uses of social science and the contribution of the scholar to policy making. Controversies over testing provide an instructive example.

The able psychologists who wrote popular articles about individual differences set out to tell the public what they knew, so that it could be weighed into policies. Human differences, however, are an explosive theme. The most dramatic fulminations were set off by Arthur Jensen's 1969 paper, and his story can be our starting place. The Jensen incident is often referred to as if his paper were an isolated effort to promote an idiosyncratic theory. Few readers realize that controversy over these issues has waxed and waned since test reports began in 1905. Views that arouse heated rejoinders in one climate of opinion have been accepted matter-of-factly in another. For perspective, the Jensen affair must be seen alongside other controversies. Particularly important to the story is the

---

[2] A disclosure of partisanship is required. I was chairman of this study committee. More generally, my professional interests make me very much a part of the testing Establishment. Among the persons to be discussed, I have had some affiliation with Freeman, Terman, Davis, Eells, Snow, and Elashoff. On invitation, I have been a public critic of Jensen.

The work leading to this paper was begun while I was a Fellow of the John Simon Guggenheim Memorial Foundation and a Visiting Scholar at the Center for Advanced Study in the Behavioral Sciences. Paul Chapman has been of great help in preparing this paper. I thank many of the persons mentioned in this history for comments and information.

role of the media in shaping controversies and, at times, in neglecting an opportunity for controversy. Nor are the media to be seen as independent agents; what catches fire depends, at any time, on the direction public opinion is blowing.

TESTING IN THE PUBLIC EYE: 1967–1974

The Political and Scientific Setting

To set the stage for Jensen, we must go back three decades. World War II dramatized the value of specialized training, and testing played a large part in allocating men to military specialties. After the war, talent was cherished as a resource. Specialized and higher education expanded rapidly, "merit scholarships" became available, and schools emphasized career guidance as never before. Even as college education became more widely available, entrance to prestige colleges became more competitive. Draft exemption, too, came to depend on test scores. The more the tests came to determine life chances, the more they became foci of anxiety; objections to elitism and meritocracy followed.

Around 1960, traditional concepts were challenged in the newly vigorous field of child psychology. The new ideas, coming from studies of child learning and colored by Piaget's views on the role of experience in intellectual development, were strenuously "environmentalist." The importance of the biological substrate was not denied, but the emphasis was on the use the child made of experience. If logical powers are constructed out of experience, it becomes natural to decry "the old belief in fixed intelligence" and to search for methods of stimulating intellectual growth. This trend within psychology crested just as the condition of blacks became a national concern. The Head Start program for the children of the poor was adopted on the warrant of demonstrations that such activities on a small scale had benefited children. Evidence that the hasty large-scale program had not produced the intended miracles was just beginning to surface in 1969.

Racial differences in ability had rarely been examined by scholars in the preceding two decades. A few psychologists had assembled the studies showing that blacks average lower on tests than whites and had tried to interpret the finding biologically rather than environmentally, but their work was considered irrelevant if not disreputable. Criticisms of the early work on the problem had convinced nearly all social scientists that no research design can disentangle genetic and environmental components of group differences, and the view prevailing after 1940 has been close to these statements of Otto Klineberg:

> The available data offer no support for the view that racial or national origins set different limits to the potentialities of a child. The teacher has the right to assume that under similar conditions both the range of capacities and the average

capacity of various groups will almost certainly be about the same. He has the
duty, therefore, to treat each child as an individual. . . .[3]

The middle sentence, however, slides from the view that the question of innate
group differences is unanswerable to the "assumption" that no differences exist.
What was an assumption in the 1940s had crystallized into a combative assertion
in the 1960s.

A few more words of preamble, and we can turn to Jensen. Much of the dispute centers around the contention that a child's standing in ability depends
largely on what genes he inherits. As Jensen has documented, the evidence is
that differences among American or British whites in the past generation have
been due more to genetic differences than to differences in upbringing. The
precise proportion of hereditary influence can be debated, but not the principle.[4]
Yet the statistic is an index of sociocultural conditions, not a biological inevitabil-
ity. Change the distribution of nutrition, home experience, and schooling in the
next generation, and the heritability index will change. Findings on heritability
within white populations tell us nothing whatsoever about how white and black
groups would compare if their environments had been equalized. Note also that
a high degree of heritability does not imply that improved environment can
have no effect. Even with an heritability index as high as .80, two children with
the same genotype may differ by as much as twenty-five IQ points, if one is
reared in a superior environment and the other in an unstimulating one.

Jensen: Scholarship, Confusion, Inferred Advocacy

Arthur Jensen, a well-recognized educational psychologist, and the geneticist
Ernst Caspari were invited to present companion lectures to the 1967 meeting
of the American Educational Research Association. Caspari dealt with biological
questions, while Jensen crossed over into social class and educational policy.[5]
The Jensen and Caspari papers agreed wherever they touched the same subject
and caused no controversy. Although Jensen dealt with heritability, he emphasized his own research on the relations among memory, IQ, and school
performance in different social groups. At the end, he recommended ways to
teach pupils having adequate memory but mediocre IQs. The one paragraph of
Jensen's paper that foreshadowed later events said only this.

I find little information about the extent to which Negro-white differences
have a genetic basis. . . . Therefore, statements . . . can at present be nothing but

[3] Otto Klineberg, in *Encyclopaedia of Educational Research,* ed. Walter Monroe (New
York, 1952), p. 953.

[4] J. Loehlin, G. Lindzey, and J. Spuhler, *Race Differences in Intelligence* (San
Francisco, 1975).

[5] Arthur R. Jensen, "Social Class, Race, and Genetics: Implications for Education,"
American Educational Research Journal 5 (January 1968) : 1–42.

conjecture and surmise. . . . But the question arises whether there has been an official decision to create the impression that such hypotheses have already been scientifically tested with conclusive results.

He cited particular government releases asserting a conclusion about biological equality that had been for Klineberg and other scholars no more than a working assumption.

During the same year Jensen produced a noteworthy but little-known paper on compensatory education[6] which entirely denied the view that came to be known as "jensenism." On comparative education, he said, "Action programs are obviously needed immediately." On race (a single page in the paper), "[T]he fact that Negroes and Mexicans are disproportionately represented in the lower . . . [classes] cannot be interpreted as evidence of poor genetic potential. . . . [I]t seems a reasonable hypothesis that their low-average IQ is due to environmental rather than genetic factors."

Jensen's famous 1969 paper arose out of the journalistic enterprise of the student editors of the *Harvard Educational Review,* abetted by his missionary zeal. Initially, an editor asked Jensen to submit the manuscript of a 1968 talk on "learning ability and socioeconomic status." Jensen meanwhile had drafted another lecture arguing that IQs do not respond to educational intervention even though compensatory programs probably could boost educational attainment. He provided both manuscripts to *HER* and after studying them the editors, in April 1968, asked Jensen to work up a complete statement of his views for their 12,000 readers.[7] Having outlined the controversial content to be covered, the editors arranged for a panel to provide comments for publication alongside Jensen's piece. Jensen was to cover, in the context of intervention programs, the contribution of heredity and environment, "his own position" on social class and racial differences, and his research on learning. Jensen, even as you and I, let other work crowd his schedule until mid-September and then put together 50,000 words in two months.

The elaborations and asides added in Jensen's hasty completion of the manuscript damaged the balance and clarity of the final version. The distribution of emphasis was not much like that of the 1967 and 1968 papers and seemed not to follow closely the weighting suggested by the *HER* editors. Even in this paper, race took up less than 10 percent of the space, but race somehow looms larger than in the 1967 AERA paper because of the interest of blacks in com-

---

6 Arthur R. Jensen, "The Culturally Disadvantaged: Psychological and Educational Aspects," *Educational Research* 10 (November 1967): 4–20.

7 Arthur R. Jensen, *Genetics and Education* (New York, 1972). This provides a 67-page history, reprints the *HER* paper, and gives other papers and bibliography. The original paper was "How Much Can We Boost IQ and Scholastic Achievement?" *Harvard Educational Review* 39 (Winter 1969): 1–123. For responses see 39 (Spring 1969): 273–356, and 39 (Summer 1969): 449–631.

pensatory education. The 1969 title came from the second 1968 speech, "How much can we boost IQ and scholastic achievement?" The 1969 reader would conclude that the answer was "Not at all; neither of them," whereas the 1968 listener had been urged to concentrate on improving achievement *rather than* IQ, a very different answer. Jensen's own research led him to the optimistic view that an alternative form of teaching could benefit the poor child whose IQ is low. Only the final two pages of the 120-page paper in *HER* offered this positive approach to compensatory education. The message was a quaver compared to the stentorian opening: "Why has there been such uniform failure of compensatory programs wherever they have been tried?"

As soon as the article was in type, the publicity broke. *HER* made the article available to the press along with the remarks of the prearranged critics. Substantial excerpts appeared in *U.S. News* and the *New York Times* and lesser accounts in other media. Within two weeks, the SDS were cruising the Berkeley campus with a sound truck whose chant was "Stop racism. Fire Jensen!" And, on the eastern seaboard, it was rumored that the Nixon cabinet had discussed whether the article could be used to justify reducing outlays to aid blacks. In denying the rumor, Nixon's aide Daniel Patrick Moynihan commented, "I know what Jensen is going through. I got the same treatment for almost exactly the opposite hypothesis."[8] (A few years earlier, Moynihan had suggested that many black difficulties in later life arise out of the conditions of child rearing.)

Style and Substance of the Controversy

There was no precise statement of a "position" in Jensen's sprawling and allusive argument. He defended at length the longstanding conclusion that a large fraction of the differences within the white population can be attributed to inheritance and acknowledged that differences between groups have some environmental sources. "But the possible importance of genetic factors in racial behavioral differences has been greatly ignored, almost to the point of being a tabooed subject, just as were the topics of venereal disease and birth control a generation or so ago."

The statement that most nearly asserts racial genetic disadvantage is this.

> . . . [T]he discrepancy in . . . average performance [of the disadvantaged, compared to the norm] cannot be completely or directly attributed to discrimination or inequalities in education. It seems not unreasonable . . . to hypothesize that genetic factors may play a part. . . . The preponderance of the evidence is, in my opinion, less consistent with a strictly environmental hypothesis than with a genetic hypothesis, which, of course, does not exclude the influence of environment. . . .

---

[8] Daniel P. Moynihan, "Comment: Jensen Not 'Must Reading' in the Nixon Cabinet," *Journal of Social Issues* 26, no. 2 (Spring 1970) : 191–92.

The language is equally moderate throughout the paper, but Jensen's many comments on race differences, alongside his massive emphasis on heredity, were read as a one-sided assertion.

The news media were not able to weigh matters as delicately as Jensen had. Fairly typical is *Newsweek*'s summary: "Dr. Jensen's view, put simply, is that most blacks are born with less 'intelligence' than most whites."[9] Journalists who had more space at their disposal did a remarkably good job of touching on the range of issues, though it was the epigrammatic or emphatic statements by the critics that were quoted.

It is impossible to summarize what was said. The first wave of solicited replies ran to the same length, in total, as Jensen's article. Further responses in the summer issue of *HER* ran to another 150 pages. The tone ranged from condemnation to applause, from polemic to technical analysis. Jensen made full use of his opportunity to reply to the first wave of criticism. Similarly, a *New York Times Magazine*[10] profile of Jensen's personality and theory drew page upon page of correspondence. Jensen had the opportunity to set forth, letter by letter, just what he agreed or disagreed with.

One display of the academic community in action took place at Berkeley. In a spring when the radicals were smiting the Establishment with any cudgel, no one took seriously the demands for Jensen's scalp. There was an attempted invasion of his classes and harassment of a research assistant that drew an editorial frown from the faraway *Times,* but most of the agitation was confined to the campus newspaper. A few faculty members opposed to Jensen's views decided that a public debate was needed to set the campus straight. The university administration assumed control and saw fair play, setting up a symposium before an audience limited to an equal number of observers chosen by each side. The three-hour proceedings were videotaped and shown to an evening meeting which drew a serious audience of several hundred—large even for Berkeley—on a spring evening just before finals.

Jensen made a brief, considered, and articulate statement. Genetic race differences he spoke of as merely a hypothesis meriting investigation, saying nothing that can be read as even a tentative judgment that the gene pool of blacks is somehow inferior. Two geneticists, two sociologists, and an educational psychologist replied. Whatever matters were capable of being posed in intellectual and disciplined terms were so posed and debated for the Berkeley students. While panel members hit hard at various points, they did not invoke ideology or passion.

---

[9] *Newsweek,* March 31, 1969, p. 84.

[10] Lee Edson, "jensenism, *n.* The Theory that I.Q. is Largely Determined by the Genes," *New York Times Magazine,* August 31, 1969, pp. 10–11+. For correspondence, see September 21, 1969, pp. 4+ and September 28, 1969, pp. 38+.

Meanwhile, there had been another type of formal reaction from academe. The executive board of the Society for Psychological Study of Social Issues was composed of eighteen leading psychologists noted for their liberal social concerns. Several of them were deep into civil rights and compensatory education activities. Six weeks after the news broke they issued a measured statement[11] denying that there is any technique for investigating innate racial differences under current conditions, asserting that the failure of compensatory education was in the planning and scope and not in the idea, and decrying heredity-*vs.*-environment statements as oversimplified. The American Anthropological Association adopted a less restrained resolution.[12]

Jensen was right about the disappointing results of compensatory efforts, inasmuch as even now we have no compensatory method, reproducible on a large scale, of demonstrated value. The article seemed to say that efforts toward compensatory education ought to be dropped, overdramatizing the failure. But buried within the paper was recognition that intensive small-scale programs often succeed, and in actuality Jensen's position was a call for invention of effective educational procedures.

Heritability was taken up by Jensen as if it has some bearing on compensatory policies. But even the most hereditarian position does not hold that ranks in performance will remain stable when the initially low-ranking children are treated specially. Jensen let this point drop from sight. He wrote strongly on heritability because he thought that other psychologists had spread a false cliché. "Speakers and writers on intelligence, mental retardation, cultural disadvantage, and the like, . . . state, often with an evident sense of virtue and relief, that

---

[11] Society for the Psychological Study of Social Issues, "Statement," *American Psychologist* 24 (November 1969) : 1039.

[12] Resolution submitted by the executive board to the membership on March 5, 1970. There were two companion resolutions, adopted at a national convention after a symposium of Jensen critics and ratified by a mail vote of the membership. The vote on the main resolution was 1,795 to 239. (Personal communication, Edward J. Lehman, July 17, 1973). The resolutions are reprinted in Jensen, *Genetics and Education,* pp. 38–39. We may skip over the statements of general liberal, equalitarian principles, and extract the comments most specifically on Jensen's work.

"All races possess the abilities needed to participate fully . . . in modern civilization. And whereas . . . Jensen . . . cast doubt on this conclusion; . . . the article reviewed is not consistent with the facts of psychology, biology, or anthropology. . . . [T]he data assembled in Jensen's article are wholly inadequate for the conclusions drawn and we reassert . . . that: There is no scientifically established evidence to justify the exclusion of any race from the rights guaranteed by the Constitution of the United States. . . ."

One can agree with the sentence of the resolution stating that "any *ad hominem* response to a scholarly paper is regrettable." It seems far-fetched to accuse Jensen of wishing to deny constitutional rights to persons of below-average IQ, whatever their race, or to attribute to him the view that blacks cannot "participate fully." To be sure, such views are held by some of those who took comfort from his article.

modern psychology has overthrown the 'belief in fixed intelligence'." Jensen did not manage to restore the balance. The conventional results that he reiterated were taken by readers to be a new and controversial doctrine.

Jensen was also attempting to balance talk about race. He rightly protested the propaganda that had science proving races indistinguishable with respect to any psychoactive genes. It seems that Jensen intended to speak for openmindedness and continued research on racial characteristics. But as the spotlight excited him he became more forceful. The *New York Times Magazine* offers this fantastic quote:

> There are no "black" genes or "white" genes; there are intelligence genes which are found in populations in different proportions, somewhat like the distribution of blood types. The number of intelligence genes seems to be lower, overall, in the black population than in the white.

This apparently is a garbled version of an explanation given to a reporter by telephone, but Jensen did not set the record straight when he could have.

For many, the distressing part of the Jensen affair was that it misdirected attention. Consider the ambivalence of Joshua Lederberg in his newspaper column on science.

> [T]he article is a thoughtful review. . . . [P]opular commentaries . . . have emphasized a few controversial (and I would say incautious) remarks at the expense of a great deal of Dr. Jensen's wisdom and scholarly reserve.

> The genetic hypothesis is almost irrelevant to Jensen's most cogent point [about adapting instruction]. . . . If a 6-year old has a deficit in abstract thinking, it is relatively unimportant for educational policy whether this is the fault of the genes or a cultural maladaptation. . . . The genetic hypothesis does matter if it discourages educators and scientists from probing more deeply into the crucial early years.[13]

Lederberg remarked on malnutrition and lead poisoning in the ghettos, cited a study in which poor children whose mothers had received dietary supplements during pregnancy averaged eight IQ points above controls, and ended, "With effects like that, why are we discussing anything else?"

The controversy reached a wide audience and Jensen's name became well-known. But outside the professional literature the dispute got little space. The usual magazine editor covered the controversy just once; the *Reader's Guide* lists just twelve articles in 1969 and only two in 1970.

The Atlantic Monthly Provides a Little War

In 1971, the Jensen episode had a peculiar echo. Richard Herrnstein offered to the *Atlantic Monthly* a paper discussing IQs, squarely within the tradition of

---

[13] Joshua Lederberg, "Racial Alienation and Intelligence," *Harvard Educational Review* 39 (Summer 1969) : 611–15.

Atlantic Monthly essays on scientific themes.[14] The editor accepted the essay provisionally but asked Herrnstein to make it livelier and to bring in questions of policy. By mutual agreement, the topic of race differences was inserted at this time. In Herrnstein's final sixteen pages (mostly on long-established psychological generalizations), less than one and one-half pages touched on racial differences. Every paragraph of the editors' 1,200-word introduction, however, brought in the racial theme. This filter distorted Herrnstein's communication and in a sense politicized a paper that had originally been almost textbookish.

Herrnstein spelled out once again the facts indicating that IQ differences within the white population, under present social conditions, have a large hereditary component, adding that such estimates of heritability "say nothing" about differences between groups. Then Herrnstein offended some sensitive souls by a single sentence saying that possible genetic differences affecting average IQs of groups should be open to investigation.

Much louder criticism was stirred up by Herrnstein's parsing of a simple syllogism: Make conditions wholesome and uniform for everyone, and the power of heredity will in the course of generations stratify any achievement-based society so that a child remains in his father's status. Herrnstein did not suggest—as many readers thought—that the offspring of the blacks or of the present poor are doomed to form the low caste of the future. His position was simply that, if there is no variance in environment, nothing save heredity (and luck) can influence status.

The Jensen drama was replayed on a small stage. The editors supplied copies of the finished article to many academics and invited publishable letters. Two issues later, the *Atlantic Monthly* carried seven pages of letters, some condemning Herrnstein and some endorsing his facts and logic. The Harvard radicals mobilized to demand Herrnstein's dismissal. Herrnstein found himself challenged to debate about a position that seems as documented and as guarded as a statement about human affairs can be. The range of complaints was confusingly broad, but there was no logical rejoinder to Herrnstein's syllogism.

The only fault of the Herrnstein paper is its silence on matters of social philosophy.[15] It is assumed that those social contributions that derive from mental ability are the proper basis for distributing rewards and respect. But the paper is not factually or logically deficient,[16] and not at all racist.

The Herrnstein affair did not live beyond three issues of the *Atlantic Monthly* and received only the briefest of attention outside Cambridge. Agitation on the Harvard campus continued for a year, fomented by radicals needing

---

[14] Richard J. Herrnstein, "I.Q.," *Atlantic Monthly,* September 1971, pp. 43–64.

[15] Robert Paul Wolff, letter, *Atlantic Monthly,* December 1971, p. 106.

[16] P. E. Meehl, "Nuisance Variables and the *Ex Post Facto Design,*" in *Minnesota Studies in the Philosophy of Science,* eds. M. Radner and S. Winokur (Minneapolis, 1970), vol. IV.

a target.[17] The controversy over Herrnstein was a journalistic stunt in the tradition of Hearst-to-Remington: "You provide the pictures, I'll provide the war."[18] The *Atlantic Monthly* provided no more than a popgun fusillade—but it is liveliness that sells papers and magazines.

Proposals to Restrict Inquiry

The controversies over race and intelligence revived the meta-controversy over social science itself to which Yaron Ezrahi's paper in this symposium is addressed. Whereas the social scientist has insisted upon his right and duty to inquire into all human affairs, the community is increasingly unsympathetic. It has become difficult for white social scientists to work in the black community; black distrust was surely increased by the Jensen affair.

To make a statement about race differences even at the level of hypothesis was to offend blacks and threaten their political interests in the America of 1969.[19] Many laymen and scholars condemned Jensen not for false impressions he might have given but for making *any* statement about race. *Vide* one letter to the *Times:* "The wise scientist will not devote himself to research on the relation between race and ability; the wise university will not honor those who do, or disseminate their work."[20]

Jensen's stance was and is that society should encourage the interested scholar to investigate *any* hypothesis.

> . . . [U]nnecessary difficulties arise when we allow the scientific question to become mixed up with the social-political aspects of the problem, for when it does we are less able to think clearly about either set of questions. The question of

---

[17] Herrnstein has published a full account of his experience with "the hostility of the radicals, the obscurantism of some academics." R. J. Herrnstein, *I.Q. in the Meritocracy* (Boston, 1973), pp. 3–59.

Interest in the Jensen and Herrnstein debates faded quickly from the national scene and might now be regarded as ancient history, but for the deliberate efforts to keep the fight going. On the one hand, the radicals at Berkeley and Cambridge have not forgotten, and surface from time to time with a new attack. On the other hand, Jensen and Herrnstein have become increasingly committed to winning attention for their views. In addition to the new books cited here and in footnote 7, Jensen has expanded the *HER* paper and his rejoinders to critics into a 400-page book that no longer suspends judgment about race differences as the 1967 and 1969 papers did. Now he concludes: "All the major facts would seem to be comprehended quite well by the hypothesis that something between one-half and three-fourths of the average IQ difference between American Negroes and whites is attributable to genetic factors. . . ." Arthur R. Jensen, *Educability and Group Differences* (New York, 1973), p. 363.

[18] It is significant that Herrnstein's book expands his *Atlantic* article to 160 pages but omits all discussion of the existence of and explanation for race differences.

[19] Carl T. Rowan, "How Racists Use 'Science' to Degrade Black People," *Ebony,* May 1970, pp. 31–40.

[20] Eleanor Greenwald, letter, *New York Times Magazine,* September 21, 1969, p. 4.

whether there are or are not genetical racial differences in intelligence is independent of any questions of its implications, whatever they may be.[21]

The root of Jensen's martyrdom is that word "Unnecessary."

Law Professor J. D. Hyman spoke for the other side: "Sensitivity to the social problems of our day requires a clear showing of the high probability of their truth before hypotheses are advanced which reinforce the stereotypes on which our caste system has been built."[22] One infers that the social scientist with a disturbing hypothesis should pursue it privately, keeping his dark suspicions secret until he has a solid case. Given the social nature of the scientific enterprise, this seems as inhospitable to heterodoxy as an outright embargo on a research topic.

Pygmalion in the Headlines

After Jensen, the work on testing that received most attention from the press was *Pygmalion in the Classroom*.[23] This work too was a matter of heated controversy, but the controversy was wholly concealed from public view. We had better wonder why.

Robert Rosenthal had ingeniously demonstrated that the psychologist experimenting with animals tends, all unconsciously, to make his results favor the hypothesis he initially tended (or wanted) to believe. Perhaps he makes nonrandom errors of observations; perhaps he preconditions subjects differently. In time, Rosenthal launched a study to demonstrate that similar effects occur in the school when teachers "know what to expect." Teachers in a California school were handed a list of pupils who supposedly had shown exceptional promise on a test but who in fact had been picked at random. Months later, we are told, these children had progressed more than their unheralded classmates. The teacher supposedly created talent by her own ministrations, to fulfill the prophecy.

In my view, *Pygmalion* merits no consideration as research. The "experimental manipulation" of teacher belief was unbelievably casual—one sheet of paper added to the teacher's in-basket, which apparently moved within seconds to the wastebasket. The technical reviews indicate that the advertised gains of the "magic" children were an artifact of crude experimental design and improper statistical analysis. (No doubt there are expectancy effects in the class-

[21] Arthur R. Jensen, "Can We and Should We Study Race Differences?" in *Disadvantaged Child,* ed. Jerome Hellmuth, vol. 3, *Compensatory Education: A National Debate* (New York, 1970), pp. 124–57. The quotation is from p. 149.

[22] J. D. Hyman, letter, *New Republic,* October 25, 1969, pp. 30–31.

[23] Robert Rosenthal and Lenore Jacobsen, *Pygmalion in the Classroom* (New York, 1968). For critical analyses and rejoinders, see *Pygmalion Revisited,* eds. Janet Elashoff and R. E. Snow (Worthington, Ohio, 1971).

room, even when tests are not used.[24] The question ought to be whether tests add to bias or instead bring expectations closer to the truth. On that there is no direct evidence.)

The *Pygmalion* study was carried out from 1964 to 1966 and was given a preliminary report in a few pages of a scholarly book on "experimenter effects," followed by fuller scholarly reports and news stories. By 1968 Rosenthal had produced *Pygmalion in the Classroom,* plus articles in *Psychology Today* and *Scientific American.* The publisher of the book sent the manuscript to referees; the opinions ranged from high praise to sharp criticism. The decision to issue the book was not unreasonable, but one might have expected the finished book to acknowledge that the methodology was in dispute. Worse, while scores of pages were given to the desired "findings" from California, fewer than 500 words were used to report a Massachusetts study by Rosenthal in which a "significant" difference favored the control group!

We need not trace here the controversy within the profession or spell out the objections. Much of the professional debate is conveniently collected in the Elashoff-Snow volume (cited in footnote 23), a project of the National Society for the Study of Education. The vehemence of the criticism is only incompletely suggested by this remark from R. L. Thorndike's review (there reprinted): *Pygmalion* "is so defective technically that one can only regret that it ever got beyond the eyes of the original investigators!"

Now what was the public being told? Nothing, about the controversy. Much, however, about the study as evidence that mental tests are doing harm. It is significant that the media ignored the loud but cloistered battle over the quality of the evidence. The *New York Times* gave sympathetic front-page play to the preliminary report. Out of thirty column inches, one inch on the carry-over page mentioned that studies in Massachusetts and Ohio "have not clearly corroborated" the California findings. Nothing said about evidence in the opposite direction—indeed the next paragraph returns to restating that teacher expectations are a powerful determinant.

Robert Coles,[25] reviewing the full-length report for *The New Yorker,* went out of his way to praise what it said about the "ethical dimensions of scientific work." If Coles had heard of doubts about the scientific dimensions of the work, no hint appears. In *The New York Review of Books,* Herbert Kohl was equally sure of the conclusions, but he found the Rosenthal work defective ethically, because the experimenters had "assumed god-like" roles and acquired

---

[24] Ray C. Rist, "Student Social Class and Teacher Expectations: The Self-Fulfilling Prophecy in Ghetto Education," *Harvard Educational Review* 40 (August 1970): 411–51.

[25] Robert Coles, "What Can You Expect?" *The New Yorker,* April 19, 1969, pp. 169–77.

knowledge "through deceit and bad faith."[26] Coles' asides—about "experts, the secular gods of the twentieth century," "the effect a pair of scientists armed with tons of paper can have," and the "dense, muddled language" of theorists—are characteristic of an antirational tone present in nearly all the recent attacks on testing and research into human differences. To be sure, some social scientists invite such criticism by writing as if numerical analyses are in themselves sufficient to settle issues of social policy.

EARLIER CHALLENGES TO MENTAL TESTING

Our thesis, that the hearing given to social evidence and issues depends on the times and the audience, is best demonstrated by stepping back to decades when the audience was attuned differently. The most useful examples are the arguments of Allison Davis in the late 1940s and the attacks by Walter Lippmann and William C. Bagley in the 1920s.

Social-Class Bias: A Charge Fails to Ignite

From 1945 to 1953 Davis, a sociologist, contended that existing tests underestimated the abilities of children of the working class. His challenge was not accepted by the profession at the time and, despite its significance, was ignored by the public. The basic scholarly document combined the doctoral study of Kenneth Eells with short essays written by Davis and others to place Eells' results in a policy context.[27] Eells compared children from higher and lower classes and found the latter weaker on nearly all test items. But verbal items, especially those referring to uncommon words and objects, magnified the group difference. Poor children would rank higher, said Davis, if the test were limited to "fair" items. He tried out tests of this kind and then reported that according to such tests "hereditary ability" is about the same in all socioeconomic groups.[28]

Davis and his colleagues sought attention for their thesis by means of numerous semipopular presentations to lay and professional groups and in articles in *Scientific Monthly, The Journal of the National Education Association,* etc. Their argument was not given much attention by educators. Benjamin Fine, the education writer for the *New York Times,* did run two pieces about a Davis speech to school superintendents. Six months later,[29] Fine included Davis' work in a pro-and-con piece on tests for the *New York Times Magazine.* Fine concluded only

---

[26] Herbert Kohl, "Great Expectations," *The New York Review of Books,* September 12, 1968, pp. 30–32.

[27] Kenneth Eells et al., *Intelligence and Cultural Differences* (Chicago, 1951).

[28] Allison Davis, "Socio-Economic Influences on Learning," *Phi Delta Kappan* 32 (January 1951) : 253–56.

[29] Benjamin Fine, "More and More, the IQ Idea is Questioned," *New York Times Magazine,* September 18, 1949, pp. 7 ff.

that tests should be used sensibly. Mild as this essay was, it provoked outraged howls from psychologists, but the published letters, while countering other criticisms of tests that Fine had mentioned, ignored the Davis material. Likewise, Davis' own popular articles and speeches were left unanswered, hence the challenge withered.

Such statements as "Half the ability in this country goes down the drain because of the failure of intelligence tests. . . ."[30] were not ignored *within* the testing profession. Professional symposia featured attacks on the new Davis tests. Although Davis expected his tests to eliminate class differences in IQ and found this in his initial studies, other investigators found as much social class difference on the Davis tests as on traditional ones. Moreover, his tests were not good predictors of success in school, and so they were dismissed.[31] Davis and his group were so discouraged that they allowed striking results they obtained on a "fair" individual test to drop from sight.[32]

As the argument developed, the central policy issue was misperceived. Davis' challenge was actually not to tests but to traditional schooling, as some material in the Eells volume shows. Traditional tests predict who will succeed in a schooling that makes use of abstract ideas and experiences the middle-class child is likely to have. At base, the Davis argument was that there are reasoning abilities in the lower class that schooling *could* capitalize upon if it were redesigned to be less verbal and less culture-laden. (This is analogous to Jensen's view that there are memory abilities in the lower class, on which schooling could rely.) Davis' campaign failed for several reasons. He challenged the testers when they were in public favor. He concerned himself with "persons of low status," and there were no militant voices to take up that cause. And, if it were true that his new tests identified potentially capable children for whom someone ought to invent better schooling, that advice was too vague for public debate or action.

Morons, Immigrants, and Efficiency Experts

The principal tenet of the Progressive movement at the turn of the century was the power of social science to redirect and reshape society. Darwin and Comte, between them, had inspired a fervor for subjecting man and his institutions to scientific, iconoclastic analysis. Within the Darwinist camp, such men as T. H. Huxley and L. F. Ward read the evolutionary message as a call for social activism, to redesign institutions so that men would prosper in them. The

---

30 Allison Davis, "Poor People Have Brains, Too," *Phi Delta Kappan* 30 (April 1949) : 294–95.

31 See a review of the Davis-Eells Test by Raleigh M. Drake in *The Fifth Mental Measurements Yearbook*, ed. Oscan Krisen Buros (Highland Park, N.J., 1959), p. 461.

32 Robert D. Hess, "Controlling Culture Influence in Mental Testing: An Experimental Test," *Journal of Educational Research* 49 (September 1955) : 53–58.

American reformers expected factual analyses to free society from ills that ranged from political corruption to prostitution, from despoliation of the environment to child labor. The social survey took its place alongside the journalistic exposé as a way of determining what should be set right and how. Efficiency and scientific management like that of industry were to be brought to social institutions.[33]

In education, few studies had more influence than Ayres' *Laggards in Our Schools* (1909),[34] which counted how many children were below the grade normal for their age and tallied up the economic and social costs of such retardation. At that same time, the child-study movement was deploring the emotional costs of a Procrustean school system. With child labor going out, the junior high school and vocational education coming in, and high-school enrollment booming, the superintendents of 1920 were greatly concerned about coping with the range of abilities. The mental test, fresh from its triumphs in the army, promised to sort out pupils who should move fast, those who should move slowly, those who should go to college, and those who should not. The testers and their audience were sympathetic with the bright child forced to poke along at the average pace and with the dull child pressed to keep up. The tests would allow grouping by ability and would pick out the talented children for special encouragement.

Virtually everyone favored testing in schools; the controversies arose because of incautious interpretations made by the testers and, even more, by popular writers. Debate was touched off by the official memoir on the army data—specifically, by the two pages (out of 800) describing the distribution of soldiers' scores. Scores had been converted to a mental-age scale and, after reporting the average score of thirteen for the white draft, the writers added two sentences by way of popularization, "A moron has been defined as anyone with a mental age of from 7 to 12 years. [By] this definition . . . almost half of the white draft would have been morons."[35] The comparability of the sample to 13-year-olds need not have been too surprising at a time when most adults had left school by age 14. But the theoretical standard of maturity had been taken as 16 years of mental age, which argued that the typical soldier was markedly deficient.

Popular writers, especially those associated with the eugenics movement, drew broad elitist conclusions from this "finding."[36] Paul Popenoe, for example,

---

[33] Raymond Callahan, *Education and the Cult of Efficiency* (Chicago, 1962).

[34] Leonard C. Ayres, *Laggards in Our Schools* (New York, 1909).

[35] Robert M. Yerkes, "Psychological Examining in the United States Army," *Memoirs of the National Academy of Sciences* 15 (1921).

[36] Paul Popenoe, "Measuring Human Intelligence," *Journal of Heredity* 12 (May 1921): 231–36. The Goddard quotation comes from *Human Efficiency and Levels of Intelligence.* Albert Edward Wiggam, "The New Decalogue of Science," *The Century,* March 1922, pp. 643–50.

wrote: "Can we hope to have a successful democracy where the average mentality is 13?" and went on to quote Henry Goddard's reading of the data: "Obviously there are enough people of high intelligence to guide the Ship of State, if they are put in command. The disturbing fear is that the masses . . . will take matters into their hands." Albert Wiggam, a popularizer of science, wrote a deliberately outrageous piece for *The Century*. He declared that efforts to improve standards of living and education are folly because they allow weak elements in the genetic pool to survive. That men are born equal is "a great sentimental nebulosity"; social classes are "ordained by nature"; and "slum-people make the slums." In the clever talk of the 1920s, "moron" claimed as large a place as "Babbitt." As Vernon Parrington mourned, "morons . . . jar one's faith in human perfectibility. In the light of intelligence tests perhaps the whole romantic theory of democracy was only a will-o'-the-wisp. . . ."[37]

Racism, directed especially against immigrants from southern and eastern Europe, was active, and the army data provided ammunition for it. The psychologist C. C. Brigham was persuaded by one of the advocates of racial purity to rework the army data on ethnic groups into a book.[38] Brigham did warn, for example, that the Italians recently come to this country were probably not representative of the population of Italy, but his attempt to confine his conclusions to immigrants was not made prominent, and it escaped the attention of most persons who cited or attacked his work. Likewise, Brigham acknowledged that tests were not pure measures of innate ability, but he was sure that innate racial differences had been proved to exist. So closed was his mind that, in what purported to be the definitive tabulation of the army data by ethnic origin, he presented no cross-tabulation by years of schooling or the like. Social scientists quickly came to realize that the evidence proved nothing about group differences, and Brigham was the subject of criticism, as I point out below. But Brigham let his book stand for years. His only published acknowledgment of criticism was a side remark; psychologists should work on their data and ignore armchair challengers.[39] Brigham did, in 1930, disavow his studies in a professional journal,[40] and since that time psychologists have been happy to point to this as evidence of the scientist's openness to correction. But Brigham's "retraction" was on the largely irrelevant grounds that the army tests were inhomogeneous; he bowed not at all to the professional consensus that ethnic comparisons themselves are meaningless.

---

[37] Vernon L. Parrington, *Main Currents of American Thought,* vol. 3 (New York, 1930), p. xxviii.

[38] C. C. Brigham, *A Study of American Intelligence* (Princeton, 1923).

[39] C. C. Brigham, "Value of Tests in Examinations of Immigrants," *Industrial Psychology* 1 (June 1926) : 413–17.

[40] C. C. Brigham, "Intelligence Tests of Immigrant Groups," *Psychological Review* 37 (March 1930) : 158–65.

Occasionally a psychologist took to a popular magazine to correct false impressions. In the *Atlantic Monthly*[41] Robert Yerkes, a principal figure in the army testing, condemned Wiggam's distortions. But Yerkes then drew indefensible conclusions of his own. ". . . [It] is quite commonly believed," he said, "that intelligence increases with schooling. This, however, is flatly contradicted by results of research, for it turns out that the main reason that intelligence status improves with years of schooling is the elimination of the less capable pupil." Not more than 10 percent of the population are capable of earning the B.A., as their earlier departure from school proves (!).

Two months later (May 1923) Walter Lippmann lambasted Yerkes and Brigham in *The Century*. He objected particularly to the claim that the tests measured innate abilities and foretold who could profit from education; also, he objected to the comparisons of ethnic groups. The essay in *The Century* was Lippmann's second position paper. The first appeared in installments in *The New Republic;* with rejoinders and extensions, he published ten articles there between October 1922 and May 1923.[42] There too, the foe was the elitist who argued that democracy, even when buttressed by education, could not work. While Lippmann was basically favorable to the tests as an aid in school management, he became increasingly vehement in attacking psychologists. By the end of the series, his language was strong indeed: "Men of science presume to dogmatize," "purely statistical illusion," "behind the will to believe, . . . the will to power," "self-deception as a preliminary to public deception." The "deception" was the claim that native intelligence was being measured.

Terman, who had been a special target, replied to *The New Republic* articles with a heavy-handed sarcasm that gave thoughtful consideration to none of Lippmann's points. Elsewhere Terman himself acknowledged the debatability of some working hypotheses, but he apparently saw Lippmann as a presumptuous layman to be routed. Lippmann, for example, had said (as we would say today) that early experience in the home might account for much of the correlation of IQ with social class. Here is part of Terman's reply.

> [If so, it would be] high time that we were investigating the IQ effects of different kinds of baby-talk, different versions of Mother Goose, and makes of pacifiers and safety pins. . . . Does not Mr. Lippmann owe it to the world to abandon his role of critic and to enter this enchanting field of research?

---

[41] Robert M. Yerkes, "Testing the Human Mind," *Atlantic Monthly,* March 1923, pp. 358–70.

[42] The Lippmann papers and rejoinders in *New Republic* appeared as follows: October 25, 1922, pp. 213–15; November 1, 1922, pp. 246–48; November 8, 1922, pp. 275–77; November 15, 1922, pp. 297–98; November 22, 1922, pp. 328–30; November 29, 1922, pp. 9–11; January 3, 1923, pp. 145–46; May 2, 1923, pp. 263–64; May 9, 1923, pp. 295–96; May 16, 1923, pp. 322–23. The more comprehensive paper is "A Defense of Education," *The Century,* May 1923, pp. 95–103. Terman's reply is "The Great Conspiracy," *New Republic,* December 27, 1922, pp. 116–20; see also pp. 201, 289.

This served only to allow Lippmann an *ad hominem* rejoinder, followed by an exchange of sharp letters. Nothing was clarified, and readers were annoyed with Terman for refusing to discuss issues soberly.

Lippmann was confused at several points, and his tactics as a debater were not above reproach. Here is an excerpt from *The Century.*

> They are determined that education and opportunity shall not count, "for we must (*sic*) assume," says Dr. Brigham, "that we are measuring *native* or *inborn intelligence.*" To this we can reply that there is no law compelling professors to assume the very thing which they set out to prove. They are quite free to assume nothing and to conclude, if the facts point that way, that they are measuring very crudely some aspects of the mixture of native ability and acquired habits. That is in fact all that modest and critical psychologists claim for the tests. But, unfortunately, the modest and critical psychologists . . . have remained in the background, while their rasher colleagues have offered to the public a yellow science. The headline professors, be it said, to the dismay and chagrin of the true scientists in this field, have succeeded for the moment in producing something like a panic, using misleading statistics to destroy confidence in the value and possibilities of education.

If yellow science there be, it inspires yellow journalism. The quoted words on which the sarcasm focuses were a target of Lippmann's own making. In Brigham's context, the words clearly meant "We must assume this *or* the contrary." Brigham had used his sentence to launch a ten-page examination of alternative explanations, not to close off thought.

While Terman and a few other psychologists were chopping savagely at every critical head, there was also a dignified response. Just two months after Lippmann's first essay objecting to the "13-year-old" interpretation, Frank N. Freeman had gotten into the pages of a professional journal a note showing that the mental-age statement was indefensible and saying to his colleagues, in effect, "We must stop talking nonsense about these important matters."[43] As the criticisms continued, Freeman put the central issues into a series of questions, obtained answers from leading testers including Terman and Yerkes, and published a consensus in *The Century* that should have satisfied Lippmann on every point. It said, among other things, that there was no logical way to judge the native ability of groups that had had dissimilar upbringings. (A close reading of Brigham shows that his book had included every one of the specific qualifying remarks required to keep his statements literally in line with Freeman's consensus. Yet the message Brigham transmitted was not muted a bit by his grudging caveats.)

With the appearance of Freeman's consensus statement and an equally judicious piece in the *Atlantic Monthly* by Henry Link,[44] the controversy vanished

---

[43] Frank N. Freeman, "The Mental Age of Adults," *Journal of Educational Research* 6 (December 1922) : 441–44.

[44] Henry C. Link, "What is Intelligence?" *Atlantic Monthly,* September 1923, pp. 374–85. Frank N. Freeman, "A Referendum of Psychologists," *The Century,* December 1923, pp. 237–45.

from the press. These papers aroused no comment: They were water on a bonfire that had already burned out. The entire debate had come and gone in an eighteen-month period. It provided some lively reading, but it changed few minds. At most, it led psychologists of the time to be as circumspect in public as in their professional writings. This apparently was the only aim of the critics; Lippmann endorsed such use of tests as Freeman's consensus called for. A more restrictive immigration law was passed, as would have happened without the army data on ethnic groups. The mental-age scale for adults was adjusted, but not abandoned even in the face of continuing intraprofessional criticism. The heredity-environment issue remained the subject of heated intraprofessional debate. Reviews by the National Society for the Study of Education in 1928 and 1940 settled little, because the contending parties put a quite different coloration on the evidence.[45] Only stray echoes of this scholarly dispute reached the public, however, until the issue was politicized in the 1960s.

Biographies Written in Advance?

William James had warned psychologists that to understand man was not to write his biography in advance, but the testers came very close in their estimate as to how much education a man could use and what careers he could thrive in. More serious, when the tests indicated who could enter the college preparatory program and before that indicated who should go into the "fast" section of an early grade, the tests began to *determine* fates. The testers intended to shield the child destined to be a worker from the rigors of an academic curriculum. Such sorting would reduce distaste for schooling, prevent failure, and retain him in school longer. Testers said that the IQ was constant, hence to make decisions early was merciful and just. Hostility to this determinism was a central theme of many essays by William Bagley,[46] a conservative educational theorist, and it entered tangentially into Lippmann's writings. This attack too was answered by Terman, Guy M. Whipple, and a few others, again in a rhetoric that tended to beg the issues.[47] Bagley's is a "Christian Science Psychology," said Terman, and his vision "blurred by the moist tears of sentiment." The peroration of Whipple's vice-presidential address to the American Association for Advancement of Science was

---

[45] *Nature and Nurture,* ed. Guy M. Whipple, *Twenty-seventh Yearbook of the National Society for the Study of Education.* (Bloomington, Ill., 1928). *Intelligence: Its Nature and Nurture,* ed. Guy M. Whipple, *Thirty-ninth Yearbook of the National Society for the Study of Education.* (Bloomington, Ill., 1940).

[46] William C. Bagley, *Determinism in Education* (Baltimore, 1925). This reprints earlier papers.

[47] Lewis M. Terman, "The Psychological Determinist; or Democracy and the I.Q.," *Journal of Educational Research* 6 (June 1922): 57–62. Guy M. Whipple, "The Intelligence Testing Program and its Objectors—Conscientious and Otherwise," *School and Society* 17 (May 26, 1923): 561–68 and 17 (June 2, 1923): 596–604. The Hoover quotation is from *American Individualism.*

... I am not ashamed to find myself supported by Mr. Hoover, who declares that, "We in America have too much experience of life to fool ourselves into pretending that all men are equal in ability, in character, in intelligence, in ambition; that was part of the claptrap of the French Revolution."

This argument requires only passing attention here. It took place in educational and academic circles more than in public, and Bagley got too little support to keep the challenge alive. It is certainly a most important theme of the 1920s and of the present, for it questions whether pupils who differ should be sorted into educations different in kind, or different in pace, or different in method of instruction. (The constancy issue as such was less important even in the 1920s than the debate suggested, for in their writings to the profession Terman and the others advised periodic retesting and recommended that decisions be adjusted when the IQ changed.) The wisdom of sorting pupils into distinct programs deserved public scrutiny it did not get. Streaming was the obvious answer to the problem of laggards and dropouts in an efficiency-minded decade. Today, with other social priorities, there is again uneasiness about sorting in school that shapes life chances. But philosophical issues remain unvoiced, while loaded, overblown issues, such as heritability, get all the attention. Society needs to think once again about the kind of equality it would prefer and about the desired relation among productivity, social status, and standard of living. Most of all, it needs to distinguish between education as preparation for service to society, education as a preparation to get more out of living, and education as a means of certifying social status.

SOME POSSIBLE GENERALIZATIONS

The Zeitgeist and the Media

Controversies over social science are not created by findings as such. At any time, the professional literature is full of socially important results that are potential raw material for journalism. The journalist, by and large, controls what becomes public (except where the social scientist himself is a talented publicist). The topics of controversy about tests were always there to be exploited, after 1905. More facts became available each year, but there were few surprises. There is complete harmony between the consensus statement of 1923 and the SPSSI statement of 1969. It is hard to see that any one of the controversies changed any minds (except as they rigidified the positions of a Terman or a Jensen) or even enlightened its public. At best, controversy corrected an incautious and unpopular statement here or there. Journalism has no corrective for misstatements that are popular.

Repeatedly, we have seen journalists mining scholarly reports for controversial copy, distorting the original to make it more exciting, pointing up disagreements, and sometimes reporting only the iconoclastic side. Man bites

Establishment is news. But the journalist cannot keep alive a message the public is not attuned to hear.

There is a tide in the affairs of issues. When the nation had ordered up businesslike public administration, Bagley could not get attention for a philosophical dissent. Around 1960, when eyes were on international competition and schools were charged with slackness, John Gardner's *Excellence* had a ready market. The same market, short years later, is avid for attacks on the competitive attitude and on the work ethic itself. The public of the 1920s was sour on immigrants; hence Brigham's racial comparisons were popular and his critics got little hearing. In the 1970s a proposal merely to do research on ethnic differences is howled down. The times were against Davis and Bagley; the times favored Rosenthal and Terman. Jensen scorned the *Zeitgeist* and became a target of scorn himself.

The usual controversy fades away quickly and seems not to alter the trend of social policy. Perhaps the controversies are evidence that broad changes in social thought and policy are taking place, more than they are determiners of policy. When a fresh spring air mass sweeps over the plains of the Midwest, brief lightning and hailstorms play upon scattered localities along its edge. The storms are dramatic, but the energy within them is trivial in proportion to the momentum of the oncoming mass and the inertia of the one in possession of the territory. In the first half of this century the American system turned from laissez-faire to rationalization, system, and an increasingly managerial government. Hoover's "individualism" and what Parrington called the "romantic idea of human perfectibility" were both pushed aside; the controversy over tests was a symptom of the shift of forces.

The world view entrenched before World War II is now under attack, and an alternative scheme that cherishes pluralism, affiliations within local communities, and fulfillment rather than "perfection" is taking shape. It is too early to judge whether the new view or the old one will dominate the next generation, but, I suggest, it is this struggle for the minds of men and not concern for specifics, such as mental tests, that has generated the recent controversies.

How the Scientist Conducts Himself in Public

Once caught up in a public issue, scholars who are not journalists at heart lose their composure, their clarity, and their judgment. Scholars typically welcome the widest possible attention to their views, because they cherish the ideas and because they prize visibility and influence. What wonder, then, that a scholar given his once in a lifetime moment in the public eye will seek to make the moment memorable?

There is a fundamental difference between the style of the advocate in law and in journalism and the style of the scholar. An advocate tries to score every point, including those he knows he deserves to lose. The advocate who bridles his partisanship places his side at an "unfair" disadvantage. The scholars we have been discussing chose to play advocate when they went before the public, and they lost their scholarly balance. Terman spoke to the public only of the "constant" IQ, whereas to the profession he recommended periodic retesting. Brigham minimized the cautionary statements that cast doubt on his conclusions. And the public Jensen remains silent about the environmentalist positions the professional Jensen set forth in 1968. (In 1974 he answered a challenge by stating that his studies in 1967–1969 had changed his views, but the manuscripts lead me to think that most of the change was subsequent to 1969.)

The American academic is ill-trained to cope with the media and the public. In his normal life he speaks to a captive, notetaking audience. He writes for archives where those who want his thoughts *in extenso* can find them and where the reader can be trusted to weigh sentences in context. But the public reads the headlines and the snappy quotes and only half-remembers even them. In the dispute of the 1920s the journalists were the first offenders, with Wiggam's flamboyance and Lippmann's irreverent pinpricks. Terman and Whipple tried to play the same game and were hopelessly overmatched. Their sarcastic jabs appeared to be a frivolous and evasive response to serious if ill-specified charges. At best, they answered peripheral points while leaving main issues in confusion. The academic needs writing skills of an entirely unaccustomed order if he is to make sure that no unwanted implication will be drawn from a buried sentence, that no sentence quoted out of context will advocate what he does not believe, and that no colorful aside will be remembered instead of his main message. We may rail against the journalist for relaying what we said instead of what we meant to say, but mind-reading is not his job. We may rail against the public for not studying the text we put before them, but the writer in public is the servant, not the master, of the reader.

Academics in public take themselves too seriously. They write too much—one thinks of Jensen solemnly answering in print letter after letter, diffusing the force a few sharp retorts on central issues might have had. In public discourse, the more one says, the more trouble he creates for himself. That lesson comes hard to the academic.

The academic cannot control the timing of controversy. When the media offer space, they write a time for delivery into the contract. And the academic who on his own decides that the time has arrived for a public report must speak while the ear is turned his way. Hence we had one party to our controversies scribbling last-minute additions in airplanes, trying to meet a deadline and still make the most of his moment on stage. If it took a full year for Yerkes to get his reply to Wiggam into print, one can scarcely fault him for not obtaining reviews of his draft; yet the logical holes in his reply made it as damaging to his cause as helpful.

The associations and informal devices of the scholarly community are tested in these conflicts. Some acquit themselves well. The National Society for the Study of Education has a particularly good record in providing forums; its symposia on tests, inheritance, and expectancy effects have laid out the issues of disputes in 1922, 1928, 1940, and 1970. Even a politically active group such as SPSSI can at times make a judicious and stabilizing statement. But associations also can be rash and one-sided—witness the American Anthropological Association. Hence one cannot assume that scholars collectively will bring a debate to a sober finale. Nor does a balanced and unexciting summing-up get the public ear.

Consequences of Knowledge and Innocence

Since Eden, there have been uncertainties about whether knowledge is good. In the scientific ethic, and even more in the vision of social science held by the Progressives, knowledge is created to be made available. But there is a higher knowledge that records the effects of knowledge, and there is a social science still to be built that will clarify when and how knowledge is likely to be used to exploit or corrupt or dehumanize.

Inquiry is best left unrestricted. But the person publishing or popularizing a study does have responsibility for anticipating what his words will suggest to the rightists and the leftists, the exploiters and the *descamisados*. He is not irresponsible when his conclusions sway public decisions; he is irresponsible if his careless writing does so.

Our greatest difficulty is our innocence. When scholars spotlight a single question, pleased that social science can answer it, it often casts closely related questions into a deeper shadow. The testers of the 1920s were innocently pleased with their new powers. Tests improved the schools' judgments about academic promise, hence they were socially good. But were they wholly good? Whose children gained by the tests? Was there any risk of undue reliance on the new "scientific" judgments? Do the tests really increase mobility? And what does the very existence of social mobility mean for the health of a democratic society?

Testers as a profession have been accused of being servants of the interests, specifically, of "corporate liberalism."[48] While it is true that there was a natural affinity between their ideas and a hierarchically organized, differentiated society, testers worked *with* the system, not *for* it. The social dislocations that concerned them were those attributable to imperfect management, and they were to be remedied by a new technique, not a new philosophy. What distorted the public remarks of the testers was their unquestioning conviction that they were rendering a public service. It was so obviously cruel and inefficient to instruct every-

---

[48] David K. Cohen and Marvin Lazerson, "Education and the Corporate Order," *Socialism Revisited* 2 (March–April 1972) : 47–71.

one in the same things at the same pace, and so obvious that systematic measurement was providing better information for teachers, that the testers of the 1920s could conceive of no risk or error save that of failure to take the tests seriously. The spokesmen for tests, then and recently, were convinced that they were improving social efficiency, not making choices about social philosophy. Their soberly interpreted research did place test interpretation on a more substantial basis. But they did not study the consequences of testing for the social structure —a sociological problem that psychologists do not readily perceive.

The social scientist is trained to think that he does not know all the answers. The social scientist is not trained to realize that he does not know all the questions. And that is why his social influence is not unfailingly constructive.

The Jensen Controversy:
A Study in the Ethics and Politics
of Knowledge in Democracy

Yaron Ezrahi

THE ETHICS OF KNOWLEDGE AND AMERICAN
SOCIAL SCIENCES

With the evolution of science as a cooperative institutionalized enterprise in the modern society, the scientific community has confronted conflicting cultural demands. On the one hand, it has had to defend and justify the claims that science is politically neutral, that it advances universally valid knowledge, and that it is objective; and on the other hand, it has had to legitimate and mobilize support for the scientific enterprise within a particular culture and political system.

The specific ways in which scientists have encountered and coped with such conflicting demands naturally tend to vary in different types of societies. In the United States and a number of other Western countries, wide segments of the scientific community have responded to these demands by evolving a sort of professional ideology or a "social ethics of knowledge" that attempts to integrate the norms that regulate the internal life of science with a concept of the external functions of science.

According to this professional ideology, science is regarded as the highest embodiment of human rationality, and the social diffusion and application of scientific knowledge are conceived as means for the realization of the cherished social goal of enhancing rationality in human affairs. The contribution of science to the social deployment of rationality thus becomes perhaps the principal basis for the social legitimation of the scientific enterprise. Implicit in this view is the

(a)
ethics
(ideology)
of
knowledge

149

assumption that when the appropriate intellectual procedures that insure the universal validity and objectivity of scientific knowledge are followed and this knowledge is then incorporated into the context of social discourse and action, the qualities of that knowledge as universal and objective are not only retained, but through such a process they are also somehow transferred to and become the properties of the picture of reality and the modes of action into which knowledge is assimilated.

As the rationality of scientific knowledge is deemed a model or a paradigm for rationality in human affairs, the ethics of knowledge defines it as the duty of the scientist qua scientist to advocate and enhance the role of science as a basis for the social perceptions and manipulations of "reality." It tends to regard the scientist's commitment to the internal professional canons of science as implying a commitment to the realization of a vision of society based on scientific rationality.

The French molecular biologist, Jacques Monod, for example, who recently used the expression the "ethics of knowledge" to indicate the scientist's moral choice of a value system within which "the standard value is objective knowledge itself," typically extends the scientist's internal commitment to the scientific enterprise to a wider commitment to the goal of substituting knowledge for traditional beliefs and helping to "lay the foundations for a value system wholly compatible with science itself and able to serve humanity in its 'scientific age'."[1]

In the United States, the belief that it is the social role of the scientist to enhance the rationality and objectivity of public discourse and public policy and offer a special contribution to the solution of social problems has gained wide— if not universal—support among social scientists. It is perhaps sufficient to mention such founders of American social science as Lester Ward, the first president of the American Sociological Society, who was devoted to the use of sociology for social reform, was a public advocate of social planning, and contributed to popular journals, such as *Forum*;[2] or Charles Merriam, one of the founders of American political science and early president of its association who, as one of the creators of the Social Science Research Council and as a member of President Franklin D. Roosevelt's Committee on Administrative Management and in a variety of other active involvements in public affairs expressed and exemplified a commitment to the idea that the social scientist has a unique contribution to offer to public affairs.[3] More recently, another social scientist, economist Gunnar Myrdal, who became central in American social science by virtue of his comprehensive

---

[1] Jacques Monod, "On the Logical Relationship between Knowledge and Values," in *The Social Impact of Modern Biology,* ed. Watson Fuller (London, 1971), p. 15.

[2] See, in this connection, Richard Hofstadter, *Social Darwinism in American Thought* (Boston, 1955), pp. 67–84.

[3] See Barry Dean Karl, *Executive Reorganization and Reform in the New Deal* (Cambridge, Mass., 1963), pp. 37–81.

study of the Negro problem in the United States, expressed the view, which many American social scientists share, that it is the unique function of social scientists to furnish "the long range intellectual leadership thrusting society forward to overcome primitive impulses and prejudices and to move in the direction of rationality."[4]

An active commitment to the ethics of knowledge, combined with a special emphasis on the importance of the social sciences and the diffusion of knowledge for the preservation and development of the democratic system, is manifest in the social history of such learned societies as the American Political Science Association. Aside from encouraging its members to engage qua political scientists in public affairs, it has adopted the goal of spreading knowledge about the workings of government and has taken other steps to educate the public to be competent and effective citizens in a democratic polity.[5]

More recently the growing financial dependence of the social sciences upon government money and the pressures exerted by students on faculty have led quite a few social scientists to advocate social involvement not so much as a contribution to society but as a necessary means for securing the financial and human resources vital to the future of social sciences.[6] By and large, however, the legacy of the rationalism and optimism of the Enlightenment and of the "classical" beliefs in the unique role of the social sciences and of science in general in rationalizing society and enhancing social progress have remained dominant in the ethos and aspirations of contemporary American social scientists. A recent report sponsored by the National Academy of Sciences and the Social Science Research Council typically states that "it is in the definition of goals and the resolution of goal-conflict that the social sciences may have a unique opportunity for service."[7] The report recommends that social scientists be given the appropriate support to develop a system of social indicators that "could help assess the performance of social institutions and of special programs or policies established to remedy social ills and to move toward a more ideal society."[8] Such advocacy of the application of science to the assessment of the performance of

---

[4] Gunnar Myrdal, *Value in Social Theory* (London, 1958), pp. 24–25.

[5] See Albert Somit and Joseph Tanenhouse, *The Development of American Political Science: From Burgess to Behavioralism* (Boston, 1967).

[6] On the dependence of science on government and the consequences, see for example, Don K. Price, *Government and Science* (New York, 1960) and *The Scientific Estate* (Cambridge, Mass., 1965); Daniel Greenberg, *The Politics of American Science* (Harmondsworth, Eng., 1969); David Truman, "The Social Sciences: Maturity, Relevance, and the Problem of Training" in *Political Science and Public Policy,* ed. Austin Ranney (Chicago, 1968), p. 278.

[7] *The Behavioral and Social Sciences: Outlook and Needs,* a report by the Behavioral and Social Sciences Survey Committee, National Academy of Sciences (Washington, D.C., 1969), p. 95.

[8] Ibid., p. 102.

government programs extends the social role of the social scientists to include not only advice in the definition of goals and the identification and choice of means for their implementation, but also the evaluation of the results of government actions. This conception of their extensive role in public affairs is typical of the meliorist spirit of social scientists who are guided by the ethics of knowledge. It is a conception that asks the social scientist to share in functions, at least in an advisory role, that have been the principal prerogatives of political leadership and political institutions.

As a still further extension of this perspective, some social scientists have concluded that the growing functions of science in social life may lead or are already leading toward a new kind of society in which scientists and scientific knowledge occupy the central place. Typical of this view are Robert Lane's concept of the "knowledgeable society"[9] and Donald Campbell's "experimenting society."[10] The "knowledgeable society" is a society in which scientific knowledge and the institutions for the production and diffusion of knowledge are central to public discourse and action; it is a society in which "the criteria and scope of politics are shrinking while those of knowledge are growing."[11] In the "experimenting society," the interaction between science and public policy is so close that social action becomes a part of experimental research. It is a society "committed to reality testing, to self-criticism, to avoiding self-deception. It will say it like it is, face up to the facts, be undefensive and open in self-preservation. Gone will be the institutionalized bureaucratic tendency to present only a favorable picture in government reports."[12] The emphasis on "problem solving and self-healing"[13] would entrust the social scientists with a leading role as the "methodologists for the experimenting society," who among their many functions would collaborate "in preparing revisions for laws which needlessly prevent social reality testing."[14]

Although such sanguine views of the power or prospects of social science as a healer of human ills are surely not shared uniformly by social scientists, it may be that they expose a hidden vein of Utopianism that has more support in the social science community than is commonly supposed. There is in such Utopianism the presupposition that scientific knowledge, valid knowledge about

---

[9] Robert E. Lane, "The Decline of Politics and Ideology in a Knowledgeable Society," *The American Sociological Review* 31 (October 1966).

[10] Donald T. Campbell, "Methods for the Experimenting Society," preliminary draft of a paper delivered in abbreviated and extemporaneous form to the Eastern Psychological Association, April 17, 1971, and to the American Psychological Association, September 5, 1971. I am indebted to Professor Stephen P. Cohen of Harvard for calling my attention to this work.

[11] Lane, "Decline of Politics," p. 660.

[12] Campbell, "Methods for the Experimenting Society," p. 2.

[13] Ibid., p. 14.

[14] Ibid., p. 29.

"reality," is a "thing" or a "cultural construct" that is not transformed or particularized in the social context. *The social context from which the scientist must emancipate himself in order to be free to obey the logic of scientific investigation and arrive at a scientific outlook on reality is perceived also as the source of resistance that, guided by the ethics of knowledge, he must overcome in order to emancipate society from the forces of prejudice, myth, and politics and to clear the way for "objective experimentation" and "reality testing."* The "ethics of knowledge," in this perspective, is therefore very much the ethics of an embattled group. Its social agents are often presented as martyrs—modeled after Galileo, who had the courage to diffuse the truth even in defiance of strong religious, social, and political forces.

The belief that scientific truths should be not only intellectually but also culturally and socially compelling regardless of the particular nature of the social context seems to be reinforced by the thought that unlike other "commodities," the distribution and application of knowledge do not have to be regulated like scarce resources by the laws of competition or struggle. Epistemologically, there is nothing in the nature of scientific truth that requires that when it is possessed or is known by some, it be less available for the knowledge of others. Similarly, knowledge as technological power, e.g., medicine, can be used to heal some people without losing its potential to enhance the health of others. If knowledge is nevertheless used to gain economic, military, political, or any other form of advantage, this is attributed to the fact that certain social groups protect their privileged access to knowledge. They impose secrecy or furnish special financial rewards to scientists to subvert their allegiance to the ethic of spreading knowledge and rationality for the general welfare.

I would like to suggest that the ethics of knowledge, insofar as it tries to integrate the role of the scientist as scholar, devoted to the life of learning and bound by the internal canons of scientific rationality, with the role of this scientist as an objective nonpartisan agent for the diffusion and application of rational knowledge in human affairs, and insofar as it puts forward the supreme ideal that science become paradigmatic for social discourse and action, is based upon a misconception of the nature of politics and of the relation between politics and science.

THE DISCONTINUITIES BETWEEN SCIENCE AND POLITICS AS DISTINCT "CULTURAL SYSTEMS"

One reason why the ethics of knowledge as defined here leads to a misconception of the relations between science and politics is that there goes with this ethics a tendency to refuse to recognize that, especially in a democracy, the influence of political forces on the structure of social discourse and action is integral to the organization and management of public affairs. This tendency manifests itself in the reluctance to view political phenomena as if they had, like economic, legal, or other distinctive systems of social behavior, a unique un-derivative internal logic or as having a degree of irreducible autonomy vis-à-vis other sociocultural phenomena. A reductionist perception of political phenomena has been, as Giovanni Sartori pointed out, widely held among sociologists, econ-omists, psychologists, and other social scientists who, from their specialized disciplinary perspectives, view political structures and processes as dependent variables.[15] Sartori considers this tendency, which he characterizes as an "ob-jectivist bias," to be manifested in the habit of social scientists of perceiving socioeconomic phenomena as "facts" while considering political phenomena as "artifacts."[16]

Once the social scientist moves to the public domain to diffuse and apply his knowledge of "facts," this "objectivist bias" is often transformed into the belief that the diffusion and application of economic, psychological, sociological, or other social scientific knowledge may rationalize and depoliticize public opinion and public policy.[17] This "objectivist bias" encourages the social scientist to overlook the political dimension of the act of using the knowledge of the social sciences to "depoliticize" the definitions and handling of social problems. Social scientists imbued with this outlook may further tend to overlook the fact that the appeal to empirical science as a basis for evaluating social actions and institutions[18] implies a politically loaded preference for an approach that evaluates the appropriateness of actions in terms of their predictable or antici-pated effects over an approach for which the test of the appropriateness of an action is in its adherence to a "right principle"—a choice, which, as Max Weber indicated, expresses a preference for judging actions by their instrumen-tal rather than intrinsic value.[19]

---

[15] Giovanni Sartori, "From the Sociology of Politics to Political Sociology," in *Politics and the Social Sciences,* ed. Seymour Martin Lipset (New York, 1969), pp. 66–69.

[16] Ibid., p. 85.

[17] Aaron Wildavsky has pointed out that the advocates of the "gospel" of efficiency and the application of such economic techniques as program budgeting and cost-benefit analysis treat politics as a negative yet removable constraint and fail to consider the func-tioning of "the laws that enable the political machinery to keep working." They ignore the political costs and benefits of alternative techniques of economizing public action. Aaron Wildavsky, "The Political Economy of Efficiency: Cost-Benefit Analysis, Systems Analysis, and Program Budgeting," in *Political Science and Public Policy,* ed. Ranney, p. 79.

[18] An appeal made, for example, by Donald Campbell as well as the NAS report. See Campbell, "Methods for the Experimenting Society," p. 11 and the NAS report, p. 107.

[19] Max Weber, "The Meaning of 'Ethical Neutrality' in Sociology and Economics," in *The Methodology of the Social Sciences,* trans. and eds. E. A. Shils and H. A. Finch (New York, 1949), pp. 16–20. Weber, of course, regarded an ethics of "absolutes" as both so-cially irresponsible and incompatible with scientific methods of inquiry into values.

A position that would recognize the discontinuities between scientific and political universes of discourse, the differences between scientific and political grounds and procedures of action and between scientific and political associations and organizations, that is, a position that would look at science and politics *as if* they were distinctive "cultural systems," may furnish alternative perspective on the social roles and functions of science in the public domain.[20] Such a perspective may help illuminate the processes by which certain elements of the cultural system of science—such as scientific images of "reality," scientific prescriptions or procedures of action, and the social norms of scientific associations—are selected for assimilation into political discourse, action, or organization, respectively, while others are rejected, neutralized, or left untouched. The cultural system of politics may be seen as inducing the operation of such mechanisms of cultural selection to protect its jurisdiction over those dimensions of public life where considerations of political utility or of costs and benefits to the political order cannot be ignored. In such cases, the diffusion and application of scientific knowledge in public affairs cannot be guided exclusively by the internal criteria of science or by scientists' visions of a perfectly rational society.

The social history of the Copernican and Darwinian theories and the history of social attitudes towards birth control techniques, for example, indicate the extent to which extrascientific considerations concerning the impact of scientific ideas and techniques on the stability and authority of social conventions or attitudes and their consequences for the established political order influence the *social* diffusion, interpretation, and application of scientific knowledge.[21]

That point can perhaps be further clarified by briefly examining the differences between the underlying ends, values, and forms of scientific and political activities. The scientific community is organized around a basic commitment to the goal of advancing systematic rational knowledge about natural and social phenomena. Inasmuch as it has such a basic goal, separated from other social goals, the normative orientation of the scientific community can be homogeneous, specialized, and differentiated from the normative orientations of other social groups and the larger society. In contrast, the political community is organized around a much more diffused, ambiguous, and wider set of ends that are often incommensurable with one another and are never fixed. Especially in democratic systems, the body politic is continually engaged in the very process of setting goals and ordering priorities. It is an association that characteristically has to

---

[20] For an interesting yet different approach which distinguishes between ideology and science as cultural systems, see Clifford Geertz, "Ideology as a Cultural System" in *Ideology and Discontent*, ed. David E. Apter (New York, 1964), pp. 47–76.

[21] See, for example, Jerome J. Langford, *Galileo, Science and the Church*, rev. ed. (Ann Arbor, 1971); Richard Hofstadter, *Social Darwinism in American Thought* (Boston, 1955); John T. Noonan, Jr., *Contraception: A History of Its Treatment by the Catholic Theologians and Canonists* (Cambridge, Mass., 1965).

order and consider the interrelations of such diffused and heterogeneous ends as the maintenance of order, the realization and regulation of conceptions of justice, the cultivation of cultural traditions, and the advancement of material welfare. At the organizational level, these differences between science and politics manifest themselves in the differing structures of the scientific community and the body politic respectively. Because its goals and value orientations are relatively narrow, specific, differentiable, stable, and homogeneous, the scientific community tends to configurate as an exclusive association. By contrast, the political community, because its goals and value orientations tend to encompass the various dimensions of collective life and because they are characteristically diffuse, unstable, and heterogeneous, tends to configurate as an inclusive and open association that can contain members with vastly different political values and orientations.[22]

The ethics of knowledge, in its ideological or Utopian version, blurs the perception of such differences. It obscures the fact that the precision, simplicity, and consensus found in the work of science depend on the narrowness of its normative perspective.[23] Insofar as it encourages scientists to overlook the operation of a specific "political logic" in the domain of public affairs, it leads them to believe that the fulfillment of the requirements of rationality and objectivity, which renders scientific modes of perceiving and manipulating reality compelling in the context of scientific investigation, is sufficient to make them compelling also in the context of public affairs. In line with this fallacy, the ethics of knowledge tends to encourage scientists to believe that the diffusion of scientific theories or research results in the larger society necessarily also serves the cause of enhancing the rationality and objectivity of public discourse on social problems.

In order to further clarify the limitations of this view, I suggest that we examine how the grounds for the willingness to accept ideas in the different contexts of scientific research and public affairs vary and how the acts of making scientific ideas or theories public have different meanings and functions in the two contexts.

Objectivity

One of the basic weaknesses of notions about the social role of the scientist

---

[22] In the United States, the "openness" of political life relates to a deeply held belief (which, of course, cannot be fully matched by practice) "that public business is everybody's business and that public decisions should be open and openly arrived at"—Edward C. Banfield, *Political Influence* (New York, 1965), p. 284. In light of this belief it can be better understood why the increasing relevance of science to public affairs would subject the exclusive professional associations of American science to growing political pressures to become more open and to relax the conditions of membership.

[23] On the differences between scientific and political associations see further Price, *The Scientific Estate*, pp. 120–62 and 209–69.

that are grounded in the ideology of the ethics of knowledge stems from the failure to recognize the discontinuities between the requirements and meanings of objectivity as an attribute assigned to scientists or their ideas in the internal context of scientific investigation and in the external context of public affairs. In the internal context of scientific investigation, scientists' communications become objective when they can be confirmed or disproved by the impersonal public procedures of scientific verification. In the external context of the larger society, the "objectivity" of a scientist's communications is determined not so much with reference to the ability to verify them scientifically as it is by the extent to which the diffusion and application of scientific knowledge appear to contribute to the general welfare—or at any rate do not appear to serve partisan political ends and interests. "Objectivity," as an attribute of scientists and their ideas in the larger social context, is enhanced by the perception that a given body of knowledge is irrelevant to the politics of public affairs,[24] or, if that knowledge is perceived as relevant, by the existence of a relatively high degree of normative consensus. The "ethics of knowledge" ideology, however, tends to presuppose that the objectivity accorded to scientists and their ideas in the context of research and the qualifications of scientists who meet the internal canons of the scientific community are sufficient to guarantee also the "neutrality" of their ideas and actions as agents of scientific knowledge in the larger society. According to this perspective, the scientific community, because it possesses procedures by which the subjective worlds and the particular sociocultural characteristics of the scientists are, as it were, extracted from the process of advancing and certifying scientific knowledge, also holds the key to the objectivity of scientists as public actors.[25]

---

[24] Thomas Hobbes alluded to remoteness from practical human affairs as a condition for the social willingness to accept the authority of knowledge when he wrote, "if it had been a thing contrary to any man's right of dominion . . . that the three angles of a triangle should be equal to two angles of a square; that doctrine should have been, if not disrupted, yet by the burning of all books of geometry, suppressed . . . ," *Leviathan* (New York, 1962), p. 84.

[25] There is of course a considerable diversity of opinion among scientists who maintain this position with regard to the means by which the subjectivity of the scientist and his particular cultural and social background are brought under control and properly separated from his scientific work. Some place their confidence in peer review of the procedures by which evidence is certified and conclusions are drawn from evidence. See, for instance, the attempts of the Operation Research Society of America to review and evaluate the evidence and arguments of scientists who were active in the ABM debate in "Reports and Documents, the Obligations of Scientists as Counsellors," *Minerva* 10, no. 1 (January 1972): 107–57. Some, like Max Weber, emphasize the professional conscience or integrity of the scientist who reports his findings honestly and who knows and makes explicit "just where the arguments are addressed to the analytical understanding and where to the sentiments." See "Objectivity in Social Science and Social Policy," in his *The Methodology of the Social Sciences,* trans. and eds. E. A. Shils and H. A. Finch (New York, 1949), p. 60. Still others take a position like that of Gunnar Myrdal, who insists on the requirement

Nevertheless, once the messages or the "recipes" of action that originate from the scientists enter the domain of public discourse and action, they may acquire a politically significant value load. Scientists cannot control the political significance and consequences of their communications simply by making them adequate by professional standards. The specific mechanisms that structure the precise meanings of communications among scientists, such as standardized training, common professional languages, penalties for ambiguity and distortion, the power to influence professional reputation, etc., tend to lose their effectiveness as controls in the political universe.[26] Scientists often tend to reject such ideas about the influence of social and political factors on the significance and functions of scientific knowledge in society, because they see these ideas as challenges to the autonomy of intellectual standards. The political dimension of knowledge, however, is not a property of knowledge proper but of the relations between certain aspects of knowledge and certain aspects of the social context. The *political relativity* of knowledge in the social context does not necessarily challenge the professional integrity of the man of knowledge, nor does it presuppose a cognitive, epistemological, or logical relativism or call into question the universal *intellectual* validity of scientific truth.

Rationality

Whereas in the context of science concepts of the nature of man, society, and the cosmos are selected and sustained on the basis of their relative explanatory and predictive value in the various fields of knowledge, in the context of politics such concepts are often bound to be evaluated primarily by other criteria of acceptability. These criteria would typically refer to such sociocultural properties of ideas as their compatibility with the world views that support prevailing conventions of justice; their agreement with operating institutions, norms, and in-

---

that the social scientist make the value premises, from which he cannot escape in his work, sufficiently explicit to alert his audience to the particular "contextual" components of his scientific work. See Gunnar Myrdal, *Value in Social Theory* (London, 1958), p. 52, and *The Behavioral and Social Sciences: Outlook and Needs,* p. 135.

[26] The great variety of sociopolitical controls that affect the influence, meaning, and functions of scientific ideas in the public domain include censure; limitations on scientists' access to the mass media; moral criticism of scientific theories that appear to challenge cherished social conventions; the co-optation of scientists as advisers and their use to justify or challenge public policies even when such use lacks any intellectual basis; attempts to relativize the social authority of the scientists by linking their opinions with their social, economic, and even ethnic situation; the development and use of "official" sociocultural doctrines concerning the relations between science and education, science and national cultural traditions, science and the economy; the utilization of the power of the state to confer recognition and professional status on experts and to provide legal basis to scientific institutions; and the use of public money and public rewards to influence the incentives of scientists.

terests; their capacity to inspire social cooperation and trust rather than conflict; and their utility in justifying rather than challenging established authority.[27]

Thomas Hobbes, who was one of the first thinkers to examine the place and significance of scientific concepts of reality in the construction of the political order, noted such differences between scientific and political criteria for the adoption and rejection of ideas when he stated, "If nature . . . has made men equal, that equality is to be acknowledged; or if nature made men unequal; yet because men that think themselves equal will not enter into conditions of peace but upon equal terms, such equality must be admitted."[28] In this statement Hobbes implicitly recognizes the unique role of social images of reality as against reality as a scientific construct in the organization of the collective life.[29] He implies that ideas that are valid in the context of scientific discourse may be considered dysfunctional for the purpose of maintaining "conditions of peace," while ideas that may be functional for the organization and maintenance of the public order may lack any foundation in, and at times may be positively contradicted by, science.[30]

---

[27] Some scientific theories that attempt to explain the origins and evolution of the cosmos, of life, and of society may constitute in some contexts a challenge to established doctrines and authority in ways similar to the functioning of what Judith Shklar calls "subversive genealogies." See her "Subversive Genealogies," *Daedalus* (Winter 1972), pp. 129–54.

[28] Following that quotation, Hobbes assigns to his idea the status of the ninth law of nature in this theory. The law is formulated as the demand that "every man acknowledge another for his equal by nature." See for both references *Leviathan*, ed. Michael Oakeshott (New York, 1962), p. 120.

[29] See, in this connection, the distinction made by Peter L. Berger and Thomas Luckmann, following Alfred Schutz, between theoretical or scientific and common sense or everyday knowledge. See Alfred Schutz, "Common-Sense and Scientific Interpretations of Human Action," *Collected Papers* (The Hague, 1962), Vol. I, pp. 3–47; Peter L. Berger and Thomas Luckmann, *The Social Construction of Reality* (Garden City, 1967).

[30] Politicians and bureaucrats tend to evaluate symbolic forms or ideas in light of the structural, organizational, and regulatory requirements of the political order rather than their truth value by some intellectual standards. This is, as S. N. Eisenstadt indicated, one of the major sources of tensions between intellectuals and political authority. See S. N. Eisenstadt, "Intellectuals and Tradition" in *Daedalus* (Spring 1972), pp. 1–19. The difference between evaluating ideas or symbolic constructs by looking at their influence on human conduct and by looking at their truth value as assertions about the world is especially a source of tension between politicians and bureaucrats on the one hand and social scientists on the other. K. E. Boulding has aptly pointed out that "where knowledge is an essential part of the system, knowledge about the system changes the system itself." See "The Economics of Knowledge and the Knowledge of Economics," in *Economics of Information and Knowledge*, ed. D. M. Lamberton (Harmondsworth, Eng., 1971), p. 30. Social science knowledge is obviously that kind of knowledge. This is why when social scientists advocate changing the premises of public policy in light of new knowledge or new ideas, they may clash with public servants who evaluate the benefits of improving the scientific grounds of a given policy and promoting certain categories of knowledge against the costs to the

When scientists ignore these discontinuities between scientific and political grounds for the acceptability of ideas and apply scientific criteria for the evaluation of political ideologies or social myths, they commit what may be termed the "fallacy of misplaced rationality." The fallacy of misplaced rationality is characteristic of scientists who ground their conception of the social role of the scientist in the ethics of knowledge. These scientists typically fail to consider the unique character of political constructions of reality that must fulfill functions distinct from the functions served by the scientific construction of reality. The latter cannot be regarded as a means for such ends as the cementing of social cooperation, the justification of public authority, or the channeling of emotions and moral sentiments.[31] This is, at least in part, why as long as there are ambiguities and inner inconsistencies among the purposes of the body politic, and as long as the incommensurability of the value commitments and interests of political actors and the emotional needs and anxieties of the people remain an integral part of the social condition of man, the attempt to enhance the influence of scientific rationality in human affairs will be constrained by the requirements of political legitimation.[32]

Publicity

One of the most significant discontinuities between the cultural configurations of science and politics relates to the purposes and functions of publicity in the two systems of communication. Within the scientific community or its subcommunities, the publication of research results is instrumental to the very work of science. Since the products of scientific research are at the same time the "means of production" of further knowledge, scientists have tended to regard publicity as a central norm of appropriate professional conduct and to penalize scientists who keep their research findings secret.[33] Historically, however, scientists have often tended to generalize this norm of publicity and to lend it an

---

stability and continuity of the involved system of behavior. See the conflict between the validity of the cost of living index and its utility as a policy tool in K. S. Arnow, "The Attack on the Cost of Living Index," in *Public Administration and Policy Development,* ed. Harold Stein (New York, 1951), pp. 775–853.

[31] Rousseau, one of the earliest political critics of the culture of science, considered these functions to be central to the body politic.

[32] If turning all the members of the community into effective participants in or a competent audience of the scientific discourse is not feasible, then making scientific criteria the basis of public decisions and actions and the standards of their evaluations would conflict with the values of participatory democracy. Making the possession of a certain kind of knowledge a condition for participation would imply a kind of return to the old principle of selective democracy according to which political participation is restricted to those who own a specified amount of property.

[33] See, in this connection, W. O. Hagstrom, *The Scientific Community* (New York, 1965) and John Ziman, *Public Knowledge* (Cambridge, England, 1968).

unquestioned external social value as well. Considering publicity to be normative for the scientist not only in professional forums but also in the larger social context, scientists have regarded the publication and diffusion of research results as a means for making scientific knowledge available for all and as a reflection of democratic ideals in the habits of scientific discourse.

Making ideas and information public has, of course, been a central value in democratic political traditions. It has been regarded as basic for the kind of open public discourse that facilitates wide participation in the political process and underlies the capacity of the public to accept or challenge intelligently government policies. At the same time, however, publicity and the control of the means of public communication have been commonly used by partisan political interests to mobilize public support and alter social attitudes and behavior. Yet while the rhetoric of the ethics of knowledge is rich with references to the idea that the publication of the findings of science is not only instrumental for science but is at the same time democratic and conducive to the rationality of social discourse and action, it ignores the partisan political functions and uses of publicity. Scientists who believe themselves to be nonpolitical when they accept a priori the duty to spread scientific ideas are thus often subjected to a rude awakening.

Especially in the heterogeneous normative contexts of democratic political systems, where different "world views" or "ideological perspectives" on reality clash and compete for influence, identical concepts of causality and reality, though made public with the authority of science behind them, may have widely different implications for different political positions. Once the communications made by scientists enter the universe of public discourse and intersect with the political symbols and ideologies that compete for influence over public affairs, scientists cannot prevent the politicization of their ideas. In a pluralistic or heterogeneous normative context, therefore, even if a perfectly equal and universal distribution of knowledge in the epistemological sense were at all possible, this would not guarantee a symmetrical distribution of knowledge as political power. In the larger social context, equal knowledge does not insure equal benefits from that knowledge.[34] The act of diffusing or publishing knowledge may thus not only fail to advance dispassionate rational discourse about social problems but may in fact be a catalyst for the further segmentation of social attitudes and the politicization of public discourse.

The anticipation of the consequences of a direct appeal to knowledge without the restraints imposed by considerations of the social and political context

---

[34] No wonder that some of the most pertinent insights into the limitations upon the "scientification" of politics appear in conservative political thought, which criticizes the norms of the ethics of knowledge as part of democratic ideology. See, for example, M. Oakeshott, *Rationalism in Politics* (London, 1962).

is probably what has led Talmudic scholars over the last few hundred years to preface their works with the warning "lehalacha lo l'ma'ase" (for speculation, not for application), which is intended to prevent the lay public from blindly or prematurely following scholarly authority and illegitimately appealing to purely theoretical discourse as a reference for imperatives of practical action.[35] In modern societies, such as America, where the discourse of scientists and especially social scientists is often inseparable from social discourse and social action, where a theoretical statement may become a catalyst of change in social attitude or behavior by the sheer fact of its publication, scientists who are committed to the future growth of science may have to learn to draw a sharper sociocultural line between the processes by which knowledge is advanced and the processes by which knowledge becomes incorporated as a factor in social life.

These observations are meant to deny neither the value of the diffusion and application of knowledge in public affairs nor the fact that some scientific ideas and techniques may in time replace nonscientific modes of perceiving and manipulating reality. My aim is rather to indicate that as long as the "scientification" of social discourse and action is not the only or the supreme end of the political association of men, and as long as the goal of enhancing the influence of scientific knowledge in public affairs appears to compete or conflict in the public arena with other social goals or needs, scientists who use their authority or ideas as instruments of social enlightenment must recognize that their actions are politically loaded and are likely to evoke political response, regardless of the innocence or disinterestedness of their motivations.

THE JENSEN CONTROVERSY AND THE SUPPOSED DUTY TO TELL "UGLY TRUTHS"

The misconceptions about the relations between science and politics, which are induced by the ideology of the "ethics of knowledge," are particularly manifest in cases where scientists see it as their role to use the mass media and the nonprofessional popular press to advance, in the name of the objectivity of scientific knowledge, the social acceptance of a theory that appears in the social context to favor the partisan political position of some social groups over others. One of the recent and most instructive of such cases is furnished by the renewed eruption in the United States and England of the nature-nurture controversy.[36] Even though this is not a new controversy, it has been renewed with great intensity following the publication of an article entitled "How Much Can We

---

[35] I am indebted to Rabbi Adin Steinsaltz for calling my attention to this fact.

[36] The ABM controversy may constitute another such case. See "Reports and Documents, the Obligations of Scientists as Counsellors," *Minerva* 10, no. 1 (January 1972): 107-57.

Boost I.Q. and Scholastic Achievement?" written by Arthur Jensen and published in the *Harvard Educational Review* in 1969.[37]

Professor Jensen, a psychologist at Berkeley, analyzed in his article the results of a wide range of studies bearing upon the relative weight of environment
and heredity in explaining differences in the intellectual performance and mental
abilities of different human groups. Public attention, however, was attracted to
a relatively few remarks that Jensen made with reference to differences in the
average IQ scores of blacks and whites. Public and, indeed, also a large part of
the scholarly response to Jensen's conclusion that the weight of hereditary factors
in accounting for differences has been underestimated and that "the lower average
intelligence and scholastic performance of Negroes could involve not only environmental, but also genetic factors . . ."[38] was, by and large, violently critical
and resentful. In turn, the criticism and attacks on Jensen provoked a number of
scholars who work in the same general field to defend him and to argue for the
desirability of an open attitude towards even "ugly truths."[39] Many of these scientists joined Jensen in charging that the uncritical tendency to explain differences in intellectual performance and mental abilities by environmental deprivation was perhaps responsible for the costly failure of several social programs
aimed at reducing such differences by manipulating environmental variables.

Among these scientists, those who became particularly visible during the
"Jensen controversy" include, in addition to Professor Jensen himself, D. J. Ingle,
physiologist from the University of Chicago, Richard Herrnstein and H. J.
Eysenck, psychologists from Harvard and London universities respectively, William Shockley, a Nobel prize winning physicist from Stanford, and C. D. Darlington, a biologist from Oxford. These scholars do not belong to a formal organization and have not coordinated their publications and actions, but their conduct
during the controversy together with the body of literature that they have produced suggests that they share not only common scientific opinions but a similar
concept of their social duties as scientists.[40]

---

[37] Arthur Jensen, "How Much Can We Boost I.Q. and Scholastic Achievement?"
Harvard Educational Review 34 (Winter 1969) : 1–123. See also the chapter by Lee Cronbach in this volume.

[38] Ibid., p. 82.

[39] Aware of the unpopularity of his ideas, Jensen devoted in his article and later in
his book considerable space to the kind of nonscientific arguments that are aimed, in the
tone of the ethics of knowledge, at persuading the lay public to prefer "knowledge of
reality" to "static ignorance," or "scientific understanding" to "ideology." See ibid., p. 79.
Also in Arthur Jensen, *Genetics and Education* (London, 1972), pp. 1–67.

[40] In addition to Jensen's article in the *Harvard Educational Review,* see the following publications: Dwight J. Ingle, "Racial Differences and the Future," *Science* 10 (October 1964); by the same author, see "The Need to Investigate Average Biological Differences among Racial Groups," in *Science and the Concept of Race,* eds. Margaret Mead,
Theodosius Dobzhansky et al. (New York, 1968), pp. 113–21; Richard Herrnstein,

I would like to suggest that their concept of the social role of the scientist is grounded in what we have defined as the ethics of knowledge. It consists of the following elements: The belief that scientific knowledge—in this particular case the results of research on the links between heredity and scholastic performance —is not only of theoretical interest but is also important for promoting human happiness and in advancing the solution of social problems on a factual basis and with the help of sound methodology;[41] the belief that scientists as objective and neutral agents of scientific rationality can and should, by urging the diffusion and application of such knowledge in the public domain, "bring society face to face with itself" and bring the knowledge about the links between heredity and behavior to bear upon the social perceptions and handling of social problems;[42] and the belief that public policies and social practices that are based upon premises that appear to be false by the standards of scientific knowledge are sustained only by ignorance and dogma and should be rejected or altered on grounds of their unacceptability to science.[43] Finally, the hereditarians believe that the attempt "to spread the truth" about "the role of heredity in human behavior" involves the old struggle between the forces of reason and unreason. They compare the violent response and resistance to their ideas to the kind of pressures that were directed against Galileo, Darwin, or Soviet Mendelian biologists for the "nonscientific reasons" of "seeming to contradict some religious or political beliefs."[44] These beliefs are, of course, not peculiar to Jensen and the hereditarians who have supported his position. The communications and conduct of the environmentalists who have opposed Jensen and the hereditarians who have supported him reveal a similar allegiance to the principles and norms of the ethics of knowledge.

Subject to attacks and accusations that they are serving the partisan political

---

"I.Q.," *Atlantic Monthly* (September 1971); Hans J. Eysenck, *Race, Intelligence and Education* (London, 1971); and by the same author, "The Dangers of the New Zealots," *Encounter* 39, no. 6 (December 1972): 79–90; C. D. Darlington, *The Evolution of Man and Society* (London, 1969) and, by the same author, "Genetics and Society, A Scientist Replies, *Encounter* 37, no. 6 (December 1971): 84–93; William Shockley, "Human-Quality Problems and Research Taboos," reprint from *New Concepts and Directions in Education* (Greenwich, Conn., 1969).

[41] "The Resolution on Scientific Freedom," *Encounter* 39, no. 6 (December 1972): pp. 88–89. (The signatories on this resolution included Jensen, Eysenck, Herrnstein, Darlington, and Monod. Not all the hereditarians signed it and some of the nonhereditarians did); Eysenck, *Race, Intelligence and Education,* p. 10; Shockley, "Human-Quality Problems," p. 85.

[42] Darlington, "Genetics and Society," p. 93.

[43] Ingle, "Racial Differences and the Future"; Eysenck, *Race, Intelligence and Education,* pp. 10, 19; Jensen, "Reducing the Heredity-Environment Uncertainty," in *Environment, Heredity and Intelligence, Harvard Educational Review,* Reprint Series No. 2 (1969), p. 215; Ingle, "The Need to Investigate," p. 113.

[44] "The Resolution on Scientific Freedom," pp. 88–89.

interests of conservative and even racist whites,[45] the hereditarians typically have tried to defend their credentials and claims to objectivity by invoking their record as scientists of professional reputation and integrity and by challenging their critics to refute them on scientific grounds.[46] In attempting to show that no political bias has inspired his work, Eysenck, for example, ventured to prove that even his political record places him as an opponent of the political interests that he was said to serve.[47] Such evidence about the objectivity of the hereditarians in the context of research and their loyalty to strict professional canons even in the context of public affairs does not show, however, that the objective consequences of their public advocacy of their ideas are neutral in their impact in the political arena.

Hereditarians, such as Ingle, Jensen, Shockley and Eysenck, who have maintained that definitions of human nature which are held by public bodies should be rejected if they do not stand the test of scientific opinion, have applied criteria of scientific rationality for the evaluation of the acceptability of ideas that function in the public domain primarily in a political capacity.[48] They have criticized certain pronouncements by public bodies including the U.S. Department of Labor, U.S. Office of Education, and UNESCO. These pronouncements, for example, that "intelligence potential is distributed among Negro infants in the same proportion and pattern as among Icelanders or Chinese or any other group" or that "the peoples of the world today appear to possess equal biological potentialities for attaining any civilizational level," they claim, are devoid of any basis in available scientific knowledge. By insisting that such pronouncements should be rejected as premises of public policy since, insofar as they lack scientific validation, they must be grounded merely in political and ideological considerations, the hereditarians have obviously committed what we have labeled earlier as the "fallacy of misplaced rationality." They have tried in fact to derive from the presumed superior intellectual validity of their conclusions the superior status of these conclusions as premises of public policy. Their position illustrates also the failure to acknowledge the political ramifications of acts of publishing or in any other way socially diffusing research results that appear outside the

---

45 See, among the reactions to Jensen's article, William F. Brazziel, "A Letter from the South," in *Environment, Heredity and Intelligence,* pp. 200–208; see also the reactions to Herrnstein's article in the *Atlantic Monthly,* December 1971, pp. 101–10 and February 1972, pp. 38–39. Numerous other, including some very violent, reactions could be found in the letters to national daily papers which covered the Jensen controversy. See, for example, *New York Times Magazine,* September 21, 1969.

46 See, for instance, Jensen's *Genetics and Education,* pp. 1–67 and Herrnstein's article in *Commentary* 55, no. 4 (April 1973) and his answer to his critics in *Commentary* (July 1973) : 12–13.

47 Eysenck, "The New Zealots," p. 79.

48 See, for example, Ingle, "The Need to Investigate," p. 119; Eysenck, *Race, Intelligence and Education,* p. 19; and Jensen, "How Much Can We Boost I.Q.?" pp. 28–29.

context of scientific discourse as messages supporting or weakening competing public positions.

In the public domain of contemporary American and British politics, where the genuine scientific debate on the relative weight of heredity and environment in the determination of differences in the behavior of human groups ties up with a political conflict on the nature and degree of government responsibility and capability for eliminating these differences, the publishing of scientific evidence and theories concerning the nature-nurture problem is not likely to be regarded as purely instrumental research communication. Once it reinforces the politically heretical belief that it is unfeasible to eliminate these differences by manipulating the environment, such an act of publication is inevitably—regardless of the contribution to the advancement of knowledge—a politically significant act.[49] As can be seen by the impact of such communications on the political conflict between segregationists and antisegregationists in the United States, such acts can be perceived as contributing to the redistribution of political power.

THE POLITICAL PROFILES OF KNOWLEDGE AND THE SCIENTIST AS A TACIT POLITICAL DECISION MAKER

In order further to clarify the ways in which scientists operating according to the principles of the ethics of knowledge may become involved in the political process, I suggest that we look at science as linked to politics in three elementary ways or as having three political profiles in terms of which scientists can be seen as acting—even though innocently—as tacit political decision makers. Science can become linked to politics by virtue of its concepts and constructs of reality, its recipes and techniques of action or manipulation, and its socio-institutional organization.

a. *The Political Profile of Scientific Concepts and Constructs of Reality*

The professional communications of scientists, once they are made public, bring into the context of the particular symbolic, cultural, or ideological systems of a given community concepts of reality and causality that can affect the nature and stability of public attitudes towards the legitimacy of government authority and the appropriateness of its actions. In particular where scientific theories refer to the nature of man and society, they can easily turn into factors in the ongoing

---

[49] On the political visibility of science, see also Yaron Ezrahi, "The Political Resources of American Science," in *Science Studies* 1, no. 2 (1971): 117–33, and Yaron Ezrahi, "The Authority of Science in Politics," in *Science and Values,* eds. E. Mendelsohn and A. Thackray (New York, 1974).

process by which modes of perceiving and manipulating social reality are politically and publicly established or challenged.

b. *The Political Profile of Scientific Procedures and Techniques of Action*

Any idea or procedure that is presented by scientists as authorizing in the name of scientific technical rationality a particular mode of action as superior to others can become politically loaded if it introduces politically significant changes in the de facto order of ends served by public action or in the social distribution of the costs and benefits of that action. Given the independent impact of political criteria on the acceptability of modes or techniques of action in areas of public concern, it is possible that one technique of action will be technically superior to another and yet, because it introduces changes in the order of goals or distribution of costs and benefits that are politically unacceptable, will have an inferior political legitimacy.

c. *The Political Profile of Scientific Associations and Institutions*

The communications or actions of scientists may become politically loaded also as a result of the properties believed to characterize the group of scientists in question or the scientific community as a whole. The lay public especially, which lacks the ability to evaluate the communications of scientists by internal intellectual standards, tends to construe and judge what they say on the basis of external indicators, such as the perceived group properties of the scientists; it evaluates these group properties in terms of their compatibility with prevailing collective identities, notions of authority, patterns of behavior, and principles of association. It regards such factors as indicators of the value commitments of the scientists and uses them to construe the social meanings and functions of their communications.

I would like to suggest that it is these political profiles of science as a bundle of messages, recipes of action, and social associations rather than the inner intentions and motivations of scientists that can account for the "social careers" of scientific ideas and the political use and abuse of science.

Scientists, according to this approach, are engaged in tacit political decisions when their decisions influence the political profiles of science, that is, the degree and nature of its involvement and interaction with the political process. These tacit political decisions or actions can be seen as falling into three elementary categories that correspond with the three political profiles of science listed earlier in the following way:

The first category of tacit political decisions would include decisions, such as the selection of place, timing, and form, including the choice of language, of publication by virtue of which scientific communication acquires a political communicative load in a given context. The I.Q. controversy furnishes an abundance of instructive examples of such tacit political decisions. They include Herrnstein's decision to publish his ideas about IQ in such nontechnical forums as the *Atlantic Monthly* and *Commentary*, Eysenck's decision to publish a deliberately popular book on *Race, Intelligence and Education*,[50] and Ingle's decision to use in his publication such a potentially politically loaded expression as "average racial differences in genetic endowment."[51] As can be measured by public reactions to these communications, these decisions contributed to the utilization of hereditarian ideas and of the scientific authority of their social carriers in current ideological controversies and political conflicts. The arguments advanced by the environmentalists, in which the "environmental deprivation" explanation for low IQ scores is couched in the rhetoric of equality, justice, and democracy, equally involve, to be sure, such tacit political decisions.

Another category of tacit political decisions or actions includes decisions or actions by virtue of which what scientists communicate or do alters the order of ends or interests served by collective social actions, such as legislative acts, the choice of public policies and public programs, or the actions of government agencies. Furthermore, decisions or actions that influence the ways in which knowledge becomes a technical power in the social context and is socially deployed or that affect the ways in which the costs and benefits of collective actions are socially distributed, would, according to our criteria, be politically loaded. Jensen's decision to open his article with the assertion that "compensatory education has been tried and it apparently has failed,"[52] insofar as it may have affected the political or ideological strength of certain choices among alternative educational programs, belongs to that category of tacit political decisions. So do the statements made by Herrnstein and others that may have affected the credibility, scope of use, and social functions of IQ tests.[53] This is manifest, for instance, in the fact that negative public response to the hereditarian thesis and in particular to Herrnstein's article in the *Atlantic Monthly* often appears to be motivated by the fear that as a result of the kind of ideas expressed by Herrnstein the social technology of IQ tests will be used not only for such agreeable ends as the spotting of retarded children but also for much more controversial ends, such as the building of a meritocratic elite or the classification of human beings into the kind of biological categories that are politically explosive in modern societies.[54]

---

[50] See Eysenck's reasons for publishing a popular book on the subject in his introduction to *Race, Intelligence and Education*, particularly p. 8.

[51] See his "The Need to Investigate," in *Science and the Concept of Race*, eds. Mead et al., and the criticism made on this usage by Margaret Mead in the same publication, p. 177.

[52] Jensen, "How Much Can We Boost I.Q.?" p. 2.

[53] See in particular Herrnstein's "I.Q."

[54] See the reflections of these fears in the responses to the Herrnstein article in the *Atlantic Monthly*, December 1971, pp. 101–110 and the responses to the Jensen article in *Harvard Educational Review* 39, no. 3 (Summer 1969): 581–631.

At a more fundamental level, the very advocacy of using IQ tests in order to evaluate the performance of the educational system and its capacity to level social differences implies a politically loaded choice between furnishing equal education as a means for narrowing gaps in human intellectual performance and as an expression of the duty to follow the imperative: "Treat all human beings as if they were of equal ability."

Thirdly, the ethnic, class, or religious affiliations of scientists are not usually the results of the kind of voluntary decisions that determine their political, social, and institutional affiliations. Both kinds of affiliations, however, can have political import when, as we have noted, the lay public reads into them *the scientists' value orientations*. In political contexts, *who* says what and when he says it and under what circumstances are inseparable questions. It is from this perspective that the social identities, political views, and institutional affiliations of the hereditarians became politically loaded in the context of the Jensen controversy.[55]

CONCLUSION

Whether they are politically innocent or incompetent, scientists who thus act as tacit political decision makers without recognizing the inevitable role of prevailing political ideas and structures in shaping the influence of their ideas and theories in the public domain are usually puzzled if not utterly shocked when political storms are stirred up by their communications and actions. They do not realize the extent to which the ethics of knowledge—even though they think of it as the ethics of the scientist as an apolitical rational man—can be politically loaded when applied in the context of public affairs. Scientists who define their social role in terms of the ethics of knowledge fail to recognize the fact that attempts to advance the influence of scientific criteria in the organization and management of the common life and to leave out considerations and ideas that appear arbitrary from a scientific point of view may at the same time be politically significant acts of introducing into public affairs ideas and considerations that appear arbitrary from the standpoint of prevailing social and ideological premises. Scientists may be free to deny but they are powerless entirely to negate the operation of "political logic" in public affairs. In an age in which science becomes increasingly involved as a factor in the public domain, scientists' ability to contribute to society without undermining the social and cultural foundations of the

---

[55] Note, for example, the response of William F. Brazziel to the publication of Herrnstein's "I.Q.": "There is little to be said about R. J. Herrnstein's article except that some *white* editors are seizing on Arthur Jensen's article to promote the cause of *white* supremacy" (my emphasis), *Atlantic Monthly*, December 1971, p. 101. See also June Meyer Gordon's response, *New York Times Magazine*, September 21, 1969, p. 14, to an article by Lee Edson on "Jensenism," *New York Times Magazine*, August 31, 1969.

scientific enterprise may very well depend, therefore, upon their ingenuity not only in discovering new truths but in evolving a new social ethics of science: a code of ethics of knowledge that is based on a deeper and wider knowledge of the social and political dynamics of public life and the ways in which it bears upon the social roles and functions of science; a new ethics that gives proper consideration to the discontinuities between the universes of science and politics; a code that reflects the realization that the norms that govern the pursuit of scientific truth in the internal forums of the scientific community are distinct from the norms that govern the process by which the integration of that knowledge into public affairs is effected. Such a code would redefine the relations between science and politics.

Scholars as Public Adversaries: The Case of Economics

Harry G. Johnson

INTRODUCTION: AN ECONOMIST'S VIEW OF THE PROBLEM

In his letter of invitation to participate in this study, the editor of this volume, Charles Frankel, wrote:

> Unlike other social sciences, economics has achieved—or so it seems to the outsider—a working etiquette which allows people to disagree vigorously without engaging in recrimination about "unscientific" or "unprofessional" behavior. Moreover, the educated public seems well accustomed to the expectation that economists will disagree, and yet the status of economics as probably the hardest of the hard social sciences is unchallenged. How has this happened? What lessons, if any, can be drawn that might illuminate the situation in other social sciences?

In that part of his description of the project relevant to this section of it, he wrote:

> Politically significant debate among scholars takes place often in explicitly political contexts. Scholars take sides before Congress, in public commissions, as advisers to the bureaucracy, before the press, with regard to issues such as the ABM controversy, wage-price guidelines, or poverty programmes. What issues affecting the authority and integrity of scholarship do such activities raise? It's hasty to assume that taking sides on a public issue is incompatible with objective scholarship and an honest examination of the alternatives. Nevertheless, partisanship may affect the selection of topics for research, the designing of the investigation, and the formulation of general conclusions based upon it. And this partisanship is all-the-more partisan, perhaps, when it is hidden, or disguised as "neutrality." The effects of involvement in controversial public issues with regard to the authority of scholarship therefore merit attention.

171

These two paragraphs defining the scope of this part of the study, read in reverse order, and critically interpreted as an economist would criticize them constitute in themselves a good starting point for the explanation sought. The reason is that they typify—or perhaps more fairly to the editor, accord, for purposes of discussion, academic respectability and potential validity to—an unsophisticated and primitive methodology that economics, at least in the United States, has long since outgrown. The second paragraph offers for consideration a general hypothesis that participation in public policy discussions must be corruptive of scientific work and of the maintenance of scientific standards; the first expresses the puzzlement that economics, which is more deeply involved in public policy discussion and formation than many other social sciences—with the exception of political science in the specific contexts of foreign policy formation and the winning of elections—seems to be an exception to this role and asks for an explanation.

An economist would observe that the general hypothesis is badly formulated to begin with and that the fact that the strongest available empirical test—economics—falsifies it is strong evidence that the opposite hypothesis possesses more validity. The opposite hypothesis is that the stronger a social science is, the more its members can afford to participate in adversary debate over public policy issues without jeopardizing scientific integrity and freedom. There are several reasons for this: first, the scientific basis of the discipline helps to develop roles in relation to public policy formation that are scientific and politically neutral; second, because of the scientific base, scholars are well aware of what they and others are doing when they step outside academia into public policy discussion and advice and can establish fairly clear lines of demarcation between scientific work and conclusions and political partisanship; and third, both the scientific base of the subject and the members of the scientific community operate to inhibit or police transgressions. These points will be illustrated in the next paragraph.

The hypothesis of the second paragraph is badly formulated both in terms of fundamental conceptions and in detailed argument. Implicit in it is the academic concept of the pure scholar searching for truth. But the raw material of the social scientist is not nature but society; he has to draw his problems from events in society, of which many consist of public policy decisions and their consequences, and his task as a scientist is to develop general principles reliably explaining the workings of society and to elaborate on their applications to particular cases; moreover, he has some obligations as a citizen or merely as a human being to feed some of his findings back into the social process. It is thus difficult either to define what purity in social science would be, or how public policy participation could corrupt it, in the terms traditionally conceived of for the natural sciences. Any such definition would have to run in terms of either violation of accepted scientific standards for the sake of partisanship or diversion of effort to scientifically peripheral studies and excessive emphasis on practical application as contrasted with "pure" research—the latter alternative being difficult to define for reasons already given. Equally important, one must distinguish between the individual scholar and the scholarly community and recognize the implications of the transition that has occurred from the few isolated scholars of past history to the large number of members in each social science discipline today.

To turn to the details of the second definitional paragraph, the various contexts of participation in politically significant debate listed in the first sentence carry widely different political overtones. Testifying before congressional committees is commonly a matter of analyzing the nature of a problem and the alternative policies that might be adopted; and while their own values may lead individuals to different policy recommendations, the procedure is not so much adversary as competitive in the presentation of economic analysis. A decision is not made, as in a courtroom, in favor of one party or the other. Who wins the scholarly debate is a side issue. Congress, having heard, goes off on its own and makes policy. As to public commissions, economists connected with them are usually research staff engaged in scientific studies of relevant problems; economist members of commissions are usually appointed to represent their profession and try to do so honestly, whereas if they are appointed on account of their political views, these must have been at least as well known to the profession as to the government that appointed them and will be appropriately discounted in professional assessments of the resulting report. Advice to the bureaucracy is usually engaged on the basis of professional expertise with respect to such matters as the effects of taxation, monetary policy, and foreign economic policy. Appearance in the communications media or before the television camera is typically a matter of explanation of economic policies and issues, though the willingness to explain often comes from political partisanship. Not on the list, but probably the most potentially dangerous corrupting influence on economic science, is actual participation in the policy-decision process, since such participation can obscure the sense of scientific integrity and objectivity in the need to achieve politically acceptable compromises and turns the object of activity from scholarly understanding and inquiry to achieving effective influence on policy making. (Very few, indeed, of economists who have served on the Council of Economic Advisers have returned quietly and happily to the calm of academic life.)

It is true enough that partisanship may affect the selection of topics for research, the designing of the investigation, and the formulation of general conclusions. However, it should be noted that, equally, partisanship may follow from the completion of a study undertaken for scientific reasons; and conversely that participation or partisanship in politically significant debate may suggest new problems that need to be tackled by scientific methods. Here the existence of the scientific community is relevant in several ways. On the one hand, it judges the value of research topics, the quality of the design and performance, and the scientific validity of the conclusions; on the other hand, both the scientific demand for demonstration of originality of topic selection and competence in execution and inference and the scientific objective of basing general principles on as wide a body of tested evidence as possible give value to the scientific study of problems even if the motivation or origination of the study was partisanship.

After all this argumentation, which in a sense is an explanation of why economics is not seriously troubled by the problem of partisanship as envisaged in the overall study, it is necessary to state that the "outside view" of economics referred to in Frankel's first paragraph is significantly rosier than the inside one, for two reasons. First, the view is based on economics as understood and practiced in the United States; economics elsewhere is very different, especially in the United Kingdom, which used to be the leader in the subject. The reasons include such factors as the much larger scale and more advanced professionalization of American economics, the politicization of British economics in the 1930s which has continued in Oxbridge ever since (in the United States a similar politicization went less deep and was halted by the McCarthy era), and the difference between a congressional and a parliamentary system of government. (In the latter, the majority government makes economic policy, and the minority opposition has to criticize it, so that economists' participation in policy formation has inevitably to be partisan or is so considered if conducted from the outside and can be conducted from the inside only by joining the bureaucracy, except for the odd consultant and royal commission.)[1]

Second, recriminations about "unscientific" or "unprofessional" conduct are significantly present in the United States, though they typically relate to the adequacy or validity of the evidence alleged to support policy conclusions and are fought out in the professional journals and meetings. There are cases of an eminent economist bending his economics to support his political party in public speeches or debates, but control over this is exercised through the grapevine, which spreads news of such lapses from scientific integrity. No economist can get away for long with disguising partisanship as "neutrality." In fact, as will be explained later, economics long ago went through the phase of believing that the integrity of the discipline was protected simply by relying on the capacities of the individual to achieve neutrality. It has come to rely much more on mutual policing by the members of the profession or on the revelatory effects of competition of biases.

---

[1] For a fuller comparative treatment of the profession in different countries, see my "National Styles in Economic Research: The United States, The United Kingdom, Canada, and Various European Countries," *Daedalus* (Spring 1973); *The Search for Knowledge,* vol. 102. no. 2, p. 65 ff.

THE EVOLUTION OF ECONOMICS INTO A SOCIAL SCIENCE

How has economics developed to the point where it maintains its own confidence and its public reputation as a science while being able to engage extensively in public policy debate and public policy formation? Part of the explanation lies in its subject matter, which is in a sense more "objective" and amenable to logical and empirical analysis than that of the other social sciences, and to its scope and method, which have from the start been concerned with whole societies as such rather than with the analysis of groups or individuals in society, and with the study of complex contemporary societies (illuminated of course by historical knowledge) rather than with small and apparently simple and static primitive societies existing in isolation from more complex and sophisticated societies. A different approach to the same point is to say that, in a world evolving from feudalism into the national state, economic issues were more important and were realized earlier to be important enough to deserve analysis, because they were immediately vital to the survival of the nation-state. In contrast, the issues that concern the other social sciences assume the continued existence of the nation-state (or of primitive societies) and are matters of internal social organization rather than of external survival.[2] (This indeed may be a fundamental factor in the explanation of the problem set: Economics is so important to the state that governments and the public perhaps naturally expect experts to disagree over such important and difficult problems.)

The remarks in the preceding paragraph are essentially static observations on the social sciences, whereas the question is posed in terms of evolution. To answer the dynamic question properly would require a tremendous knowledge of both economics, in the sense of mainstream economics as the core of economic science, and of the evolving social context in which economics itself evolved. The following sketchy treatment of the subject is confined to English-language economics, which has been dominant in the historical evolution of the subject— though with important importations into general equilibrium theory, capital theory, and monetary theory from various European traditions after World War I. In English-language economics the lead was taken by the British classical and neoclassical traditions, and in the 1930s by the "Keynesian Revolution" until somewhere in the late 1930s. Then it shifted decisively to the United States, in part as a result of the involvement of British economists in the economic management of the British war effort and their subsequent involvement in British

---

[2] This applies also to political science, though it has a longer history as a subject of scholarly study, because the great historical figures were concerned with explaining the need for the existence of government and in particular reconciling the medieval "divine right of kings" with the fact of successful revolutions.

politics and economic policy and in part as a result of the vastly greater numbers
of well-trained American economists.

While both British and American economists had from time to time before
the Great Depression of the 1930s been involved in public policy formation, it
was almost exclusively as expert witnesses or as professionally representative
members of public commissions. (It is necessary to emphasize that economics
was from the start concerned with public policy issues. Adam Smith, founder of
the subject, enunciated the doctrines of laissez-faire, Malthus produced his population theory as an answer to the utopian socialism of William Godwin, Ricardo
enunciated the principle of freedom of trade, and later Marshall, Sidgwick, and
especially Pigou turned utilitarianism into a case for reducing the inequality of
income distribution). It was not until after the crash of 1929 that governments
began to seek the help of economists in solving immediate issues of economic
organization—and economists became extensively involved in the kind of political participation with which this study is concerned.

By that time, and indeed since the emergence into dominance of the neoclassical (marginal utility and marginal productivity) school in the last third of
the nineteenth century, economics had a hard and consistent scientific core of
both real and monetary theory.[3] It thus should have been ready to cope with the
new public policy demands being made on it. Unfortunately, the monetary
theory, while a logically beautiful and sophisticated structure, rested on the assumption that the economy reacted quickly enough to monetary changes to maintain full employment of labor, so that such disturbances would produce price
changes and not fluctuations in employment. When economists were faced with
the fact of mass unemployment caused essentially by monetary deflation (which
prevailed in England from World War I on and throughout the capitalist world

---

[3] To explain this distinction very briefly, "real" theory is concerned with what determines the price of potatoes relative to the price of ham, shoes, and other things. If we can
assume the prices of these other things to remain roughly constant on the average, we can
take the short-cut of using the money (dollars and cents) price of potatoes to represent the
value of potatoes in terms of their purchasing power over goods in general. But we cannot do this if all money prices on average are falling (deflation) or rising (inflation), because in a deflation a fall in the money price of potatoes is consistent with an increase in
their purchasing power over other things, and in an inflation a rise in the money price of
potatoes is consistent with a decrease in their purchasing power over other things. "Monetary" theory, by contrast with "real" theory, is concerned with the causes and consequences
of general movements up or down in the average money prices of goods and services and
finds the explanation of such movements in one formulation or another of the balance
between the demand for and the supply of money. The problem for economists, and still
more for policy-makers, is to distinguish between cases in which "real" theory is approximately adequate and cases in which it is not. A case in point is inflation, with respect to
which even many professional economists persist in seeking for "real" causes, such as union
monopoly power.

from 1929 until World War II), they did not question their assumptions about price flexibility and admit that real quantities rather than their prices might make the adjustment to monetary disturbance. Instead they sought explanations in terms of other real factors, such as excessively high real wages or a glutting of wants. These explanations appeared as silly and stupid to the public as they in fact were in terms of scientific method. (If the facts do not fit the predictions of the relevant theory, reexamine the assumptions of that theory rather than retreat into an alternative theory.)

The scientifically correct answer was provided by Keynes: Wages and prices are "sticky," and quantities bear most of the brunt of short-run adjustment. But Keynes's answer, aside from being cluttered with new terminology and concepts and specifically British controversies that produced much bitter but on the whole fruitless scientific debate, disregarded the background of monetary deflation that had produced the problem of mass unemployment and instead made mass unemployment the characteristic condition of a capitalist society. This proposition was quickly seized on by economists of socialist persuasion. In addition, Keynes pointed to certain conditions under which expansionary monetary policy would be incapable of producing full employment, and government expenditure involving budget deficits might be necessary. These propositions were quickly translated by his followers, especially the Americans led by Alvin Hansen of Harvard, into the proposition that monetary policy was powerless and that fiscal policy (specifically, deficit financing) was necessary to the management of a capitalist economy, the reverse of the traditional view that government, like private citizens, should balance its budget and that the central bank and not the Treasury should be responsible for stabilizing the economy.[4]

Both messages made the scientific division between Keynesian and "orthodox" economists a political division between radicals and conservatives, and this division has survived into present times, though it has gradually ceased to exercise the strong influence either on academic appointments or politicians' choices of economic advisers and evaluation of economic advice that it once had.[5] Three reasons for the fairly rapid blunting of the sharpness of the adversary conflict of the 1930s and early postwar period can be adduced.

---

[4] For an analysis of the reasons for the scientific success of the Keynesian Revolution and the speed of that success, see Harry G. Johnson, "The Keynesian Revolution and the Monetarist Counter-Revolution," *The American Economic Review* 61, no. 2 (May 1971): 1–14; also *Encounter* 36, no. 4 (April 1971): 22–23.

[5] The author can remember, as an instructor at Toronto in 1946–1947, being assailed by a pamphlet attacking a new textbook, written by an eminent Keynesian in a midwestern university, as being subversive. As a graduate student at Harvard, he overheard a telephone conversation in which the anti-Keynesian department chairman at Harvard assured a chairman elsewhere that the man he was recommending for appointment was definitely not a Keynesian.

First, Keynesian economics proved essential to wartime economic management, though the reason was less the theory itself than the fact that it emphasized "real" aggregate variables and relationships rather than "monetary" variables, and so indicated that the crucial wartime problem was the allocation of labor among armed forces and productive sectors and that the monetary and financial side of wartime management should be secondary to the real side and coordinated with it. (This was an approach that Keynes himself had espoused during the British conscription debate in World War I and successfully got implemented as government economic adviser in World War II.) This emphasis was right and gave Keynesian economists a lasting edge over the more orthodox financial approach in terms of levying additional taxes and raising war loans, even though the postwar consequences of Keynesian war finance proved strongly inflationary.

Second, and most important, the problem of capitalist countries since the war has been that of a chronic tendency toward inflationary excess demand for labor; hence the debate has centered around the issue of a little more versus a little less unemployment in the management of the economy, a practical problem in the management of a capitalist system as contrasted with the 1930s debate on whether capitalism could produce satisfactory results without radically new methods of management. This is a question that politicians have to decide, and advice on which does not threaten the system from which they derive their political power. Moreover, it is a question on which there are legitimate reasons for differences of opinion. Accordingly, economists pronouncing on the issues can disagree in public without jeopardizing their status as scientific experts. (Indeed, the fact that they can give both logical expression to, and quantitative information on, matters that the politician or civil servant senses only vaguely may be important probably enhances the public esteem economics enjoys as a scientific subject.)

Third, the Keynesians commanded the most prestigious economics departments (Oxford and Cambridge in Britain, Harvard in the United States), and, what is perhaps more important, those that attracted the best graduate students. Through successive generations of undergraduates, particularly in the United Kingdom, Keynesian economics has become part of the intellectual culture of the elite and eventually of the common culture. Through successive generations of graduate students who became teachers and economic civil servants, it gradually conquered academic economics and became the orthodoxy on the macro-economic side of economics. There was, however, and remains, a noteworthy difference between the United Kingdom and the United States in the way in which Keynesian economics came to dominance, and it is relevant to the problem of this study. In the United Kingdom it remained politicized and identified with the left-wing in politics; and it became dominant through the left-wing Keynesian conquest of Oxford and Cambridge and the automatic influence over the minds of prospective civil servants, politicians, and academics, and of academic appointments in other universities that Oxbridge commands. The orthodox tradition was not so much reasoned with; it was stamped out or retired without replacement, the process resting on the fact that, in contrast to the United States, graduate work involving formal instruction and leading to a formal graduate degree has not been a requirement of either academic or civil service employment in Great Britain until very recently (less than a decade ago). Hence economic advice is regarded in Britain as political advice, sought from economists of proven loyalty to the party or, if offered uninvited, treated as propaganda either for the government or the opposition party and discounted as such. The effect is that in Britain economics is publicly regarded not as a science but as a set of ground rules and techniques for a rather arcane type of political debate, and the economist enjoys far less public respect (if he enjoys any) than does his American counterpart. (In fact, the public respect he gets is proportioned to his academic rank and the public status of his university and not to his professional accomplishment.)[6]

In the United States, on the other hand, with its large size and democratic tradition, its large number of good universities, its already long-established tradition of formal graduate instruction, leading to a Ph.D. and drawing students from all over the country, and the general practice of requiring such education as the prerequisite for academic appointment or for good prospects in the civil service, it was impossible for Keynesian economics to conquer the profession by conquering one or two major universities. Even if it had been possible, the standards of professionalism already achieved by American economics, together with the pragmatism characteristic of pioneer societies, would have prevented the parading of political partisanship as neutral scientific recommendation. In the United States, Keynesianism had to compete for attention with the more orthodox approaches (or sometimes, as in the case of "institutionalism," more radical approaches) on the scientific grounds of being able to produce better answers to scientific problems. And, in a competitive process, one attempts to take over and use as many of one's competitors' good ideas as one can, while still advertising that one is producing a far better product than he. Hence, in the United States, Keynesianism became dominant in economic science on the basis of its scientifically valid and useful new ideas, as sifted by the competition

---

[6] When the author was a professor of economic theory in Manchester, virtually no one in the communications media, let alone the civil service or the Parliament, solicited his views on any public policy issue. When, after an interval perhaps significant in terms of the increasing emphasis of the British political process on economic growth as the panacea for the country's problems, he became the professor of political economy at the London School of Economics, he found himself deluged with such solicitations from all quarters of the Establishment.

in and judgment of the economic scientific community, rather than on the basis
of its political overtones or of an all-or-nothing choice between Keynesianism
and professional success, and orthodoxy and professional failure.

In an important sense, the statement is true that, scientifically, "we (economists) are all Keynesians now." But this permits, on the one hand, plenty of
room for scientific debate over specific theoretical and empirical issues, and, on
the other hand, the identification of themselves alternatively as "Keynesians" or
"monetarists" by economists to explain their personal political orientation without implying basic disagreements on the nature and methods of economic theory
and enquiry. Controversy among economists, when exposed to the public in the
context of public policy debate and policy formation, does not detract from the
public esteem of economics, because it displays the esteem that eminent economists have for each other—the only possible basis for reasoned debate among
them—far more than it advertises their disagreements in political stance or in
the diagnosis of particular cases calling for the application of economic analysis.
The public, after all, is accustomed to the idea that medical doctors may disagree
on the diagnosis of and prescription for a particular patient. It does not lose its
general respect for the medical profession because this happens; it continues to
believe that that profession is genuinely concerned about the patient's health
and that the patient's doctor is not motivated by the desire to kill him in order to
inherit his wealth.

The foregoing account relates to the central issue that has divided economists
into bitter scientific controversy in this century—the causes of mass unemployment
and the policies required to deal with it. But once, either as a result of economic
good fortune or of the acceptance and application of Keynesian analysis,[7] the
economy returns to and maintains a normal state of full employment, the "real"
economics of resource allocation subject to overall limitation of available quantities of resources—the crowning achievement of the evolution of economics from
Smith's *Wealth of Nations* to Marshall's *Principles of Economics* and Pigou's
Economics of Welfare, which may be regarded as the flowering of neoclassical
economics—comes into its own again.[8]

This is for two reasons: First, apart from the conditions of a great depression
such as followed the crash of 1929, in which idle resources could be reemployed
at no social cost and the capacity of man to satisfy his wants thereby improved,
the normal condition of man is a shortage of resources and the necessity of
making choices among alternative uses of them—and this is what the science
of economics is fundamentally concerned with, both the positive (descriptive)

" Micro-
economics

---

[7] There is a strong disagreement among economists over whether the full employment
of the past quarter-century has been due to the transformation of the Keynesian revolution
into economic policy or to "natural forces" independent of policies of governments.

[8] See Harry G. Johnson, "Individual and Social Choice," in *Man and the Social Sciences,* ed. William Robson (London, 1972), pp. 1–22, for a more detailed discussion of
the development of economic theory in these terms.

and normative (prescriptive) analysis of the results and implications of these choices. Second, by far the majority of the policy issues that concern the public and the politicians pertain to questions of resource allocation and the effects of resource allocation on the incomes of individuals and social groups (e.g., farm price supports, tariff policy, government regulation of industry, minimum wage laws). The exception to this rule is the transitory periods of either mass depression or abnormal inflation, both of which disrupt private and social calculations of optimal allocations, and also lead to the mistaken effort to use micro-economic resource allocation policies to compensate and correct for errors of macro-economic policy. (For example, during the stagnation and abnormal unemployment period of the early 1960s, the idea that unemployment was due to automation or to inadequate education of workers became very popular; in the late 1960s and earlier 1970s, the idea that inflation was due to the greediness of monopolies and trade unions became equally popular. In both cases the result was the adoption of policies that distorted resource allocation without correcting the fundamental error in macro-economic policy.)

In the context of micro-economic resource allocation policies (assuming that macro-economic policy is being managed reasonably satisfactorily), the problem in establishing an economic science as distinct from political propaganda is to separate the value judgments of individual economists from the scientific logic and empirical facts and to develop a methodology for establishing those facts. From this point of view, three episodes in the history of the development of economics are important.

First, as already mentioned, the neoclassical economists of the late nineteenth and early twentieth centuries, on the basis of utilitarianism and the hedonistic calculus, believed firmly that a more equal distribution of income would contribute to increased social welfare and, in consequence of the same principles as those, that an all-round increase in individual incomes contributes to increased social welfare. Thus the desirability of income redistribution from rich to poor became one of the presumed scientific findings of economics—and remains so both in the minds of many economists and in popular economic mythology. Lionel Robbins, in his *Nature and Significance of Economic Science,* published at the beginning of the 1930s, exploded this belief by pointing out that it required interpersonal judgments, which the economist as scientist is not entitled to make, about the comparative welfare of different individuals—specifically that an extra dollar for a rich man adds less to total welfare than an extra dollar for a poor man. A number of younger noneminent economists attempted to get around this point by proposing "compensation tests" of economic changes —i.e., a change is an improvement if the gainers could compensate the losers— but this was a logically unacceptable dodge unless the compensation were actually made, which it normally is not or cannot be. The resulting "new welfare economics" arrived at the position that potentially welfare could be improved, but actually it might not be, by a change that increased total output. This implied that the economist could usually say nothing about the effects of such changes on economic welfare, and therefore nothing about economic policy. But nature abhors a vacuum or a position of abstention from the social process of those engaged in understanding it. The end result has been that economists are conscious that their own values are not necessarily those of society and that they need information on society's values in order to make policy recommendations.

An alternative view of this matter, propounded by Gunnar Myrdal and still influential among his followers in Sweden, Oxford, and elsewhere, is that a social scientist should state his personal values at the beginning of his work on a problem and leave it to the readers to evaluate his conclusions in the light of this knowledge of his values. The difficulty with this solution is that any real social scientist who is aware of his own biases will attempt to prevent them from interfering with the objectivity of his work. Consequently the serious problem concerns the biases the individual has that he is not himself aware of, and that no amount of introspection can make him aware of. (Myrdal's own work exemplifies the failure of the methodology he propounds.)

Myrdal's position on the role of individual values in the social sciences parallels a larger debate over social science methodology initiated by Mannheim's *The Sociology of Knowledge* and answered by Popper's *The Open Society and Its Enemies*. Essentially, Popper's argument as it relates to the present study is that the problem of values is to be overcome, not by investigating values themselves and attempting to develop a "value-free" social science, but by applying the tests of scientific experimentation and proof. In short, it is the community of scholars policing and accepting or rejecting each other's work according to scientific standards of verification, not the individual scholar researching his own soul, that produces a social science that is genuinely scientific and not propagandistic.

Of course, to Popper's Marxist opponents, this reply has the limitation that social restrictions on entry to the social sciences may produce a community of scholars that is thoroughly scientific in its approach to the questions it asks, but blind to certain kinds of questions, especially those raising fundamental issues about the nature and justification of the existing economic organization of society. One can indeed argue both that the McCarthy era in America strengthened economics in the United States as a hard social science, by squelching the freedom of scholars to ask questions of this kind and forcing them to concentrate their attention on the more innocuous question of how the capitalist system works (or by confining the rewards of the academic career to those interested in the latter type of question), and also that it laid the profession open to legitimate student protest when American capitalism lost its self-confidence as a result of the war in Vietnam. However, it was the Marxists who initiated the debate by claiming to base their analysis of capitalist self-contradiction on a scientific economic foundation. Popper was thoroughly justified in challenging their assertion that no scientific economics other than Marxism could exist in a capitalist society and in pointing to Marxists' failure to satisfy the standards of science.

Popper's book, though largely unread now, constituted the second relevant episode in the recent development of economic science. The third was the methodology of positive economics propounded by Milton Friedman in his *Essays on Positive Economics* (Chicago, 1953), though its roots lie in a book by Keynes's father, John Neville Keynes, *On the Scope and Method of Political Economy,* published before the turn of the century. The background of Friedman's contribution was the climate of economic debate that grew out of two revolutions in economic thought that occurred in the 1930s—the Keynesian Revolution already referred to, and a somewhat prior "revolution," known variously as the "imperfect" or "monopolistic competition" revolution (the two terms incorporate the key adjectives in the titles of two books published almost simultaneously by the Cambridge economist Joan Robinson and Harvard economist E. H. Chamberlin).

The Keynesian Revolution, as already explained, attacked the assumption of neoclassical economics that capitalism tends to produce full employment. The imperfect/monopolistic competition revolution attacked the assumption of neoclassical value theory that competition tended to produce the lowest-cost production of goods for consumers and payments to the owners of factors of production equal to their contribution to the social product, on the grounds that in the real world of observation firms had some degree of monopoly power. As a consequence, it became standard practice among self-proclaimed radical economists to attack the more orthodox opponents on the basis of the "unrealism" of their assumptions about the nature of the real world. Friedman's positive methodology asserted that the question to be asked of a theory is not whether its assumptions are realistic or otherwise, but whether it possesses predictive power. This position too has some philosophical difficulties, since the assumptions of one theory may be the predictions of another, and the methods for testing predictions are themselves controversial, but it did a great deal to shift the emphasis of economics from the interpretation of the economic system to the ability to say something about how it works.

The importance of these background episodes, however, can only be appreciated in relation to the vast increase in the numbers of competent professional economists that has occurred since the 1930s. The United States, in particular, now has perhaps fifty academic economics departments of an average quality of the four or five best departments in the whole world in the pre–World War II period (though not, it should be remarked, ten times the number of really original minds, because one of the laws of intellectual society is that originality is measured by comparison with the average, and the higher the average the smaller the proportion of those rated as genuinely original). The consequence of this expansion is that, in contrast to the preceding period when academic scholars in economics could set themselves up as across-the-board personal adversaries expounding conflicting holistic views of the subject, the modern economist's adversary is a faceless host of his professional colleagues, and to be effective he must accept most of what they accept and choose carefully a limited piece of the territory on which to challenge them collectively.[9] For this very reason, economists can afford to engage in public debate over policy issues without sacrificing either their own reputations among their colleagues or the reputation of their science among the public at large.

THE LESSONS TO BE DRAWN

On the stipulation that lessons have to be drawn, the main lesson for the other social sciences to be drawn from the experience of economics would seem strongly to be that participation in the public policy formation process will be less corruptive of the scientific work and of the public reputation of a social science, the more of a science it is and the larger the scientific community it comprises. From the viewpoint of the economist—to the extent that there is one —the problem of the other social sciences is that individuals become qualified as "scientists" competent to hold academic posts by virtue of an ill-specified academic process, and thereafter feel free to abuse their academic positions to advocate their personal and social prejudices, without being subject to the discipline of the judgment of a professionally trained and scientifically competent academic community agreed on the nature of scientific procedures as applied to their discipline, and armed with an extensive body of well-tested and validated empirical knowledge. With no real science at his command, but with the pretense of having one, the academic pseudo-scientist can command undue attention for his own propaganda only at the price either of exposing his alleged science to public contempt for the pseudo-science it is, or of demeaning the efforts of his more scientifically minded and responsible colleagues to improve its scientific quality by honest hard work. The key to individual policy participation by the individual without degrading the scientific community is to have a profession that has a common scientific core; and this means a consistent body of theory validated by empirical knowledge and testing and policed by professionals, in place of a congeries of conflicting untested hypotheses carrying conviction only proportional to the persuasive power of their proponents.[10]

---

[9] The most obvious exception to this generalization in American economics is the rivalry between Milton Friedman of the University of Chicago and Paul Samuelson of M.I.T., but even this is largely confined to monetary theory, and there is little but peripheral disagreement between them on issues in "real" economic theory. Similarly, though Friedman as leader of the "Chicago School" of monetarists and James Tobin as the leader of the "Yale School" of post-Keynesians are sharp adversaries in monetary theory, both when confronted with the question of the best way of dealing with the poverty problem came up independently with the proposal for a negative income tax.

[10] These remarks are not meant to be condescending. The author's experience of economics outside the United States is that much of the practice as distinct from the science of economics is, deplorably, of exactly the same description.

Science Advising and the ABM Debate
Paul Doty

With the signing of the treaty limiting anti-ballistic missile (ABM) systems, in Moscow in May 1972, the decade-long ABM debate came to an end. It had its roots in the 1959 decision of Neil McElroy, then secretary of defense, to make the Army responsible for missile defense. Many talented and dedicated officers were thereby committed to this mission. Since it was the only license the Army had in the new dimension of space, it was certain to be pursued with alacrity. Despite the growing opposition of many technical experts in responsible government positions and on scientific advisory councils, successive systems were developed and tested. By 1966 the controversy had become a pitched battle. It culminated in a meeting that took place in the White House in January 1967. In addition to President Johnson, Secretary of Defense McNamara and the joint chiefs of staff, there were present all past and current special assistants to the president for science and technology and all past and current directors of defense research and engineering.[1] "The place where the buck stops" had been reached. The question was: "Will it work and should it be deployed?" The context was that of a country-wide defense against a Soviet missile attack. The answer from the assembled experts was "no"; there was no dissent. There was, however, a minority favoring a thin ABM system oriented toward a hypothetical Chinese attack. The question of a Minuteman defense alone was not posed.

The controversy receded but was suddenly rekindled by the surprise announcement by Secretary McNamara in September 1967 that the United States would build a light, country-wide ABM system, known as Sentinel, to cope with

---

[1] H. York, *Race to Oblivion* (New York, 1970), p. 194.

185

a hypothetical Chinese attack. The reasoning behind this decision has never been made public.[2] Without much debate, Congress soon approved funds for beginning the deployment of the Sentinel system.

It was only some months later when representatives of the army began to acquire land for missile sites near Boston, Chicago, and other major cities that a public awakening occurred. By this time many of the government experts had left office where they had been unable to oppose the deployment decision: They moved quickly to join with groups of private citizens in urging Congress to halt the building of Sentinel.

Subsequent developments hardly need recounting. The Nixon administration, sensing the magnitude of the opposition and being, initially, uncritically responsive to Pentagon advice, focused on the protective role for Minuteman; the administration was supported by the buildup of large Soviet ICBMs that could with years of further growth and development put much of the American land-based Minuteman system at risk. The result was a regrouping of essentially the same weapons as were to have been used in Sentinel to produce the Safeguard system whose fourteen sites were to provide substantial defense of the 1,000 Minuteman missiles in the Northwest and a light area defense of almost all the continental United States and Hawaii.

The climax came in August 1969 when the Senate voted 50–50, and the vice president's tie-breaking vote launched the actual deployment. On that occasion *Newsweek* reported:

> Not since Franklin Roosevelt's draft law cleared the House of Representatives by one vote in the summer of 1941 had a President been put to so stern a challenge by Congress on a major question of national defense. Richard Nixon had staked his prestige on a no-compromise commitment to the view that a beginning on the Safeguard anti-ballistic-missile (ABM) system was "absolutely essential" to America's security. Precisely half the U.S. Senate said he was wrong. In the showdown last week, Mr. Nixon won.

While the first site was being constructed, the Moscow Treaty of 1972 came into force limiting the Soviet Union and the United States to two ABM sites, one for missile protection and one for defense of the national capital. In July 1974 both sides agreed to reduce ABMs to one site each. The American site at Grand Forks, N.D. reached full operational status on October 1, 1975. In November 1975 both the House and the Senate voted to dismantle the installation

---

[2] Since this change in position could be viewed as a rejection of what seemed then to be the dominant independent technical advice or else a conversion to the minority position by Secretary McNamara, it is useful to record an alternative interpretation. That is, this switch bought for McNamara the freedom to oppose an expansion in numbers of missiles in the ICBM force, which was being strongly advocated at that time. If so, it would not be the first time that technical advice has become the subject of bargaining in the political decision-making process at a higher level.

knowing that the Department of Defense was planning to place it on a stand-by basis on July 1, 1976. This major military system, costing $5.7 billion, is destined to have the shortest "on-line" time in recent military history. Its epilogue was spoken by Representative George Mahon (Democrat-Texas), chairman of the House Appropriations Committee, who had stoutly defended the Safeguard system until 1975. He observed, "We have spent $5.7 billion preparing to defend ourselves against the intercontinental ballistic missile. The Safeguard system has not been effective, except perhaps from a cosmetic standpoint. If we had done nothing, it would have been the same."

This finale underlines the importance and consequence of the decision of the Soviet Union and the United States to terminate ABM deployment at an early stage: it clearly represents the most far-reaching restraint in strategic weap- onry thus far undertaken.

This is the barest outline of the titanic struggle over whether or not to deploy and eventually whether or not to limit one of the most ambitious and costly weapons systems ever undertaken. Because the record is almost completely public and since the public was intensely involved in the later years, this debate is certain to become a classic case for examining the processes of decision making, the interaction of technical advice and advisers with government and public, and the role of developing weapons systems in strategic negotiations.

Our intent is to examine this case from the viewpoint of the role of the scientific or technical adviser in a national decision in which such advice is clearly important. Such an examination will reveal a striking number of difficulties and complexities, particularly in the intertwining of the political and technical factors, as well as a quite inadequate system for eliciting and evaluating scientific and technical advice. Moreover, it allows us to follow the interesting attempt made in 1971 by a professional society to judge the scientific contributions to the Senate debate in terms of the guidelines it proposed for scientific analysts serving as advisers.

Before turning to these matters, however, it is useful to note some conclusions reached in a related study of scientists and the ABM by Anne Cahn.[3] Her principal concern lay with assessing the influence scientist advocates had with their several audiences (executive, congressional, and public) and the identifiable characteristics associated with those who took pro and anti positions. She assessed the influence of scientists with the Senate as being intermediate between the lesser role they played with the executive and the unexpectedly popular role they played in public. In the congressional arena she suggested that

> According to most of the senators interviewed thus far, the scientists' most notable contribution to the ABM issue was that they gave senators and their staffs

---

[3] A. H. Cahn, "Eggheads and Warheads: Scientists and the ABM," Ph.D. thesis. Massachusetts Institute of Technology, Cambridge, Mass., 1971.

the courage and confidence to express their views on complex technological issues, bolstered by their newly acquired knowledge and expertise.

Furthermore, it was evident that the scene was not the simple one in which the Senate committee called in expert witnesses but rather a more complex one in which numerous scientists were pressing to be heard. At a critical juncture Senator John Stennis consented to have outside (nongovernmental) scientists testify before his committee, because Senator Albert Gore would have offered the forum of his subcommittee if they had not been invited by Stennis. Clearly this suggests a state of advanced advocacy rather than the summoning of detached testimony.

Shortly after the Senate vote, a professional society, the Operations Research Society of America (ORSA), appointed a committee to prepare a set of guidelines for systems analysts involved in advisory capacities, and in the course of doing this, the committee also assessed the quality of advice provided the Senate on the ABM debate: This became a highly controversial appendix to the final report.[4] Inasmuch as the writer has examined this particular part of the episode previously,[5] the main part of this article will draw heavily on that examination.

In focusing on the 1969 period covered by the report, it is important to keep in mind that this was only a small although crucial part of the much longer debate. This concentration seems justified, because the 1969 period is such a well-documented one, and much comment has been stimulated by the ORSA report that dealt with it. The report itself is the product of an investigation by an ad hoc committee of operational research specialists appointed by the council of ORSA to investigate the professional conduct of the debate, at the instigation of Professor Albert Wohlstetter, one of the most vigorous participants. The report was accepted by the council of ORSA on May 5, 1971, and published in the September issue of the society's journal. In a minority statement five of the twelve members of the council objected to the society's "quasijudicial function of investigating and reporting on professional behavior of individuals" (see citation in footnote 4).

Putting aside for the moment the ethical and legal aspects of an investigation of professional conduct, it is evident that the debate preceding the vote in the Senate was a milestone in the history of scientific and technical advice in matters relating to military decision making. Consequently, a definitive investigation that was impartial and comprehensive would be of great interest and value. It is possible that the aim of the ad hoc committee was no less than this. But when one takes into account the length and heat of the debate and the fact that the issue

---

[4] "Guidelines for the Report of the ORSA *ad hoc* Committee on Professional Standards," *Operations Research* 19 (1971) : 1123–1258.

[5] P. Doty, "Can Investigations Improve Scientific Advice? The Case of the ABM," *Minerva* 10 (1972) : 280–94.

at its heart was to continue unresolved for some time to come, an investigation that would have reasonably satisfied all the contending parties would have been a superhuman achievement indeed.

My own impression of the reception of the report in the four months following its publication is as follows. Of all those persons known to me, who had intimate knowledge of the substantive questions, all who supported the ABM have, with one exception, favored the report, and all who were opposed to the ABM have been critical of the report. Comment in the press has been equally partisan: Mr. Joseph Alsop's praise of the report[6] and the White House letter of congratulation to the president of ORSA[7] were roundly criticized by Professor George Rathjens and by Drs. G. B. Kistiakowsky, H. Scoville, and H. F. York.[8] The *Wall Street Journal* saw the report as a vindication of Professor Wohlstetter.[9] Professor Philip Morse, one of the founders of ORSA, expressed strong objections to the report,[10] as did Professor W. K. H. Panofsky.[11] Apart from a privately circulated set of comments by Professors Rathjens, Steven Weinberg, and Jerome B. Wiesner, the most detailed criticism of the report is that by Dr. Richard Garwin.[12]

Other reviews and comments were solicited by several senators and were published together in the *Congressional Record.* Subsequently a selection of comments was published in *Operations Research,*[13] and several articles,[14] in addition to mine (see footnote 5), commenting on the issue of the obligations of scientists as advisers appeared in *Minerva* in 1973.

At this point it may be useful to record some unwritten comments that seem representative of private discussions of the report in the months following its publication. These fell into two categories. The first was from several senior scientific advisers who had not taken public positions on the ABM and several senior government officials in relevant departments: They remarked that the report was biased and constituted a further stage in the ongoing debate; they considered that it avoided the main issue and would, therefore, be quickly judged

---

[6] J. Alsop, *New York Times,* November 9, 1971.

[7] V. K. McElheny, *Boston Globe,* November 7, 1971.

[8] Letters to the editor, *Boston Globe,* November 19, 1971.

[9] R. L. Bartley, *Wall Street Journal,* October 12, 1971.

[10] Letter to the editor, *Boston Globe,* November 19, 1971.

[11] W. K. H. Panofsky, *Scientific American,* January 1972, p. 6.

[12] *Congressional Record,* November 12, 1971, pp. S-18320–24.

[13] *Operations Research* 20 (1972): 205–46.

[14] A. J. Miser, "The Scientist as Adviser: The Relevance of the Early Operations Research Experience," *Minerva* 11 (1973): 95–108; M. J. Moravcsik, "The Universal Intellectual versus the Expert," *Minerva* 11 (1973): 109–12; Duncan MacRae, Jr., "Science and the Formation of Policy in a Democracy," *Minerva* 11 (1973): 228–42; A. Mazur, "Disputes between Experts," *Minerva* 11 (1973): 241–62.

irrelevant and drop from view. The second type of response was from several persons experienced in policy making in other areas but not acquainted in a specialized way with the substantive details of ABM technology. From a careful reading of the report, they concluded that a strong case had been made for the shortcomings of the scientists criticized in the report. These two types of response —negative and positive—have not been put into written form, and my impression of the distribution of these unwritten responses might have been different if I had encountered different persons. They are, however, probably representative of the types of view held outside the polarized groups of congressmen, members of the executive branch of the federal government, and scientists who have been closely involved in the debate, and they therefore deserve consideration.

o These impressions of the early response to the report are not meant to be a guide in any way to a more definitive evaluation of the report. But they do suggest the range of possibility and the difficulties that face anyone attempting to assess what might be learned from this inquiry.

However, beyond the special illumination provided by the ORSA report and its attempt to codify acceptable behavior for technical witnesses, there remain several other questions of perhaps equal importance and even greater refractoriness. How can Congress get better advice from the scientific and technical community? How can Congress and the public keep scientific components in perspective in relation to larger political issues; in other words, how can they beat the "a little knowledge is a dangerous thing" syndrome? And finally, assuming that some scientists can be expected to remain uncommitted and capable of giving objective and relevant advice in the real world where knowledge is power, how can they be identified and put to best use? Nor is this the entire sum and substance of the matter. Many scientists can enter into policy formulation only as advocates either because they have the interests of their employer uppermost or because they have become personally persuaded that a particular policy direction is right. How can the input of advocate scientists also be used in national policy determination? With these questions in mind, we return to the ABM debate.

*   *   *   *   *

Two features make the assessment of the ABM debate, and the ORSA report as well, particularly difficult and complex. Yet it is these two features that make this such a useful case for studying the interplay of scientific advice and governmental decision making. The first is that none of the experts could be considered neutral in 1969, when President Nixon's administration proposed the deployment of the Safeguard system and the Senate was faced with the decision of whether or not to provide the necessary financial support for it. Most disputes on public policy involving scientific evidence or prediction are settled at low levels. Others rise in public visibility and are sometimes judged by allegedly neutral bodies of experts, such as committees of the National Academy of Sciences. A few others cannot be contained and eventually explode into public view as full-fledged conflicts. By this time most, if not all, experts have taken sides. The question of how to proceed beyond this point in the most rational manner has not been well answered, and examination of the ABM conflict may offer some suggestions.

The second feature that gave this debate its distinctive character was the complexity of the issue, coupled with the fact that the debate was carried on at different levels. As with many major policy decisions, the problem faced by the Senate of whether or not to appropriate funds for the deployment of Safeguard for Minuteman defense required working through several groups of questions in order. It is useful to specify these in detail, since they also correspond to the different levels at which the debate proceeded.

1. *Assessment of Need.*

Here one had to ask whether the American land-based ICBM force (1,000 Minutemen and 54 Titans) would become vulnerable to almost total destruction in the foreseeable future of roughly five to ten years. Clearly the answer depended on the outcome of several subsidiary questions. First, what different estimates or assumptions of the growth of Soviet forces, both in numbers of missiles and in payload capability, should be considered for the next decade? Secondly, what would be the vulnerability of the American force to each of the assumed growth patterns of the Soviet force? Thirdly, to what extent would the bomber and submarine parts of the American deterrent force become vulnerable, and to what extent would the American tripartite deterrent force remain capable of launching a retaliatory strike of unacceptable intensity?

2. *Assessment of the Adequacy of the Solution.*

If the protection of some or all of the land-based missiles and some or all of the bombers is shown to be necessary, one must then ask if the proposed solution, in this case Safeguard, is adequate. The reply to this question requires careful analysis of the effectiveness of the composite system against the variety of attack options and tactics available to the Soviet Union. Such analysis must include the degradation in performance that may be produced by the environment of a nuclear attack, the special vulnerability of the radars, the probability of maintaining the system in a state of instant readiness indefinitely, and the ability of the attacker to exhaust the defense. After defining as well as possible the range of threat for which Safeguard may be effective, the cost must be estimated and compared with alternative proposals for maintaining a roughly equivalent deterrent force.

3. *Assessment of the Political Value of Acceptance of the Solution.*

The criterion at this level is largely political rather than technological; the aim is to estimate the net benefits of the solution in terms of national security, diplomatic advantage, and domestic needs and pressures. In the context of the ABM decision, the question is: Will having Safeguard help attain a political goal that is worth the price and risk? This question remains urgent in all circumstances short of a decisive negative answer to questions 1 and 2. The less affirmative the answers to questions 1 and 2 are, the greater the burden placed on the political perception of the decision maker and the more he risks turning diplomacy and military posture into bluff.

*   *   *   *   *

Viewing the ABM debate retrospectively in this framework, one cannot avoid observing that the pro-ABM scientists concentrated on questions of the first type, i.e., need, while the anti-ABM scientists focused on questions of the second type, i.e., adequacy of the solution. Meanwhile, the administration was not seriously challenged on its political decision (question 3), the only articulated basis for which was the need for Safeguard as a "bargaining chip" in SALT.

The pro-ABM scientists argued that the American ICBMs could soon be in danger, that American security demanded the retention of all three components of the deterrent (ICBMs, submarines, and bombers), and that Safeguard was the only available response to the growing Soviet SS-9 force, which was endangering the ICBMs. By concentrating the force of their arguments on Minuteman vulnerability, they left the technical merits and shortcomings of Safeguard essentially unexamined.

The anti-ABM scientists argued that a linear projection of the Soviet arsenal of SS-9s, coupled with increased accuracy and the use of MIRVs, would ultimately lead to the obsolescence of Minuteman, perhaps in a decade. But they insisted that this would not give the Soviet Union the equivalent to a first-strike capability since the other parts of the American deterrrent could not be simultaneously attacked: Enough was certain to survive to devastate the Soviet Union. More important, however, the opponents of the ABM concentrated their fire on the ineffectiveness of Safeguard in providing significant protection to Minuteman, even if it performed optimally.

Turning now to the ORSA report, and particularly to Appendix III, which makes up the bulk of the report, we find that the investigation does not deal with all these three levels of the debate but is limited almost exclusively to questions of type 1. Even its treatment of questions of type 1 is incomplete, for it does not examine the adequacy of the tripartite deterrent when one part fails. This limitation of scope not only imposes severe restrictions on what is being examined but prejudices the outcome, because it cuts out most of the ground on which anti-

ABM arguments were made and gives undue emphasis to the narrow terrain on which most pro-ABM arguments rest.

Although it is not my purpose to examine the many findings of the committee that seem to be open to question, two of them are sufficient to illustrate what appears to be a lack of impartiality and comprehensiveness in the investigation. Perhaps the most dramatic finding was the difference in the numbers of ICBMs calculated to be able to survive a Soviet first-strike attack, using the 420 to 500 SS-9 missiles it was then predicted the Soviets might have in 1975. Clearly such a calculation depends on the assumptions one makes about the number of reentry vehicles per missile, their accuracy, their megatonnage, the tactics employed by the attacker, and the hardness assigned to the ICBMs attacked. Since the range of reasonable choice for these variables is considerable, it is understandable that no great weight should be attached to any particular set or the result that is derived therefrom. That two different assessments should produce figures as different as 5 percent and 25 percent surviving ICBMs is not surprising. If the assumptions had been the same, the calculated results would have been the same: High-school mathematics are sufficient for the calculation. Professor Wohlstetter considered the difference a matter of high principle; Professor Rathjens looked upon it as a "back-of-the-envelope" calculation. After identifying the assumptions used and some small errors made by Professor Rathjens, the report praises Professor Wohlstetter for doing his "homework" correctly and criticizes Professor Rathjens rather severely for his errors and the bias that the committee found in some of his assumptions.

Having been treated in so much detail, this incident assumes the importance of a pivotal point in the debate. Yet the committee fails in its obligation to put the calculation in perspective. It does not suggest that the choice of 500 missiles made the best possible case for Safeguard effectiveness.[15] A significantly smaller number would leave too many ICBMs surviving, and any significantly larger number would so overwhelm the Safeguard system that it would be useless. The critical role of the choice of 500 goes even further. Since the effectiveness of Safeguard is sharply peaked at this number, it is clear then that an adversary could overwhelm it by waiting until he had a larger striking force. The main point is that, in an environment of constantly growing forces, Safeguard offers *at best* a brief period of marginal effectiveness. Whether this period would occur in 1975 or in some later year is very uncertain. This is a situation that occurs repeatedly in technically based decision making. The fine tuning of a calculation involving a number of parameters having substantial uncertainties is seldom justified, particularly if it obscures larger issues. Yet Professor Rathjens is taken to task in the report for being inattentive to small details, while a testimony that

---

15 The "Guidelines" in the body of the report recommend that analysts should "check the sensitivity of the results to variations in assumptions and inputs. . . ."

consciously avoids the main point—that Safeguard can be effective against only a very narrow band of transient threats—is praised.

Indications of dual standards can be seen in many other places. An interesting example is the report's treatment of two tactical options that might possibly be used by the Soviet Union if it were planning a first strike. One of these involves reprogramming—the retargeting of some missiles to replace those that failed to function in the original salvo. The inclusion of such a tactic improves the hypothetical destructiveness of a Soviet first strike when large weapons are used. Since it supports the point Professor Wohlstetter was making, the inclusion of this tactic in his assumptions is understandable, although comparable choices by Professor Rathjens are criticized. But consider the justification that Professor Wohlstetter uses for assuming that the Soviet force has this capability. In this testimony he states: "There are very familiar, well-known methods of arranging it so that you can reprogram missiles to replace a very large proportion of your failures. . . ." Professor Rathjens replies: "There is no basis that I am aware of for believing the Soviet Union employs such a technique, and I do not believe we do." The report agrees, but allows the assumption since Professor Wohlstetter "does not claim that either we or the Soviets have such techniques now." The standards that Professor Wohlstetter must meet could hardly be lower. To help him, the report devotes nine pages to suggestions of how reprogramming might be done. Yet it does not admit the central point: that this "quite likely tactic" requires selection of standby missiles, the switching of their targeting instructions, and possible internal readjustments, all within seconds. This very heavy additional burden for computer and guidance systems would require extensive tests in salvo firings before the confidence level of 95 percent single warhead kill probability assumed by Professor Wohlstetter could be achieved. It is the great cost and the near impossibility of achieving and maintaining high reliability for this tactic that makes it so unlikely; the necessary but insufficient numerical criteria elaborated in the report to legitimate this assumption miss the point.

Compare, now, the way that this assumption was handled with the treatment given to Professor Panofsky, who had argued that it was unreasonable to assume that in a first strike the Soviet Union could force the United States to hold Minutemen in their silos while bomber bases were being attacked by exploding submarine-launched warheads over the Minuteman fields. Professor Panofsky concludes his argument by saying:

> [Such an attack] . . . would require an enormous increase in the numbers of Soviet missiles, their accuracy, and in the confidence the Soviets would have to have in their system. Moreover, the SAC fleet would have to remain on the ground as "sitting ducks" even in times of stress, that is, they would have to be not on airborne alert; moreover the SAC airfields would have to be within reach of the Soviet's SLBMs [submarine-launched ballistic missiles] a fact that we are presently changing. . . . We are giving the Soviets credit for a degree of performance and reliability of military systems which we could not dream of achieving ourselves.

The committee was unimpressed and formulated the unrealistically high standard that Professor Panofsky (and Professor Wiesner) should have met: "Those who wish to challenge the possibility of a pin-down attack by the Soviets must treat *all* reasonable tactics that might lead to pin-down, and demonstrate that *none* of them will succeed." Just as ABM systems can always be exhausted by being presented with more incoming warheads than they can handle, so can scientific witnesses, if they accept the charge to evaluate all kinds of "contrived threat which totally ignore the kind of realities the Soviet planner would have to face" (Panofsky).

The gap between the capability that the Societ Union would have to have to employ this tactic with confidence and that which they are estimated to have in the foreseeable future is very great. Only arguments using classified data could elaborate this in detail, but it is most unlikely that the U.S. Department of Defense is so derelict in its duty as to have allowed this kind of vulnerability to develop. This attitude of allowing maximum capability on one's opponent's side and minimum capability on one's own, like the asymmetry between capability and intent, permeates all strategic debates and is probably unresolvable by any professional committee. Being unresolved it offers a tool, perhaps unconsciously used, to impose an unacceptable demand for precise discrimination on technical witnesses.

*   *   *   *   *

Let us now turn to the propriety of the ORSA investigation and examine the extent to which this effort might affect the conduct of public policy debates and the technical advice that they require. It is evident upon examining Appendix III that what took place in some ways resembled a judicial procedure. The findings read like a judgment, and the potential impact on the careers of those "found guilty" could be substantial. Yet this was carried out without any prior communication of rules, without a prior limitation of jurisdiction and without any provision of safeguards. These features are considered necessary in a court and even more so in an ad hoc proceeding where the reputations of individuals are at risk. Even if one argues that justice was done in this case, the precedent is set for other investigations of this kind, any of which may bring substantial harm to individuals whose conduct and, hence, whose ethics, since ethics are the complex of rules that govern conduct, are publicly judged by a group to which they do not belong and on which they never conferred such prerogatives. Only the state with its judicial apparatus can claim such powers.

The authority that ORSA and its ad hoc committee presumed to have in this investigation derives solely from itself. None of the six persons[16] whose conduct was found at fault was a member of ORSA; Professor Wohlstetter was.

---

[16] At least one of the six, Professor Panofsky, received no notification of the investigation until he was sent the report.

Only one of the six considers himself to be engaged in operational research. More importantly, almost none of the individual points investigated involved matters obviously within the domain of operational research. Instead the questions that led to the severest judgment dealt with how a graph was read or misread, or whether certain data or others were employed. Distinctions such as that between 500 and 600 are not matters requiring an expertise in operational research. Nowhere except in the ten-page section supporting Professor Wohlstetter's assumption on reprogramming can one see any requirement of the professional discipline. Hence one must ask why a group of persons who are not members of an operational research society should be investigated by a group who are, on matters that do not require an expertise in operational research.

Many, perhaps most, professional societies have faced the problem of propagating a standard of professional behavior, particularly with regard to the professional-client relationship. The "Guidelines" that are set forth in the first ten pages of the report—the rest consists of appendices—appear to be a sound statement of standards of procedure and conduct for operational research workers doing work on contract and serving a client as advocate. If the appendices dealt with the application of these standards in typical situations, the result would be professionally useful and conform to the practice of other professional societies, which, in setting professional standards of conduct, confine themselves to issues that are sufficiently narrow and central to the discipline to command a nearly unanimous consensus in the profession. Thus the ORSA investigation is a radical departure from the traditional roles of professional societies and is in principle in conflict with the due process of law.

These considerations lead me to conclude that it is unlikely that the quality and effectiveness of scientific advice to government will be improved by investigations of the type undertaken by the ORSA committee, although some persons may indeed do their sums more carefully as a consequence. Even if such procedures were modified so as to avoid infringement of legal guarantees, they would be harmful to the process of advice and debate, because they empower a professional group, no matter how narrowly constituted, to apply its particular standards to issues that are almost certain to be very much larger. Yet the general respect that professional societies still receive from the public is such that the condemnations arising from such procedures would be widely accepted and the persons who would be willing to be judged publicly by such standards would become fewer.

*   *   *   *   *

How then can the contributions of technical experts to such important policy debates be made more responsible? How can conflicting conclusions involving scientific concepts and analyses be fairly resolved or understood in time to be useful? And how can one insure that a reasonable balance of attention will be given to both the arguments that depend on detail and the wider issues that depend on experience, judgment, and perception of the political context? Let us consider only those few major issues, such as that concerning the ABM, in which the debate becomes extensive and the technical component is substantial. The SST debate is also in this category, as are the debates of the early 1960s over a nuclear test ban and their recurrence in the future if a complete test ban becomes the subject of negotiation.

Ideally such conflict should be resolved and some approach to a consensus reached before congressional hearings begin. This consensus should be worked out in the relevant government departments or agencies and the scientific advisory committees, and through their interplay. When properly appointed, these committees form a

> parallel communication network within the federal government which to a very considerable extent circumvents the customary bureaucratic channels. In science and engineering no level of the bureaucracy has a monopoly on new ideas, and the loose nature of the advisory system provides one means by which ideas originating at a low level in the bureaucratic structure can be brought directly to the point of decision without going through regular channels, and new ideas from outside the federal structure (or its contractors) can be introduced quickly into governmental operations.[17]

When this system fails to bring about consensus, the administration generally recommends its choice among the alternatives to Congress and the debate develops in hearings before the appropriate committee(s). The content and value of the hearings is then shaped by the work of the staff of the committees and the choice of witnesses invited to testify. While experienced and competent staff members can arrange very useful hearings on many bills within their normal range of work, the issues of large scope, such as the ABM, involve matters, especially technical matters, with which they cannot deal adequately. The selection of witnesses can be done in such a way as to bring out the important differences and to aid in finding compromises. But in issues about which opinions have already become highly polarized and politicized the choice of witnesses is likely to be strongly influenced by those members of the committee who are acknowledged exponents of one or the other of the polarized viewpoints. This allows little opportunity for introducing less partisan testimony; it polarizes the debate further and converts the taking of testimony into an adversary proceeding. Obviously it was this kind of situation, and the inevitable haste, that contributed to much of the unnecessary misunderstanding in the ABM hearings.

Since the hearings in such cases are so close to adversary proceedings in spirit, there are recurring suggestions to go all the way and introduce the actual procedures of a court of law. The attractiveness of this diminishes, however, when one appreciates that this would require a congressional committee to im-

---

17 H. Brooks, *The Government of Science* (Cambridge, Mass., 1968), p. 82.

merse itself in the technical details as a judge does. Given the tasks and schedule requirements, such a process would be ludicrously cumbersome and would paralyze decision making. Moreover, any reform of existing procedures should encourage convergence rather than intensify the polarization of viewpoints.

Perhaps the most practical way of improving the advisory process at this stage is to build on the process that keeps scientists honest and relevant in their professional lives. That is, a means should be found to have witnesses confront peers of equal competence. To be specific, congressional committees, after being formed in each two-year congressional period and assessing the major issues that are likely to come before them, could, with adequate advice, engage a small and balanced group of consultants of acknowledged technical competence and reputation for the remainder of the congressional session. As consultants, they would agree not to engage in public discussion or serve on other advisory committees on subjects that would overlap with or touch on those that are expected to come before their particular committee.

In actual operation a consultants' panel would be selected for a given set of hearings. These consultants would advise the staff on witnesses, organization, and schedules. They could suggest the most useful form of testimony and specific questions that should be put to the witnesses. At the hearing itself they would be able to question each witness and require written answers to questions that could not be dealt with in the hearing. In cases of continued conflicting testimony, they could recommend additional sessions and the questions that should be pursued further. After the hearings they could meet with the committee in both open and executive session to discuss their evaluation of the presentations and provide a written summary.

Of course, the success of such a course depends on choosing and enlisting as consultants scientists of considerable experience and stature, so that the witnesses will feel that they are being judged by their peers. In some circumstances it might be possible for the panel of consultants to meet with witnesses prior to testifying to resolve issues that are obviously due to misunderstanding or insufficient data and thereby avoid wasting time in the hearings proper.

Another device that might prove useful and would rest on the judgment of peers is one by which the chairman of a committee of the Senate or the House of Representatives requests an external body, such as the National Academy of Sciences, to provide an advisory report in an area of potential committee concern. This was done in 1965 and 1967 by the House Committee on Science and Astronautics, which requested reports on *Basic Research and National Goals* and *Applied Science and Technological Progress*.[18] In both cases the panels were chosen to represent a balance of views. Individual members were asked to prepare

---

[18] Reports to the Committee on Science and Astronautics, U.S. House of Representatives, by the National Academy of Sciences (Washington, D.C., 1965, 1967).

papers outlining their own views on specific topics but were then required to present and defend them *in camera* before the entire panel. There was considerable revision of papers as a result of this confrontation of peers. The conclusions prepared by the staff and the chairman clearly reflected the quality and conviction of the arguments before the entire panel. These recommendations eventually became the basis of legislation reorganizing the National Science Foundation. Although the subjects in these instances allowed a more leisurely approach than issues such as the ABM might, the usefulness of such a procedure and the balanced and judicious quality of advice that it can produce justifies its being tried on other major issues. For example, consider the possibility that the administration proposed that a complete nuclear test ban become the subject of negotiations in SALT. As before, an enormous amount of seismological and other data would be involved and used. Early in the next congressional session, the appropriate committees could request an examination of this problem in the form just outlined. Members of the panel who carried out this task, or some of them, could then also serve as consultants on hearings dealing with the administration's proposals. Such a procedure could be much more effective and much less abrasive in dealing with an issue, which may have the emotional potential of the ABM, than the procedures now followed.

Both of these proposals have the additional virtue of increasing the contact between congressmen and scientific and technological advisers. Moreover, they do so in a manner that exhibits the procedures and modes of reasoning that are used in science itself. A scientist recognizes that his standing in the scientific community rests on the degree to which his research is verified by subsequent events and provides results that other scientists can build on. A scientific adviser will function best if his influence in government rests on the degree to which his advice is vindicated by subsequent events and provides results that others can build on.

*   *   *   *   *

We now come to the second of three questions raised near the end of the first section: How can Congress and the public keep scientific or technical components of public policy debates in perspective? "In perspective" implies that the technical issues are only part of the whole and, as in the ABM debate, may assume a disproportionate importance. In that debate the narrow issue of the number of Minutemen likely to survive a very specific kind of Soviet first strike mushroomed into a seemingly pivotal issue. In the broader context this issue is seen to be only a part of questions of type 2, and yet it tended at times to dominate the whole debate.

This compulsive preoccupation with that part of a policy debate that can be cast into a simple, one-dimensional numerical form seems more and more to be a recurring trap in major technological debates. The test-ban debate became overly preoccupied with the number of on-site inspections, the SST debate with the estimate of increased incidence of skin cancer, and the ABM debate with quantification of missiles surviving a Soviet first strike. While all of these had some relevance and deserved the best technical assessment, they did not deserve to become primary, decisive issues. They did become so nevertheless, because the numerical dimension in which they could be argued provided welcome escape from the much more complex policy issues that were actually at stake.

The suggestions made in the foregoing section to improve the format of congressional testimony so as to filter out misleading or biased testimony would not by themselves insure that policy debates remain focused on policy issues. In this regard Professor F. A. Long of Cornell University wrote as follows:

> . . . you do foreshadow these broader issues by your Type 3 question in out-lining the various levels of discussion. And you do point to ways in which this entered in the ABM debate. On the other hand, to the degree that these hearings and the testimony which goes with them frequently are directed more toward national goals than to the specific technical or military problem at hand, one can be a little skeptical of your otherwise sensible recommendation for improved procedures for the giving of technological advice. In other words, if Congress by bad organization or by deliberate intent insists on substituting technical discussions for policy discussions, large elements of policy are likely to creep in under the door and confuse things almost no matter what is the structure.

To the extent that the Congress can be criticized for allowing the quantitative aspects of technological arguments to assume exaggerated importance, one can criticize the ORSA report and some reactions to it of similar shortcomings. Just as members of Congress have the obligation to impose balance on their deliberations, so do members of the scientific and technical community have the obligation of assessing and communicating the relative importance of technical input to policy debate and of not exaggerating it to promote an overall preference that has been reached on other grounds.

*   *   *   *   *

This admonition leads directly to our final question: What are the professional and ethical standards that are appropriate for a scientist who is advocating a particular position in a policy debate? At one end of the spectrum of acceptable behavior is the person of totally uncompromised personal integrity who separates analysis from any desired outcome, who is completely open about his assumptions as well as his ideological commitments, and whose record displays an unassailable detachment from his employer, his professional associates, and his governmental connections. Such individuals are rare, but that is no reason to abandon such an ideal of behavior.

The other end of the spectrum is much more heavily populated and institutionalized: It is the scientist or technical expert who contracts with a party to a dispute to help him insofar as scientific or technical matters affect his case. Often this relationship requires the expert to select the evidence favorable to his client and impose unusually severe standards on unfavorable evidence. Such behavior is perfectly normal in the legal profession and among many scientists in industrial employment. It is also the norm for many technical employees in government agencies, and in more subtle ways many academic scientists have used favorably selected scientific or technical data or exaggerated the feasibility and promise of their own line of research in advancing applications for funds. It is to this end of the spectrum that the guidelines of the ORSA report seem to refer. On page 1128 of the report, we find:

> Scrupulously observe any ground rules about confidentiality laid down by the organization being served.
>
> Report the study's results only to the organizational elements sponsoring the study, unless specifically directed by them to report to a wider audience.

Later (p. 1134), the report states that:

> An analyst called upon to testify on behalf of a client whose decision he has helped to shape by his analyses should support his client's case.

Although such guidelines may be acceptable in typical employer-client relations, they surely fall far short of what should be expected in testimony before Congress or in contributions to a public debate. What is at issue here is a problem that the legal profession solved a long time ago, and perhaps their solution can be of some guidance to the dilemma that confronts scientists. Professor Milton Katz made this point recently in addressing the National Academy of Sciences.[19]

> [The legal profession] has tried to protect itself and others—by formalizing the distinction between a legal *opinion* and a legal *brief*. When the lawyer renders a legal opinion, he is expected to give a coldly analytical objective opinion, letting the chips fall where they may. When he presents a brief, it is understood that he is making the best argument that he can make under the circumstances, whatever his objective analysis may be. When the stakes are high or when energy, patience, and time are short, the distinction may become blurred; but the lawyer's code of professional conduct enjoins him to keep it clear. When he is at his best, he does so.

Recognition of this distinction in ethical and intellectual posture would go far to resolve the dilemma of the scientist as adviser. Surely almost all the actors in the final stages of the ABM debate were advocates filing briefs; under the conditions of time and pressure, they could hardly have been other. But it should have been more clearly revealed that this was indeed their posture, and that what they said should not be confused with an opinion in the legal sense.

The public and the Congress can, however, expect more from scientist-

---

[19] M. Katz, *News Report, National Academy of Sciences* 22, no. 6 (1972): 4–5.

advisers. Our final prescription focuses on three possible elements in reaching national policy decisions. First, there is the role of the scientific advocate whose mode of testimony consists of an honest review of the way he reached his position of preference—an open cost-benefit listing of the pros and cons and the uncertainties and the reasoning by which he concluded that one position was superior to others. Acting as a citizen, he openly reveals his value judgments in reaching his conclusion. A scientist serving a client cannot assume this position, for his commitment to his client would be part of such an account and would nullify the independence of judgment that is the heart of this mode.

Second, there is the forum in which witnesses are examined by other experts who attempt to establish an atmosphere of impartial inquiry and finding of fact. To succeed, such a system requires a tradition that accords the examiners the detachment and authority that can only be established by a record of having been seen to have acted in such a principled manner in the past. It is this quasi-judicial atmosphere of insistent inquiry that we have suggested earlier as a means of reforming congressional hearings. Only in this kind of environment would most of the "guidelines" of the ORSA Report for client-sponsored witnesses make sense. Otherwise the operation would be comparable to outlining the standards of behavior for patent lawyers without recognizing that their ultimate test was in their confrontation with patent examiners.

Thirdly, and perhaps anti-climactically, there is the traditional device of seeking expert assessment and judgment—the overworked, often abused advisory committee composed of experts of diverse backgrounds. The frequently unrecognized premise of this institution lies in the expectation that if the committee members are chosen so as to represent relevant expertise and a wide array of private and public interests, positions based on strictly partisan or client-oriented interests will not receive unanimous or near unanimous endorsement. Consequently the advisory committee structure, at its best, combines and optimizes expertise and filters out narrow parochial interests. Failure to meet this standard can be monitored by a separate body that reviews the advisory committee's findings in a neutral, detached context, as does the Report Review Committee of the National Academy of Sciences. But no structure or procedure can insure that novelty or originality will occur and survive in such a counterbalanced scene and therein lies the particular weakness of many advisory systems.

It is evident that these three modes of bringing expert technical and scientific knowledge to bear on national policy decisions represent only a stage in society's still rudimentary understanding of how best to utilize these rapidly growing resources. Improvements are urgently needed, structurally, institutionally, and ethically. In this larger panorama professional societies, with their newly formulated guidelines, have a small but important role to play. One can hope that they will be modest in their goals, for they can do no more than warn against the most obvious excesses of professional practice. In particular they are not designed for or capable of resolving doctrinal disputes, which I believe is what made so inappropriate the ORSA committee's attempt to apply its guidelines to the ABM debate. Of all professional groups only the church pretends competence in settling doctrinal disputes, and even then with the expectation of divine guidance and, it would seem, with mixed results.

Scholarly Rights and Political Morality
Kenneth E. Boulding

A famous exhortation of the Quakers is that Friends should "speak truth to power."[1] Many of them followed this advice, according to their lights, with considerable energy and often at considerable cost. Indeed, the visits of earnest Quakers "under concern" to crowned heads, presidents, and other powerful people make a fascinating little chapter, or perhaps no more than a footnote, in the history of the last three hundred years. George Fox himself delivered the truth, as he saw it, to Oliver Cromwell, and William Penn to Charles II. A servant girl, Mary Fisher, even visited the sultan of Turkey and was apparently received kindly. American presidents have received a good many of these visitations.

What the effects have been, of course, is hard to say—probably not very much. Nevertheless, there is a pattern here that has much wider implications. In a very real sense, speaking truth (as it saw it) to power has been characteristic of the scholarly community for a long time. The list that goes from Aristotle to grand visiers, to privy counselors, and to the Council of Economic Advisers is a long and impressive one. There is hardly any profession indeed, whether the army, the navy, the church, or even the stage, that has not felt itself called upon at various times and places to give good advice to the sovereign. Of all the academic communities, economists have been particularly prone to this activity. The role of economists in the world today indeed is almost distressingly like that of the bishops in the British House of Lords or the cardinals in medieval Euro-

---

[1] This phrase was used as the title of a pamphlet issued by the American Friends Service Committee in 1955.

pean courts. The ecological community has now moved into the business of giving good advice in a large way. Sociologists advise the Supreme Court, and the principal presidential adviser in foreign affairs at the moment is a political scientist, or what in the absence of a proper name we have to call an "I-R type."

In examining and trying to appraise this phenomenon we have to draw a very large picture, hardly smaller indeed than the totality of the social process itself. We start off with the proposition that all decisions of any kind, from those of the powerful ruler deciding questions of war and peace to those of his humblest subject making a purchase in the store, follow much the same principles. They all depend on some kind of cognitive structure within the mind of the decision maker. This includes alternative images of the future. These images of the future, on the whole, are derived from the whole cognitive view of the past, as projecting the past into the future is the only way to form images of it. In order that images of the future should form what might be called "decision agenda," that is, things that are chosen amongst, the decision maker must believe that they are feasible, in other words, that he has power to choose one alternative future rather than another. In making the decision to buy or not to buy a shirt, I must have money in my pocket, I must be close to a store that sells shirts, and I must at least be somewhat aware of the consequences of either buying the shirt or not buying it.

This does not mean, of course, that a decision maker chooses among all alternative futures stretching into the infinite time ahead. Our image of the future always has a rather limited horizon, and often what we are choosing is not so much the future itself as some parameter that will affect that future. Indeed, often all we are choosing among is futures of varying degrees of probability. The king who decides to go to war will certainly change the future by so doing. Presumably he made the decision because he thought this would be a better future for him, but of course he may be wrong and very often is. Disappointment, that is, the failure of an expectation for the future, is one of the most important sources of human learning, provided that the disappointment is not fatal and that reaction to disappointment is "realistic," whatever that means. The progress of science indeed depends very much on the institutionalization of disappointment, which is the process known as "testing." This is a process, however, which also goes on all the time in daily life, and there is a constant interaction in all decision-making processes between the decision itself, which is a result of certain images of the world, and the revision of these images of the world as the result of the perception of the consequences of the decision.

Decisions, however, involve not only knowledge in the sense of images of the world; they also involve values, that is, an ability to order these images in some order of preference. The simplest theory of decision making is that we simply order our images of feasible futures in the rank order of preference and select the one that is at the top of the list, that is, the most preferred. This is essentially the theory of maximizing behavior as it is expounded by economists. This theory may be carried to great degrees of elaboration, though it is in considerable danger of falling into mere formalism. If it simply says that people do what seems best to them at the time, this is no doubt true, but it is not the sort of truth that speaks very much to anything. It does not give us any predictive power, and a theory that cannot lead to disappointment can hardly lead to verification.

If any content is to be put into the theory, it must be done by what I have called "plausible topology," which is one of the principal methods of economics, that is, postulating certain general properties or shapes of utility or value functions and drawing deductions from these. This procedure has at least some degree of testability, as we have it, for instance, in the theory of consumer demand, where certain assumptions about preference functions lead to certain conclusions about demand curves, which are at least halfway verifiable by statistical and econometric analysis.

These procedures, while not to be despised, do not really get at the crucial problem of the learning of values. In the case of pigeons, we can perhaps assume that the value structure of the pigeon's nervous system, whatever it is, is built into it by the genes in the process of growth from the original fertilized egg. In the case of human beings, we cannot assume this. There are indeed genetic values, but they are quite primitive and elementary, such as the values of the newborn baby, but by the time there is anything that could be called decision making, even in the child, a huge value structure has been added to the original genetic values by a process of learning. The actual processes by which values are learned are very inaccessible and are little understood. This indeed is one of the greatest handicaps to the social reformer. His main objective is usually to change people's values and preferences to conform to his own, but the total process of society by which this is done is so little understood that it is hard to be confident that any reforming behavior will have the hoped-for results.

There are two sets of questions in the "learning of values" problem. One is the general problem of how we learn to prefer the things we actually do. Some people like cheese or cabbage or caviar, and some do not. Many tastes do in fact depend on our taste buds and may have a physiological base. Thus, there are substances that taste bitter to some people, but not to others. Tastes in art, nationality, and religion are obviously much more complex, but are related closely to the socializing process by which the child grows up to be like or unlike his parents. There does seem to be a strong tendency for cultures and subcultures to perpetuate their own value systems in their children, in the way, for instance, that the Amish have perpetuated certain values now for about two hundred years. On the other hand, there are also very important failures of socialization; without these failures indeed there would be no social change. It is those who rebel against the socialization process who create new cultures. Exactly what are the circumstances, however, under which a generation will rebel or conform, and even more puzzling, what a generation will rebel into even if it decides to rebel, are questions to which there seem to be no easy answers.

The other problem in the learning of values is: What determines the general shape or character of a preference function, particularly in regard to the strength or weakness of the orderings involved? If we think of the value or preference function as a mountain, higher points on which represent higher values, raised over some plane that represents a field of choice, the critical question here is whether the mountain is a "peak" or a "mesa," that is, whether there is one point in the field of choice that is very strongly preferred, all other points being much inferior to it, even those fairly close to it, or whether there is a large area where we do not care very much, our orderings are weak, and we would just as soon have one thing as another. The distinction between "weak orderers" and "strong orderers" is something that seems to have received little attention in the psychological literature, but it is a very important characteristic of human beings, characterized by wide differences that often make themselves apparent even in childhood. The weak-ordering child, who eats placidly what is set before him, almost no matter what it is, contrasts sharply with the strong-ordering child, who insists on having chocolate ice cream and will eat absolutely nothing else.

The very fact that we use the words "weak" and "strong" in this connection tells us a good deal about the moral values of our society. Nevertheless, there is a great deal to be said for the mature weak orderer. The strong orderer, who knows exactly what he wants, will accept no substitutes, and is miserable unless he gets precisely what he has set his heart on, is likely to be a very high-cost person, both to himself and to those around him. The immature weak orderer, who in the words of the famous English slander upon the Irish "doesn't know what he wants and won't be happy until he gets it," may be in not much better shape. But it is the mature, relaxed, wise, and tolerant weak orderer, who likes a great many things about equally well, who learns to like what he gets instead of fussing about getting what he likes, who holds both families and the larger world of society together, even though he does not have a very good press. Just how "mature ordering," to give it a good name, is learned is something that we do not understand. Certain subcultures produce more of it than others, but when in a single family it is possible to produce easygoing mature orderers on the one hand and cantankerous immature orderers on the other, one realizes how very little we know about this extremely important property.

Our ignorance in this area is all the more deplorable because the strength or intolerance of preferences is a very important element in determining both the patterns and costs of social change and the impact of the knowledge producer on the decision maker. Neither new persuasions nor new knowledge are likely to affect the value structure of a decision maker who has strong intolerant preferences. His decisions, he feels, are at the peak of his value function. He stands triumphantly on the summit of his Matterhorn and any other part of the field seems disastrously low. A decision maker, on the other hand, whose value function looks like a mesa with a flat top may have his decisions changed quite readily by new perceptions either of value or of fact. It is indeed the vacillating quality of the weak orderer that has given weak ordering a bad press. Weak orderers (there are probably a great many of them, because it pays off so well in ordinary life) often have a sneaking admiration for the decisiveness of the strong orderer who comes to look like a heroic father image, and the high costs of strong ordering are thereby often overlooked. Our evaluation of strong and weak ordering depends also on what is ordered. Things judged to be important should have strong orderings; unimportant things should be ordered weakly. Further, if people are in a condition of high uncertainty about the facts, they may very well act like compromisers or temporizers precisely because they do not wish to endanger the topmost values about which they feel strongly.

The economist tends to think of the value problem as consisting of a single set of orderings of a field of choice. This assumption is clearly too simple because we also have ethical valuations, which may concern themselves with the whole hierarchy of evaluations of value systems themselves. Thus, if I say to you, or even to myself, "You (or I) prefer A to B, but we really ought to prefer B to A," this is criticism of a preference system. This can be done from all sorts of points of view, but it is usually done from the point of view of a smaller or larger group. Thus, we may say "As an individual, I prefer A to B, but as a father or as a citizen or as a member of the human race, I prefer B to A."

This problem is very closely related to what in economics is known as the problem of interdependence of utilities, in which my welfare is perceived as affected one way or the other by my perception of an increase or a diminution of the welfare of somebody else. This is the problem of benevolence or malevolence. In the case of benevolence, I perceive that my welfare is improved if I perceive that the welfare of someone else is improved; in the case of malevolence, my welfare is diminished if I perceive that the welfare of someone else is improved.

Another factor that complicates the situation is the preference for principles, that is, for rules for decision making. Decisions are often costly in time and effort. A rule or a principle is a decision economizer. Thus, if one decides to be clean-shaven, one does not have to struggle over the decision every morning whether to shave. If one decides to be a teetotaler, this is a decision economizer on how much to drink. Rules of thumb may be quite rational under circumstances where each individual situation is so difficult and complex that accurate decision making, in the sense of looking over the whole field of choice and evaluating it carefully, is not worth the effort. The conventional morality of the past has often perhaps laid excessive value on principles as such, and "situational ethics," which emphasizes the peculiarity and uniqueness of every situation and the necessity for deciding each case as it comes along, is a not-surprising reaction to too rigid principles. Nevertheless, "situational ethics" does not perhaps recognize sufficiently the rationality of principles, particularly under conditions of uncertainty. There are conditions under which even bad principles may be better than none, simply because of the time and effort that they save. This principle about principles is important in the present context because, essentially, academic independence is a principle; that is, it is really a decision not to make decisions about whether any particular academic is worth his independence, on the grounds that this kind of decision is more trouble than it is worth. A few bad apples are not worth the trouble of sorting when the good apples are so good! Besides, once the sorting starts, who knows whether the bad or the good apples will be discarded? Principles are a way of keeping long-term prices down even at the expense of momentarily inflated prices on certain occasions.

Now we return to the larger problem of the impact of academic knowledge and the academic subculture that produces it. In the decision-making process of society, and particularly in the decisions of powerful decision makers, we face what is really the interaction of three evolutionary systems. On the one hand, we have the evolution of the whole "noosphere," to use the great word of de Chardin. This includes all the cognitive structures and value orderings present in the nervous systems of the human race, plus the cultural deposits in the forms of artifacts, buildings, ruins, records, books, computers and computer content, and so on. It is hard indeed to avoid including the whole human capital structure in this concept, for capital consists of improbable arrangements imposed on the material world by the still more improbable arrangements within the human nervous system. Capital is simply frozen knowledge.

This whole system is an ecosystem of interacting populations of different species. It is harder in this case to identify the species than it is in the biosphere, particularly when we do not really know what it is that constitutes the elementary particles or species elements of the cognitive structure. Nevertheless, the system can be partitioned into species, each species consisting of all those elements of the system that conform to some common definition. These definitions may even be fairly arbitrary, and the system will not change much. Even in the biosphere the definition of species is by no means easy, as Darwin knew very well. Thus, a biological species is usually defined in terms of individuals that are capable of procreating. Where the same procreational species has individuals living in diverse habitats, it may not be a particularly homogeneous group from the point of view of its ecological interaction, whereas two different procreational species occupying the same niche may be a very significant group ecologically. All that is really necessary for an ecological system is the partitioning into species, however arbitrary, and then the postulation of functions that relate "births" (additions to the population of the species) and "deaths" (subtractions from the population of the species) to other populations or parameters of the system. In the case of procreational species, births are very closely related to the number, age, and sex composition of the population of the species itself, which is a great convenience, but this is a special case and is not essential either to the concept of a species itself or to the concept of its birth and death functions.

It is quite reasonable, therefore, to think of the whole "noosphere" as an ecological, evolutionary system in which different kinds of images, ideas, or value functions constitute the species, each of which at any one time has a certain population and each of which is added to and subtracted from. Any species that is added to faster than it is being subtracted from will grow, and any species that is being subtracted from faster than it is being added to will decline. If a species goes on declining long enough, it will become extinct. New species are created by mutation, which consists of the process of "birth" or adding to a previously non-existent species. In the "noosphere" this happens through the development of new ideas and new insights, new values, new theories, and so on. All the species of the "noosphere" are continually being subtracted from through the processes of human aging and death and, unless they are added to in younger minds, they will soon disappear. This process of transmission from old minds to young ones is of enormous importance. It is, of course, the principal function of formal education, but it also happens in innumerable other relationships of life. A language, for instance, can be thought of as an ecosystem of words within the "noosphere," and this has to be transmitted every generation or else it will rapidly die out.

Just as in the biosphere, some of the species of the "noosphere" are cooperative with each other and some are competitive. Two species are cooperative if an increase in one tends to increase births or diminish the deaths of the other; two species are competitive if an increase in one diminishes the births or increases the deaths of the other. The evolution of a language is a fascinating example of these principles. If there are too many words serving the same purpose, one or more of them will tend to fall into disuse. If there is a purpose for which there is no word, it soon tends to be invented.

The preceding is an example of another very useful concept in evolutionary theory, that of the niche. This may be defined as a situation in which there is a certain "full niche" population, below which conditions will be favorable for expansion, additions will exceed subtractions, and the population will grow, and above which, however, conditions will be unfavorable and the population will decline. The population then tends to reach an equilibrium at the capacity of the niche. We see many examples of this in the "noosphere" where the niche is frequently some kind of institutional or organizational structure within which certain ideas or complexions of ideas flourish, outside of which they do not. Thus, inside a monastery a certain complexion of ideas and values flourishes and is continually reinforced, as people who do not hold this particular pattern of ideas simply leave the monastery. Outside the monastery, however, these ideas do not flourish. Sometimes, however, a niche does not have very clear boundaries. We may have an equilibrium of a given population, which is determined by the pressures of other various populations that surround it, but which does not correspond to any clear physical or institutional boundary. Another very useful concept is that of territoriality, which is essentially the creation of artificial niches by various forms of behavior. This phenomenon is particularly noticeable in university departments.

The scholarly subculture occupies a niche or complex of niches, often created in ways that have very little to do with the intellectual product itself. The most essential part of the "noosphere" exists only in persons; libraries and other records are only significant in so far as they are the food and shelter, as it were, of the knowledge structure of the present, and in the absence of persons they have no cognitive significance. Persons, however, have to find a place in an economic ecosystem; they have to be fed, clothed, sheltered, and motivated in order to participate in the "noosphere" at all. Very often it is the grants economy in one or another of its many forms—that is, the system of one-way transfers of goods rather than of exchange—which in fact supports them, whether because they are independently wealthy, like Boyle or Darwin, or because they are in an endowed college or are the recipients of government grants, or because they are able to support themselves, like John Stuart Mill, with occupations that have very little to do with their intellectual product. Teaching, of course, is the principal exchange system that supports the academic subculture, and this fortunately is almost certainly symbiotic with the intellectual product itself, for the effort to teach seems to improve what we know.

The critical question here is how the truth of the images that constitute the "noosphere" relates to their probability of survival. That there is a relationship cannot be doubted, that is, the truth of an idea or an image must be one element of the survival function. It is, however, by no means the only element; ideas and images do survive within the cognitive structure that are not true, in the sense that they do not correspond to the pattern that they purport to represent in the external world. Ideas survive that are not true if they reinforce the identity of the person who holds them, if they fit into a highly valued syndrome or pattern with other ideas that are regarded as true, if they are held by some other person who is respected and followed as a model, and so on.

Nevertheless, there is a certain asymmetry between truth and error, as there is between truth and lies, which introduces a profound bias into the whole evolutionary process by which 'the "noosphere" develops. This asymmetry rests on the fact that, whereas error can be detected by disappointment, truth cannot, and whereas lies can be found out, telling the truth cannot. There is, therefore, a certain inherent instability in images that are not true, in the sense that, other things being equal, they are more likely to be discarded, that is, "die," than images that are true. The difference in likelihood may not be very great, but cumulatively it has a profound impact. Thus, man started out with the image of the world that it was flat and had an edge. As long as man's mobility was small, this image was relatively realistic, in the sense that for small movements, we can treat the surface of the earth as a plane without any serious errors. As man's mobility increased, however, and as his image of the world became more sophisticated, the view of the earth as flat had to be rejected in the sheer practical interest of navigation. And now, of course, the image of the world as a sphere or spheroid is almost universally accepted and is likely to persist. It could be, of course, that a man with an immense charismatic power, who believed that the earth was flat, might rise to the position of ruler of the world and compel everybody to assent verbally, at least, to his beliefs, but if his airplane pilot believed him he would be in a bad way very soon.

The more complex the system, of course, the harder it is to find out the truth about it. A very severe difficulty also is encountered with probabilistic systems, that is, systems that have some kind of ineradicable randomness in them, for here testing is extraordinarily difficult. If a meteorologist predicts a 50 percent chance of rain tomorrow, it is very hard for him to be wrong, although by a vast amount of data collection over a large number of cases, his probability might be shown to be in error. As we move into social systems, the complexities and the irreducible uncertainties become still larger and it is not surprising, therefore, that truth seems to retreat over the horizon and we fall back into ideologies that at least appeal to people through their coherence.

In considering the relations of knowledge to power, we now have to consider another evolutionary ecological system, which is that of the development of the distribution of roles in society of greater or less power. A role is a kind of one-person niche; that is, it is part of the images of usually a considerable number of other people who surround it and who feed communications into it and accept communications out of it. These communications may demand obedience and respect and may modify the behavior of those receiving them. Any organization is essentially a set of roles and role expectations, both of the occupants of the roles and of others, which permit a network of communications to produce certain effects.

Powerful roles are generally those at the center of a large network. It is the essence of hierarchy, for instance, that communications follow a tree-like pattern from the center or "top" of the hierarchy to the periphery or "bottom," and that the further toward the top we go in such a system, the more effect decisions have, simply because they are transmitted through longer and longer lines of communication to more and more people. The question of distribution of power in society, therefore, is very much bound up with the evolution of communication networks. In the case of hierarchical networks, the question of the survival of power roles is very much the same as that of survival of the organization itself. Organizations form species, and they have births and deaths just like any other species, although there may be examples here of species with only a single member, which is virtually unknown in the biosphere.

Organizations that are in existence at a given time consist of all those created in times past, minus those that have not survived. An interesting question in regard to the birth of organization is how far this is due to random elements. Death takes place through conquest in the case of states, bankruptcy or amalgamation in the case of businesses, suppression or attrition in loss of membership in the case of churches, fraternities, clubs, and so on. Here again, there are both competitive and cooperative relationships among different species.

We also have to reckon with nonhierarchical communications and nonhierarchical forms of power. These have become particularly important as means of communication have become more widespread and diffuse. The power of a prophet, a poet, a song maker, or a philosopher is of this sort and in the long run may be much more significant than the power of hierarchy.

Observe also, although there is not time to develop the point in this chapter, that there are at least three major sources of power arising from essentially different kinds of communicative or other relationships.[2] These I have called "threat power," where the communication is "You do something nice for me, or I will do something nasty to you"; "exchange power," where the communication is "You do something that I want, I will do something that you want"; and "integrative power," where the communication is "You do what I want because of what I am and you are, or because you love me and respect me, or follow me, and so on." Threat power comes from threat credibility, which may only be quite distantly related to capability, particularly in the case of spiritual threats or magical threats. The relation between credibility and capability is stronger in the case of physical threats, and even here it is surprisingly loose. Exchange or economic power comes from having a lot of things to exchange, preferably at good prices. It may emerge as a by-product of the threat system, in the case, for instance, of priests or kings. It may arise from unusual productivity or unusually favorable terms of trade, and it may arise from property relationships and the ownership of large amounts of valuable property. Ownership in turn is related to threat power, frequently at its origin, but later on to integrative power, that is, the ability to occupy generally recognized roles, such as that of the landlord. Integrative power is closely related to the structure of legitimacy, which has a very dominant but extremely puzzling dynamic. The loss of legitimacy is more fatal to power than any other process, as the imperial European powers had to recognize, and as the United States was forced to recognize in Vietnam. The new social significance of the scholarly community could be described as the result of the fact that, thanks both to the triumphs of modern learning and the secularization of society, the "integrative power" and the legitimacy of scholarship has grown and has now been joined by the "exchange power" of the academics, who have something to sell that others, for good reasons or bad, think they need.

---

[2] K. E. Boulding, "The Three Faces of Power," in *50 Years of War Resistance: What Now?* (London, 1972), pp. 18–21.

Closely linked with the processes by which roles and especially the distribution of power in role structures are created is another process that does not fall so easily into the patterns of evolutionary theory and is the process by which role occupants are found and roles are filled with persons. There are some fairly well-recognized principles here, especially in hierarchical role structures, where roles are generally filled from the next level in the hierarchy below, and the people rise to more powerful roles through promotion. Two famous self-named principles are Parkinson's law, which is that roles proliferate to fill any budget space, and the Peter principle, which is that everybody rises in a hierarchy to a point that he is ill-fitted to occupy, because then he is not promoted any further. Both suggest that hierarchy has costs that can easily become excessive. One way of getting around the Peter principle is the introduction of randomness, particularly in the selection of top members of hierarchies. This is presumably the main justification for elections, whether for the pope or for the president. Another alternative is the development of a market, particularly a labor market, so that people can be brought in from other organizations, and who therefore rise by impressing their peers rather than by impressing their superiors. Finally, roles may be filled by a person creating the role that he then occupies, such as the entrepreneur, the prophet, the guru, the revolutionary leader, and the exerciser of mass charisma of all kinds. The historical record here is not too encouraging.

The reader may now feel that I have walked all around the central problem of this essay, which in the large is the relation of knowledge to power, and in the small the relation of the academic community as a specialized purveyor of specialized knowledge to the political power structure. However, circumnavigation is one way to show that the earth is round, and the problem that we are dealing with here is a very round globe of interrelated matter indeed. Perhaps all I have really suggested so far is how to look at the problem, and here we are faced immediately with the fact that perhaps because of the absence of any large theoretical structure this is a problem on which very little data has been systematically collected. A casual glance at the historical record certainly suggests that the exercise of political power may require special skills, both in the assessment of alternative images of the world and in the development of value systems that permit survival.

In the academic community these skills may well be selected out. The record of intellectual advisers to the powerful, stretching the word "academic" a bit perhaps to include the bishops and the cardinals, the Beckets and the Cromwells, the Wolseys and Richelieus and Rasputins, as well as the Schlesingers and Kissingers, is not wholly encouraging. The intellectual in power, indeed, is frequently a dangerous man, perhaps because his very capacity for analysis often gives him illusions of certainty in the situations that are objectively uncertain. This is the greatest danger indeed in the sophistication of decision making of any kind, whether coming from cardinals or from computers. Decision making, even powerful decision making, under uncertainty is a very different affair from what it is under certainty. Under certainty, we find the best thing to do and do it. Under uncertainty, we often do not know what is the best thing to do, so we postpone decisions, we try to avoid commitment, we stay liquid, we leave alternatives open, even at the cost of not ultimately doing as well as we might have done if we had been certain. Under conditions of objective uncertainty and subjective certainty we usually zero in on disaster. How far the Vietnam war, for instance, was a result of sophisticated decision making at high levels of government and military is a history that still remains to be written.

We do see a creeping increase in the ability of the intellectual and academic community to affect the decisions of the powerful. Partly this is a result of the rise in the complexity of society that has demanded development of the disciplines in the social sciences and hence necessitates specialized expertise—at which the academic, of course, is very good—in situations that previously could be disposed of by common sense. Herbert Hoover had very good common sense and in many ways was a good and wise man. But he was a disaster also, because neither he nor his advisers, nor for that matter anybody, really understood what was happening to him. Today we have a Council of Economic Advisers whose power fluctuates, but whose members have access to presidents and who have whatever prestige comes with expertise. The model of institutionalizing expert advice is probably a good one. One of the problems in the international system is that, in the first place, there has not been an adequate body of genuine expertise, the experts being simply camp followers of the powerful and, in the second place, whatever expertise exists is collected and used in a random and haphazard manner. Moreover, around many specific problems, there is a tendency for experts to be collected who are, or become, artificially like-minded and not representative of expert opinion in the discipline as a whole. Institutionalizing competition among advisers is a basic desideratum.

If we are looking for an evaluation of the relationships between the academic and the political community, perhaps the most important component of the value function is respect. The academic community, even today after its huge inflation, is still a powerful source of legitimacy, mainly because, with all its vices, it is of all the subcultures in the society that one where truth has the highest coefficient in the survival function of ideas. It is a community singularly free from mortal sin, especially outside the more prestigious institutions where pride has a pretty good following. Its venial sins—the petty jealousies, the jockeying for position, the exploitation of students, the occasional laziness—are not enough to destroy the feeling of those who are in it, that it is a pretty good world to be in. Supposedly intellectual institutions, like research groups and lobbying organizations, which do not command the respect of the academic community, perhaps because it is felt that they are not sufficiently committed to truth, operate under a severe long-run handicap.

The corruption of power is primarily a corruption of the information system of the powerful. If this is to be overcome, those who provide information must be independent, in some sense, of those who use it. Here again, however, we run into a dilemma, that if the independence of the information providers is too great, the decision makers will be out of touch with them and will not use them. This is where the intermediate organization, like the Council of Economic Advisers, can be of great value, provided that it is staffed mainly from the independent intellectual and academic community and for fairly short terms of office. The business community has not yet learned to an adequate degree the relationships of mutual respect that are necessary if the business community is to draw legitimacy, and in a legitimate manner at that, from the academic community, which is such an important source of it. The relationships between the religious and the academic community are likewise of enormous interest, but we do not have time to go into them here.

To end the chapter with a call for further research is a low trick, but in this connection I find I cannot resist it. Academics, or more broadly intellectuals, in positions of power, whether in direct power or as advisers to the powerful, constitute a fairly recognizable species in the social system. As far as I know, it has never been studied as a species, and one would like to encourage both historians and sociologists to do this. Data are readily available, academics in power having been much prone to writing memoranda and memoirs. I would suggest as a tentative hypothesis for such a study that, on the whole, the impact of this species on others is not very favorable, but this hypothesis may easily be the result of a rather biased sample arising from the haunting feeling that the Vietnam war has been a most sorry example of the impact of academics on policy. Once a species has been identified, however, one hopes that at least a subdiscipline might develop to study it and that, whatever the evaluative conclusions, careful study would lead to a subsequent improvement, not only in the impact of powerful academics on human betterment, but also on the internal economy and productivity of the groves of academe themselves.

Federal-Academic Relations in
Social Science Research

H. Field Haviland

Since mankind is the reason for, and principal resource of, government, no area of governmental-academic interaction would seem to be more significant than the study of human behavior. Yet this is one of the weakest sectors of public-private research collaboration. Both sides are inadequately oriented, structured, staffed, and linked in order to plan and administer strategies of social science research relevant to public needs. The limited progress that has been made has been dominated more by crash responses to traumatic crises—particularly wars (hot or cold) and economic calamities—than by careful advance planning geared to more balanced long-range development. The decision-making process is influenced by, and helps to perpetuate, imbalances both between the "hard" and "soft" sciences and among the individual "soft" ones. And the current penny-pinching mood of Washington, demand for quick "practical" results to be measured by "scientific" cost-benefit analysis, and a shift of support from academic institutions to private firms raise serious questions for the future.

The central purpose of this essay is to probe the mysteries of current governmental-academic interaction in establishing goals, formulating programs, and administering operations of social science research. The intent is not only to understand but to appraise and improve. The analysis begins with a brief retrospective look at the historical road that has brought us to where we are now. We then examine major institutions and relationships that are presently involved in the scrimmaging between Washington—both "downtown" and on the "hill"—and the intellectual community—academia and other relevant enterprises. Finally we consider the major problems posed by these relations and try to suggest some constructive possibilities for the future, recognizing that these are complex and difficult issues for which there are no easy or ideal solutions.[1]

THOUGHTS ON HISTORICAL TRENDS

If there is one dominant theme in the development of governmental inter-action with the social science community, it is that the principal spurts in this activity have been in response to major crises confronting the federal government. Only when a giant and traumatic challenge has arisen for which the social sciences seemed to offer some useful antidote has the government been prepared to offer substantial encouragement and support. The principal triggering events have been wars and depressions. Fortunately, pioneering and aggressive entrepreneurs of the social sciences, such as Wesley Mitchell, Charles Merriam, Frank Goodnow, and William Willoughby, were prepared to ride these waves of crisis in order to advance the development of the social sciences.

Throughout the experience, the government has given the overwhelming portion of its research support to the natural sciences—whether to create new engines of defense or of material progress—but there has been an increasing trend, primarily during the twentieth century, to give greater attention to problems of human relations. Within the social sciences, the major emphasis has been on applied aspects of economics, psychology, and education, but there has also been a gradual, though modest, increase in the support of more comprehensive and less "applied" research.

The major governmental agencies that have nourished these developments have been those most directly concerned with the dominant crises. Because defense has been the primary stimulus, the military agencies have been the principal cornucopias of support, with the Office of Naval Research being generally regarded as the most imaginative, courageous, and long-range in behalf of the social, as well as natural, sciences. On the civilian side of defense management, agencies concerned with economic policy, political analysis, and psychological problems, both internal and external, have played important roles. In the war against depression, agencies, such as the Departments of the Treasury, Agriculture, Commerce, Labor, and, more recently, Health, Education and Welfare, have been sup-

---

[1] Among recent analyses of this subject that I have found most useful are the following: Daniel S. Greenberg, *The Politics of Pure Science* (New York, 1967); Gene M. Lyons, *The Uneasy Partnership: Social Science and the Federal Government in the Twentieth Century* (New York, 1969); The Behavioral and Social Sciences Survey Committee, *The Behavioral and Social Sciences: Outlook and Needs* (Englewood Cliffs, 1969); National Science Foundation, *Knowledge Into Action: Improving the Nation's Use of the Social Sciences* (Washington, D.C., 1969); *Science Policy and the University*, ed. Harold Orlans (Washington, D.C., 1968); and Don K. Price, *Government and Science* (New York, 1954).

porters of social science research. The weakest sector of governmentally supported research has been those civilian agencies chiefly concerned with external affairs: the Department of State and the foreign aid and information agencies. The major recipients of governmental support of social science research have been the principal universities, interdisciplinary councils, and nonuniversity research institutes.

The establishment of the National Science Foundation in 1950 was a landmark in emphasizing more varied and basic research in the social, as well as natural, sciences. In the beginning the scientific community and the government encouraged the Foundation to give primary support to the natural sciences and gave sustenance to the social sciences only in miniscule portions and for projects that were most obviously policy relevant and most like the natural sciences in method. After heated and voluble debates, the Foundation became more generous and comprehensive in its support of social science research. At the present time, however, there is great stress throughout the government on economy and rigorous application of cost-benefit evaluations of governmentally supported research.

PRESENT STRUCTURE: THE EXECUTIVE SUMMIT

Within the Executive Office of the President, the principal agency for general planning, including guidance of social science research, is the Office of Management and Budget (OMB), successor to the Bureau of the Budget, which was created in 1921 to help the president formulate his program supported by the necessary financial resources. The mission of the OMB is crucial because it serves the president as his most comprehensive planning arm and makes many important decisions, most of which the president cannot personally review. At the same time, its staff resources are extremely limited. To review the entire $628 million research program of the National Science Foundation for fiscal year 1975, for example, there is only one professional staff member of OMB, a physicist, who gives most of his time to this task. Thus the agency wields extraordinary power, but does not have the capability to do an effective job of analyzing and resolving the many complex programmatic issues confronting the president. Yet it intervenes substantially in the details of program planning, promoting some programs and demoting others, without adequate evaluative capacity to make such judgments.

Close to the summit are more specialized advisory bodies relevant to the social sciences. The first general social science advisory body attached to the White House was the Research Committee on Social Trends, created by President Hoover in 1929, which produced an extraordinarily thorough and far sighted report entitled *Recent Social Trends in the United States,* arguing for the more systematic application of the social sciences to problems of national policy. As the storm of the depression broke upon the nation, President Roosevelt's New Deal was influenced by the strategy suggested in the *Social Trends* report and created a National Planning Board in 1933 which, in various forms and under various names, did an unprecedented job of using the social sciences at the highest governmental level to try to find better answers to major national problems. Despite pleas to coordinate the efforts of both the "soft" and "hard" sciences, Isaiah Bowman and other members of the National Academy of Sciences persuaded President Roosevelt to create a separate Science Advisory Board. Soon this effort was supplanted by a Science Committee, under the National Resources Committee (successor to the National Planning Board), in which representatives from the National Academy, the Social Science Research Council, and the American Council on Education participated.

When World War II came, other more defense-oriented people and agencies, such as the Office of Emergency Management, assumed the planning lead, and what was then called the National Resources Planning Board was quietly laid to rest in 1943. The most powerful presidential-level science planning body was the Office of Scientific Research and Development (OSRD), created in 1941 under the direction of Vannevar Bush, which was primarily concerned with mobilizing the natural sciences to fight the war and whose most extraordinary achievement was the atomic bomb. Most recently, the principal successor of the OSRD was the President's Science Advisory Committee, which was dominated by the natural sciences and had virtually no social science staff. Both the committee and its staff were disbanded by President Nixon in 1972, and their advisory functions, minus defense and health matters, were assigned to the director of the National Science Foundation. President Ford has recommended the reestablishment of the post of Presidential Science Adviser with a relatively small staff and with heavy reliance on ad hoc advisory committees.

A descendant of the National Resources Planning Board, but with a far narrower mission, is the President's Council of Economic Advisers, created by the Employment Act of 1946 to provide general economic guidance. Another presidential planning arm employing substantial social science analysis is the National Security Council, which advises on major foreign policy issues.

BELOW THE SUMMIT

As one descends from the peak of power to lower levels of the executive establishment, one is struck by the overwhelming emphasis on the nonsocial sciences. In the most recent fiscal year for which there are comprehensive data, 1975, the federal government estimated that it would obligate only 5 percent of its research funds for all of the social sciences compared to 31 percent for the "life" sciences (biology, medicine, etc.), 30 percent for engineering, 18 percent for the physical sciences, and 11 percent for the "environmental" sciences (atmospheric, geological, oceanographic sciences).² The principal dispensers of this federal largesse, totaling $7,674 million, in order of magnitude were: the Department of Defense (24 percent of the total), the Department of Health, Education and Welfare (23 percent), the National Aeronautics and Space Administration (19 percent), the National Science Foundation (8 percent), the Atomic Energy Commission (7 percent), and the Department of Agriculture (5 percent).

If one looks only at the agencies primarily concerned with dispensing the modest support given the social sciences, totaling $374 million, one finds that the relative standing of the agencies is quite different. The principal agencies, in order of their obligation of funds for social science research, in fiscal year 1975, were: the Department of Health, Education and Welfare (40 percent of the total), the National Science Foundation (13 percent), the Department of Agriculture (13 percent), and the Department of Housing and Urban Development (9 percent). As for the allocation of federal research funds among the social sciences, the ranking in obligations for fiscal year 1975 in order of magnitude was as follows: economics (36 percent), "miscellaneous" (30 percent), sociology (20 percent), anthropology (5 percent), political science (3 percent), and history (2 percent).

If one examines how the principal executive agencies concerned with social science research are organized to deal with relevant nongovernmental communities, one is struck by certain general characteristics. It is evident that a key ingredient is the availability of qualified personnel both to engage in intra-agency utilization of social science and to collaborate with external counterparts. Yet it has been difficult for all agencies to attract superior personnel and, despite substantial long-term progress, only a few have been able to recruit and maintain an adequate critical mass of talented people. The favored agencies are those that are securely established, have substantial resources, and are most prestigious. The National Institute of Mental Health is probably at the top of the heap. Unfortunately the present level of personnel and current balance (or imbalance) between the "hard" and "soft" sciences and among the social sciences tends to perpetuate itself and is extremely difficult to alter.

All of these agencies exert some effort to consult with appropriate counterparts outside the government and to engage some of them in the process of determining governmental policy, but these arrangements vary widely. The weakest part of the apparatus is at the top. While some of the agencies have high-level advisory bodies with comprehensive jurisdictions, none of these bodies is sufficiently broad in its membership or adequate in its analysis to do a sufficient job of giving general guidance to the agency concerned.

---

² The source of these data is: *Federal Funds for Research, Development and Other Scientific Activities, Fiscal Years, 1973, 1974, and 1975*, vol. 23 (Washington, D.C., 1974). These figures include funds obligated for both "basic" and "applied" research to be done by both governmental and nongovernmental agencies.

The agency with the broadest mandate, the National Science Foundation, has a top-level National Science Board of twenty-five members, of whom only five are currently engaged in professional social science work. This body meets infrequently, for brief periods, to consider general policy questions and to review projects of special significance. It does not have the time, staff, or methodology to formulate adequate guidelines to determine the general direction of the program and to establish priorities among the several disciplines and projects.

Thus, in this key forum where top public and private scholars meet, there is no analysis or negotiation that can provide a strong foundation for general program planning. Crucial decisions regarding general substantive objectives are determined by a small group of influential governmental and nongovernmental leaders with a maximum of informal consultation and power politics and a minimum of open, systematic, and broadly representative analysis. The same is true of all of the other agencies concerned with social science research.

At lower levels concerning narrower and less significant decisions, the process works better. Here the typical task is to have public-private consultations regarding specific projects. The usual procedure is to have a panel composed of relevant scholars review proposals for federal support of research in a particular field. Care is normally taken to strive for a reasonable balance among institutions, geographic areas, sexes, color, etc. Appointments to the panels are limited in time, and members do not vote on projects with which they are directly connected. This "peer" system is generally thought, by both insiders and outsiders, to work reasonably well, although there continue to be complaints about excessive over-representation of favored individuals, institutions, and disciplines.

THE CONGRESS

If the executive branch is highly decentralized, meagerly staffed, relatively neglectful of the social sciences, and inadequately equipped to plan and evaluate general strategies of social science research, Congress is in even worse shape. There is the usual atomistic splintering among chambers, parties, committees, and individuals. Staff resources are far thinner than "downtown." There is, for example, only one trained scientist, a specialist in "science policy," on the staff of the House of Representatives Committee on Science and Technology, who is responsible for overseeing the National Science Foundation. The staff can call upon the Congressional Research Service, various agencies in the executive branch, and the private community, but its own extreme limitations set severe restrictions on its capacity to seek and digest advice from other quarters.

The general atmosphere that emanates from the members of Congress tends to be skeptical of the social sciences. They doubt social scientists' credentials, and they emphasize the need for immediate and direct relevance and utility to national policy.

Consultation with the nongovernmental community tends to be sporadic and superficial. It is usually focused on specific legislative issues, especially those that generate controversy, and the selection of witnesses is relatively unsystematic and strongly influenced by the staff and key committee members. Occasionally there have been continuing panels of consultants, such as the Panel on Science and Technology, composed of sixteen distinguished scientists (only three of whom were social scientists), which advised the House Committee on Science and Astronautics, but such consultations have been infrequent and shallow and have had relatively little influence on key policy decisions.

THE PRIVATE SECTOR

On the other side of the fence are the nongovernmental scholarly organizations, which are the major partners of the public programs: chiefly the universities, professional associations, interdisciplinary councils, nonuniversity research institutes and foundations. While all of these institutions comprise a mighty army of intellectual capacity, it should be remembered that they receive only a small proportion of federal research funds. In fiscal year 1975, the federal funds obligated for all research in universities, totaling $7,674 million, were only 33 percent of the total federal research budget. Industrial firms got 25 percent. Another 34 percent was obligated for "intramural" projects within the government. At the same time, it is clear that the relative importance of the private scholarly community, especially the universities, is not to be measured primarily in terms of financial resources but in terms of quality and impact. By these measures, the nonprofit scholarly sector continues to be the most important source of intellectual initiative and development.

As one considers how this community is organized to do business with the government, it is clear that it suffers from at least as many disabilities as the public sector. The most intimate and effective relations with the government are concentrated chiefly among the major universities that have superior financial resources, faculties, and research programs. This is reflected in the fact that the ten states leading in federal research and development support currently receive approximately 70 percent of the total obligations. While both the private and public communities have made efforts to broaden the circle of participation, relatively little progress has been made in this direction.

Even within the more favored institutions, the decision-making process to determine general institutional policies regarding interaction with the government is usually as uncoordinated and unsystematic as it is within the government. Top leadership—presidents, provosts, deans, chairmen, and others—tries to impose some order on the process, but the centrifugal pressures are usually dominant. Not only are the various competing programs aggressively independent, but they are reinforced by equally independent interests within the federal government.

The primary negotiations take place between relatively specialized units in both the public and private institutions with a minimum of intrauniversity or intra-governmental coordination.

Another problem that afflicts the scholarly community is its constant quest for long-term support for "basic" research, while the government tends to em-phasize relatively short-term support for "applied" research that will have demon-strable and immediate utility. A few governmental agencies, such as the Office of Naval Research, the National Institute of Mental Health, and the National Science Foundation, have tried to be more supportive of long-term basic research, but the counter-pressures continue to be dominant.

Within the professional associations there is considerable lack of symmetry between those disciplines that have received the most generous share of govern-mental support—especially psychology, economics, and education—and others that have been less fortunate. And these differences are self-reinforcing and perpetuating. The stimuli that gave rise to governmental support of certain dis-ciplines, especially the major crises mentioned earlier, have helped to develop stronger scholarly capabilities which, in turn, generate more governmental sup-port.

All of the social science professional associations are interested in receiving federal nourishment. Their various activities give some attention to governmental relations and sometimes strive to influence governmental support. The staffs and officers of the associations consult from time to time regarding their relations with government and occasionally take action to affect relevant governmental policies. For example, the top officials of the American Political Science Association waged a vigorous and successful campaign to increase National Science Foundation support for political science. Yet none of these groups has done a very systematic or intensive job of mobilizing continuous and comprehensive analysis of its disci-pline's interests with regard to governmental support or of communicating with governmental agencies regarding these interests.

The American Psychological Association, representing one of the most favored disciplines, utilizes the usual channels—conventions, committees, publi-cations—to conduct its business, and its various activities give some attention to interaction with the government. Yet, according to the testimony of one of its officials, it engages in no effort specifically designed to review the general research needs of the discipline in relation to actual, or potential, governmental resources and to persuade appropriate governmental agencies to respond to those needs.

Other major cadres of the intellectual world are the four councils that strive to coordinate the activities of various interests in four main areas: the natural sciences, social sciences, humanities, and academic administration. These are the National Research Council of the National Academy of Sciences (NAS–NRC), the Social Science Research Council (SSRC), the American Council of Learned Societies (ACLS), and the American Council on Education (ACE).

The National Academy of Sciences, the oldest and most powerful scientific body, was founded in 1863 especially to mobilize science and technology in response to one of our earliest crises, the Civil War. Its affiliate, the NRC, was created in 1916, at the request of President Wilson, to assist the government in fighting World War I. While both organizations have been chiefly concerned with the natural sciences, they have gradually expanded their activities in the social sciences until now one of their three major "assemblies" (advisory councils) concentrates on the behavioral and social sciences. Its functions include cooperation with the government in identifying national problems requiring social science inputs, helping to organize relevant social science research, giving advice to the government, and evaluating social science programs related to governmental functions. The National Research Council is especially close to the government, emphasizes the interaction between the natural and social sciences, benefits from its long and influential collaboration with the government, and is willing to undertake studies, mainly evaluative, under its own auspices and management.

The council that is most directly in the mainstream of the social sciences is the Social Science Research Council, founded in 1923, largely under the leadership of Charles Merriam, to help develop the social sciences and to improve collaboration among them. The council has tended to be less intimately connected with the government than the National Research Council, more ambivalent about its responsibility to give direct aid in tackling problems of governmental policy, and less involved in the direct administration of research projects. Nonetheless, its board and various specialized committees have been concerned with the relevance of the social sciences to governmental problems. Individuals associated with the council have played important roles in collaborating with the government. And occasionally the council has engaged in a comprehensive review of its domain with important implications for governmental utilization of the social sciences, such as its joint effort with the National Academy of Sciences to produce a general study, *The Behavioral and Social Sciences: Outlook and Needs* (1969).

The American Council of Learned Societies (ACLS), a close cousin of the Social Science Research Council, was organized in 1919 to perform much the same functions in the field of humanities as the SSRC does in the social sciences. The ACLS has collaborated with the SSRC in a number of areas where their interests overlap, e.g., African, Asian, Latin American, and Slavic studies.

The fourth major council is the American Council on Education whose membership represents university administrative leadership and whose mission is to improve collaboration among its constituents, including their relations with the federal government. The council is concerned with the social sciences as one of its many responsibilities and is generally interested in strengthening federal support of all academic functions. At the same time, there are occasionally differences between professors and administrators that are reflected in the relations between the ACE and the other councils.

The nonuniversity, nonprofit social science research institutions vary considerably in their dependence on the government, the scope of their interests, and their concern with governmental policy. Among the first to be established was the Brookings Institution, created in 1928 to concentrate entirely on social science research, mainly economic and political, with particular relevance to national policy problems. A more recent example is the Rand Corporation, created by the United States Air Force in 1948 to advise the government chiefly in the defense field. Rand has been primarily supported by governmental resources, has engaged in security-oriented social science studies, but has had considerable difficulty with criticism of its activities and restriction of its freedom by both the executive and legislative branches of the federal government.

Finally, there are private foundations that are not consumers of governmental support but have occasionally played a significant role in stimulating and supporting social science research relevant to governmental needs. The Rockefeller Foundation, Carnegie Corporation, and Russell Sage Foundation were among the first to make invaluable contributions to the social sciences and thereby perform functions useful to the government and often in compensation for lack of governmental support, e.g., assisting institutions, such as the Social Science Research Council and the Brookings Institution, to get established. More recently the Ford Foundation and other newer foundations have entered this field. While these institutions have the advantage of independent funds and staff and have used these to try to improve private-public collaboration, they have also had their independence threatened by governmental criticism and regulation.

"HARD" VS. "SOFT"

As one reflects on the key policy issues posed by the current pattern of interaction between the government and the scholarly community, one of the major questions concerns the balance between the natural and social sciences. The fact that only 5 percent of federal research obligations are currently devoted to social science compared with 31 percent for the "life sciences" (mainly physical medicine) and 59 percent for the physical and environmental sciences and engineering is not insignificant.

There is no easy or simple answer to this question of balance between the "hard" and "soft" sciences. Those who generally support the present pattern, strongly favoring the natural sciences, argue that the problems dealt with in these fields are high on the list of national priorities, that these disciplines are more developed than the social sciences and hence more reliable and productive investments, that their research is inherently more expensive due to a larger input of sophisticated methodology and hardware, that federal support of social science research has gradually increased and is currently commensurate with the capacity of the social sciences to make good use of such funding, and, finally, that there are no generally accepted criteria that would make a persuasive case for any substantially different allocation of funds.

Ranged against these considerations are counter-arguments that call for a significant increase in the relative support given social science research. All of our national problems, including those dealt with by the natural sciences, are crucially dependent upon human behavior, and thus research in this field deserves high priority. Despite the methodological difficulties of studying social behavior, the relevant disciplines, including those generally classified as "social sciences," already have a capacity for productive analysis that far exceeds the opportunities afforded by the current level of support and are making rapid progress in expanding that capacity. As for the costs involved, modern social science methodologies, including possibilities of massive worldwide research on all aspects of human behavior, could justify programs that would be as expensive as any conceived by the natural sciences.

While the level of federal support for social science research has grown in recent years, many leading social scientists, including those in major governmental agencies, have testified that this rate of growth is inadequate and that both the relative and absolute levels of support given the social sciences should be substantially increased. One key official has indicated that his program could absorb at least twice as much money for fully qualified programs, and that the capacity to make good use of federal support could be expanded considerably further if such efforts were encouraged. As we have seen in all fields, the absorptive capacity of a discipline is significantly affected by the prior investment made in that area.

True, there is no formula that can indicate, beyond debate, how much should be devoted to the social sciences, but neither is there in the hard sciences. We have seen that past patterns of allocation in all fields have been crucially affected by human perceptions of critical needs, with a mixture of logical analysis and pressure politics. Future patterns of allocation are likely to be affected by similar influences. The thesis of this analysis is that there are critical needs in the social sciences, amply documented by various studies, such as the BASS report, that deserve stronger intellectual and political support. Only by the generation of such support is the pattern of allocation likely to be altered.

One major organizational issue related to the problem of balance is the perennial question of whether there should be a separate National Social Science Foundation. Ideally, one is inclined to espouse the principle of the unity of science and therefore to favor a single governmental foundation to help develop all aspects of science, natural and social. This was the preferred position of the joint NAS–SSRC Behavioral and Social Science Survey Committee. But that group went on to say that, if the National Science Foundation failed to give adequate support to the social sciences within a reasonable time, consideration should be given to creating a separate independent agency to support the social sciences.

At present, it does not seem that the NSF or the federal government generally is yet giving adequate support to the social sciences. Unless the situation improves substantially within the near future, the alternative of a separate foundation should be given urgent consideration.

GENERAL PLANNING AND PRIORITIES

No function is more crucial than surveying research needs from the most Olympian perspective, scanning the horizon for new problems, weighing alternative needs in relation to some guiding criteria, suggesting priorities, and injecting these judgments into the bloodstream of policy making. Yet there is evidence on all sides that these critical tasks are the weakest links in the policy process both within and between the scholarly and governmental communities.

There are understandable reasons for these difficulties that cannot be easily altered. There always have been, and always will be, legitimate differences of opinion, among experts as well as amateurs, about the relative importance of various substantive areas of "applied" vs. "basic" approaches and of different analytical methodologies (e.g., quantitative vs. nonquantitative). Even if more precise substantive guidelines could be agreed upon, there is no generally acceptable and reliable technique for applying such criteria to the selection, administration, and evaluation of research projects. There will always be different interests, responsibilities, and approaches characteristic of different scholarly and governmental institutions that cannot be easily reconciled. One must be realistic in recognizing that the intellectual planning process can never be definitive and that much will depend on power politics.

If one looks at the academic world, both within and among educational institutions, one finds certain general characteristics that make it difficult to engage in very systematic comprehensive analysis of competing research needs as a basis for fashioning general guidelines for governmentally supported research. Each individual scholar, department, institute, division, and school has its own interests, does its best to cultivate its own relations with counterparts in Washington, and resists any intra- or extrauniversity effort to coordinate research planning with other units. There are academic officials who are supposed to orchestrate university-wide research plans, but these suffer from all of the disabilities mentioned.

The main responsibility for communicating, advising, and negotiating with the government generally rests with each interested party, and neither academic nor governmental procedures encourage a very comprehensive communication or planning process. Intra-academic relations are strongly affected by past and current governmental policies and operations that have favored some fields more than others and have engaged in positive missionary efforts to cultivate scholarly interest and participation. The National Science Foundation is reported to be more active in cultivating university participation in the natural sciences than the social sciences. Few academic institutions have mobilized sufficient critical masses of intellectual capacity and organized their efforts with sufficient effectiveness to be able to respond adequately to governmental needs. Associations that represent educational institutions in Washington give scant attention to trying to sort out research priorities and to negotiating with the government on general research strategies.

In addition, there are the professional associations and interdisciplinary councils that should play a major role in continuous examination of research needs relevant to government, suggestion of priorities, and consultation with government to promote such plans. Each disciplinary association has a staff, governing council and committees to help manage its affairs, but little effort is made to engage in general analysis of research priorities relevant to governmental concerns and in negotiation with government to seek support for those needs. The major councils that serve as bridges among the disciplines, especially the three mentioned earlier, NAS–NRC, SSRC and ACLS, occasionally try to review competing research needs within the broadest perspective and to suggest program priorities to guide governmental support. The more typical pattern, however, is for such councils to establish committees to deal with more narrowly specialized problems, with little reference to any general research strategy, and, with the exception of the NRC, to deal with governmental involvement as a relatively marginal matter.

The resistance to any broader or more systematic coordination of decision making regarding the allocation of support within these academic institutions is buttressed by a number of arguments. One is that there are no reliable and generally accepted analytical guidelines, especially across disciplinary boundaries, to indicate what the proper pattern of support should be. Even if such guidelines existed, who should apply them? The broader the substantive area involved, the more difficult it becomes to achieve agreement on the criteria or procedures to govern allocative decisions. Finally, it is argued that lack of such coordination is positively good. Even those who denigrate the "free-marketplace" concept in other areas of human endeavor often extol it in determining research priorities. The dangers of coordination, it is said, including the influence of those not competent to judge, are greater than the dangers of no coordination. In the competitive process, quality will be recognized and supported.

The strongest counter-argument favoring broader, more systematic coordination within the academic world is the need to do a better job of making optimum use of scarce resources. True, it is difficult to develop criteria and procedures that will be widely acceptable, but it is both necessary and feasible to move further in this direction. The fact that substantial progress has already been made along these lines is reflected in coordinating methods now used in academic institutions to help guide the development of future research programs. The "free market-place" is no guarantee of wise allocation of support. Because organized coordination is usually accepted as the preferred method of allocative decisions within relatively circumscribed specialized fields, where peer-group relations are well established, it makes sense to try to expand such methods, especially by consciously broadening and deepening communication and collaboration among disciplines.

On the governmental side, there are similar difficulties of achieving adequately comprehensive, systematic and rigorous sifting of needs and priorities as a basis for guiding federal policy regarding social science research. At the summit one finds an assortment of staffs and agencies that are the closest aides of the president in determining social science, as well as other, objectives, including the Office of Management and Budget, the National Security Council, the Council of Economic Advisers, and the National Science Foundation. It is obvious, however, that this conglomeration of executive appendages is not adequately comprehensive or balanced in its jurisdiction or personnel. The agency with the broadest purview is the Office of Management and Budget, but our earlier discussion of that organization emphasized the gap between its vast responsibilities and limited capabilities. Both at the presidential level and within the "line" agencies there continues to be a gross imbalance between the hard and soft sciences, reflected in the statistics cited earlier and in the difficulty of mobilizing and maintaining staffs of the requisite caliber to plan and manage viable social science programs.

Despite these difficulties, it is both desirable and feasible to strive to improve the network of communication, analysis, consultation, and general policy guidance at the highest levels of both the scholarly and governmental worlds in order to do a better job of weighing competing needs and formulating guidelines for the allocation of resources and evaluation of results. One should not assume that any "scientific" cost-benefit decision-making system can produce guidelines that will be universally valid and acceptable. Considerable pluralism is healthy and desirable, leaving room for the maverick who may be a truly original pioneer. Nonetheless, we need a more effective and comprehensive system for planning coordinated strategies of future research and for sorting out priorities to guide the allocation of scarce resources.

IMBALANCE AMONG DISCIPLINES AND INSTITUTIONS

There is still considerable imbalance in the pattern of governmental support among social science disciplines and institutions. For various historical reasons, governmental programs still strongly favor a few disciplines, especially psychology, economics, and education, and a few of the leading universities and related nonprofit institutions. While some efforts have been made to break out of this self-perpetuating pattern, far more needs to be done through both governmental and nongovernmental channels to improve the balance among disciplines and institutions.

"APPLIED" VS. "BASIC"

Another problem concerns the relative emphasis placed on "applied" and "basic" research. The government tends to favor the first approach, with a few notable exceptions, while the nongovernmental scholarly community generally favors the latter. Although it is impossible to draw any neat boundary between these two approaches, the distinction retains some validity. It is natural for those responsible for governmental policy to try to maximize the demonstrable utility of publicly supported research, and they are justified in trying to identify areas that may be especially productive in relation to governmental concerns. Nonetheless, review of the history of scientific development should be a reminder that too narrow and short-term a concept of utility can be self-defeating and that all programs should be relatively permissive in supporting a substantial portion of research that may have no obvious or immediate relevance to current problems. While we may try to apply rigorous cost-benefit analysis to some aspects of social science research, such methods may not be very helpful in judging the long-range utility of other research.

"NORMATIVE" VS. "SCIENTIFIC"

In some quarters, including the National Science Foundation, it is said that the government does not, and should not, support "normative" research but only truly "scientific" research. It is appropriate that the government not support that kind of "normative" research that begins with certain value preferences and simply proceeds to build a case that will support them. On the other hand, all research is based on certain normative judgments, including the decision to study one set of phenomena rather than another and to pursue the solution of certain problems in certain ways. The development of the atomic bomb is a classic example of such normative decisions. The government is correct in insisting on the most rigorous scientific methods in dealing with problems in the social sciences as in the natural sciences. Those methods have to do with accurate and comprehensive data, objective analysis of causal relationships, and systematic appraisal of alternative strategies guided by stipulated criteria. Thus one does not have to choose between "normative" and "scientific" research but between good normative scientific research and bad normative scientific research.

THE ETHICS OF COLLABORATION

Finally, there is the central issue of ethical considerations affecting inter-action between private scholars and the government. On the nongovernmental side, there is the problem of how far scholars should go in adjusting to the inter-ests and requirements of government, e.g., what subject matter to research, what emphasis to place on immediate relevance and utility, and whether or not to render specific advice regarding governmental policy. The scholar must realize that some degree of adjustment is necessary whether he deals with governmental or nongovernmental patrons. He must decide how far he is prepared to com-promise consistent with his own basic values and purposes. Some academics, especially in the wake of the recent war, argue that it is not appropriate for a private scholar to give any policy advice to government, but this is an extreme position. Knowledge is power and carries with it the responsibility to use it for constructive purposes. The history of private-public collaboration supports the thesis that it is legitimate and useful for the scholar to give policy advice to the extent that he does so of his own free will, on the basis of professional competence and analysis, and without violating his own scholarly standards.

Governmental personnel face equally difficult questions: To what extent should they accommodate private scholarly objectives and needs, how much should they support untrammeled basic research, what should they expect in terms of scholarly participation in governmental decision making, and how best can they minimize conflict of interest on both sides? There are no easy answers to these questions, and the government must also compromise if it is to get the best results out of such collaboration. Although the government went some dis-tance in recent decades to meet the needs of the scholarly community, it has appeared recently to revert to a narrower, more rigid, and less generous posture. This is unfortunate. The government cannot serve the nation's needs well unless it is more flexible in enabling superior private scholars to pursue generally relevant research with maximum freedom and with a minimum of limitations imposed by governmental requirements.

The Federal Government and the Autonomy of Scholarship

Harvey Brooks

THE MEANING OF AUTONOMY

The concept of scholarly autonomy is derived from nineteenth-century liberal ideas; its origins and original meanings are well described in the chapter by Robert Nisbet entitled "Max Weber and the Roots of Academic Freedom" in this volume.[1] Perhaps its purest ideological expression was given by M. Polanyi in "The Republic of Science." This "liberal model" of science is summarized by J. J. Salomon, who characterizes it as an assertion of "the blind duty of society towards science, without any counterpart duty on the side of science except the truth."[2] The scientific system is a kind of "intellectual marketplace" analogous to the idealized economic "free market," such that "the slightest external intervention is enough to distort the mechanism of the free market, and the self-regulation of the network of initiatives and ideas, of which scientists are the sole judges, is the only guarantee of the progress of science."[3]

In this model the progress of science is at least partly an end in itself, and scholarly autonomy is essential to the efficient functioning of the system, i.e., the greatest scientific output for a given investment of resources, in much the same

---

[1] R. Nisbet, "Max Weber and the Roots of Academic Freedom," pp. 103–122 of this volume.

[2] J. J. Salomon, "Science Policy and Its Myths: The Allocation of Resources," *Public Policy* 20, no. 1 (Winter 1972) : 3–4.

[3] Ibid., p. 4.

sense that the working of the economic market is conceived as providing the most efficient allocation of productive resources. In the scientific system the "consumers" are other members of the scientific community; the transactions are exchanges of scientific ideas; and the "market" is the system of evaluation provided by the refereed and cited scientific literature. The distribution of individual rewards is measured in the coinage of scientific prestige, which is indicated in the scientific marketplace by citations of papers, awards and prizes, election to selective academies, invitations to lecture, and appointment to the most prestigious chairs in universities. The autonomy of the system is preserved to the degree that the distribution of prestige and recognition reflects "objectively" the contributions of the scholar to knowledge, of which his scholarly "peers" are the sole judge.

As scholarship becomes more dependent on public money for support questions arise as to how much the reward system and the allocation of resources become distorted by considerations and pressures external to the workings of the self-regulatory systems of the "community of scholars." This community of scholars is by no means identical with the academic community, especially in the sciences, but the ideal of scholarly or professional autonomy is expressed in identical terms with that of university autonomy. Nisbet in his chapter in this book quotes from Humboldt's theory of university autonomy as follows:

> The state must not ever demand from the university that which would serve its purposes directly, but should hold to the conviction that when the universities fulfill their true aims, they will also thereby serve the state in its purposes, and from a far higher point of view.[4]

Thus the true aim of the university, in the view articulated by Humboldt and developed by Weber, is the "discovery, advancement, and teaching of that kind of knowledge to be found in all the learned disciplines."

This view of the university and of the scholarly community in general encounters increasing doubts in the modern world, for it seems clear that the tremendous upsurge in the support of even the purest research in the past twenty-five years was not much related to the purity of scientific purpose embodied in the ideas of Polanyi, Humboldt, and Weber. Few today could take the optimistic view of Polanyi that "there is no reason to suppose that an electorate would be less inclined to support science for the purpose of explaining the nature of things than were the private benefactors who previously supported the universities."[5]

It seems at least unlikely that an egalitarian society will support science for other than its visible utility, at least in the long run, the brief love affair of the American public with the space program notwithstanding. What is surprising,

---

[4] Quoted by Nisbet, "Max Weber," p. 108, from *Gesammelte Schriften* (Berlin, 1903–1936), X, 255.

[5] Quoted from M. Polanyi, "The Republic of Science," in Salomon, "Science Policy," p. 4.

perhaps, is the degree to which the nineteenth-century ideal of scholarly autonomy has actually been able to survive the injection of massive governmental support ultimately motivated by pragmatic values. It is a tribute to the political skill of the wartime leaders of American science that they were able to convince a skeptical public and Congress that only by permitting a high degree of self-governance and autonomy to the scientific community could the country hope to reap the practical benefits that would ultimately flow from scientific progress.[6]

In considerable measure the problem of autonomy in the sense I have attempted to define it here is different for the natural and the social sciences. In the case of the natural sciences the polity seldom intervenes to influence the substantive conclusions of science. It "distorts" the system primarily through the allocation of resources to particular fields of science presumed by conventional wisdom to be related to particular political purposes or social goals, such as national defense or the cure of a specific disease. When one is talking about "pure science" the relationship between a scientific discipline and particular social purposes is speculative and uncertain. Distortion of research occurs when such speculative potential applications become the major basis for choice between alternative research projects, in contrast with the logical structure of the science itself. Thus political authority attempts to influence the presumed "purpose" of research in the natural sciences, though this purpose may not coincide with that of the researcher, but it seldom attempts to intervene with respect to substantive conclusions or methodology, except when this methodology itself raises ethical issues, as in the use of human subjects in biomedical or psychological experimentation.

The potential for distortion in the social sciences is of another order, however. In these fields the tradition of expert autonomy is less well established, and the line between professional expertise and conventional wisdom less sharply drawn. The conclusions of social science research frequently have apparent policy implications that the public can understand and that attract the interest of the news media. Scientific discourse thus tends to "leak" much more rapidly into public discourse, often in distorted and oversimplified form, with cautions and limitations in assumptions forgotten. Social science research has a more obvious impact on widely held values and prejudices and often has implications for the redistribution of wealth or political power, or is so perceived.

Recent research and public controversy over the heritability of intelligence as it relates to social performance and the distribution of social rewards or over the effects of busing on the attitudes and learning performance of minority children are only two examples of this phenomenon.[7] There is less public acceptance

---

[6] V. Bush et al., *Science the Endless Frontier,* reissued as part of the tenth anniversary observance of the National Science Foundation (Washington, D.C., 1960), see esp. p. viii.

[7] For an interesting detailed example, see D. Armor, "The Evidence on Bussing," *The*

of the claim of social science research to be objective and free of political bias, and indeed the concept of a value-free social science is under serious attack from within the social science disciplines themselves, especially among the younger generation of social scientists.[8]

Today, attacks on the objectivity of the social sciences come particularly from the left, but only a few years ago they were more frequently from the right, and indeed many a politician confused the term "social science" with the advocacy of "socialism." The low public acceptance of the social sciences as science was a principal reason why natural scientists opposed the inclusion of the social sciences in the original act creating the National Science Foundation, except in the category of "other sciences." It was feared that social science research would attract political attacks on the agency that would impair its capacity to support the natural sciences.[9] Even as late as the early 1960s many leaders in the social sciences preferred not to have a separate social science foundation, thinking that social science research would be safer under the mantle of natural science prestige within the National Science Foundation.[10] The National Science Foundation did not create a Division of Social Sciences until 1958. Public distrust of the social sciences led the NSF to confine its sponsorship of social science research initially to the more quantitative and descriptive aspects of the social sciences, those which could be most easily defended as "value-free" and were generally regarded as noncontroversial.

The natural sciences themselves are not entirely free of the threat of political criticism or suppression of their conclusions, but this happens mostly when they tread directly on political and economic toes as in the ADX-2 battery additive case or the controversy over the genetic effects of nuclear radiations.[11] In these

---

Public Interest 28 (Summer 1972), and rebuttal and commentary in *The Public Interest* 30 (Winter 1973): 88–134.

[8] Some well-known discussions of the issue can be found in Gunnar Myrdal, "A Methodological Note on Facts and Valuations in Social Science," *An American Dilemma,* vol. II (New York, 1944), and also his *Objectivity in Social Research* (New York, 1969); Alvin Gouldner, "Anti-Minotaur: The Myth of a Value-Free Sociology," *Social Problems* 9 (Winter 1962): 199–213 and his *The Coming Crisis of Western Sociology* (New York, 1970).

[9] *Technical Information for Congress,* Report to the Subcommittee on Science and Astronautics, 91st Cong. 1st Sess., April 25, 1969, prepared by the Science Policy Research Division, Library of Congress; see ch. 5, "Inclusion of the Social Sciences in the Scope of the National Science Foundation 1945–47," pp. 97–125.

[10] Hearings on S. 836, a Bill to Provide for the Establishment of the National Foundation for the Social Sciences in Order to Promote Research and Scholarship in Such Sciences, Subcommittee on Government Research, Committee on Government Operations, U.S. Senate, February 7, 8, and 16, 1967.

[11] See ch. 3, "ADX-2: The Difficulty of Proving a Negative," in *Technical Information for Congress,* pp. 14–56; also, "The Effects on Populations of Exposure to Low Levels of Ionizing Radiations (The 'BEIR' Report)," NAS/NRC (Washington, D.C., 1972).

examples the controversial issue is not central to the conceptual structure of the pertinent science; it is the policy implications that draw attack, and these are incidental to the underlying scientific issues. Natural scientists are usually accused in public of suppressing or distorting known facts rather than of putting forward false data or theories. When one examines closely the controversies among scientists regarding radiological hazards, the effects of smoking on health, or the effect of detergents on eutrophication, one finds that they are mostly disputes in which the parties differ in their implicit value judgments and exploit uncertainty of evidence in an incompletely researched field to provide different interpretations of the evidence consistent with their policy predilections. However, these are seldom differences of fundamental theoretical perspectives within science, and historically the controversies have gradually been resolved as new evidence accumulated. Other recent examples of controversies in the natural sciences that have erupted into the public arena were the Velikovsky affair[12] and the public furor over UFOs.[13] These involved more ideological sorts of controversies within science, but although they were taken quite seriously by the public the scientific community was never in much doubt as to where the truth lay. Neither the theories of Velikovsky nor the possible existence of UFOs were taken seriously by any but a tiny minority of scientists. In neither of these cases was there any attempt at official political intervention in the substance of the scientific issues involved. More serious perhaps was the recent California school textbook controversy, involving the teaching of alternatives to Darwinian evolution in biology courses in the schools, but this was more an educational than a scientific issue.[14] Yet, by and large, even in an area as politically charged as the abortion issue, there is little disposition on the part of politicians to question those conclusions of science that pertain to the physiology of reproduction or to interfere with fundamental research on the biology of the process. Even in totalitarian societies, scientific truth has largely won out over politically sanctioned doctrine in the fields of genetics and quantum theory, and in the Soviet Union there has been widening toleration for the conclusions and methods of Western economic research. The creation in Vienna of a joint East-West Institute for Applied Systems Analysis with multinational financing demonstrates a belief on both sides of the Iron Curtain that there exists some body of value-free applicable knowledge and techniques in the social sciences.[15]

---

[12] D. H. Menzel, "The Debate Over Velikovsky, An Astronomer's Rejoinder," *Harpers*, December 1963; *The Velikovsky Affair*, ed. A. de Grazia (New Hyde Park, N.Y., 1966).

[13] *News Report*, NAS-NRC-NAE 19, no. 2 (February 1969) : 6–8.

[14] "Creationists and Evolutionists: Confrontation in California," *Science* 178 (November 1972) : 724–729.

[15] "Charter is Signed for the International Institute of Applied Systems Analysis," *News Report*, NAS-NRC-NAE, 22, no. 9 (November 1972) : 2.

In dealing with the question of scientific freedom, it is important to distinguish between freedom with respect to the substance and conclusions of research and freedom with respect to methods. Despite occasional abuses, the claim of scientific freedom has never been extended to tolerate the violation of widely held ethical norms in experimenting on human beings or animals. There have, of course, been examples of abuses, but the scientific community has recognized society's right to enforce some sort of trade-off between the potential intellectual or social benefit to be derived from research and the hazard to the health or well-being of individual human subjects or their right of privacy. It has also recognized the principle that the infliction of pain and suffering on animals is justified only to the extent that it is necessary for the benefits obtained and that potential benefits are sufficiently great in ultimate human terms to outweigh the suffering inflicted on experimental animals. There is, of course, no precise calculus by which such trade-offs can be computed; ultimately the balance of values will depend upon the general climate of opinion among all those with an awareness of the issues. On the other hand, there is a serious question concerning the relative weight to be accorded lay and professional judgments in making such trade-offs, and this appears to be an area of growing controversy in both the natural and social sciences. For example, at the very time when increasingly numerous and stringent animal tests are required to justify the introduction of new therapeutic drugs to the market, there is also much closer political scrutiny over the treatment of animals in such experiments.[16]

In the physical sciences there has been little questioning of either the methods or the substance of research, although there have been attempts to question the objectives of research when it seemed to have a fairly apparent relation to an obvious or probable military application. Occasional controversies have erupted over the responsibility of the individual scientist for the ultimate social uses made of his results, with an implied obligation not to work in areas where there is reason to believe that the results might or could be used for purposes that would contravene the values of the individual. As a political movement, however, this trend has always floundered on the high degree of uncertainty that exists regarding the ultimate applicability of pure research.[17]

A problem raised by the Weber-Humboldt view of the autonomy of scholarship is the difference between institutional or professional autonomy on the one hand and the activities and responsibilities of individual scholars on the other. Does the principle of autonomy and the injunction to the state not to ask institutions and collective associations of scholars to serve its purposes directly extend

---

[16] M. B. Visscher, "Animal Welfare Act of 1970," *Science* 172 (May 1971): 916–197; M. B. Visscher, "The Newer Antivivisectionists," *Proceedings of the American Philosophical Society* 116, no. 2 (April 1972): 157–162.

[17] D. Nelkin, *The University and Military Research: Moral Politics at M.I.T.* (Ithaca, 1971); see also my review of that book in *Minerva* 11, no. 3 (July 1973).

to the whole individual or only to his role as a scholar? To what extent is the scholar justified in serving the state, or indeed any other political purpose, provided he clearly separates his role as scholar from his role as citizen and whole human personality? Can the same individual serve the state, or participate in political action, and still preserve his integrity as a scholar? Does the Humboldt view preclude the channeling of money to universities in categorical grants whose purposes are defined by the state, however pluralistic or decentralized the allocation and decision mechanisms may be? Or does university autonomy imply that government money should be channeled only through block grants to the institution, with the internal allocation among various research and teaching activities being the collective responsibility of the community of scholars? Can a scholar serve as a government adviser or as a consultant to a political candidate without compromising his entire scholarly role? According to Nisbet, Weber in his personal capacity was a political activist,[18] so apparently he felt that *Wertfreiheit* applied only to the role, not to the whole man. On the other hand, the problem may be more complicated if the scholar is paid for his external role or accepts some limitation on his freedom, such as the obligation to protect security classified information or administratively privileged information obtained in the course of his external activities. Even more debatable is the use by scholars in their research of information or personal communications that cannot be documented or made public. Yet a great deal would be lost in terms of richness and accuracy if scholars had to confine themselves to publicly documentable sources. In my opinion this is not an area in which absolute principles should obtain. Undocumented evidence should be used with great restraint and should be corroborated with public documentation to the maximum extent possible, but it should not be excluded as unethical or improper within the canons of good scholarship.

In the United States both government policy and the conventions of the scholarly community have tended to accept a sharp dichotomy between institutional and personal roles. Harvard University, for example, has, except during World War II, prohibited the conduct of classified or proprietary research under its auspices, but has seldom discouraged and has often actively encouraged the outside consulting roles of its faculty members and placed no limitations on the types of activities in which they might engage outside the university, provided such activities did not conflict directly with formal obligations to Harvard (e.g., teaching a course for credit in another university while a full-time teacher at Harvard).[19] But this separation of roles has been steadily challenged in recent years by students and political activists on the faculty. For example, a medical school dean was criticized by medical students for serving on the board of direc-

---

18 Nisbet, "Max Weber," p. 104.

19 Harvard University, *Report of the Committee on Criteria for Acceptance of Sponsored Research in the Faculty of Arts and Sciences* (Cambridge, Mass., December 1970).

tors of a drug company, and several professors of government have been attacked for their alleged roles as government advisers with respect to United States policies in Vietnam. In one case, a professor was criticized both for his role as an adviser on Vietnam and for his operation of a private consulting firm that did extensive social science studies for the Department of Defense. However, for the most part, these attacks were not made in the name of the autonomy or neutrality of scholarship, but rather because the individuals involved appeared to be on the opposite side of the political fence from the critics.

Within universities there is a fairly widespread consensus that the external advisory or consulting activities of its scholars enhance the prestige of the university as well as the research and teaching capabilities of its faculty, provided there is no direct interference with university responsibilities. Because of general acceptance of the involvement of university scholars in external affairs, the fact is that the purest "ivory towers" probably now exist in the basic research divisions of large industrial laboratories, where outside activities for pay are rigidly proscribed, and even unpaid outside professional consultation is subject to administrative approval. The same situation exists in some government laboratories and federal contract research centers or private research institutes. Few of the organizations that follow this practice, however, are involved in social science research.

The Weber argument for university autonomy and the Polanyi argument for the republic of science were both based on a postulated dichotomy between the pursuit of truth and engagement in social action and on the necessity of protecting the scholar in the pursuit of truth from external pressures either to distort the truth or to conform to current public prejudices or official doctrine, or to alter his intellectual priorities to conform to the social demand for immediate practical results. An extension of this concept of academic freedom, popular in some quarters today, says that a function of the universities is to harbor disinterested criticism of existing society, and that any external relations that bind the scholar or the university to the existing institutions and power structure of the outside society compromise their primary role as critics of the status quo. The purists of this school would argue that money should be channeled to the universities free of any limitations as to purpose set by the outside society. Government money is all right only if it flows in the form of a free institutional grant or of unrestricted funds derived from the fees paid by or on behalf of students. But categorical grants from government or private gifts for special purposes are inevitably biased as to purpose in favor of the status quo, and hence they potentially compromise the social critic role of the university and its members. Thus it is argued that university scholars should not provide external services for pay; their outside earnings should be confined to royalties and lecture honoraria that are without strings and hence without biasing influences from the established power structure of society. In fact such honoraria are the principal means by which critics of the status quo can derive income from the existing system without compromising themselves, morally or politically. At least that is the claim.

The other side of this argument is that honoraria and royalties often reward sensationalism and exaggeration rather than intellectual honesty and objectivity. Hence they introduce their own political biases. Extreme proponents of this view have argued for the existence of a "knowledge industry" that has an inherent vested interest in social change and in attacking the status quo. Thus, on balance, it would appear better to support a free market of contending ideas, accepting the occasional risks of distortion or bias both for and against the existing institutions of society.

AUTONOMY AND OBJECTIVITY

To a considerable extent the notion of scholarly autonomy depends on a belief in the existence of such a thing as value-free knowledge, i.e., a truth that can be agreed upon by large numbers of people with widely different personal values and social preferences according to neutral criteria that are independent of value assumptions. This is the concept that Ziman has characterized as "public knowledge."[20] Such public knowledge has the same characteristic as paper currency or checks. It can circulate freely and be widely believed without being frequently tested as long as people believe that it *can* be tested on demand by publicly specifiable and reproducible procedures. Public knowledge is thus the universal legal tender of scientific truth. Its hallmarks are communicability and verifiability. Part of our continuing confidence in the verifiability of scientific knowledge lies in the fact that each element of truth is part of an exceedingly complex network or interdependent structure of truths. Even when a given element does not appear at first to be empirically verifiable or seems to contradict common sense, we can have confidence in its truth by reason of its place in the network, like a single missing piece of a huge picture puzzle with a few empty holes, which can only fit in one place. We are prepared to believe the rest of the network and disbelieve the failure of empirical verification for a long time before accepting a change in the overall articulated framework. That is why the "paradigm-breaking" discoveries or concepts of science take so long to break their way into the corpus of public knowledge.[21]

Public knowledge enjoys especially great authority in pluralistic democratic societies just because it purports to be value-free. In a society with many different values, interests, and opinions, it derives social authority from the fact that it

---

[20] J. Ziman, *Public Knowledge, the Social Dimension of Science* (Cambridge, England, 1968).

[21] T. S. Kuhn, *The Structure of Scientific Revolutions* (Chicago, 1970).

can command a consensus that no other form of authority, except perhaps the common law, can command. In fact the common law enjoys much the same authority in the moral sphere that science and scholarship command in the cognitive sphere, and for the same reasons. It is an element of a cumulative nexus, and no single element can be denied without doing great violence to the nexus. The credibility of the university and of professional or scholarly societies as institutions derives from their adherence to the notion of public knowledge in the sense described earlier, and of course this implies a general belief that there is such a thing as public knowledge, much as the acceptance of currency and instruments of credit depends upon the belief that all such instruments can be redeemed in some universal medium of exchange, such as gold or a reserve currency.

Perhaps nowhere outside the United States is the appeal to value-free knowledge relied upon so extensively as an instrument to achieve political consensus for governmental actions. In American politics there is constant pressure to convert political questions into technical questions, so that they can be referred to experts without actually confronting the value differences that frequently are the real origin of conflict. This is one of the functions of presidential commissions. Although such commissions are usually composed of "public-spirited citizens" representing a spectrum of political opinion on an issue, the actual work is almost invariably done by expert staffs, and the commission itself is used as a bridge between expert research and general public opinion. The work of the commission thus has the form and appearance of an apolitical investigation, and the president feels obliged to take it seriously even when he disagrees with its conclusions on political grounds.

This tendency to refer sensitive political issues to experts poses a special hazard to the social sciences because of their closeness to policy. There is first of all the tendency of experts to present their political preferences as disguised technical recommendations and of politicians to recruit experts who can cloak the politician's goals with the respectability of apparent scientific objectivity. In a society that places a high value on practicality, the expert is often trapped in front of politicians into ascribing to his data and conclusions a degree of validity that he would defend much more cautiously before his scientific peers. He is so flattered that the politician is interested in what he has to say, and that his work has apparent relevance to real world policy issues, that he forgets normal scientific caution. The politician wants sharp answers and would like to shift the burden of decision to the expert, especially when the expert seems almost but not quite ready to say what the politician wants to hear. Furthermore, scientific results expressed in probabilistic or statistical terms must often be translated into more value-laden language, such as "insignificant risk" or "best alternative." Thus the very process of interpreting science for the politician and the exigencies of necessary concrete action involve some compromise in the original objectivity of a scientific result.

The notion of objective knowledge in the social sciences has been under attack from many sides in recent years. The grounds of this attack are threefold. First is the argument that most social science propositions involve hidden and often unconscious value assumptions that are usually biased in favor of power and rewards in society. Second is the assertion that social scientists, especially when they deal with issues close to policy, address questions as formulated by a client and are thus compelled to accept the value assumptions and preferences implicit in the client's formulation of the problem, which, again, is usually biased against radical alternatives. Both of these criticisms come mainly from scholars on the political left. Third is the well-known sociological fact that the members of each scholarly discipline have a definite political bias along the spectrum from left to right,[22] and that this quasi-consensual political orientation of the peer group strongly biases conclusions on any supposedly scientific question that has high salience in current political debate. An example is the strong pro-egalitarian (as opposed to meritocratic or "elitist") bias of most sociologists. This third criticism is quite similar in principle to the first, but paradoxically its formulation comes most often from the political right in the form of an accusation that social scientists as a group are against the status quo. This bias, furthermore, can be enhanced by government support, since the middle level bureaucratic professionals responsible for detailed resource allocation are also toward the left of the political spectrum. Thus, the conservative critique goes, government-supported research or action programs involving social science knowledge are biased toward providing intellectual backing for federal programs that create jobs for social science professionals.[23]

The attack on the objectivity of the social sciences is bound to become sharper in a period of disintegration of the national consensus on values, which we have witnessed during the past ten years. When there is a general consensus on fundamental values, at least among the politically articulate segments of the population, it is more likely that the unspoken value assumptions underlying social science research questions will pass unnoticed or be given little attention. The great flowering of social science research in the United States occurred in the 1950s and early 1960s when there was relatively little overt value conflict in American society. The Great Society programs were launched in an atmosphere in which there was belief, fostered in some measure by previous social science, that poverty and racial underprivilege were technical problems that could be solved by technical means without politically painful redistribution of power or wealth. Poverty and underprivilege were thought of as absolute rather than rela-

---

[22] S. M. Lipset, and E. C. Ladd, "Politics of Academic Natural Scientists and Engineers," paper presented at the annual meeting of the American Political Science Association, Chicago, September 7–11, 1971; also *Science* 172 (June 1972) : 1091.

[23] D. P. Moynihan, "Equalizing Education—In Whose Benefit?," *The Public Interest* 28 (Summer 1972) : 74–78, esp. fn. 5, p. 78.

tive conditions. That is, they were ascribed to an absolute lack of opportunity among the poor and minorities, and it was widely believed that the removal of this absolute disadvantage would solve the problem.

Probably no responsible social scientist ever believed this, but it was a view quite attractive to politicians, as evidenced by Arthur Schlesinger's report of a conversation between President Kennedy and André Malraux in 1962. According to Kennedy the real issue at that time was not capitalism vs. the proletariat but the management of industrial society, an administrative problem rather than an ideological one.

> . . . the fact of the matter is that most of the problems, or at least many of them, that we now face are technical problems, are administrative problems. They are very sophisticated judgments which do not lend themselves to the great sort of "passionate movements" which have stirred the country so often in the past. . . .[24]

Recent research has thrown considerable doubt on the assumption that poverty can be cured by education and opportunity alone,[25] an assumption that was the natural and comfortable one for politicians and a public interested in maximizing consensus and avoiding conflict outside the rules of the game. It also throws doubt on the meaning of an absolute poverty level, since perceived deprivation appears to be more a function of economic status relative to median income than of absolute material living levels.[26] The failure of the Great Society programs to live up to the expectations that were generated for them, often based on social science advice, has shaken the faith not only of scholars but of the public in the efficacy of social science and in doing so has legitimatized a widening of political conflict at the expense of technical argument. To be fair it must be conceded that the Great Society programs were never funded on the scale that their early proponents thought necessary to achieve significant results, and therefore the evidence of their "failure" is inconclusive at best. Nevertheless, many later studies, such as the Coleman report, threw doubt on the assumptions underlying these programs.

In a rather similar fashion, faith has been shaken in the efficacy of economic theory as a tool for the management of the economy. The success of the 1963 tax cut in restoring a full employment economy in the United States, after a decade of partial stagnation, placed objective economic theory on a pedestal of prestige not enjoyed by any scholarly discipline since the beatification of the nuclear physicists following the explosion of the first nuclear bombs in World War II. In the words

[24] A. Schlesinger, Jr., *A Thousand Days* (Boston, 1965), p. 644.

[25] Moynihan, "Equalizing Education"; see also C. Jencks, *Inequality: A Reassessment of the Effect of Family and Schooling in America* (New York, 1972).

[26] L. Rainwater, "Work, Well-Being, and Family Life," Working Paper No. 15, Harvard-MIT Joint Center for Urban Studies, prepared for Secretary's Committee on "Work in America," Department of Health, Education and Welfare (June 1972).

of *Business Week* in 1966, a record of five years of "remarkable growth—and remarkable stability—in the United States economy . . . has raised the prestige of economics—especially in those who espouse the so-called new economics—to an all-time high."[27]

This success provided a license for economists to spread their influence and methodology throughout American politics—in the analysis of the strategic balance, in the assessment of the situation in Vietnam, in the introduction of PPB into the federal budget process. This last was going to depoliticize the allocation of federal resources.[28] All of these initiatives were disappointing in various ways, because the assumptions on which they were based were not fulfilled in real life. What I am describing, of course, is to some extent a caricature of a position. The early prophets of economic theory applied to public issues put forward much more modest claims than their less perceptive disciples and thought only that it would provide a useful instrument of self-analysis, not a substitute for the value decisions of politics.[29]

As the public became more assured that depression was impossible, the wage-price spiral took over. Political competition between various groups for a larger share of the national product gradually eroded the stabilizing forces of macro-economic management. Political intangibles (which a better historical knowledge might have taken into account) defeated supposedly hard logistic calculations about Vietnam. PPB overlooked the possibility of its own use as an instrument of bureaucratic infighting. Fortunately, the theory of mutual strategic deterrence has never been tested directly by experience.

In short the new economics tended to underestimate politics, and yet paradoxically this was its great attraction to politicians, at least those of the executive branch. More broadly, in the 1960s there was an alliance of interest between the politicians who saw "objective" social science as an argument for the enhancement of executive power and a certain school of social scientists who saw the needs of politicians as enhancing the opportunity to apply this knowledge.

What has emerged from this experience is an erosion of confidence in the social sciences as instruments of policy. This erosion stems not only from the disillusionment of politicians and the public, but also from a greater appreciation on the part of social scientists of the complexity of the real world of politics.[30]

---

[27] *Business Week,* February 5, 1966, p. 125, quoted in Walter W. Heller, *New Dimensions of Political Economy* (Cambridge, Mass., 1966).

[28] Executive Office of the President, Bureau of the Budget, Bulletin No. 68–2 (July 18, 1967), reprinted in *Planning Programming Budgeting: A Systems Approach to Management,* eds. F. J. Lyden and E. G. Miller (Chicago, 1968), p. 430.

[29] C. J. Hitch, "Economics and Operations Research: A Symposium II," *Review of Economics and Statistics* (August 1958) : 209.

[30] A. Wildavsky, "The Political Economy of Efficiency: Cost Benefit Analysis, Systems Analysis, and Program Budgeting," *Public Administration Review* 26, no. 4 (December 1966) : 292–310.

There is an interesting parallel here with the disenchantment with the physical sciences as automatic instruments of economic growth and general welfare, which occurred much earlier in the decade. This disenchantment among the public was accompanied by a growing appreciation among specialists of the complexity of the relationships between science and the economy.

To some extent, of course, disillusionment with the social sciences has also come from the disappointment in what the social sciences have been able to produce intellectually. There has been less in the way of undebatable conclusions and generalizations than might have been originally hoped for. Some of the disappointment within the social sciences themselves has seeped down to the more perceptive politicians.

The image of all the social sciences has been somewhat tarnished by their encounter with government, but it is not clear whether this is a net gain or loss for the sciences themselves. Could the lessons of the inadequacy of the assumptions, particularly the lack of consideration of political factors, have been learned less expensively? Was progress of the social sciences on their own intellectual terms delayed or diverted by their encounter with the real world of government policy, or were they refreshed and sobered by this cold dash of reality? Did the social sciences help divert the country from the true path of social reform by lulling it into a belief that the problems facing it were technical, rather than political? Did government support tempt the social sciences into promising more than the state of their understanding made it possible for them to perform? Was scholarship corrupted by hubris? Or did the social sciences succeed in introducing a small increment of rationality into situations that would have developed much as they did anyway? If the latter was the case, then perhaps the social sciences learned from the laboratory of experience without much affecting policy. I must confess I can only raise these questions, not answer them.

THE SOCIAL SCIENCES AND THE PENTAGON

In no area has the question of the effect of government support on the autonomy of the social sciences received more attention than with respect to the relations between the social science community and the Department of Defense. The issue first surfaced publicly in connection with Project Camelot in 1967. This aborted project in foreign area research, intended for support by the army, but never implemented, brought the whole matter to the attention of Congress, and several hearings by the Senate Foreign Relations Committee resulted. Actually, as in other pioneering areas of basic research, the military services were the first to appreciate the practical potential of the social sciences and to stimulate research effort in several new fields. One of these fields was foreign area research.

The rationale for military support of such research was succinctly stated by McNamara in his May 1967 speech in Montreal. He said:

> There is still among us an almost ineradicable tendency to think of our security problem as being exclusively a military problem. . . . We understand that for our military mission to be most effective requires understanding of the political, social, and economic setting in which we fulfill our responsibilities.[31]

The point was further amplified by Dr. John Foster, director of Defense Research and Engineering, who said that

> at the outset of hostilities or the possibility of hostilities, the Defense Department is frequently asked to consider just what kind of action it might take in the interests of the country affected—in supporting the United States allies. . . . So it is in our interests to understand the nature of such instabilities, as well as the various countries in which instability might occur.[32]

On its face this seems an enlightened recognition of the fact that the application of force in international affairs is an extension of political action and that the nature and amount of the force must be tailored to the political goals sought and the political and social environment in which force is to be exercised. Indeed it could be said that the failure of this perspective to penetrate the decision processes about Vietnam is the basic explanation of that fiasco. It is a great advance in sophistication over the doctrines of "unconditional surrender" or "massive retaliation" that characterized the conduct of World War II and the early period of the cold war. It could be argued that bringing in social science research could moderate fixed positions and prejudices entertained by conservative military officers. In this view, failures of American policy have stemmed in large part from inadequate injection of social science research perspectives into the policy process, not from the corruption and distortion of the social sciences by their contact with the sources of political power. Putting the worst possible face on things, it may be that DOD calls primarily on its sympathizers when it recruits social scientists for consultation and advice. Nevertheless, these social scientists have associations and loyalties to the larger social science community and represent the application of more critical standards to the assessment of specific situations than might otherwise be employed.

On the other hand, to the extent that the social science research or advice to the military is either classified or privileged it may be argued that the assumed objectivity of science merely provided a cloak of scientific respectability for policies that the military was determined to pursue anyway and that the military supported and used social science research only to the extent that it helped it to

---

[31] Hearings Before the Committee on Foreign Relations, U.S. Senate, "Defense Department Sponsored Foreign Affairs Research," May 9, 1968, quoted on p. 11.

[32] J. S. Foster, ibid., p. 17.

carry its arguments before the academically oriented key policy makers of the Kennedy and Johnson administrations.

The heady wine of being taken seriously by top level decision makers may also have distorted the interpretation of data by social science advisers. While this may have been in part true, I am inclined to feel that to the extent that objective evidence and knowledge about foreign nations and societies replaces stereotypes and prejudices all too likely among politicians and military officers, the involvement of social scientists with the military was a net gain for policy, though not necessarily for the social sciences.

Indeed, for foreign area studies, the indirect price of military involvement in the support of research may prove to be intolerably high. The support of some social scientists with military funds throws suspicion on the motives or concealed purposes of any American social scientist working in a foreign country. Thus even a small amount of military support can poison a whole field of research, as much for those who do not accept military support as for those who do. In addition, because of the generally conservative bias of the professional military establishment, the suspicion is bound to arise that unique information on foreign areas obtained under military sponsorship may be used to suppress social and political change in the areas studied on the unproven assumption that such change is inimical to United States interests.[33]

The sensitivity of scholars to military sponsorship became significant only after major United States involvement in Vietnam. Up until the early 1960s there was a remarkable American consensus on foreign policy, dating from World War II, and with some exceptions this consensus was widely shared even by the liberal academic community.[34] Thus it was perfectly respectable to work for the CIA or for the weapons laboratories of the AEC or to consult on military "summer studies" on defense policy or weapons development problems. Many leading young theoretical physicists participated in Project Jason, a consulting group set up by the DOD-sponsored Institute for Defense Analyses to engage younger scientists in the part-time study of technical problems of defense. It was during this period of academic support for (or at least acquiescence in) the cold war that many of the leading universities set up or administered special laboratories for the Department of Defense. Thus by the time of the great reversal of academic opinion in the mid-1960s, a few institutions, such as Stanford and M.I.T., were deeply engaged in defense research and were indirectly dependent on the

---

[33] H. Brooks, "Impact of the Defense Establishment on Science and Education," in *National Science Policy,* pp. 935–63, H. Cong. Resolution 666, Hearings before the Subcommittee on Science, Research, and Development, Committee on Science and Astronautics, U.S. House of Representatives, 91st Cong. 2nd Sess., no. 23 (Washington, D.C., 1970), esp. p. 953.

[34] Ibid., p. 942.

Defense dollar for the support of their primary missions, through overhead cost recovery on their defense contracts and through reimbursement of some faculty salaries. In addition they had acquired long-term moral commitments to research employees specializing in defense technology or military policy issues. A much larger number of institutions was dependent on the Defense dollar in particular departments, such as electrical and aeronautical engineering. When the switch in opinion came, dependence of most universities on Defense support had already receded drastically from what it was in the mid-1950s when there was little concern with the issue. For example, dependence of all universities on military support dropped from 70 percent of all academic research support in 1954 to only about 11 percent in 1972 and was around 20 percent in the mid-1960s. Despite the continuous decline of the relative importance of defense support of academic research during the 1960s, the rhetoric of the critics continued to speak of ever-increasing involvement of the military in all corners of American life.

Ironically, the money received by the universities from the military had for many years fewer strings attached to it than did funds from any other source of government support. This was true for the social sciences as well as for the natural sciences. In the immediate postwar years the Office of Naval Research was charged by law to support "pure and imaginative" research, and for many years thereafter the ONR was noted for its pioneering support of newly emerging areas of fundamental science: low temperature physics, molecular biology, radio astronomy, X-ray and gamma-ray astronomy with sounding rockets and balloons, behavioral psychology, and statistical decision theory. It was able to recognize and move quickly into emerging areas of science, and the fact that it was part of a large agency with many more consequential budget issues meant that its scientific initiatives were enthusiastically backed without any requirement for detailed pragmatic justification. As long as the public remained supportive of the general mission of the Department of Defense and accepted the prime need for a large defense establishment, it accepted the ONR program with little question, and later the research branches of all three military services remained friendly and protective homes for basic research, outlasting by several years public disillusionment with the rest of the military establishment. The doctrine of scientific autonomy was never so strongly and consistently defended as by the military research offices during the 1950s and early 1960s. It was only after the research support of civilian agencies grew to comparable size that ONR could no longer justify almost any program of acknowledged scientific merit with the argument that the defense of the United States required a broad strength in science across the board without too much reference to its immediate applicability to specifically military problems.

The suspicion that attached to support of the social sciences by civilian agencies in the minds of conservative congressmen did not extend to the military agencies, which were less suspected of socialistic tendencies. Thus it was, for example, that the navy was able to make effective use of ONR-supported anthropological research in providing governance for the mandated Pacific islands.

However, American policy in Vietnam ultimately poisoned the relations between the military and a large segment of the academic community. Although the military might argue that they were only the instruments of politically determined national policy, they were a visible symbol and were suspected of excessive influence over nominally civilian decisions through their monopoly of information sources, their expensive tax-supported public relations, and their network of alumni throughout industry and in Congress. A strenuous debate arose on campuses not only as to the morality of any university association with weapons work, but even as to the appropriateness of any military sponsorship of basic research. No matter how pure the research, it was argued, the military would not sponsor it unless they had some ultimate military use in mind. A program officer in Washington could assemble a significant program of militarily applicable research out of seemingly innocuous unclassified pure research projects, in which no one investigator would be aware of how his own work contributed to the real objectives of the program. This opinion was reinforced by the rhetoric that program officers in Washington were increasingly forced to use to sell their programs to skeptical budget officers and congressional committees. The academic scientist with DOD support was thus caught in a cross fire between two opposing constituencies to which he was accountable. To his colleagues and students he defended his research on the grounds that it was basic, having only a remote relation to military applications. It was published and available to the scientific community and could be used for many nonmilitary purposes beneficial to mankind. The potential military application was only incidental. To his sponsors he was increasingly forced to demonstrate some sort of relevance of his work to a military function or problem, and his immediate sponsor in turn often took his words out of context to make the work appear even more relevant to *his* bosses. There was no overt, or even conscious, deception in this process. Both sets of statements were true to a degree. But the net effect was to surround military sponsorship of basic research with an aura of duplicity that steadily eroded its political legitimacy in the eyes both of its sponsors and its recipients.

This problem emerged with particular intensity in the controversy that boiled up over Project Cambridge, a proposed large joint contract to the Harvard-M.I.T. social science community for the development of new computer methodology for the handling of social science data. This was to be supported by the Advanced Research Projects Agency (ARPA) in the Office of the Secretary of Defense.[35] The debate rolled along through the fall of 1969 while a subcommittee

---

[35] Faculty of Arts and Sciences, Harvard University, *Report of the Subcommittee on Research Policy on the Participation of the Faculty of Arts and Sciences in the Cambridge Project* (Cambridge, Mass., December 1969), esp. App. I.

of the Harvard faculty examined the pros and cons of the project and the philosophical issues involved in the acceptance of institutional support of this magnitude from the Department of Defense for research in the sensitive field of social data management. Though it had little or no relevance to such matters, the purposes of Project Cambridge excited emotional overtones of government dossiers on individuals and the development of a social technology that might be used by a police state to suppress dissent and keep minorities in line. A broader contention was that, because of its cost, any new computer technology for social data would augment the power of those who could afford to pay for it over those who could not. The proponents of the project, on the other hand, were adamant in their belief in the intellectual validity of the proposed research and in its potential constructive social value. But they especially vehemently denied the right of students and a group of their own noninvolved colleagues to legislate morality for them at no personal cost to themselves. Thus they not only defended the project but questioned the right of the university community even to consider its legitimacy on substantive grounds.

After considering five alternative policies ranging from endorsement of the project to outright prohibition against any faculty or student participation, the Harvard subcommittee split between two alternative policies. The first would have permitted full institutional participation, with Harvard assuming joint responsibility with M.I.T. for the administration of the funds and the selection of individual research projects. The second would have permitted participation by individual faculty members and students, guided by their individual consciences, but would have left to M.I.T. the administration of the contract and formal responsibility for the selection of projects and research strategies. Although the subcommittee favored the first alternative by a small majority, the Harvard faculty as a body voted against institutional participation. The practical effects of the choice of the second policy rather than the first were small, since individual Harvard faculty members could act as principal investigators on subcontracts from M.I.T. to Harvard and in their individual capacities could accept invitations from M.I.T. to serve as consultants on the selection of research projects. Thus violation of the principle of freedom of research was avoided, but Harvard as an institution abjured collective responsibility for the research.[36]

The resolution of the Project Cambridge controversy was effected on the principle of the separation between collective and individual responsibility for the consequences of research. Each individual could participate or not according to his own conscience, and the formal management responsibility for the project resided in faculty members only in their individual roles external to the university. Four years later the project was still in being and operating with a low profile on both campuses. The individual projects satisfied all the criteria of

---

[36] Ibid., section II, alternative A-1, p. 10.

freedom of publication, freedom of participation of personnel without prior approval of the sponsor, and individual, not collective, responsibility for the results of the research. These are the criteria that apply to all government-sponsored research at Harvard, embodying the principle that it is the conditions of sponsorship rather than the identity of the sponsoring agency or the specific subject matter of the research that should determine the acceptability of research at Harvard.

Described thus baldly, the resolution of the Cambridge Project has the appearance of an intellectual dodge, the maintenance of a distinction without a difference. Yet the dilemma could not be resolved by any simple decision. To start down the road of limiting the freedom of research of some faculty members, because their research was offensive to a minority of their colleagues seemed intolerable, but there were also many who felt it equally intolerable that the university as an institution appear to be lending its endorsement to a research project that was offensive to a significant body of community opinion. Even if the research were offensive to a majority of the community, there were few people prepared to impose their views on a minority who believed in the intellectual validity of what they were undertaking.

POLICY SCIENCE AND INTERDISCIPLINARY RESEARCH

The present debate is not over the direct relation between government support and scholarly autonomy. As the Department of Defense, prodded by its congressional committees, moves further away from the "enlightened" philosophy of the early ONR days, it seems unlikely that the issue of Defense sponsorship will again emerge as a political bone of contention on campus, but the problem of university involvement in applied and policy-oriented research for federal purposes will emerge with increasing urgency as the external managers of funding agencies become increasingly hostile to self-motivated, individualistic scholarly research. Not only in government agencies, but also in the management of private foundations and in the attitudes of university administrations, one perceives an increasing demand that scholarly research be both policy relevant and "coherent," that is, that individual pieces of scholarship within a single institution fit into a pattern that "adds up to something" and that can be used for the construction of public policy.

The issue is not so much whether the research is "basic" or "applied" but rather whether it should be "investigator-originated" or centrally managed so as to be effectively channeled to potential users. Increasing emphasis on the management of research effort both at the federal agency and at the university level comes into conflict with the traditional concept of scholarly autonomy and academic freedom. The practical issue is that individual scholarly merit will be less and

less the sole criterion for the allocation of resources to research projects. More and more sponsors are likely to demand evidence of how an individual piece of proposed research will fit into some master strategy involving many scholars crossing several disciplines. There is less and less appreciation among research sponsors of the effectiveness of the internal coordinating mechanisms of the scientific community, of mutual criticism of scholarly peers, and the strong sanctions against duplication of research efforts.

There is also likely to be more insistence by sponsors on institutional specialization and less on supporting merit wherever found. This also means that judgments of scholarly merit will be made less by scholarly peers in the same or a closely related discipline and more by educated generalists who take a more pragmatic view towards research and will judge social relevance in narrower and more literal terms. This attitude is already clearly discernible in the administration of the RANN (Research Applied to National Needs) program of NSF and several other national and international programs supported by that agency. A narrower focus will be demanded of scholarly programs with less freedom to follow where curiosity or the logic of the inquiry may lead.

This is not a question only of government policy, but of the whole fiscal and intellectual climate in which academic research is likely to be living in the next decade or so. In a sense it is an outcome of the increasing dependence of the universities on government support, in that it results in part from the effort to stretch limited resources. In research, universities will not be able to aim to be all things to all men, and new programs may increasingly have to be started at the expense of old ones even when resources can be secured from outside sponsors. This is so because the long-term commitments of outside sponsors seem less and less secure, as funding agencies, both private and public, respond to intellectual fashions and swings in popular opinion as to what is important. In addition, sponsors will increasingly seek to use personnel and capabilities already in place rather than to create new opportunities for competitive recruitment of new people on a long-term basis.

The consequences of all this for the spontaneity and originality of scholarship are hard to foresee. Undoubtedly there will be both gains and losses. When basic research was fashionable in the early 1960s, a highly dispersed national research capability was fostered. Many universities were encouraged to imitate the leaders by expanding their research capabilities in order to attract the products of the major graduate departments to their own faculties. Official pronouncements encouraged universities and colleges to believe they could not aspire to teaching excellence, unless they could recruit research-oriented faculties and offer glamorous research opportunities. Funds were available to start new ventures without injury to work in progress. Increasingly in the future, however, novelty may come only at the expense of established work. Investment in a risky intellectual venture—that is, a project with high potential payoff but a high risk of failure—will have to be undertaken at the expense of the "blue chips" of demonstrated productivity and worth, but with less possibility of changing the "paradigms" of existing knowledge. It is difficult to foresee how this balance will be struck, but the likely shift of intellectual initiative away from the individual scholar will be a serious loss. This individual initiative is the source of most of the new paradigms of science,[37] and the trend towards greater "management" of research may buy more coherent evolutionary progress at the cost of losing those "mutations" of insight that radically alter the direction of a discipline. It is true that once these mutations have occurred they can often be exploited by more managed programs, but in a period of limited resources there is an inevitable tendency to be so selective as to limit the possibility of mutations.

The question also persists as to whether present expectations from policy-oriented research are not excessive. Despite the alleged growth of anti-science and anti-rational opinion, the legitimate pressure on decision makers to use analysis to clarify issues and redeem decisions from entire dependence on prejudice will continue. In addition, there will be a temptation to appeal to seemingly neutral rational principles to avoid painful overt political choices. The involvement of the social sciences in policy can import a realism into basic research that will be healthy and productive of novelty, but it can also introduce the creeping corruption of telling the client what he wants to hear, or accepting his formulation of the research issues. There is always a time lag between the perception of research questions at the frontiers of current scholarship and the perceptions of well-educated generalists informed by the social science insights and paradigms of a few years ago. One sees already in all the sciences a tendency to be unduly sensitive to contemporary rhetoric and conventional wisdom, and this sensitivity is present not only in those who hold the purse strings but tends with time to penetrate the thinking of researchers themselves, first only in the rhetoric of their proposal writing, but gradually in their actual research.

Already this tendency is seen in the spreading of the holy water of "interdisciplinarity" over practically every research or educational program, whether it merits the adjective or not. More dangerous is the belief that the disciplines are somehow parochial and inferior, and only interdisciplinary research will contribute to the solution of society's problems. Weber's concept of scholarly autonomy does, after all, imply a central role for the disciplines, since it is only in the evolving disciplines, and in the coherent communities of scholars that they represent, that the cumulative character of scholarship is strongly developed and the standards of intellectual excellence are passed on from one intellectual generation to the next. Interdisciplinary research is successful to the extent that it derives constant sustenance and renewal from the disciplines. An interdisciplinary field either becomes a new discipline with its own cumulative standards and

---

[37] V. Bush et al., *Science.*

criteria of quality, or it decays into mediocrity, unless it continues to recruit to itself new people trained in the latest techniques and concepts of the more traditional disciplines. The temptation to escape the standards of the disciplines and then defend oneself against the application of those standards by accusing the disciplines of "parochialism" is sometimes valid, but more often simply a psychological defense mechanism. The difficulty is compounded by the fact that laymen are incapable of evaluating the controversy and tend to sympathize with the individual who defies disciplinary standards.

On the other hand, the disciplines are justly criticized for their conservatism, for their attachment to the well-established paradigms. Most new ideas are not any good, and science would become very inefficient if it tried to pursue every new intellectual lead. It ought to be difficult to step outside the established conceptual frameworks, but not impossible. The disciplines ideally provide just the obstacles necessary to discourage all but the most brilliant and determined, and this is perhaps as it should be. But the conflict between interdisciplinary research and disciplinary attitudes and vested interests can be a healthy and creative one if it is not too one-sided in favor of one or the other. A victory for either the traditional disciplines or for interdisciplinary "problem-oriented" research would lead to the institutionalization of mediocrity. The biggest problem will be to provide careers of equivalent security and prestige to those in the disciplines for those working outside them without at the same time weakening the disciplines.

This situation poses especially difficult problems for the universities because of the difficulty in expanding interdisciplinary work with fixed resources without injuring the vitality of teaching and research in the disciplines. Interdisciplinary work was fine as long as it could be added onto a strong and healthy disciplinary structure. This is really the fundamental problem posed to scholarly autonomy by the combination of declining resources and increasing preoccupation with coherent and policy-oriented programs, especially in the social sciences. There is no simple answer to the conflict except to recommend in the strongest terms to funding agencies that a certain minimal percentage of the funds devoted to research be expended for the support of individualistic, self-generated investigations not too narrowly defined by the sponsor, for it is most usually from such research that the really new ideas spring, even though it may take more coherent and managed programs to bring such ideas to full intellectual realization or to practical application. The greatest threat of government, and indeed of foundation support, to the autonomy of scholarship may come from selective emphasis on pragmatic problem solving without adequate consideration of the long-term health of the individual disciplines and the key importance of individualistic scholarship as a standard setter for the research process as a whole.

How Good Was the Answer?
How Good Was the Question?

Adam Yarmolinsky

In the course of six-and-a-half years of government service in the Kennedy and Johnson administrations, I sought and received a good deal of scholarly advice on a wide range of subject matter from the nature of the problem of poverty in the United States to the anticipated consequences of France's withdrawal from the NATO military structure.

Despite the range of this advice, there were many more opportunities to seek scholarly advice neglected than exploited, and the advice was often less than fully useful. Difficulties arose on both sides, but at least as much in the governmental as in the scholarly sphere. The principal difficulties will be examined here, and some ways will be suggested by which they might be reduced. The discussion that follows assumes a fundamental openness to ideas, which unhappily is not always to be found in recent administrations.

I

The movements of affairs and the movements of the reflective mind are on different time schedules. Accordingly, the bureaucratic and political pressure of events is probably the greatest obstacle to seeking and receiving scholarly advice. Although I have sought advice on timetables as accelerated as that of the Cuba missile crisis or as extended as that of the early affirmative action programs, designed to increase the proportion of minority government employees and government contractors, in fact, no timetable was extended enough to permit advice to be solicited carefully and considered fully. One might almost conclude that by the time government is ready to ask a specific question of scholars, it will not stay for a scholarly answer.

The Cuba missile crisis is an extreme example: One day I was asked to find out all I could about the impact of a possible oil embargo in the three hours between sessions of the National Security Council Executive Committee. When I went to the Dominican Republic to direct the emergency relief operation there, I barely had time to collect a few books on the island, which I read on the way down and during my first few days in Santo Domingo. But even the questions asked by the President's Committee on Equal Employment Opportunity were tied to a timetable, created largely by political events that could not wait on considered investigation. The issue, for example, that arose in the early days of the Kennedy administration, whether it would be useful or counterproductive to take a formal ethnic census within the federal civil service became so intense on both sides of the controversy that it was decided before it could be thoroughly explored. Once it began to be asked about seriously, it had to be settled.

The question must be asked whether, in these three instances, more time would have produced more useful results. The answers are difficult, partly because the pace of events in government never really lets up, and I never had the time to acquire real expertise on any of these issues, even after the fact. There is one observation that seems applicable to all those situations: It is unlikely that scholarship applied in the event, even with the most deliberate speed, would have made a difference. But if thoughtful scholarship could have been initiated over a broader range of issues and its results made available well before the event, it might well have dictated a different policy decision: One that might have been nowhere on the continuum of options actually considered, but off in an entirely different direction.

A scholarly investigation can be launched in order to defer decision, when, despite pressures, the moment seems impolitic. But that kind of study is unlikely to result in action or even in significant communication between scholars and government.

Even the commission of inquiry, honestly constituted by government in a search for solutions, stands in serious danger either of being left behind by political events or of moving too far ahead of them. In the latter case, the commission's report may have great value for the country, as in the case of the Scranton Commission on Violence or the Lockhart Commission on Pornography, but it will not be directly useful to those who commissioned it. A major inquiry has a life of its own, both bureaucratic and ideological, that may diverge widely from the continuing political life of the issue that gave rise to it. The results of such an inquiry can, however, change the general context in which the issue develops and, therefore *pro tanto,* affect the development of the issue itself. The idea, presented in the report of the National Advisory Commission on Civil Disorders (the Kerner Commission), that the black and white races in the United States were becoming two nations probably had a significant impact on the terms in which new civil rights legislation and regulations were framed.

Here one must distinguish sharply between research commissioned by government to advance the state of the art and research commissioned by government to answer specific operational, or even potentially operational, questions. Government provides institutional and project support for the most basic kinds of research, both in the natural sciences (e.g., through the National Science Foundation, the National Institutes of Health, and the Department of Defense) and in the social sciences (e.g., through the new National Institute for Education and the Department of Housing and Urban Development, as well as the three agencies just mentioned). Government also provides institutional and project support in both the natural and the social sciences and, through some of the same agencies, for research that is "applied" from the viewpoint of the discipline, but "basic" from the viewpoint of government, in that it is not related to specific operational objectives of government. If HUD supports research on new building materials or DOT supports research on a new people-mover, they are generally not looking for information directly related to government policy decisions—although there may well be eventual indirect effects—and the constraints of the public decision timetable will not apply or will be very considerably attenuated. The classical paradigm is the work of the agricultural experiment stations, some of which might affect government policies, but which was really of more direct interest to farmers.

II

Closely related to the problem of time pressures is the political equivalent of the uncertainty principle. If to observe a phenomenon is somehow to change what one observes, then to call in an outside observer is to risk real—and unpredictable—consequences. This is part of the reason for executive privilege: to encourage policy makers to seek, and their advisers to give, advice by minimizing the possibility that the advice will be publicized. Executive privilege really serves three purposes, in ascending order of relevance to our concerns here. It protects the adviser from adverse public criticism, and thereby helps assure the policy maker of advice that is frank and honest, even if unpopular; it protects the policy maker from the public consequences of advice that he may not want to take, but that may be hard to resist once it is publicized; and it protects the situation itself from the impact of words publicly spoken.

Just because politics is the art of the possible, a policy maker is very sensitive about examining possibilities. Commissioning research on civil defense, with the consequent hysteria that it engendered, would be an extreme example, but to commission any research is to give an indication of which way policy may turn.[1] And while a scholarly inquiry may not be front-page news, neither can it be conducted behind the screen of executive privilege. When the Defense Department asked the Potomac Institute to study possible mechanisms for putting into effect an equal opportunity program for defense contractors, it created a major stir, in Congress as well as among the contractors. And when the department considered a more radical plan to use the off-limits sanction to enforce nondiscrimination off-base, it did not seek outside assistance in preparing the plan.

Some scholarly research may even arouse political sensibilities, quite apart from what clues it may provide to policy directions, as in the case of the famous Moynihan Report on black family structure. The Moynihan Report, named after the then young assistant secretary of labor, Daniel P. Moynihan, who commissioned it, did not grow out of any administration policies, nor did it result directly in any policy shifts. Pat Moynihan had no line responsibilities; he was a staff officer in the department in charge of research and development. But the report touched an extraordinarily sensitive nerve, and the reaction bore no relationship to the operational significance of the report itself. What it did in fact was to make any rational consideration of policies in matters related to the subject matter of the report impossible for a considerable period after its publication, thus presenting an object lesson to policy makers on the dangers of encouraging government-sponsored scholarship.

It is not only the fact of the special political sensitivity of policy makers that is relevant here, but the distinction between the political and the scholarly attitude. For the scholar, everything is open to inquiry, and it is particularly difficult for him to deal with a client for his research who cannot accept that premise.

III

Policy makers and policy advisers are not only sensitive to the political consequences of the act of inquiry. They are also peculiarly sensitive to the limited range of options open to them. Policy making in practice follows the model of what Charles Lindblom has called "disjointed incrementalism." It moves, almost always, in very small steps, and it starts only from where it left off. There is a good deal of discussion currently of a new budgeting technique known as zero-

---

[1] One recalls the difficulties that then Ambassador Philip Jessup got into during the McCarthy era over the question of whether he was *considering* the admission of Communist China into the United Nations.

base budgeting[2]—making up next year's budget without using this year's budget as a base line. Policy makers know that zero-based budgeting never really happens. They are therefore reluctant to look at a zero-base budget, even as a tool of analysis, for which it may be quite useful. By the same token, they resist the leaps of imagination that come naturally—or at least happily—to scholars. This resistance expresses itself in the way research assignments are defined—accepting the basic assumptions about the task at hand, whether it was the war against poverty, to be pursued without massive public expenditures for job creation, or the war in Vietnam, to be pursued without limitation on massive public expenditures for domestic programs.

There is also a certain reluctance to seek scholarly advice at all. Or the resistance may emerge, somewhat more subtly, in a tendency to seek advice only from scholars whose views are likely to coincide with the course of action that seems most feasible. In Vietnam, those who pursued, or acknowledged the possibility of achieving the stated United States objectives were consulted, more or less to the exclusion of those who denied that possibility. On NATO, where the government was divided within itself on the feasibility and desirability of a European nuclear force, each side had its favorite partisans in the academic world, and there was very little consultation across the intellectual battle lines.

Since policy makers are so much concerned about choosing immediate next steps and feasible recommendations, they are inclined to turn to scholars primarily for instrumental advice: not what should we do, but how should we do it. During the mid-1960s, advice was frequently sought on methods of warfare, particularly so-called counterinsurgency warfare in Vietnam, but it was seldom, if ever, sought on the wisdom of pursuing the war. It could be argued that the executive branch was getting a gracious sufficiency of advice from the congressional doves. But political argumentation is no substitute for documented scholarship.

Occasionally, policy makers will want an outside estimate of what is likely to happen in a particular situation, where the course of events is largely beyond their control. They will want these estimates only occasionally, for several reasons. First, most of their calculations deal with events that they can influence or believe they can influence substantially, and a good deal of their expertise as policy makers or policy advisers lies in their own calibration of how much effective influence they can exert. Even where that influence may be overborne by the tide of events, it is difficult for policy makers to acknowledge tides that they cannot measure with their own techniques. When the first long, hot summer of rioting in the

---

[2] See, e.g., Arthur Hammann and Aaron Wildavsky, "Comprehensive Versus Incremental Budgeting in the Department of Agriculture," in *Planning, Programming, Budgeting: A Systems Approach to Management,* ed. Fremont J. Lyden and Ernest G. Miller (Chicago, 1967), pp. 140–62.

cities came along in 1964, policy makers were still reasonably confident that the political network could encompass the problems. And over the next four years they were more ready to turn to the military—the experts in instrumentation—for solutions, than to the scholars.

IV

The question needs also to be asked whether government officials may not do better in relying on scholarly resources inside the government than in turning to outsiders. Even where an event occurs that is clearly outside the network of political controls—the building of the Berlin Wall or the invasion of Czechoslovakia or the French decisions to withdraw from NATO military arrangements—the government has substantial internal resources to which it can turn before seeking the assistance of the scholarly community. In the foreign policy arena, the work of the CIA provides a constant flow of information and opinion of a generally high caliber. On critical issues, the opinion is likely to be divided or somewhat ambiguous, which leads policy makers to suspect that outside advice will be equally divided. The authors of National Intelligence Estimates are masters of the "on the one hand . . . on the other hand" style, induced in part by the fact that they represent a consensus of all the intelligence agencies in the government.

In-house scholarship suffers a good deal from review if not authorship by committee. Its production can never be extracted completely from the hierarchical structure of government. There is always someone who must add the caveat that the author is not speaking for his department or his agency—and who will then communicate his worry that the caveat cannot be fully effective.

The very fact that the products of in-house scholarship are by and large not for attribution to particular individuals discourages a virtuosity that is also a scholarly virtue. There is a kind of dull, gray pall over in-house scholarship that seemingly cannot be cast off.

On the other hand, the in-house scholar has access to extraordinary resources. To the extent that documentation is a true mirror of events (and, as later argued, that is not always so), in-house scholars have to spend less time on the outside with their noses pressed up against the glass trying to peer in. But the act of pressing one's nose against the glass does tend to cultivate a more lively curiosity and a greater resistance to received doctrine and conventional wisdom. Scholars are probably less susceptible than most people to material bribes, but they can be bribed with information and even more effectively with a card of admission (even as observers) to the corridors of power.

V

In part, the problem is one of the political problems of a functioning government. National Intelligence Estimates are, of course, secret documents. Secrecy is a major concern for policy makers and policy advisers in dealing with scholars and not only the kind of secrecy that is associated with classified documents. For people who spend most of their lives talking, policy makers are remarkably secretive, especially so by contrast with the openness of the scholarly community. They try whenever they can to compartmentalize information, like the pieces of the map that shows where the treasure is buried. Knowledge is power, and power is not to be shared lightly. This was so even in administrations that did not, by and large, regard scholars as communist sympathizers, as effete snobs, or merely as a separate and suspect category.

As recently as the 1950s, the Joint Chiefs of Staff reportedly told the secretary of defense that he could not look at their war plans, while at the other end of town the members of the Federal Trade Commission have been known to conceal their litigation strategy from their opposite numbers in the Anti-Trust Division of the Department of Justice, who are dealing with restrictive practices in the same industry.

The practical consequences of this attitude are that even apart from the classified area, scholars are likely to find real difficulty in getting the facts they need to try to answer the questions put to them by policy makers. These facts will be particularly hard to come by when they suggest deficiencies in past performance, which most policy-relevant facts do. Even when scholars can get access to the written record of events and decisions, they discover that most of the process of policy making is not written down (unless transcribed from a tape recorder), and the written record is often used to present a self-justifying—and distorted—version of the actual course of events. The general skepticism about summaries of the Nixon tapes, for example, is even stronger among old Washington hands. Making a memorandum of a conversation is not like making a record of a laboratory experiment; it is more likely to be an act of aggression, or self-defense. The point is perhaps best illustrated by the story of the captain who, after the mate had been drunk on watch, made an entry in the log. "The mate was drunk last night," and, when he refused to expunge it, found another entry in the log, after the mate's next night watch, "The captain was sober last night."

By the same token, a general policy statement is seldom if ever a simple expression of intention. It is rather an attempt to resolve (or, in some instances to paper over) a number of disputes within the government as to the course of policy, without, so far as possible, making any direct reference to those disputes. If one does not know the history of the disagreements that led up to the policy document (and most of it is very difficult to dig out), the primary operational significance of the document is lost on the observer. For example, the discussion of so-called "non-curricular education," in the report of the House Education and Labor Committee on the Economic Opportunity Act of 1964, masked an attempt to increase the availability of funds to parochial school pupils in a regional dispute over the division of resources between the rural South and the urban Northeast.

Most policy makers are in fact extraordinarily reluctant to commit themselves to general formulations of policy, where those formulations have any bite. For some months after the Kennedy administration came into office, it was under pressure from within to issue a revised edition of the three-inch-thick "Basic National Security Policy" that had been the national security bible of the Eisenhower administration. The pressure came from the senior military, who were concerned that they had no formal guidelines for the new directions that policy was taking, and from some former academics, who felt the need to articulate the premises on which their chiefs were acting. After a good deal of debate, the matter was resolved with a one-sentence memorandum from the White House, rescinding the Eisenhower administration document and announcing that thereafter the basic national security policy of the United States was to be found in the statements of the president and other high public officials. Comprehensiveness and systematization gave way to flexibility and timeliness.

Political risks are generally uppermost in the minds of policy makers. Probably the primary reason that fundamental policy decisions both on nuclear strategy in Europe and on the course of the war in Vietnam were not explored more fully with scholars was a hesitation to risk exposure of one's thinking to political enemies, rather than conventional considerations of military security. In the early 1960s, to express doubts about the validity of official NATO doctrine, for example, would not have been telling the Russians anything they were not already aware of. But it might have triggered a major political onslaught from the hawks in Congress. The doubters in the bureaucratic ranks were constrained by personal and political loyalties to their chiefs, who were themselves not yet prepared to shift ground, and even by a certain "militarization" of thinking, in the context of national security issues and a still very active cold war. Indeed, persons who expressed their doubts publicly were less likely to rise even in the most lively governmental hierarchies.

Policy advisers, even more than policy makers, have difficulty accepting the fact that scholars will continue to comment on and criticize publicly policies on which their advice is sought. The habit of keeping their advice for their masters is so ingrained in policy advisers, and the lessons of disaster from breaking the habit have been so dramatically demonstrated—as in the Nixon administration by the departures of Walter Hickel as secretary of the interior and Lee Dubridge as assistant to the president for science and technology—that anyone serving in this capacity finds the scholarly approach essentially antipathetic and even puzzling. It is hard to remember that what is essential for the adviser's function is impossible for the scholar, and vice versa. An adviser who shares his advice with the general public, or even with a section of it, loses his effectiveness if not his job. A scholar who does not share his ideas with whatever public is interested loses just as much for opposite reasons.

Since "effectiveness" is a highly charged word, it may be worth elaborating briefly: Policy makers rely on their inhouse advisers to present to them facts, pleasant and unpleasant, and frank opinions, including the adviser's own opinions and those of critics and adversaries. They expect to be able to thrash out their own views with their advisers in free discussion. If the adviser expresses in public the personal views that he conveys to the policy maker, he risks premature exposure of the whole policy-making process, and this exposure is likely to be unacceptable to the policy maker. He may keep the adviser on, but he will probably cut off genuine give-and-take discussions. There are occasions when an adviser will decide it is better for the country, and for his conscience, if he quits rather than remain silent or even if he remains in office as a sort of publicly acknowledged devil's advocate. But these are decisions he must make in the knowledge that the roles of adviser and advocate are almost always mutually exclusive.

VI

If policy makers and policy advisers have difficulty understanding why scholars behave as they do, scholars seem to have at least equal difficulty in understanding their opposite numbers in government—and in adapting their work product to the needs of government. When and how far they ought to make the effort is a separate question, discussed later. But if policy makers can overcome the various obstacles described and reach out for help, we need to examine what are the difficulties that prevent or inhibit scholars from helping them.

The principal difficulty on the scholarly side is the disinclination of scholars to address operational questions. Their overriding concern with "why" tends to limit their interest in "how." They want to understand the problem even more than they want to solve it, with the result that they overdetermine it to the extent that, as restated and refined, it may be impossible to solve. The epidemiologists who found a way to control yellow fever before they understood the mechanism for its transmission were better policy advisers than they were scholars. The approach of disjointed incrementalism, or "little steps for little feet," referred to earlier, permits policy makers to whittle away at problems that scholars might prefer to attack head on. A health care delivery program, for example, that proposes to try some incentives to better organization and distribution of health manpower, and some extension of public funding for certain classes of recipients of care, does not face up to fundamental issues of public versus private management of health care, but instead it closes in on the problem. A welfare program that provides an inadequate supplement to the incomes of some of the working poor may not face up to the problem of reconciling adequate income support with adequate work incentives, but it may, by reducing the size and thus increasing the manageability of the welfare problem, make the underlying issue more amenable to resolution.

Operational thinking is manageable for some scholars, and not for others. In the early days of the Anti-Poverty Task Force, we brought together substantially all the scholars who had been working on the subject of poverty in the United States—which was not a very large number of people—and sought their judgment about the shape and content of the program that we were charged with putting together. Very quickly, over a period of days, the group sorted itself out into those who could adapt themselves to the fact that our assignment was to prepare a specific piece of legislation on a specific timetable, and those who could not. The latter group drifted away of their own volition without being dismissed.

Conversations with scholars in the nonoperational category provided some quite useful insights, but because they could not or would not focus on the problems that necessarily occupied the center of the field for the task force, a continuing working relationship was impossible.

Similarly, when the Office of International Security Affairs in the Department of Defense was concerned with the consequences of French military withdrawal from NATO, we consulted a number of scholars who were interested in Western European affairs. The consultations were not particularly fruitful, however, because we were operating under the gun of the French deadline, requiring withdrawal of the complex NATO infrastructure from French soil, while the people we consulted could not seem to focus on our problem but wanted to talk about their interests in their context.

This is not by any means to say that useful scholarship in policy fields is confined to answering questions put by policy makers. Asking the questions that the policy makers have not thought of is at least equally and probably more important. But the questions need to be related to the task at hand, if scholarship is to have a direct and immediate utility for policy. Perhaps the most creative contribution that a scholar can make is to persuade a policy maker that he can in fact effectively and properly enlarge the scope of his activities and the nature of his jurisdiction. But for a scholar to ignore issues of jurisdiction is to risk rendering his advice useless, at least to the people he is currently advising.

This kind of advice can still find a niche in the back of the policy maker's mind and eventually stimulate him to a new initiative that may be more valuable than his current preoccupations. But the scholar does not need a working relationship with the policy maker to have that kind of influence. Ideas do have considerable osmotic power of their own, apart from the ability of their creators to penetrate the bureaucratic maze.[3]

Bureaucrats are not the best or the most effective agents of change. But in some situations they are the only possible agents of change, and to ignore their limitations is to remove the possibilities for change. The scholars who walked away from the Anti-Poverty Task Force might have sharpened its perceptions

---

[3] Witness the attention given by policy makers to Michael Harrington's *The Other America* (New York, 1962) and Dwight MacDonald's essay "Our Invisible Poor," *The New Yorker,* January 19, 1963.

considerably about what it was doing. They might have induced some major changes in the legislation, as it was introduced and as it emerged from the legislative mill.

Specifically they might have helped to shift more emphasis to job-formation —the one provision proposed was advanced less than wholeheartedly and dropped during the first cabinet presentation. One of the fundamental assumptions of the Task Force was that it should concentrate on preparing people for jobs rather than on preparing jobs for people. The first objective was assumed to take longer, and the anticipated federal income tax cut was counted on to produce the job opportunities. A program of public works employment, financed by an increase in the cigarette tax, was put together at the last moment and not surprisingly rejected by the president, primarily on the ground that he could not simultaneously be proposing a tax cut and a tax increase. But closer examination might have made it less clear that the jobs to be created by the tax cut would be available to the people to be prepared for employment by the Job Corps and the Neighborhood Youth Corps. A job-formation piece of the anti-poverty program, relying on incentives to private employers, instead of meeting the whole wage-bill, and financed out of the regular appropriations for the program, might have made the overall anti-poverty program more successful.

The scholars might have pointed out some of the unanticipated consequences of the "maximum feasible participation" formula in defining the role of inhabitants of high poverty areas in anti-poverty programs and thereby helped to prepare for some of those consequences. Widely differing notions obtained within the Task Force as to the purposes of "maximum feasible participation": job training, consumer control, antidote to enervating feelings of powerlessness among the poor. No one, however, saw it as a stimulus to political battles between the organized poor and city hall. If this development could have been anticipated, some preparations could have been made to contain the conflict (some of it quite useful) or to channel it away from purely destructive activities.

The scholars might even have rescued the concept of testing pieces of the program in a few localities from the Republican congressmen who were using it, in the view of the task force, to try to kill the program completely. The Task Force itself was preoccupied with trying to design a program that would produce impressive enough national results within a year to convince a skeptical Congress to provide the second-year funding. Large-scale social experiments, such as the New Jersey negative income tax experiment and the subsequent housing allowance and health care experiments, were still over the horizon in 1964. Still, the scholars might have been able to help build in a few experimental designs with appropriate controls that could have contributed a good deal to program decisions in later years.

But the scholar-advisers could not do any of those things without determining—for themselves—the limits of what the Task Force could accomplish and what lay beyond those limits.

VII

It is all too easy, however, for scholars to veer to the other extreme and to try to become amateur political decision makers. The trappings of power are beguiling, particularly to those who have not had the opportunity to measure their costs. It is only natural to concentrate on political effects without worrying about the causes, and a scholar turned amateur politician can be the least analytical of men.

And just because policy makers generally work under pressure, they may throw assignments at consultants fresh from the world of scholarship without enough regard for their consultants' capacities and limitations. This is particularly so in the early stages of a program, where scholars, finding themselves in the exciting hurly-burly of political decision making, may be tempted to overlook the question of their fitness for the work to be done.

Timing is a critical factor. Once the anti-poverty program had been established, it could afford to commission much more deliberative and speculative studies, as it did in creating the Institute for Research on Poverty at the University of Wisconsin. The Institute has been responsible for most of the work on the urban and rural negative income tax experiments (the first really large-scale social science experiments commissioned as such by the federal government). These experiments were well-timed in that they came in a lull between legislative initiatives, but even then there was at least one real conflict between the administration's need for some evidence to show to a congressional committee in the fall of 1972 and the reluctance of the scholars to discuss incomplete results. Now that the experiments have been wound up, the Institute seems to be returning to much smaller scale projects, oriented more toward continuing lines of inquiry in individual disciplines. This was perhaps a natural consequence of the loss of momentum and direction in the Office of Economic Opportunity. With the shift in sponsorship to the Office of the Assistant Secretary for Research and Evaluation in HEW, there may be a new working relationship developing.

One of the advantages of an academic research institute is that it permits and even encourages scholars to make some efforts to cross disciplinary lines. The fact that public policy problems seldom if ever fall neatly within the confines of a single discipline is a serious obstacle to scholarly attention to these problems. There is a bad fit between established disciplines and current problems. Scholars make their careers and find their rewards within disciplines. They are understandably reluctant to take on responsibilities outside their main career lines. But the issue goes even deeper: The discipline provides a framework within which the scholar does his best work. It offers historical perspective and rigorous procedural standards. Outside his discipline the scholar tends to relax his guard against implicit biases and unexpressed major premises and to offer generalizations (about war, poverty, social services, fiscal policies) that he would be ashamed to venture on his own turf.

VIII

Further, scholars do import the biases of their disciplines into policy research and too often without realizing that they do so. Economists have moved more boldly and broadly into policy research than perhaps any other major discipline. But they naturally tend to put economic costs ahead of political costs. In studies of the domestic consequences of defense budget cutbacks, for example, there has been more emphasis on finding new kinds of jobs for defense industry than on identifying new claimants for resources released from the defense budget. Reconversion of the defense industry may be a troublesome economic problem, but it may or may not turn out to be a major political problem, depending on the countervailing political power of big-city mayors and education and housing lobbies. Government-sponsored studies have not reached this issue, because they have been dominated by policy researchers trained as economists.

Scholars are members of their disciplines, but they are also and above all individualists. They do not take naturally to shared efforts. If a bureaucrat is a man who never writes anything he signs or signs anything he writes, the scholar wants to write everything himself and to sign it too. The idea of completed staff work is often completely alien to him. If he has defined the problem, or even come up with an interesting idea about it, he is ready to publish, and the notion of spending endless amounts of time shaping his idea into a proposal that is both intrinsically workable and politically acceptable may not appeal to him at all. This is not to ignore the fact that some academicians are very skillful politicians inside the academic world and have learned to do all the things in that world that political decision makers have to do in the world of affairs. But by and large, and with notable exceptions, the academic politician lacks the time or the inclination to develop the kind of talent and expertise in public affairs that government looks to in scholars. He is simply too busy on the inside, dealing in the politics of academic affairs.

This situation is changing, however. Government has been commissioning very large social science research projects, in some ways more complex than big science, to try out the negative income tax, or housing allowances, or education vouchers. To undertake a research task of this magnitude is perforce to learn most of the lessons of working with others and working with government. Even to participate in such a venture is to be exposed to bureaucratic and political processes, not as aspects of a strange and glamorous world of policy making, but as part of one's everyday life as a scholar.

At the same time, scholarship, particularly social science scholarship, is discovering the political process as not only an essential but also an interesting aspect of its substantive concerns. Allisonian analysis[4] is having an extraordinary vogue

---

[4] Graham T. Allison, *Essence of Decision* (Boston, 1971).

in the universities. A recent arms control summer study devoted one-third of its energies to examining the domestic political context of the problem. There is a new scholarly interest in trying to answer the political decision maker's question: "How do I get there from here?"

IX

Social science research is potentially a major tool of policy making. It is much more than a helpful device to accomplish predetermined purposes, and it does not always confirm expected conclusions. In the work of the President's Crime Commission, social science research first produced the astonishing statistic that the probability that an American male would be arrested during his lifetime for other than a traffic offense was one in two. Rigorous additional research confirmed the correctness of the calculations, and the newly discovered fact had significant policy consequences—including removal of the question about arrests from the standard Civil Service employment form.

For social science research to perform its most important service for policy makers, the policy makers must be more open to what scholars have to offer, and scholars must be more aware of the limitations within which the policy makers operate. It seems unlikely that any formal organization can contribute much to this rapprochement. Moynihan's proposed fourth branch of government would rapidly sink to the routine level of another Legislative Reference Service,[5] while an interdepartmental social indicators staff would produce useful documentation, but few, if any, great ideas.

What is required is a shift of attitudes on both sides. More exposure, under circumstances of relatively low stress, can help. During the early 1960s I tried to organize an activity in the Pentagon that I called "opening windows on the Potomac," which involved bringing in scholars for occasional discussions of middle- and long-range issues. But the pressure of short-range problems was so great that the program existed more in hope and imagination than in reality. By hindsight, the time might have been better spent on this kind of activity. Perhaps with the eventual return of an administration that is willing at least to consider the contribution that scholars can make, more windows will be opened on both sides of the Potomac.

---

[5] This is not at all to suggest that increased attention by scholars to the research and evaluation needs of the legislative branch is inappropriate; quite the contrary, it may be more timely and productive, at least over the next few years, than attention to the executive branch, as witness the work of the Office of Technology and the Congressional Budget Office.

Legitimating the Social Sciences: Meeting the Challenges to Objectivity and Integrity

Edward Shils

THE HISTORICAL BACKGROUND: ESTABLISHING THE COGNITIVE LEGITIMACY OF THE SOCIAL SCIENCES

The effort to establish the legitimacy of the truthful study of society has a long and distinguished history. In the ancient Greek world, historians pondered the reliability of the various sources of information available to them; they were concerned with finding and asserting the truth as distinct from myths and legends. The task was taken up again in the sixteenth and seventeenth centuries by natural scientists who sought to demonstrate the superiority of inductive methods to speculative and ratiocinative procedures. The social sciences emerged as part of the movement to establish a reliable method of truthfully understanding the universe and all that went on within it. The various efforts to found a science of "social physics" were not only intended to construct a more truthful picture of society, but also to vindicate a certain way of going about the task that would be superior to previously employed methods.

In the eighteenth century, a more fundamental theoretical attempt to establish a scientific social science was undertaken by Condorcet, who took his point of departure in the theory of probability and contended that a science of society based on postulates similar to those of the natural sciences could be no less scientific than the natural sciences. Subsequently, the work of nineteenth-century German philosophers, such as Windelband, Dilthey and Rickert, to clarify the epistemological foundations of the *Kultur-* and *Geisteswissenschaften*—and to distinguish thereby the character of the procedures appropriate to the study of human action and the works of the human mind—was likewise impelled by the intention to show how objective, i.e., valid, knowledge could be produced.

The German movement reached its culmination in Max Weber's essays on "objectivity" and "ethical neutrality."[1] Weber insisted on the possibility of establishing the truth about social phenomena. He asserted that the truth of factual propositions could be established objectively, even though evaluative judgments were significant in the selection of problems. The validity of such propositions, Weber further asserted, would be compelling to all who had the intellectual capacities and qualifications to perform the necessary observations and analyses.

In these reflections, which extend over two millennia, there has always been a recognition—sometimes at the center of attention, sometimes more peripheral —that the intellectual activity involved in the attainment of a truthful understanding of society is carried on in a matrix of other human concerns. The effort to gain knowledge of society is performed by human beings with religious experience and beliefs, with political ideas and interests, with attachments to family and locality. The critical assessment of sources—i.e., of the data available for and gathered by disciplined inquiry—was intended to establish procedures through which the intellectually distorting influence of these extra-intellectual concerns could be held in check. Social scientists have also had to contend with the pressures exerted by the institutional structures and the cultural patterns within which social science has been carried on. As members of academies patronized by rulers or subsidized by government, as members of universities supported by state or church or wealthy private persons, as members of classes and nationalities with distinctive values and aspirations, social scientists have nevertheless attempted to assure that they could meet an overriding obligation to truth. The study of statistical methods, the mastery of rules of observation, the dispassionate scrutiny of evidence, and the criticism and revision of theories in the light of facts—all were intended to serve this purpose. Similarly, the affirmation of the ideals of freedom of thought and inquiry, of academic freedom and university autonomy was intended, and did in fact serve, to sustain the exclusion of noncognitive concerns and attachments from the sphere of cognitive activities.

"IS" AND "OUGHT" IN THE SOCIAL SCIENCES: HISTORICAL RELATIVISM

In antiquity, ideas about the relationship between ethical standards and the cognition of the world appear to have been diametrically opposite to those now

---

[1] "Objectivity in the Social Sciences" and "The Meaning of 'Ethical Neutrality' in Sociology and Economics," in Max Weber, *The Methodology of the Social Sciences* (Glencoe, Ill., 1949), pp. 1–112.

prevailing. The discovery of the nature of an activity also disclosed its inherent ethical obligations. There were, to be sure, counter-currents of skepticism and sophistry that denied this, but they made little headway against convictions of the identity—or at least the logical continuity—of what really "is" and what "ought" to be done. Cognitive activities and normative judgments were conceived to be inevitably part of the same process.

This point of view, so difficult to comprehend in an age in which the ethical silence of the infinite spaces haunts consciousness, has nevertheless had an extraordinarily hardy life. It persisted well into modern times, and it is only with Hume and Kant that the view finally emerges full-blown that a scientific outlook offers no basis for ultimate value judgments.

After the revolution wrought by Hume and Kant in the fundamental conceptions of "is" and "ought," the idea of the normative imperativeness inherent in the stratum of reality laid bare by cognitive processes took refuge in theories of history. God and Nature, having lost the imperative power resident in their timeless permanence, found a new home and a new form in the evolution of events in time. No longer did the permanent nature or the essential quality of things provide imperatives for action; rather, the "true nature" of their particular stage of development would provide those imperatives. Thus, man's ethical obligations were laid down for him by his location in the historical process. (Historicism has many variants: It may be seen not only in Marxism but also in the efforts of Julian Huxley and other evolutionary humanists to construct ethical principles from scientific analysis of the "evolutionary imperative.") Each stage of development—of the mind, of the economy, of the species—prescribes the tasks and ethical obligations inherent in its nature. Once the nature of the stage of development was correctly discerned, there was no room for disagreement.[2]

THE SEPARATION OF "IS" AND "OUGHT" IN MODERN SOCIAL SCIENCES: THE STRUGGLE AGAINST BIAS

Twentieth-century social science was the product of a confluence of two nineteenth-century movements, one scientific and the other philosophic. Subsequent to the philosophical revolution wrought by Hume and Kant, the reality to which social scientists—like any other scientists—could penetrate was per-

---

2 "Ethical historicism" was the antithesis of "ethical relativism." The ethical relativists were impressed by the random variety of standards of conduct and modes of arrangement of institutions in the newly disclosed societies and continents, which ethically had not hitherto been taken seriously. Their "ethical relativism" denied the classical view that there was an unchanging reality beyond the bewildering diversity of the phenomenal world. As a result, reality laid bare no uniform ethical obligations, for there was no ethical norm derivable from heterogeneity except that "the mores make anything right."

ceived as ethically mute. The understanding of this reality became an end in itself; the cognitive experience, per se, was a sufficient and autonomously valuable end. It ranked with the sphere of ethical judgment as an autonomous sphere of intrinsic dignity. The classical relationship between the two spheres was thus profoundly altered. Ethical beliefs were not in themselves improper for espousal by a social scientist; rather, he would find it advantageous to avoid them while conducting his observations and analyses. The faith emerged that this could be done and that it had to be done; not to do this would cloud the mind's eye and cause the observer to fall into observational error.

The early figures of American social science saw no incompatibility between the search for truth by the most reliable methods available and the desire to improve the life of man by means of science—and they were not apprehensive lest their detachment in the assessment of events be diminished and the accuracy of their perception blurred by their practical interest. Very few American social scientists of the 1920s and early 1930s knew Max Weber's writings on "objectivity" and "ethical neutrality," but in a less elaborate and more positivistic manner, they occupied a not very different position. Of Marx, American social scientists knew little aside from some studies of the "economic interpretation of history." The Marxian theory of ideology was scarcely known, and, to the extent that it was known, it was not taken seriously.

On the other hand, William Ogburn, one of the social scientists who led in the campaign to make the social sciences more scientific by the use of quantitative procedures, was very sensitive to the pitfalls into which bias might lead the investigator. He called attention[3] to the possibly deleterious effects of unconscious bias. The deformative potentiality of extra-scientific interests and the need to guard against them by studious adherence to scientific methods was also pointed out by Albert B. Wolfe.[4] Following Herbert Spencer, Graham Wallas[5] and John A. Hobson[6] likewise showed an awareness that extra-intellectual interests could mislead the mind in its quest for truth, yet they were confident that due care could overcome this danger.

At the same time, American social scientists pressed for a clear distinction setting off social science from social work and reform movements. Although generally sympathetic with the aspirations of social workers and reformers, they feared that close association with these groups would make sociologists "sentimental."

---

[3] In an essay entitled, "Bias, Social Science and Psychoanalysis," in *On Culture and Social Change,* ed. Otis Dudley Duncan (Chicago, 1964), pp. 289–301.

[4] Albert B. Wolfe, *Conservatism, Radicalism, and Scientific Method* (New York, 1923).

[5] *Human Nature and Politics* (London, 1906); *The Art of Thought* (London, 1926); and *Social Judgement* (New York, 1935).

[6] John A. Hobson, *Free Thought in the Social Sciences* (London, 1926).

This detachment of social science from engagement in practical affairs was in part impelled by a genuine conviction about the right way to do intellectual work and about the rational scientific foundations of social improvement. But it was also impelled by the desire to raise the public standing of social science by appearing to be as nonpartisan as the natural sciences and as free as they from association with quackery and nostrum-peddling. And even when the younger American academics became more interested in politics in the 1930s, and more social scientists asserted political preferences, their espousal of objectivity, or their belief in its feasibility and in the separability of ethical and scientific propositions, was not abandoned.

THE CONTEMPORARY SCENE: TWENTIETH-CENTURY CHALLENGES TO THE INTELLECTUAL LEGITIMACY OF THE SOCIAL SCIENCES

The initial challenge to the stance of American social science came from abroad in the work of Karl Mannheim. Mannheim argued[7] that there was a multiplicity of distinctive intellectual outlooks, corresponding to distinctive social scientific approaches, political intentions, and social positions. The English translation of *Ideologie und Utopie* (1936) directly influenced Louis Wirth, and through him, Mannheim's ideas acquired considerable influence in American social science. Mannheim's views about the "total ideology" that penetrates into the "categorical structure of thought" were adapted by Wirth into the idiom of "bias." Wirth's conception of bias assimilated it to prejudice, i.e., erroneous beliefs resulting from rigid attachments to ethnic, political, and other such groups. At times he seemed to believe that by self-scrutiny and the will to purify one's own mind, the bias could be expelled and objective knowledge established; at other times, Wirth seemed to think that bias could not be eliminated but only made explicit. This view intimated that what remained after "discounting" or "making allowance for" bias would be objective knowledge.

Wirth, in turn, had a marked influence on Gunnar Myrdal.[8] Myrdal postulated the possibility of objective knowledge, but compromised by leaving the task of establishing it to the reader. Given the ineluctability of bias, no work of social science could be taken at face value; its objective truth could, however, be discerned by the reader's correction for the investigator's avowed bias. Nonetheless, both Myrdal (in the text of *The American Dilemma* and in his *Asian Drama*[9]) and

---

[7] *Ideologie und Utopie* (Bonn, 1929).

[8] See especially *The American Dilemma*'s "methodological appendix" (New York, 1944), vol. II, pp. 1041–45; see also his *Values in Social Theory* (London, 1958).

[9] *Asian Drama,* 3 vols. (New York, 1968).

Wirth, in the various essays that he published in the last decade of his life,[10] wrote as if what *they* said about society was true and did not need to be "discounted" by corrections for their bias. Their practice in the writing of sociological analysis and in the conduct of sociological research continued, therefore, on the line of their American predecessors. Truth was attainable by systematic, disciplined procedures that suppressed the passions and desires, or at least excluded them from the operations involved in observing and analyzing. Those who were not partial to quantitative methods and who preferred "case studies," "participant-observation," "sympathetic introspection," and *Verstehen* were equally confident of the possibility and practicability of objectivity.

Just before World War II, the publication of Robert Lynd's *Knowledge For What?*[11] represented both a foreshadowing of what was to come more than a decade later and an echo from the past. *Knowledge for What?* was not a criticism of objectivity. Lynd criticized American social scientists not for presenting a false picture of what they studied, but rather for contributing to a distorted picture of American society as a whole by their avoidance of certain problems of central importance. Above all, he charged them with failure to deal with the distribution of power in the United States and its implications, thereby serving the parochial interests of the powerful. In effect, Lynd shifted the focus of concern from bias in the conduct of research to bias in the selection of problems.

Lynd's views did not arouse immediate response among American social scientists. But when they were taken up again in the late 1950s by C. Wright Mills in *The Sociological Imagination,*[12] they received a much more sympathetic response, especially from the younger generation of social scientists. Mills' critique of sociological research was written at Columbia University, where Lynd's earlier critique seemed most pertinent; for it was at Columbia that large-scale sample surveys were being conducted more elaborately than ever before, and the training of graduate students in survey techniques was most advanced. As at other large universities with survey research centers, dissertations were often chips off the huge blocks of data assembled on large-scale research projects. Thus, Mills' criticism of empirical research had an audience ready at hand. With more research now conducted on contract for business enterprises and government bodies, the charge of serving the "interests" of the powerful and of obscuring the "realities" of society by technical concerns appeared to have a more evident foundation than in Lynd's era.

Until the late 1960s however, the critics and the criticized seemed to occupy common ground. Both camps apparently accepted the view that objective knowl-

---

[10] Louis Wirth, *Cities and Social Life* (Chicago, 1964).

[11] *Knowledge For What? The Place of Social Science in American Culture* (Princeton, 1939).

[12] (New York, 1959).

edge, given the correct techniques, was achievable. The chief critics, Lynd and Mills, censured the social sciences for their alleged failure to study modern society as a whole and particularly for failure to study the exercise of power and authority on a society, or nationwide, scale. This was an assertion not of epistemological incapacity, but only of a failure to study important problems. In the more recent criticisms of social science, much, of course, is made of the latter. But it is also linked with epistemological incapacities, i.e., with the "class position" of the academic social scientists, their political intentions, and their sources of support. All are said to have a crippling effect on the truth and moral standing of what social scientists claim to discover.

Only a short time after Mills' death, when the new radicalism was beginning to afflict the universities, the ghost of Mannheim's sociology of knowledge was conjured up in its service. The social sciences were charged not only with being "ideological" but also with being part of the "ideology" of the ruling stratum of American society. Their "ideological" intention and function were stressed, and their cognitive dignity implicitly or explicitly disparaged or disregarded. Their aim was alleged to be practical and manipulative. All the techniques that social scientists had so laboriously devised to enhance and enforce objectivity were now considered only actions to aid in the co-opting or coercion of the victims of the present system of domination, while offering comfort and service to the powerful and assuring that social scientists enjoy ample rewards for their subservience. From this warmed-over and vulgarized version of Mannheim's assertion of the *Seinsgebundenheit* of all beliefs about society has come the denial of the possibility of "objectivity."

The chief work in this attack is Alvin Gouldner's *The Coming Crisis of Western Sociology*.[13] Its main argument is very simple: "Background-assumptions" determine what human beings perceive in their own society; and since the "background-assumptions" of sociological studies are conservative, nationalistic, etc., American social scientists must necessarily believe that American society is just, beneficent, conflict-free, etc. Sometimes Gouldner acknowledges that "background-assumptions" may represent intellectual propositions arrived at by observation and reasoning, subject to modification by further observation and reasoning. At other times, Gouldner takes the extreme relativist position and argues as if "background-assumptions" are entirely arbitrary in character, unaffected by disciplined intellectual exertion but dependent entirely on "social position." Although he occasionally shows some awareness that if he accepts this proposition, then his own arguments have no claim to anyone's respect, he seems to believe, for the most part, that his own "background-assumptions" are compatible with truthful observation and analysis.

---

[13] (New York, 1970).

CURRENT MORAL AND POLITICAL PROBLEMS
OF THE SOCIAL SCIENCES

Social Science as Enlightenment: Ethical Benefits

The ethical value of social science knowledge was taken for granted in the nineteenth century in those countries that inherited the traditions of the Enlightenment. Truth was one of the highest goods; man's self-knowledge a moral obligation; the exercise of the observational and rational analytical powers must be good. Only obscurantists, whose position in society and whose self-esteem rested on prejudice, ignorance, and error, could fear the continuing growth of truth. The mind had to be freed from the hindrances that impeded its continuous expansion into all corners of the universe. Not only was man's pursuit of knowledge of himself, his society, and the universe a morally elevating activity, but its accomplishment and diffusion could bring nothing but benefits. Philosophical knowledge, including political and social philosophy, was envisaged as having its effect through the clarification of the mind and the elimination of superstitious and traditionally founded beliefs that had no rational or empirical basis. The diffusion of such knowledge would result in the self-transformation of the person: Conduct would be more reasonable, more tolerant, more benevolent. Improvement of conduct by any means other than the extended diffusion of knowledge was not envisaged.

Social Science as Research: Ethical Problems

Prior to the nineteenth-century scientific revolution, observations about the individual and society were derived from books and from life experience. Except for cases of ethnological observation, acquisition of such knowledge did not involve direct, intentional, firsthand observation. Even the introduction of fieldwork in social anthropology—carrying on the traditions of inquisitive travelers, missionaries, and colonial administrators—did not raise explicit concern for the ethical nature of the relations between investigator and investigated. It was perhaps not necessary where the investigator dwelt for an extended period in an alien group, because he could gain their confidence only by rendering himself acceptable. There was not much point in explaining his scholarly interests to those who did not have sufficient education to appreciate the intentions of social anthropological investigation. Furthermore, the indigenous peoples accepted the investigator as a person connected with their colonial rulers and submitted to his inquiries accordingly. What he ultimately published about them was most unlikely to come to their attention; it would be read only by a narrow circle of colleagues and perhaps by a few officials. Finally, its effectiveness, if any, would expire before it ever reached those who were the objects of inquiry.

Similarly, the large-scale social surveys of the conditions of the urban poor in the late nineteenth and early twentieth century had an immediate moral justification so strong that little question was raised about their propriety. The Springfield Survey, for example, was regarded by those who carried it out as a communal undertaking that would provide the basis for an effort at collective self-improvement. Thus, prior to World War I, social scientists generally had a good conscience in the belief that no harm could come from knowledge disinterestedly sought by means of procedures accredited through their success in yielding already acknowledged achievements of scientific research.

But this situation began to change with the development of a new technology of observation. The use of such devices as one-way screens, amplifying and recording devices, and hidden cameras created both opportunities and temptations. They created new dilemmas, such as withholding or not withholding information from the subjects of research, of giving them false information or not performing the experiment, and, in a variety of other ways, of treating them as objects to whom the investigators had none of the ordinary obligations of social life. Early social psychological experiments were often carried out on school children and college students. Observing aspects of their behavior that they had not been told were to be observed—perhaps embarrassing or even frightening them—all seemed to fall within the rights of scientists whose ascendancy was reinforced by their pedagogical authority. Although in recent years the ethical problems raised by medical experimentation on human beings have been extensively discussed, there is little indication that the proponents of large-scale "social experiments" have considered the ethical questions entailed in the manipulation of human beings without their personal consent or that of their elected representatives. Nor is there parallel concern with the problem of defining the limits beyond which everyday methods of industrial production and marketing become manipulative, and the social sciences play a role in the enterprise. The movement towards the establishment of data banks also raises ethical problems concerning privacy that are not yet acute but may become so. Thus, the greater availability of financial and institutional resources for social research, the increased technical capabilities of social scientists, and their greater concern with affairs beyond those of the poor, the immigrants, ethnic minorities, children, and criminals have all contributed to bringing the social sciences into a state of potential tension with regnant moral opinion.

SOURCES OF FINANCIAL SUPPORT VIS-A-VIS THE INTEGRITY OF THE SOCIAL SCIENCES

When the social sciences were the affair of private scholars or university teachers who worked on subjects largely of interest only to themselves and when their results received little or no attention in outside circles, the ethic of dispassionate objectivity seemed adequate to deal with whatever ethical problems might arise. The social scientist's obligation was to the truth and to the truth alone. Even when research became an integral part of the role of the academic social scientist, the situation still did not seem to raise any ethical problems. Patronage at first was scant and its distribution ad hoc. Thomas' and Znaniecki's *Polish Peasant in Europe and America,* for example, was supported by Mrs. Ethel Dummer. No questions were ever raised about the propriety of this patronage, and no one ever suggested that Thomas' and Znaniecki's views about the Polish peasant were in any way affected by Mrs. Dummer's provision of financial support.

The role of private foundations began after World War I and increased greatly in the 1930s. Following World War II, the Rockefeller and Ford foundations and the Carnegie Corporation became the chief private supporters of social science research in the United States. These foundations supported social science in the belief that the study of socially important problems would contribute to the improvement of society, but this was not interpreted by social scientists as an attempted deflection of their own interests. The particular problem might have been selected by the patron, but the interpretation of results was not influenced by the funding source. Critics of the academic social sciences, on the other hand, have alleged that "corruption" stems in part from dependence on the great foundations, which, having been founded by capitalists and connected by many ties with the federal government, are part of the "system of oppression." The charge that the system of authority in the United States today is "oppressive," in any sense resembling that in which the term has traditionally been used, cannot stand scrutiny. It is not, however, unreasonable to inquire into the question of whether the support of social science research by private foundations or the federal government has affected the intellectual integrity of the social sciences. By "integrity" I mean unswerving adherence to intellectual standards in the choice of problems and in the assessment of findings.

It is true that American social scientists have not studied all the problems that subsequent generations, or even some contemporaries, might regard as important. But to grant this is not to accede to the view that social scientists study some problems in order deliberately to avert their gaze from others of more importance. The social sciences have usually focused on matters of deep and lasting practical concern, "practical" being understood very broadly and not as referring only to immediate social objectives. Thus, the study of various forms of order and disorder, their sequences and combinations, have nearly always been at the heart of social scientists' concern, whether they have studied juvenile delinquency, military behavior, relationships among ethnic groups and nationalities, or the operation of status groups and organizations. The macrosociological problems were never as neglected as Mills and Lynd alleged. Indeed, the rather unsystematized collection of vague concepts and loose hypotheses of American social science did not require any fundamental transformation to accommodate the macrosociological problems that Lynd and Mills wished to make salient. Nor have the critics of American social science shown, or even attempted to show, that the conceptual apparatus of the social science they criticized could not accommodate the problems that they recommended for study. And they certainly did not substantiate their allegation that these problem areas were passed over out of "class interest" or the like.

In point of fact, the problems studied by American social scientists have shown a stability as marked as their diversity. Although choice of subject matter has undoubtedly been influenced by commissioning and supporting bodies, the topics selected have never been wholly or even substantially extraneous to the traditions of the various social science disciplines. The Carnegie Corporation did not bring American social sciences for the first time to the study of the Negro in the United States; the Hoover Commission did not discover social trends and seduce social scientists into studying them; the American Jewish Committee did not discover ethnic animosity. More important, the going thematic concerns of American social sciences have not been imposed or repressed or deflected by commissioning contracts. Social scientists choose the problems they study, because they cannot do otherwise; they cannot jump out of their intellectual skins at the sign of a prospective grant for research. Let us review relevant cases and see whether or not the critics' charge of "corruption" can be documented.

The Americanization studies that the Carnegie Corporation sponsored at the end of World War I, conducted by Robert Park and William I. Thomas, were in the direct line of those scholars' previous work on ethnic groups, initiated entirely on their own. Charles Johnson's work, *The Negro in Chicago,* was commissioned and paid for by the Commission on Race Relations, but the work itself was within the scope of the Chicago school of sociology of that time. The greatest commissioned collaborative inquiry of the interwar period, William Ogburn's *Recent Social Trends,* was privately financed, but the initiative came ultimately from President Hoover. Intellectually, however, it was entirely within the tradition of quantitative description of which Ogburn was the chief exponent. Myrdal's study of the Negro was, of course, off the path of his own previous research, but he applied to this investigation ideas that he had developed earlier. In the analysis presented in *The American Dilemma,* there is no evident trace of the biases or interests of the Carnegie Corporation. The next great scheme of commissioned research was that of the Adjutant General's Office in the Department of Defense on the behavior of soldiers behind the lines and in combat during World War II. Even though the subject matter was surely different from what most of the participating social scientists would have studied had there been no war and had the government not employed them, methodologically *The American Soldier* was largely a continuation of earlier analytical and technical interests of the chief investigators and a development of ideas that had been incubating for a long time, e.g., the study of small groups, the function of reference groups, the theory of relative deprivation, and the technique of latent structure analysis. The military setting provided data for elaborating ideas and techniques that were already present in the intellectual traditions of modern social sciences. Furthermore, the ideas developed in the course of these army studies lived on after the war in numerous nonmilitary applications. Thus, at least in their early encounters with financial support from government and private foundations, the tradition of objectivity that had been cultivated by leading American social scientists served them well.

Sociology—and those parts of anthropology and political science that have become associated with it—has been called an "oppositional science." Initially, it focused its attention on those aspects of modern society that were repugnant to a traditional conservative outlook: the breakup of the old order and the features of the liberal bourgeois society that constituted the new order. The impersonality and individualism of modern society and the large place held in it by instrumental rationality came to be stressed in sociological theory. At the same time, these features were also singled out by radical and progressivist critics as those which ought to be overcome through reform or revolution. The reforming interest of sociologists, i.e., their desire to contribute their scientific knowledge to the effective improvement of their society, led them to do their early empirical studies on those situations that they deplored and that there seemed to be some practical chance of improving. The radicals, too, no less than those they criticize, are the heirs and prisoners of this tradition. Their accusation that liberal democratic society is dehumanizing, unintegrated, and bureaucratized is exactly what they have learned from the sociology they denounce.

In the recent criticisms of the social sciences that focus on their "contamination" by support from private and public establishments, there is an implication that any sort of positive relationship with authority is ipso facto corrupting. The evil intentions of the patron are bound to result in the investigations' being used for evil purposes. The argument is naively unrealistic. It would be easy for social scientists to decide not to do research that could be used only for evil ends, just as it is easy to decide that it is unqualifiedly wrong for social scientists to do research that entails evil actions on their part. But the matter is obviously not so simple. For one thing, the consequences of the application of knowledge—assuming these consequences to be susceptible to accurate measurement—might be evil in some respects and in others beneficial. Furthermore, how can it be foreseen whether the results of a research project, itself morally unexceptionable, will be used for evil ends at some time in the future?

Most of the discussion about this matter has been academic in the most pejorative sense; it does not deal with real cases. There are, in point of fact, few cases in which the specific results of social science research have been applied. Except for public opinion surveys, which are taken into account by politicians and administrators, the empirical research of social scientists is still not usually taken very seriously by those who make decisions. Those aspects of social science that go beyond descriptive and particular propositions and that make generalized assertions about causal connections have, except for economics, relatively little effect on the behavior of public officials. For instance, whereas DDT might be prohibited by a government department or legislative body when it has been shown that it enters foodstuffs with demonstrably deleterious effects on health, research that shows that variations in the composition of school classes affects learning by children in those classes seems less likely to be acted on by school administrators. Thus, despite the widespread assertion of the need for empirical research of the sort done by sociologists, social anthropologists, and political scientists, the intention of the early social scientists to improve society through studying it scientifically and communicating their results to the wider public has not met with great success thus far.[14]

INSTITUTIONAL MECHANISMS FOR THE SUPPORT OF OBJECTIVITY AND INTEGRITY IN THE SOCIAL SCIENCES

The main ethical obligation of the social scientist before the recent expansion of the social sciences and the many-sided complication of their relations with society and government was simply the appreciation of the value of truth and the duty to strive for objectivity. Until the twentieth century there was no systematic institutionalized mode to inculcate even these cognitive obligations. When the social sciences were amateur activities, they benefited from the powerful personalities attracted to them, who were seriously devoted to the truth and scrupulous in their efforts to meet the high standards that had been set in Western intellectual history in philosophy, science, and humanistic scholarship. The subsequent emergence of critical general reviews, scientific journals and societies, and governmental commissions staffed by educated laymen provided the check of scrutiny by other competent persons who examined evidence and arguments. In the second and third quarters of the twentieth century, when the social sciences became well institutionalized and offered professional careers for large numbers, they perhaps ceased to draw such a large proportion of persons of deep inner propensity to seek the truth. But this change was compensated by the pressures of the institutional controls of selection, training, promotion, and assessment.

---

14 The diffusion of the social sciences does, however, occur at least among the educated and literate members of society. David Riesman's *The Lonely Crowd* is one such influential work. Riesman has written a thoughtful assessment of the impact of his book on American opinion in the two decades following its publication. He observed that ". . . the book has contributed to the climate of criticism of our society and helped to create or reaffirm a nihilistic outlook among a great many people. . . ." "*The Lonely Crowd* 20 Years After," *Encounter* 33, no. 9 (October 1969) : 36.

These helped to guarantee the assimilation and the maintenance of the ethos in which objective truth was the major value. And to all this was joined a growing body of literature on the methodology of the social sciences, focused primarily on the problems of enhancing the reliability of observation and analysis. The machinery of "refereeing" papers submitted to scholarly journals also reinforced the internalized controls.[15]

The standards of academic publishers of social science works are generally very similar to those of the professional journals. Since the audience is ultimately an audience of social scientists, editors and referees apply the usual standards of competence, objectivity, and importance. In this process, nonintellectual criteria play only a small, probably negligible, part. Where this standard is departed from, there is little evidence that political considerations and solicitude for the interests or sensibilities of the "establishment" are of any importance.

Book reviews in the scholarly journals, unfortunately, tend to be brief and fragmentary in their discussions of the merits of the work being assessed. They are generally recommendations of acceptance into, or, more infrequently, rejection from the corpus of social-scientific knowledge. Close-grained and stringent analysis of a particular work is rare. Among the few exceptions deserving of mention are the careful scrutiny given to *The Sexual Behavior of the American Male* (Kinsey et al.) and the studies of *The American Soldier* and *The Authoritarian Personality*.

On the whole, these various institutions of the community of social scientists have worked fairly efficiently. But they have suffered somewhat from the vagueness and instability of the concepts that are current in the social sciences as well as from the imprecision and incomparability of the results of empirical investigations. Rigorously articulated analysis and verification—which, in the natural sciences, comes from the continuous assimilation of prior investigations—have been lacking for the most part in the social sciences. Meticulous analysis of what has just gone before as the basis for the next stage in research is still relatively rare in the social sciences. In the final analysis, therefore, the ethic of the search for objective truth is largely a matter for the conscience of each individual social scientist. As an external spur, he has only his belief that if he falls short, sooner or later the assessment of his achievements will disclose his shortcomings and result

---

[15] It does seem, however, that social scientists submit more papers that are not up to standard than do natural scientists. A 1967 study found that the proportion of articles rejected range from 84 percent by two political science journals, 78 percent by fourteen sociological journals, 70 percent by seven psychological journals (excluding physiological and experimental psychology), 69 percent by four economics journals, to 40 percent by two anthropological journals; in physics and geology, by contrast, only 27 percent and 22 percent, respectively, were rejected. Harriet Zuckerman and Robert Merton, "Patterns of Evaluation in Science Institutionalization; Structure and Functions of the Referee System," *Minerva* 9, no. 1 (January 1971) : 76.

in damage to his reputation and career. The fact that the ethos works as well as it does rests on the belief of social scientists that they are writing for an audience of their professional colleagues. If they were to write largely for the general public or for an audience of "users" who are technically unqualified, the results might be different.

THE CURRENT DILEMMA OF THE SOCIAL SCIENCES: SEARCH FOR TRUTH OR FOR PUBLIC SERVICE

The recent radical criticisms of the social sciences are by-products of the enormous changes in the situation of the social sciences. Intellectual immaturity and frivolity have been allowed to flourish as a result of the ambiguous standards of assessment in the social sciences. The differences between the amount and tone of radical criticism in sociology, political science, and anthropology, on the one side, and economics on the other reflects the differences in rigor in these different disciplines. The central fact that must be acknowledged, therefore, is that the state of objective knowledge in the social sciences is far from satisfactory. This holds both for empirical findings and for generalized knowledge, which is commonly abstract to the point of inapplicability to empirical observations and therefore extremely difficult to confirm or disconfirm.

These deficiencies call for two remarks. One is that research that is based on intimate understanding derived from direct observation over an extended period by one person—less frequently by several individuals—is inevitably impressionistic. Even when efforts are made to control observations through sampling procedures, precise recording, etc., the amount of labor involved in such procedures is beyond the powers of one or a few persons who must complete their work within a relatively short time. As a result, the statistically disciplined parts of such investigations are usually only a small part of the whole. On the other side, investigations on a large scale—necessary if statistical treatment is to be applied—require a considerable number of collaborators and a division of labor.

Further, they require that the categories of observation—questions for interviewers—be so simplified that they can be utilized in brief interviews and so standardized that many persons can be instructed in a short time to apply them in a way that will not vary from interviewer to interviewer. The work in these investigations is thus so differentiated and internally specialized that no one on the project has an intimate relationship to the classes of events studied. This being so, the "sense of reality," which is a product of prolonged and intimate contact with the persons being investigated, does not develop, and the questions asked are often not adapted to the subtlety and complexity of the events, beliefs, or actions being investigated.

Interpretive constructions that do not conform to the "shape" of the events studied are the result. Despite the intention of concreteness and particularity, the accounts arising from empirical research are often as abstract, in relation to the events studied, as the sociological theory that is so unmanageable for purposes of empirical study. Both situations allow for arbitrariness in interpretation; some arbitrariness may be inevitable, but it is more probable under these circumstances. Some erroneous judgments might be the product of political or ethnic or class attachments and the beliefs connected with them; others might be simply the result of insufficient experience, poor reasoning powers, lack of sympathy, or deficient imagination.

There is, of course, nothing new about these difficulties of ascertaining the truth in an objective manner. Ever since men began to be critical of the sources of the ideas accepted as contributing reliable information—i.e., ever since classical philosophy and the emergence of hermeneutics as a means of establishing the meaning of texts, sacred or profane—this problem has bedeviled the scholarly mind. The physical and biological sciences were able to deal with it to some extent by the use of instruments that standardize observations. In their endeavor to achieve precision and rigor, they were greatly aided by the use of purified substances consisting of determinate properties and by the use of experimental methods as well as by quantitative analytical techniques. The social sciences, by contrast, have progressed unevenly and haltingly, hampered by the fact that these methods move them away from concrete phenomena and from the awareness of social realities growing out of direct experience.

Most of the events with which social sciences deal, and about which it is worth having a well-founded belief, do not at present show themselves wholly amenable to the treatments that permit rigorously founded beliefs. The things that are important to know about, whether for practical or intellectual purposes, are at present very inadequately understood. Yet we must have beliefs about them; practical concerns and the need for a coherent picture of society require them. But how is this picture to be composed when we have only fragments of factual evidence susceptible to diverse interpretations? We have, in addition, our own sense of reality arising from our experiences, refined by reflection and study, and we have our theories. So we must scrutinize ourselves as well as the data.

This brings us back to the solutions suggested by Wirth and Myrdal. It is necessary to be aware of our biases, not only our political, religious, ethnic, and cultural biases but also the biases arising out of our personal vanity and intellectual traditions. But being aware of them and telling our audience that we have them is a poor substitute for overcoming the operation of these biases. It is more important to avow the uncertainty of our knowledge than to couple an allegation of certainty with an avowal of bias.

Is there a way out of the present disorder in the social sciences? Several remedies suggest themselves. The first and most important is hard intellectual work in the improvement of theories and techniques of observation and analysis. More exigent programs of training for the profession of social sciences are needed; the examination of dissertations, in particular, should become more demanding. In other words, the professional institutions of social science must raise their standards. Even if this were accomplished, however, genuine political and ethical problems will remain and perhaps become really acute. The relationship of the investigator to the investigated remains problematic. The relationship between the social scientists and those who commission or subsidize their work will become even more worthy of critical study. If those in authority begin to make use of social science studies in constructing and carrying out their policies, social scientists will find that their intellectual accomplishments have consequences running far beyond contributions to the progress of knowledge. The question is whether and how they should take responsibility for such consequences, both for those whom they have actually studied and for others not involved as subjects in their investigations.

There are various ways by which social scientists can control the use of their findings. The first is to avoid doing research that might produce such usable findings; another is not to publish the findings. Refusal to accept financial support from a potential "user" is no guarantee against their use, once published. If social scientists insist on their right to publish their results, they have only the recourse available to any other citizen to try to prevent the government from following a particular policy. It is certainly not open to a social scientist to accept a grant from a public body and then claim that the results of his research must not be used. These are, however, all very unrealistic hypotheses. What some social scientists have done is to "gang up" on others who have accepted grants from certain government agencies, charging that the recipients have collaborated with a "wicked" government. This "ganging up" has taken the form of harassment and denunciation for "collaboration" with nefarious activities.

As regards research that is immoral in itself, doing physical or mental harm to its subjects, cheating or degrading them, there is a greater need and opportunity for control—but at present the machinery does not exist. The legal and medical professions, by contrast, have the power to deprive their members of the right to practice if they transgress certain standards of "professional conduct." Social scientists have no such procedures, nor do they enjoy a relationship with the state that would permit them to exercise the authority of exclusion. I doubt, incidentally, whether those social scientists who have recently been most vehement about these issues would be willing to cooperate with the state to establish such a system of authoritative professional licensing. And what would exclusion from the American Political Science Association, or the American Sociological Association, or the American Anthropological Association amount to? Membership in such bodies is not necessary for appointment to universities, nor for receipt of grants from governmental agencies or foundations. Moreover, it would be contrary to the principles of academic autonomy if universities were to accept their criteria of appointment from these professional bodies.

A last word. One of the causes of the present dilemma of the social sciences is a gross overestimation of the intellectual accomplishments of the social sciences. This has led to an intertwinement with the larger society, which is neither necessary nor beneficial to the profession or to the society. More modesty and greater realism are called for.

Index

ABM debate
  assessment of, 190–92
  ORSA report, 188–90
  science advising and, 185–203
Academic community
  decision-making in government, role, 215–16
  role of, 7
Academic freedom
  German universities and, 119–21
  Weber, Max, and, 103–22
Academic rank, sex status and, 68–69
ACE. *See* American Council on Education
ACLS. *See* American Council of Learned Societies
Adams, Charles Kendall, 96
Adams, Herbert B., 91, 99
Advanced Research Projects Agency, 252
Advertising, 26
Advisory committee, 202
AEA. *See* American Economic Association
Affirmative action plans, 83–86
Alsop, Joseph, 189
American Council of Learned Societies, 227
American Council on Education, 227
American Economic Association, 96–98
American Political Science Association, 99
American Psychological Association, 226
American Social Science Association, 90
American Sociological Society, 99
American Soldier, The, 283–84
Andrews, Charles M., 92
Anti-Poverty Task Force, 267–68, 268–69

Anti-semitism, 80–82
Applied research, 233
Army Alpha Examination, 123
ARPA. *See* Advanced Research Projects Agency
Arrow, Kenneth, 37
Astin, Helen, 66, 69, 77
Atlantic Monthly, 131–33, 168
Atwood, Cynthia, 78
Autonomy, 5–6
  meaning of, 235–43
  objectivity and, 243–48
Ayres, Leonard C., 138

Background-assumptions, 279
Bagley, William, 142
Basic research, 233
Bayer, Alan E., 77
Beard, Charles A., 100
Bernard, Jessie, 72, 77
Bias, 275–76, 288–89
Black Americans, scientific recognition and, 78–80
Blondlot, Rene, 51
Boulding, Kenneth E., 204
Bowman, Isaiah, 222
Brentano, Lujo, 111
Brigham, C. C., 139
Bronowski, Jacob, 13
Brookings Institution, 228
Brooks, Harvey, 235
Burckhardt, Jacob, 112
Bureau of the Budget. *See* Office of Management and Budget
Burgess, John W., 91
Bush, Vannevar, 222

Cahn, Anne, 187
Campbell, Donald, 152
Carnegie Corporation, 228, 282, 283
Caspari, Ernst, 126
Chamberlain, E. H., 183
Cole, Jonathan, 27, 54
Cole, Robert, 135
Cole, Stephen, 27, 54
Coleman, James, 4
Collaboration, ethics of, 234
Coming Crisis of Western Sociology, The
    (Gouldner), 279
Compensatory education, 130, 168
Conformity, 25
Congress (U.S.)
    scientific advice and, 190–92
    social science research and, 224–25
Congressional hearings, 197–98
Consultants, 198
Cori, Getty, 66
Council of Economic Advisers (U.S.),
    216, 222
Crime, punishment and, 25–26
Cronbach, Lee J., 123
Cuban missile crisis, 260
Curie, Irene Joliot, 66
Curie, Marie, 66

Darlington, C. D., 163, 165
Davis, Allison, 136–37
Davis, James A., 77
Decision-making
    academic knowledge and, 210
    future and, 206
    principles for, 209–10 ·
    values and, 206–208
Defense, Department of (U.S.), 248–54
Dewey, John, 121
Discrimination, 64–82
Doty, Paul, 185
Double penalty, principle of, 76–77
Droysen, J. G., 96
Dunbar, Charles F., 91
Dunbar, Charles L., 97
Dunning, William A., 92

Economics, 8
    Keynesians, 177
    neoclassical, 180–81
    public adversary role, and, 170–84
    as social science, 175–84
    unemployment issue of, 178
Economic theory, 246–47
Economists
    advisory role of, 204–205
    United Kingdom and, 178–80
    United States and, 178–80
Eells, Kenneth, 136
Ely, Richard T., 91, 96
England. *See* United Kingdom
Equality of opportunity, 83
Ethical standards, 274–77
Evaluation
    scientific research and, 42–43
        credit for, allocation of, 52–53
        research findings, dissemination of,
            47–48
        research goals, 44–45
        research methods, 45–46
        scientific misinformation, control
            of, 48–52
        standards of proof and, 46–47
    values as an object of, 30–42
Exchange power, 214
Executive Office of the President, 221–
    22
Experimenting society, 152
Eysenck, H. J., 163–65, 168
Ezrahi, Yaron, 30, 148

Facts, values and, 17–18
Fallacy of misplaced rationality, 160
Federal government. *See* U.S. Govern-
    ment
Fichte, J. G., 110
Fine, Benjamin, 136
Flew, Antony, 18
Folger, John K., 77
Ford Foundation, 228, 282
Foster, John, 249
Frankel, Charles, 2, 8, 170

Freeman, Frank N., 141
Friedman, Milton, 183

Gardner, John, 144
Gardner, Martin, 50
Garwin, Richard, 189
George, Stefan, 113
George-Kreise, 113
Germany
  university ideal of, 105–10
    academic freedom and, 119–21
    George-Kreise and, 113–14
    Humboldt, Wilhelm von, role,
      106–108
    nationalism and, 110–11
    socialism and, 111–12
    Tolstoyanism, 112–13
    Weber, Max, and, 114–22
Gierke, Otto von, 111
Gilman, Daniel C., 95
Gore, Albert, 188
Gouldner, Alvin, 10, 279
Great Society programs, 245–46

Haldane, J. B. S., 49
Hansen, Alvin, 177
Harvard University, 253
Haviland, H. Field, 218
Hawkins, Hugh, 88
Head Start program, 125
Heller, Walter, 8
Herrnstein, Richard, 131–32, 163, 165,
  168
Higham, John, 91
Hobbes, Thomas, 159
Hobson, John A., 276
Honorific awards, women scientists and,
  69–71
Hoover, Herbert, 216, 221
Human purpose
  contingent foundation of, 32
  instrumental vs. pragmatic justifica-
    tion, 39–41
  preference and, 36–38
  welfare and, 38–39

Humboldt, Alexander von, 106
Humboldt, Wilhelm von, 106
Hume, David, 16–17, 275
Hume's guillotine. *See* Ought and is
Huxley, T. H., 137
Hyman, J. D., 134

Ideology, 22–24
Immigrants, racism and, 139–42
Imperfect/monopolistic competition
  revolution, 183
Ingle, D. J., 163, 165, 168
Inquiry, restriction of, 133–34
Institute for Research on Poverty, 270
Institutional facts, 20, 21
Integrative power, 214
Intellectual advisers, 215–16
Intelligence
  genetic factors and, 4
  race and, 126–36
Interdisciplinary research, 254–57
IQ
  Atlantic Monthly, article on, 131–33
  determinism and, 142–43
  tests, 168, 169

James, Edmund J., 96
James, William, 142
Jay, James M., 79
Jensen, Arthur, 124, 126, 145, 163
Jensenism, 128–31, 162–66
Jews, 80–82
Johnson, Charles, 283
Johnson, Harry G., 170

Kant, Immanuel, 275
Katz, Milton, 201
Kennedy, John F., 246
Kerner Commission, 4
Keynes, John Neville, 177, 183
Keynesian economics, 177
  United Kingdom and, 178–80
  United States and, 178–80
Kistiakowsky, G. B., 189
Klineberg, Otto, 125–26

Knowledge
  ethics of
    Jensen controversy and, 162–66
    social science and, 148–53
    political profile of, 166–69
Knowledgeable society, 152
Knowledge for What? (Lynd), 278
Kohl, Herbert, 135
Krieck, Ernst, 115

Ladd, Everett Carll, 81
Lane, Robert, 11, 152
Laughlin, J. Laurence, 97–98
Lederberg, Joshua, 131
Lehrfreiheit, 119–21
Lernfreiheit, 119–21
Lindblom, Charles, 262
Link, Henry, 141
Lippman, Walter, 140
Lipset, Seymour Martin, 81
Long, F. A., 200
Lovejoy, Arthur, 121
Lowell, A. Lawrence, 100
Lynd, Robert, 278

McElroy, Neil, 185
McNamara, Robert, 185, 249
Mahon, George, 187
Mannheim, Karl, 182, 277
Marx, Karl, 276
Mayo-Smith, Richmond, 93, 98
Mead, Margaret, 46
Mental testing, 123–47, 227
  determinism and, 142–43
  experimental bias, 134–36
  immigrants and, 139–42
  morons, 138–39
  social-class bias, 136–37
Merriam, Charles, 150, 227
Metzger, Walter, 91
Mill, J. S., 32–33
Mills, C. Wright, 278
Mill's fallacy, 32–33
Minorities, discrimination against, 64–
  82

M.I.T., 253
Mitchell, Joyce M., 69
Monod, Jacques, 150
Morality, political, 204–17
Moral philosophy, 93
Morse, Philip, 189
Moynihan, Daniel Patrick, 4, 128, 262
Moynihan Report, 262
Myrdal, Gunnar, 150, 182, 277, 283

NAS-NRC. *See* National Research
  Council of the National Academy
  of Sciences
National Academy of Sciences, 227
National Institute of Mental Health, 223
Nationalism, 110–11
National Planning Board (U.S.), 222
National Research Council of the Na-
  tional Academy of Sciences, 226–27
National Resources Committee (U.S.),
  222
National Science Foundation, 221, 224,
  229, 238
National Society for the Study of Educa-
  tion, 146
Natural sciences
  autonomy, scholarly, and, 237, 238–
    39
  federal-academic relations and, 228–
    30
  social science and, 90–92
Negro in Chicago, The (Johnson), 283
Neoclassical economics, 180–81
Newman, Cardinal, 109
Niche, 211–12
Nietzsche, Frederick, 112
Nisbet, Robert, 103, 241
Noosphere, 210–11
Normative research, 233

Objectivist bias, 154
Objectivity, 5–6, 10–13
  autonomy and, 243–48
  decline of, 13–15
  experiences leading to, 13–15

Objectivity (*cont.*)
    inherent validity of beliefs in
        question and, 15–24
    ideal of, 88–102
    social science
        challenges to, 277–79
        institutional mechanisms for sup-
            port of, 285–87
        social scientists and, 156–58
    Weber, Max, and, 116–18
Office of Management and Budget, 221,
    232
Office of Naval Research (U.S.), 220,
    251
Office of Scientific Research and Devel-
    opment, 222
Ogburn, William, 276, 283
OMB. *See* Office of Management and
    Budget
Operations Research Society of America,
    188
ORSA. *See* Operations Research Society
    of America
ORSA investigation, propriety of, 195–
    96
ORSA report, 188–90
    assessment of, 192–95
    guidelines, 201
    unwritten comments concerning, 189–
        90
OSRD. *See* Office of Scientific Research
    and Development
Otis, Arthur, 123
Ought and is, doctrine of, 16–21

Panofsky, W. K. H., 189, 194, 195
Park, Robert, 283
Parkinson's law, 215
Parrington, Vernon, 139
Patten, Simon N., 96
Pentagon, the. *See* Defense, Depart-
    ment of
Peter principle, 215
Polanyi, M., 235, 236
Policy advisers, scholars and, 266

Policy debate, scientific
    perspective, maintenance of, 199–200
    scientists and ethical standards, 200–
        201
Policy makers
    executive privilege, role, 261–62
    general policy statements and, 265–66
    options open to, 262–64
    political risks, role, 266
    scholars and operational thinking,
        267–68
Politics, 29–30, 53–62, 166–69
Power
    knowledge, relations to, 215–17
    sources of, 214
Preferences, 36–38
President's Science Advisory Committee,
    44, 45, 222
Price, Derek, 51
Price, Don K., 12
Principles, decision-making and, 209–10
Project Cambridge, 252–54
Project Camelot, 248
Project Jason, 250
PSAC. *See* President's Science Advisory
    Committee
Pseudo-science, research and, 51–52
Publicity, 160–62
Public knowledge, 243–44
Published research, 59–64
Punishment, crime and, 25–26
Pygmalion in the Classroom (Rosenthal
    and Jacobsen), 134–36

Race, intelligence and, 126–36
Racial status, scientific recognition and,
    78–80
Racism, immigrants and, 139–42
Rand Corporation, 228
RANN. *See* Research Applied to Na-
    tional Needs
Rathjens, George, 189, 193, 194
Rationality, 158–60
*Recent Social Trends in the United
    States* (report), 221–22, 283

Religious status, scientific recognition
    and, 80–82
Rescher, Nicholas, 31
Research
    government sponsored
        in-house scholarship, 264
        options open, role, 262–64
        policy makers and, 261–62
        secrecy and, 264–65
        time pressures and, 260–61
Research agenda, formulation of, 25–26
Research Applied to National Needs,
    255
Research Committee on Social Trends
    (U.S.), 221
Research findings
    credit for, allocation of, 52–53
    dissemination of, 47–48
Research goals, 44–45
Research methods, 45–46
Research subjects, 6–7
Respect, 34–35
Robbins, Lionel, 181
Robinson, James Harvey, 100
Robinson, Joan, 183
Rockefeller Foundation, 228, 282
Roles
    filling of, 215
    societal distribution of, 213–14
Roosevelt, F. D., 221–22
Rosenthal, Robert, 134
Ross, Edward A., 92, 96
Russell Sage Foundation, 228

Safeguard system, 186
Salomon, J. J., 235
Sartori, Giovanni, 154
Schmoller, Gustave, 111
Scholarly rights, 204–17
Scholars, 4
    biases influencing government re-
        search, 271–72
    as government advisors, 259–61
    government research
        inside government, 264

Scholars (*cont.*)
    instrumental advice, role, 263
    secrecy and, 264–65
    policy advisers and, 266
    policy makers and, 267–68
    as political decision makers, 270
    as public adversaries, 170–84
    public conduct and, 144–46
    role of, 7
Science
    autonomy, scholarly, role, 235–36
    cognitive content of work and, 86–
        87
    discrimination
        against women and minorities, 64–
            82
        for unpopular political ideologies,
            86–87
    politics, relation to, 153–62, 166–69
    social stratification in, 54–88
Science advising
    ABM debate and, 185–203
    advisory reports, role, 198–99
    consultants, role, 198
Science Advisory Board, 222
Science as a Vocation. *See Wissenschaft
    als Beruf*
Scientific advisory committees, 197
Scientific freedom, 240
Scientific recognition
    black Americans and, 78–80
    racial status and, 78–80
    religious status and, 80–82
    sex status and, 66–71
Scientific research, 233
    evaluative dimension of, 42–43, 45–
        46
        credit for, allocation of, 52–53
        goals and, 44–45
        research findings, dissemination of,
            47–48
        retrospect on the, 53
        scientific misinformation and, 48–
            52
        standards of proof, 46–47

Scientists
  ABM and, 187–88
  objectivity and, 156–58
  public conduct and, 144–46
Scoville, H., 189
Searle, John, 19, 20, 21
Self-discipline, 24–28
Seligman, E. R. A., 92
Sentinel, 185–86
Sex status
  academic rank and, 68–69
  honorific awards and, 69–71
  prestige of academic affiliation and,
    67–68
  productivity and, 71–74
  recognition controlling for scientific
    role performance and, 74–78
  scientific recognition and, 66–71
Shaw, Albert, 98
Shils, Edward, 273
Shockley, William, 163, 165
Small, Albion, 90, 100, 101, 102
Socialism, 111–12
Social science research
  bias and, 275–77
  Congress, the (U.S.), and, 224–25
  federal-academic relations, 218–34
    collaboration, ethics of, 234
    fund allocation, 222–23
    general planning, 230–32
    historical trends, 220–21
    natural science and balance, 228–
      30
    priorities, 230–32
    private sector and, 225–28
    use of nongovernmental communi-
      ties, 223–24
  as government policy making tool, 272
  values, role in
    conduct of, 42–53
    as object of evaluation, 30–42
Social Science Research Council, 227
Social sciences
  autonomy, role, 5–6, 8–30, 237–38
  bias and, 288–89

Social Sciences (*cont.*)
  changing concept in America, 2–4
  cognitive legitimacy of, 273–74
  controversies and, 4–5, 10, 143–44
  Defense, Department of (U.S.), and,
    248–54
  economics, evolution into, 175–84
  an economist's view, 170–74
  financial support sources vis-à-vis
    integrity of, 281–85
  independence of, 4
  intellectual legitimacy of, challenges,
    277–79
  is and ought in, 274–77
  knowledge, ethics of, and, 148–53
  moral philosophy and, 93
  moral problems, 280–81
  mutual criticism, role, 26–27
  National Science Foundation and, 238
  natural sciences and, 90–92
  objectivity and, 5–6, 11–13, 88–102,
    285–87
  as policy oriented, 36
  political problems, 280–81
  political viewpoints, 6
  politics and, 29–30
  proposals to restrict inquiry, 133–34
  public science and, 287–90
  reward systems of, 54–88
  scholar, role, 4
  self-discipline and, 24–28
  social function of, 7
  truth and, 287–90
  universalistic reward system
    affirmative action plans and, 83–86
    published research and, 59–64
    unpopular political ideologies and,
      86–87
  value assumptions, 245
Social stratification in science, 54–88
Society for Psychological Study of Social
  Issues, 130, 146
Sociological Imagination, The (Mills),
  278
Sociology, ideology and, 22–24

Sphere and Duties of Government
(Humboldt), 106
SPSSI. *See* Society for Psychological
Study of Social Issues
SSRC. *See* Social Science Research
Council
SST debate, 200
Standards of proof, 46–47
Starr, Rachel, 69
Stennis, John, 188
Strong orderer, 208–209
Sumner, William Graham, 99

Taylor, Charles, 10
Terman, Lewis M., 123, 140, 142, 145
Testing, 123–47
Theoretical issues, definition of, 25–26
Thomas, William I., 283
Thorndike, R. L., 135
Threat power, 214
Tolstoy, Leo, 112
Twilight of the Idols (Nietzsche), 112

Unemployment, 178
United Kingdom
Keynesian economics, 178–80
social science, view of, 12–13
United States Constitution, 12
United States Government
academic relations, historical trends,
220–21
imbalance among disciplines and
institutions, 230–33
Keynesian economics and, 178–80
scholarship, autonomy of, and, 234–
57
social sciences, view of, 12–13
use of nongovernmental communities, 223–24
Universities
England and, 109
German ideal
academic freedom and, 119–21
George-Kreise and, 113–14

Universities (*cont.*)
Humboldt, Wilhelm von, role,
106–108
Tolstoyanism, 112–13
Weber, Max, and, 114–22
in Germany
nationalism and, 110–11
socialism and, 111–12
transintellectual conception of, 110
University of Jena (Germany), 110

Value-free social science, 14
Value judgments, 17
Values
as an object of evaluation, 30–42
decision-making and, 206–208
facts and, 17–18
human purpose and
instrumental vs. pragmatic justification, 39–41
preferences, 36–38
welfare, 38
learning of, 207–208
Mill's fallacy, 32–33
respect of persons, fundamentality of,
34–35
social science and, 182, 245
social science research, role, 30–53
Weber, Max, and, 116
Velikovsky, Immanuel, 51
Verein für Sozialpolitik (Germany),
111–12
Vietnam, 4, 249, 252
Voliva, Wilbur Glenn, 51

Walker, Francis A., 97
Wallas, Graham, 276
Ward, Lester, 90, 99, 137, 150
Waterson, J. J., 49
Weak orderer, 208–209
Weber, Max, 12, 17, 154, 274
Weinberg, Steven, 189
Welfare, 38–39
Wertfreiheit, 10, 17, 29, 116–18

Whipple, Guy M., 142
White, Andrew D., 95
Wiesner, Jerome B., 189, 195
Wiggam, Albert, 139
Wirth, Louis, 277, 278
Wisconsin Idea, the, 99–100
Wissenschaft als Beruf (Weber), 102, 103
Wohlstetter, Albert, 188, 193, 194
Wolfe, Albert B., 276
Women, discrimination against, 64–82

Women scientists
honorific awards and, 69–71
productivity of, 71–74
Wood, Robert W., 51

Yarmolinsky, Adam, 258
Yerkes, Robert, 140
York, H. F., 189

Zero-based budgeting, 262–63
Ziman, J., 243